From Missions to Mission

UNITED METHODIST CHURCH

HISTORY OF MISSION SERIES

From Missions to Mission

The History of Mission of The United Methodist Church, 1968–2000

Robert J. Harman

GENERAL BOARD OF GLOBAL MINISTRIES
The United Methodist Church
New York, New York

Published by GBGM BOOKS
Copyright © 2005
The General Board of Global Ministries
The United Methodist Church
475 Riverside Drive
New York, New York 10115

LIBRARY OF CONGRESS
Control Number 2003107310

ISBN 1-890569-68-2 CLOTH
ISBN 1-890569-76-3 PAPER

COVER PHOTOS *(left to right, from top left):*
Response cover of Lake Titicaca, Bolivia; Côte d'Ivoire student
peace demonstration; U.S. Hispanic; Aleut fishermen;
missionary Esther Mabry in India; two African-American girls;
and center, short-term missionaries
in Washington, D.C.

This book is dedicated to the faithful of
the last half-century who awakened United
Methodists to the dawning of a new missionary
age—a journey from supporting the church's
missionaries and mission outposts to
becoming a church in mission.

And to Marcia, with thanks for every blessing.

[Contents]

[Illustrations]

[Maps]

[Photographs]

[Foreword]

*M*ORE THAN FIFTY years have passed since a history of mission series was begun by The Methodist Church Board of Missions. Wade Crawford Barclay wrote *Early American Methodism, 1769–1844* as the first of what would become a four-volume series.

In that first volume, Barclay explained that the series was "designed to present a comprehensive, detailed, and accurate history of American Methodism in its character as a Christian missionary movement." He laid out the publishing program as including the content of volume one, early American Methodism, and then the mission histories of the three divisions of mainstream Methodism prior to 1939: the Methodist Episcopal Church (MEC), the so-called northern church; the Methodist Episcopal Church, South (MECS), the so-called southern church; and the Methodist Protestant Church (MPC).

By the time of the third volume, however, Barclay was apologetic: "The writing of this volume has required more time than was anticipated." The second volume had brought the history only up to 1844, and that only of the MEC. The third volume advanced the MEC history to 1895. A fourth volume, written by J. Tremayne Copplestone after Barclay's death, completed the MEC mission work, ending in 1939. With the publication of this volume in 1973, however, the project stopped. The four volumes had taken a quarter century, and the Board of Missions had by then evolved into the Board of Global Ministries of a new denomination, The United Methodist Church. The Board decided the histories did not articulate an adequate vision of mission.

By the end of the twentieth century it seemed apparent to many that a continuation of the history of mission was needed. There were several reasons. The Women's Division almost alone in The UMC had continued to educate an important constituency about mission, supporting the National Council of the Churches of Christ in its publication of annual mission resources and publishing many resources of its own. When the

NCCC found it could no longer continue publishing these books, the Women's Division led the General Board of Global Ministries to continue their publication. The Women's Division more than most was conscientious in publishing works about mission. Yet many in the rest of the denomination remained untouched by any serious study of mission, present or past.

A second large reason consisted of the bridges that had gone under the water since the conclusion of the Barclay/Copplestone series. The history of mission of The Methodist Church, in existence from 1939 to 1968, had never been written. The history of mission of the Evangelical United Brethren, in existence from 1946 to 1968, had never been written. Since these two merged to become The United Methodist Church, critical changes had occurred in the comprehension, strategy, and practice of mission in the newly united denomination. The very nature of the denominations had altered greatly in relation to the rest of the culture and in relation to the ecumenical movement. A need existed to write all these histories taking these changes into account. Furthermore, the MECS and MPC histories needed to be written and published.

A third reason lay in the religious and cultural changes that affected the way history is conceived and written. At the time Barclay began his series, women were almost totally absent from the official leadership of the mainline churches. African Americans, Hispanics, Asian Americans, and Native Americans were not well represented in that leadership. Bishops, officers of the major program boards like the Board of Missions of The Methodist Church, and other denominational officials consisted almost entirely of white men.

The need, then, was to develop a history of mission that did justice to the role of women, ethnic minorities in the United States, and also indigenous leaders in various countries. For most of the histories of mission previously published had ignored the leadership and contributions of indigenous leaders as well.

Finally, the field of history itself had changed. Chronicles of official events and even large-scale interpretations, or "metahistories," had given way to more detailed studies of local and culturally specific developments. "Thick description" was preferred to chronicles of facts and dates. Traditional histories are still being written, those that take a large field and attempt to provide an overriding image or concept for interpretation and those that relate personal histories. These efforts, while entertaining and even popular, eventually fail because of their biases, the inevitable inability of a single historian to know that large field, or simply because they ignore the diversity of the human race.

This series might seem to be attempting such large-scale interpretations. Writers were advised to provide an interpretive framework while avoiding the attempt to create "repositories of facts," to "provide readable narratives" that would be placed "within the context of culture/religion interaction." We were keenly aware of the dangers of attempting histories "from the center," as it were, rather than "from the periphery," that is, from the perspective of previously neglected people. We hoped, however, that by breaking the histories into periods of fairly brief epochs and by seeking diligently to give voice to the voiceless inasmuch as the historical record allowed, we could fill the vacuum left in mission history since the conclusion of the Barclay/Copplestone series.

We hoped even more that we could produce histories that might actually be read by United Methodists and others committed to mission. This may seem an even more dubious undertaking, since the advent of electronic media has threatened to abolish reading entirely. Yet the publication of books and magazines on the electronic media itself gives us some hope that reading may extend into the next generation.

The General Board of Global Ministries, through grants provided by the office of the general secretary, initiated the "United Methodist History of Mission" in 1999. It was conceived as a way to accomplish four goals:

1. To complete the outlines of the history of mission of The Methodist Church and its predecessors as given in *The History of Methodist Missions* by Wade Crawford Barclay and J. Tremayne Copplestone.

2. To provide readable narratives or thematic treatments that can be used by both scholars and the general church membership.

3. To do justice to the contributions of women, ethnic minorities, and indigenous leaders to the history of mission.

4. To provide the basis for a video and other resources to be used in orienting GBGM staff and missionaries in our history.

This volume is one of a series that will consist of the following:

- the history of mission of the Methodist Protestant Church, 1830–1939
- the history of mission of the Methodist Episcopal Church, South, 1845–1939

- the history of mission of The Methodist Church, 1939–1968
- the history of mission of the Evangelical United Brethren, 1946–1968
- the history of mission of The United Methodist Church, 1968–2000
- reflections on Christian mission in the early decades of the third millennium of Christian history
- first-person accounts of presidents and directors of the United Methodist General Board of Global Ministries in undertaking significant mission initiatives from 1980 to 2002.

These histories are dedicated to past and present generations of Methodists, EUBs, and United Methodists who helped to fulfill the commitment "to reform the Continent and to spread scriptural Holiness over these lands." They are also offered in the hope that future generations will find in them not only information and interpretation of Christian mission but also inspiration to continue that mission in the future. Although a reading of these histories will reveal failures as well as successes, contemporary Christians cannot but be grateful for the accomplishments of our foreparents in the faith. "We feebly struggle, they in glory shine."

Charles E. Cole, EDITOR

From Missions to Mission

[Introduction]

*P*ROMINENT AMONG the questions asked of participants at the earliest connectional meetings of the Wesleys' movement was: "What is the purpose of the church?" The response was the oft-repeated refrain of Methodist Church leaders down through the years: "To reform the nation, and, in particular, the Church; to spread scriptural holiness over the land." Methodists have a passion for mission. Social reform and personal redemption are its hallmarks.

Even before it was organized into a church in the North American colonies, the Methodist movement was engaged in a mission. There was no need for a standing clergy — only for itinerant preachers on horseback willing to travel between frontier preaching posts. Revivalist preaching and a strong commitment to serve the social welfare of a developing nation shaped Methodist doctrine. Methodists created strong communities of faith and founded viable institutions of learning, healing, and caring. Preaching grace upon grace for the forgiveness of sins, Methodism also established standards of Christian perfection for accountability from all, including church leaders and organizational structures invested with authority over others.

For the past century and a half, Methodism has been at the forefront of the missionary movement, planting the gospel and establishing churches throughout the world community. Its proclamation of a holistic message of spiritual and social renewal was peculiarly suited to the revolutionary changes confronting the world in the final quarter of the twentieth century. Methodist mission has produced leaders for independence movements and offered guidance for the governance of new nations. Its many social institutions effectively serve cities and villages, giving a sense of purpose and well being to those who live there.

Ironically, the period of mission history extending from 1968 to 2000 opens with The United Methodist Church (UMC) in the throes of its own reformation. Consummating the 1968 union of the Evangelical

United Brethren Church (EUB) and The Methodist Church required the customary acts of institutionalization. But the new church found itself faced with a demanding social and political context. The rising spirit of independence and self-determination convinced mission churches to exercise their rightful autonomy. The civil rights movement, which successfully challenged discriminatory laws and social behaviors in the United States, prompted minority groups within the denomination to exact institutional reforms to ensure their full recognition and participation in the church.

A proud new denomination with a successful mission history was now beginning a period of mission to itself. Its mission board became engaged in a painful process of listening to representatives of constituencies that were violated by policies and practices reflecting the sins of prejudice, paternalism, exclusion, and indifference. These representatives challenged the Board of Missions to reshape its own life and mission around inclusive values and principles. This reform required an intentional process of rooting out institutional racism and opening up the ranks of the Board's policymaking body, its staff, and its missionary community to full representation by race, gender, and age.

Redefining a United Methodist theology of mission was inspired by dialogue within the church's membership and with ecumenical mission partners serving marginalized peoples of Third World communities in both U.S. and international contexts. Stewardship of the financial assets needed to undergird United Methodist mission shifted from traditional programs aimed at alleviating social ills to higher-stake experimental programs that promised transformation of unjust social structures. These measures of reform appeared to be too far-reaching for some in the general constituency, and a counterforce was mobilized within the church that aggressively aimed at restoring a more conservative or traditionally evangelical mission philosophy.

The story of United Methodist mission from 1968 to 2000 follows the journey of a church on a mission of self-correction and reform, but it also focuses upon growth in a global context. This journey begins with a strong Board of Missions executing sole authority for managing programs and personnel by the hundreds and thousands. Along the way, the Board learns a new methodology for doing mission that honors mutuality and respects partnership in program development and administration. The directors of mission learn to become recipients as well, humbly receiving

Mrs. Porter Brown, general secretary of the Board of Missions of The Methodist Church, greeted the Reverend Harold Hazenfield, executive editor of Church School Publications for the Evangelical United Brethren Church, at the service uniting the two denominations to become The United Methodist Church in Dallas, Texas, in 1968. *(Photo from* New World Outlook, *courtesy of UM Archives and History)*

and recognizing mission personnel and program strategies of partner churches and ecumenical agencies. These strategies do not emanate from but are aimed at the United States, the traditional base of the missionary "sending" church.

Throughout the period, the church is intensely engaged with a constituency benefitting from a growing awareness of international connections, within and beyond church structures. The supporters of mission become less dependent upon denominational and ecumenical agencies to channel their response via mission activities. In fact, the church encounters a strong grassroots movement among the mission-minded to engage in direct mission experiences through participation in volunteer projects and mission travel in the U.S. and other countries. Nevertheless, the goodwill of its members and the coordinating efforts of the worldwide Methodist connection have enabled The UMC to respond to new mission opportunities in regions such as Russia, the Baltic States, other parts of Eastern Europe, Cambodia, Vietnam, and East Africa, where for generations mission outreach had been prohibited or restricted. Within the U.S., program priorities have been focused upon strengthening the church's ministries with racial/ethnic minorities. This focus has helped position the church for potential membership growth among the fastest-growing segments of the U.S. population.

The conclusion of the twentieth century finds The UMC in mission shoring up church structures and programs undermined by the destructive forces of economic globalization. While advocating a taming of these global economic trends, the church ponders how its own connectional life can foster a model for a fairer and healthier global relationship. Even as these discussions increase, confidence in the ecumenical commitment to achieving visible unity in the church is fading. While there is no unanimity about the form such a global church might take, basic mission principles promote respect for the unique manifestations of the church in each culture, along with reaffirmation of the values of a common religious tradition and structural accountability. The legislative hurdle is the most daunting. The membership of the General Conference of The UMC reflects the same political imbalance as the larger world community. The membership in the Northern Hemisphere, which historically supports the mission of the church with its disproportionate influence and wealth, has yet to recognize or value fully the contributions and resources of the impoverished, but growing, membership in the Southern Hemisphere. The future of a global connection for United Methodism remains impaled upon this institutional reality.

A primary focus of this volume is the chronicling of major mission events, issues, and policy considerations of United Methodist mission between 1968 and 2000. The content is not presented chronologically but is organized around mission trends, developing themes, and structural manifestations. The evolution of The UMC in mission — from a church with missions, to a church with a vision of responsible partnership in God's universal mission, to a church contemplating a global church connection — is not yet complete. It is too complex a story to lend itself to a telling by a single author or in a single text. This author acknowledges a dependence upon the documentation of the denomination's General Board of Global Ministries (GBGM) and its predecessor mission boards. GBGM is not only the official mission program agency but is the one place where one finds records of substantive dialogue on issues of United Methodist mission for the period of study.

Also significant is the experience of mission partners that contextualize United Methodist mission in a variety of cultures, languages, traditions, and political arrangements. An attempt is made to identify and listen to stories of their mission encounters in this historical period of revolutionary change. To that end, the text contains cameo regional and country briefings in an effort to record the responses of representative mission partners throughout the world.

When asked to write this history, the author was keenly aware of his limitations and unworthiness for undertaking such a task. It was not until receiving the critique of his first draft from a panel of readers that he realized just how unworthy he was. Incorporation of their valuable commentary has improved this text, but the final product is neither as comprehensive nor the story line as precise as readers deserve. Rather, this book is a beginning to which other scholars can contribute. It is offered with the hope that future generations of United Methodist mission practitioners will find in the text appropriate guidance to take up God's unfinished and unfolding work of redemption for humankind and transformation for the world.

CHAPTER 1

Rising Expectations

In discerning God's activity in the world, mission partners often are humbled and moved to confess complicity in past and present actions which exploit and oppress peoples and nations. Such actions are exhibited in political and economic arrangements or personal attitudes which dishonor the divine image of God's children and oppose the reclamation, renewal, and redemption of human life. But partners in mission also are moved to celebrate the wondrous ways of God in transforming human frailties, failures, and disobedience to create something new and to fulfill God's will and purpose.[1]

"A New Church for a New World"

In the throes of the many revolutionary changes occurring in the 1960s, The United Methodist Church (UMC) found itself at the crossroads and embarked upon a historic new beginning. The General Conference met in April 1968 in Dallas with two major institutional goals on its agenda: first, dissolving the racially segregated structure of the Methodist Central Jurisdiction; and second, consummating the union of The Methodist Church and the Evangelical United Brethren Church (EUB) into The UMC. This church union, the largest religious merger in United States history, was accomplished after several years of negotiation, aided by the strong ecumenical spirit prevailing among the churches at the time.

For these churches to be truly "united" in fellowship and witness, more was required than blending memberships and joining articles of incorporation. A Commission on Religion and Race (CORR) was established to help the new church be proactive in addressing the divisive issue of

[7]

institutional racism in its life. As part of this task, the commission was to oversee the merger of the racially structured entities of the Central Jurisdiction into the five geographically organized jurisdictional conferences. It was also agreed that only a total restructuring of the denomination would sufficiently address new and changing organizational realities. So a special commission was mandated to complete a plan to reorganize The UMC structures — a plan to be considered by the next quadrennial meeting in 1972.

The uniting General Conference also expressed a clear resolve to strengthen the mission of the new church. Bishop Eugene M. Frank of St. Louis, the first president of the United Methodist Council of Bishops, reflected upon the actions of the General Conference: "Mission has constantly taken precedence over structure. . . . There has been a very obvious mood to shape this small part of the Body of Christ so that it would be best equipped and prepared to make real in our society the love of God for all [people]."[2]

A program theme adopted for the new quadrennium sought to mobilize the energies and resources of the church around efforts of reconciliation, witness, and renewal. In recommending this theme, "A New Church for a New World," the Coordinating Council described the moment of crisis and the opportunity for a significant witness for the new church: "Every person is a child of God . . . yet social structures, many prejudices, economic orders, and international relations threaten human dignity and freedom. The new church should use its structure and power [to address these problems and thus become] a dramatic sign of hope and symbol of compassion."[3]

The new theme was backed up by directives that would take the church into controversial new initiatives aimed at social reconciliation. The church was called upon to make "special efforts to listen to and minister to those victimized by 'manifold social dislocations,' particularly racial and ethnic minorities, the poor in both urban and rural communities, and young persons."[4] Local churches were instructed to engage in processes of self-examination to determine whether their ministries were relevant for a time of crisis. Members were urged to study the Sermon on the Mount for learnings about how "to correct the long-standing attitudes which have brought about the present crisis in the nation and around the world, especially as this crisis is prompted by racial injustice."[5] A "Fund for Reconciliation" was established, with a goal of $20 million to be raised during the 1969–1972 quadrennium through voluntary contributions over and above regular giving. The fund would underwrite new programs, such as a United Methodist Voluntary Service Corps to enlist young adults in local projects of reconciliation and reconstruction, and it would support other mission ventures proposed by UMC boards and agencies.

Confrontation and Change

In September 1968, as the United Methodist Board of Missions gathered for its first organizational meeting, members were anticipating further structural changes ahead. It was not the usual institutional issues that would dominate the Board's agenda but the impact on the organization of the social upheavals occurring in North American urban centers, on university campuses, and in many nations of the world. The Board president, Bishop Lloyd Wicke, attempted to chart the course in his opening address: "As we gather to discuss the ongoing life of this Board as an institutional arm or branch of the universal Church, we are presented with two foci: the one, the eternal nature of the Gospel, and the other, the molten sea of the human spirit to which it seeks to speak and in which it strives to live and serve. How shall this Board conduct its mission so that from these two foci an inclusive ellipse, an inclusive family of the spirit, may evolve? This is our task."[6]

The rising voices of the powerless in the world population stirred the spirits of their corresponding constituencies within the membership of The UMC. These advocates not only provoked the church to respond with programs and projects aimed at meeting newly recognized human needs but also called upon the church to reform and to support movements of political and social change. It was, after all, the unjust systems that produced inequality and human suffering which preoccupied the minds and actions of demonstrators and protesters in U.S. streets and institutions and beyond.

Because the Board of Missions was the largest agency of the denomination, having substantial resources to channel into programs of renewal, advocates of reform from within and beyond the church singled it out. The dialogue that follows documents the origins of a progressive shift in the locus of mission initiative. It moved from official agencies of the denomination to caucuses or ad hoc groups organized to exert pressure and assume leadership in shaping the direction of the mission of their church.

The Reverend Cain Hope Felder, left, a member of Black Methodists for Church Renewal, works with Tracey K. Jones, Jr., general secretary of the United Methodist Board of Missions, during negotiations after a sit-in by African Americans at the Board offices in 1969. *(Photo courtesy of UM Archives and History)*

Black Demands

The Black Economic Development Conference, headed by civil rights activist James Forman, called for reparations to African Americans from institutions that benefitted from the slave labor of their ancestors. Forman turned first to the churches in a dramatic confrontation at historic Riverside Church in New York City. He demanded $500 million for investment in various African-American controlled enterprises, from a land bank to media and publishing concerns. He started with the church, he said, because it is one of the principal "sources of capital in the United States. . . . We know that to get reparations from the government you, in fact, have to defeat it in a military war. And we felt that the most fluid source of capital was the church."[7]

A response was demanded from all churches—not just the well-established Riverside congregation. To communicate this message, Forman's group focused on the Interchurch Center, headquarters of several major denominations. Forman recruited sympathetic black students from Union

Theological Seminary and Columbia University to join him in occupying the offices of the National Council of the Churches of Christ in the U.S.A. (NCC) in New York.[8] The poignancy of the case notwithstanding, the churches found it difficult to respond to a movement lacking accessible structures for channelling resources to effectuate lasting change. The Board of Missions was the focus of a response from The UMC. Black staff members, encouraged by the organization of Black Methodists for Church Renewal (BMCR), sharpened the appeal in ways the Board of Missions could not dismiss.

The Black Staff Task Force Proposal to the Board of Missions had five points of emphasis: (1) *Education:* It called upon the Board to provide financial and technical assistance to the fund-raising efforts of denominational black colleges. It also recommended that the Board help with the raising of the $2 million Race Relations Day offering in the churches. (2) *Economics:* It summoned the Board to contribute $1.3 million to economic-development initiatives in black communities through organizations such as BMCR, United Methodist Commission on Religion and Race, Black Economic Development Conference, and the Interreligious Foundation for Community Organization (IFCO). (3) *Decision Making:* It demanded a greater role for blacks to participate in policy development and decision making in the Board. Specifically, it proposed the election of black staff to three key positions: an ombudsman for the entire Board, an assistant general secretary for the National Division in the area of economic and secular development, and an assistant general secretary for the World Division to oversee African affairs and administer the Africa regional program staff. (4) *Resources Office*: It recommended the establishment of an office in the Joint Commission on Education and Cultivation to address needs of minority groups. (5) *Special Missionary Training:* It called for the retraining of Board missionaries to "understand the trends in the black revolution."[9]

The Board of Missions was prompt to accept these recommendations at the same meeting in which they were presented (the annual meeting in October 1969). Only the promotion of the Race Relations Offering, managed by another general agency, was left unaddressed. The programs of IFCO, the National Committee of Black Churchmen, BMCR and other minority caucuses, the World Council of Churches (WCC) Program to Combat Racism, and black colleges related to the Board all received sizeable grants, totaling $1.3 million, from sources determined by the National, World, and Women's divisions.[10]

The decision to place African Americans in three key personnel positions was a breakthrough for ethnic-minority representation in mission board leadership. The Board promoted the Reverend Negail Riley, an executive with the National Division, to the rank of assistant general secretary. Isaac Bivens of Mission Personnel was elected assistant general secretary for the Africa program in the World Division. The Reverend Harry Gibson, a pastor and superintendent in the Northern Illinois Conference, was recruited to be ombudsman. In 1972, the Board took a further step in electing the Reverend Randolph Nugent — the first director of its New York–based Metropolitan Urban Service Training (MUST) program and head of the Division of Overseas Ministries of the NCC — to the post of associate general secretary for the National Division. African Americans had finally penetrated the racial barrier of The UMC mission board.

Hispanic Demands

In subsequent meetings of the Board of Missions, spokespersons from other racial/ethnic minorities in the church made their appeals for recognition and resources. Hispanics were represented by MARCHA (*Metodistas Asociados Representando la Causa Hispano-Americanos*, or Methodist Association Representing the Cause of Hispanic-Americans). At the 1970 annual meeting, Dr. Elias Galván, chair of MARCHA, presided over a panel presentation on the conditions facing Hispanics in Los Angeles, Salt Lake City, and Chicago. The churches and social organizations were neglecting growing populations of Latin American immigrants to these communities, being locked into patterns of discrimination based on language and culture. Successes in community organizing were presenting new opportunities for Hispanics in the areas of education, housing, job training, and economic development. An appeal was made to the Board to participate in the funding of organizations dedicated to community development among Hispanics. But the panel members also called for reforms in Hispanic representation at the Board of Missions to make this happen more effectively: "We want to underscore the petition for adequate and significant representation on the Board of Managers and on the staff of the Board of Missions. MARCHA is distressed at the numerical inadequacy of Hispanic-American representation in this Board. This kind of tokenism speaks loud and clear about the historic indifference with which the Board has viewed the Hispanic-American people of this country. We urge the Board to take immediate action to correct this injustice."[11]

César Chávez, the founder of the National Farm Workers Union, here shown with Coretta Scott King, worked to organize migrant farm workers and demand recognition of their basic human rights. *(Photo courtesy of UM Archives and History)*

Advocacy for expanding the focus on Hispanic mission and ministry was not intended to displace or diminish the importance of the historic Spanish-language mission of the Río Grande Conference, which the Board administered through its National Division. The Río Grande leadership participated in a disciplined planning process and presented a comprehensive package of program proposals for the Board's support. These proposals centered primarily upon leadership development for Río Grande clergy and laity—the primary source of personnel recruitment by annual conferences and churchwide agencies seeking Hispanic leaders to help them better serve this growing and increasingly vocal constituency.

The Board of Missions gradually turned its attention to filling its discernible void of Hispanic staff. The only full-time Hispanic staff position was related to the National Division administration of the mission work in Río Grande. Key portfolios of the World Division called for experience and expertise in the Latin American cultural context, but they were usually filled by missionary personnel, completely overlooking Hispanic-American United Methodists. This would eventually change, but the need for National Division staff with Hispanic church- and community-development skills was readily addressed. Positions in parish ministries, congregational development, and interpretation were soon identified and filled by Hispanics.

Native American Demands

The voices of Native Americans were also heard. A position paper from the Oklahoma Indian Missionary Conference (OIMC) summarized the issue with these words: "The call for self-determination is the call to be involved in the total ministry of the Church. We can no longer sit in the balconies of the Church or appear as mere observers while decisions that

Russell Means, center, the leader of the American Indian Movement, met with the Reverend Homer Noley, a United Methodist, during the standoff at the Wounded Knee Reservation in South Dakota in 1973. The man with the belt of bullets is unidentified but was a member of the security force of the village of Wounded Knee. *(Photo courtesy of Nebraska United Methodist Historical Center)*

ultimately affect us are being made by the Church and its boards and agencies."[12]

The claims upon the Board by the Native American constituency were not as detailed and specific as those of the African and Hispanic Americans, but Native American complaints documented a long history of benign neglect by the mission organization. On the occasion of the Board's annual meeting in 1970, the Reverend Homer Noley, director of American Indian work in the Nebraska Conference, criticized the Board for being "over-organized": "By official cynicism, I refer to the arbitrary manner in which decisions are made in boards and agencies regarding American Indian work. We react to this with a kind of cynicism as well. . . . What has happened here . . . is that we are organized about like the Bureau of Indian Affairs. [It] started out with 12 members . . . with instructions that they would work themselves out of a job. They now have over 24,000 members. . . . What happens when you become over-organized is that you have to go to one office for this and another for that. . . . A system like this causes people to act toward one another without regard to feelings and humanity of the people involved."[13]

Ironically, Rev. Noley then urged the creation of a new department for American Indian ministries within the Board. He maintained that such a position would provide greater access to Indian concerns. While the department was never established, a new Native American staff portfolio was created, which Noley eventually filled.

United Methodist concern for a witness among Native Americans was not limited to the structures and constituents of the denomination. When organizers of the American Indian Movement (AIM) protested the injustices at the Wounded Knee Reservation in South Dakota, Noley, then with the Board of Global Ministries, and the Reverend John Adams, executive staff member of the General Board of Church and Society, participated. Dennis Banks, executive director of AIM, noted their presence in an address to the Board at its annual meeting in 1974: "During the past years the American Indian Movement has wondered about the social principles of organized churches. What exactly is their total goal? What is the church? At Wounded Knee the questions were answered. Our only criticism may now be that there are not enough men like Homer Noley and John Adams. Other churches should now be commanded to follow the examples set by The United Methodist Church. For had it not been for the direct involvement of Homer Noley and John Adams, which started the negotiations to end the crisis, there may very well have been a repeat of the 1890 Wounded Knee massacre."[14]

Youth and Young Adult Demands

The most articulate and analytical appeals to the Board of Missions for sweeping changes in focus and mission agenda came from youth and young adult leaders. Aware that most organizations pointed with pride to the presence of youth but seldom let young people be heard or be given a role in decision making, the youth and young adult leaders developed several strategies for increasing their impact on the Board of Missions. When the Board established a Special Committee on Involvement of Young People in January 1969, the leadership did not create a laundry list of programs and policies that would benefit from Board funding or more youth participants. Instead, the leaders asked for more time and resources to form a youth task force and charge it with producing a comprehensive report to the Board. The task force members dedicated a whole summer to researching and analyzing social issues and developing the rationale for findings that focused on the need for system change. Their recommendations were incorporated into a major position paper presented by the Special Committee to the Board's annual meeting in October 1969.

This final report emphasized cause-and-effect relationships, charging the church with "complicity" in the forces of colonialism, racism, and oppression. The youth had not heard the voice of the church firmly raised against the social injustices that perpetuate poverty and political oppression. They were looking for models of social change in the mission programs of the Board. Until the church became part of the solution, they said, it was itself causing the kinds of human suffering that blacks, Hispanics, and Native Americans were reporting. They wanted the church to confront and redress its own institutional racism and own up to its own status among the economically privileged and corrupt institutions of society.

The chair of the Special Committee on Involvement of Young People readily dismissed self-interest as a motivating force behind its work. Rather, he characterized the role of his committee as "an aggressive enabler in Christian mission, enabling the Board to face issues presented by minority groups."[15] Indeed the committee's report admonished the Board to adopt the recommendations of other groups, for example, full funding for the requests from BMCR with which the Board was struggling. But the major thesis of the youth task force report was distinctive. It established new parameters for the church's self-understanding and, consequently, its mission purposes. The youth concluded that the North American church had too easily identified "with the nature, assumptions, goals, and values of the American society. This has led to the theological corruption of the Church's own nature, message, and mission . . . and the misdirection of its resources towards its own self-perpetuation, power, and aggrandizement instead of towards the service of the poor, the weak, and the oppressed."[16] The youth envisioned a role for the church that supported movements for social change rather than identifying with social institutions that only defended their own status and privilege. "Specific changes in the Church's programs, policies, or structures," they concluded, "will have little significance unless they are accompanied by a commitment to a new world and new values of life other than what the industrial and technological society of the West has hitherto provided."[17]

In the prologue of their report to the Board, the youth uncritically adopted the perspective and rhetoric of the revolutionary movements for social change. They called upon the Board to "dissociate itself from competitive capitalism," engage the whole church in a process of "anti-racist training," disavow secular organizational patterns that produce "the stratification and isolation of people . . . in the church bureaucracy," along with a host of other generalities. But then they began "meddling" in the specific and historic values and actions of the missionary enterprise. They called for decision making over the use of funds to be devolved to local

control, especially to those organizations that represent poor and oppressed peoples' legitimate claims for self-determination. "Supremacist
assumptions" of the missionary movement were to be reviewed and their
impact upon other religions and cultures addressed. Duplicity was alleged
in the fact that, while the church accepted reparations from governments
that seized church properties and resources in acts of war, it refused to
consider restitution for damages caused by its own racism.

Youth critiques of Board policies and program directions included
specific mission venues. Regarding Korea, the youth alleged that the
church's mission to society was preempted by the church's fascination
with self-development. The young critics singled out Cuba for a critique
of failure by mission churches to accept the realities of the revolution and
to contribute to positive developments. They rebuked the ministry in the
suburban U.S., where they said the church was squandering mission resources in building churches for the wealthy. All these matters were referred to units of the Board for consideration. The Special Committee on
Involvement of Young People reviewed reports from Board divisions and
other sources. Each report was met by new proposals or recommendations, taking the Board deeper into the agenda for social change laid out
by the youth. The World Division was challenged to review its charter
and to challenge any prohibitions on the use of its funds for programs
within the U.S. The Board's financial officers were encouraged to participate in socially responsive and politically sensitive investments. A bond
fund for pretrial detainees in the U.S. was recommended as a missional
responsibility.

Over time, the youth agenda turned from an exclusive focus on human
rights and civil rights to its own constituency's concerns. Helping the
church understand and interpret the "youth culture" became its major
objective. Then, as the Board moved through a series of restructures, appeals for larger and broader-based representation on Board committees
and in other internal matters began to dominate the youth agenda. Thus
young people successfully confronted the Board over its mission in the social and political context and then saw to it that their generational issues
were also included within the scope of the church's mission focus.

Women's Empowerment

The women's movement in the secular society produced corresponding
actions within The UMC. The Woman's Division petitioned the 1968

General Conference to authorize a churchwide study commission to research the implications for the church of the changing role of women in the worldwide community. The aim of the study was to "see how [the church's] woman power is used in this time of growing recognition of basic equality of men and women."[18] The concern of the Woman's Division was the empowerment of women in the program and policymaking arenas of the church. The Program Council, the official coordinating body for denominational agencies, turned to the renamed Women's Division to fund the study. The division refused on the basis that the research was to be a priority for the whole church, not for one division alone.

The Women's Division did not hesitate in contributing to the critique and analysis of barriers to full participation of women in the life of the church. The Ad Hoc Committee on Churchwomen's Liberation was formed, and it developed policy proposals and recommendations for the 1972 General Conference. These proposals included a formula to ensure women's membership on church boards and agencies and supported a similar formula for minority-group members and youth. The committee also focused on the participation of minority-group women in the life of women's organizations in annual conferences and local churches, especially in light of the ongoing merger of the Central Jurisdiction into the geographical jurisdictions of the church.[19] The combined efforts of the Women's Division and the study commission resulted in the establishment of a churchwide Commission on the Status and Role of Women (COSROW) by the 1972 General Conference.

The laity was the primary focus of the Women's Division advocacy for women in the church. Over the years, women had been systematically excluded from the ranks of clergy. The organizational predecessors of the Women's Division (and similar organizations in other denominations) were formed with an adamant determination that women would not be frozen out of the missionary movement. The women's independent activities in missionary recruitment and sending accounted for the rapid increase in denominational missionaries in the late 1800s and early 1900s. Since these women leaders were unconvinced that the wives of missionaries would be singularly devoted to the development of mission work among young girls and women, the primary targets of their recruitment efforts were single women. They recruited women of great vision and ability, many of them professionals in education and medicine. The success of these women in mission and their supporting mission board was especially evident in Asia, where major colleges, universities, and professional schools for young women were established and still represent an important aspect of the Christian commitment to community service.

In 1964, the General Conference had merged the independent work of the Woman's Division of The Methodist Church with the administration of its World and National divisions. It was following a pattern established by other Protestant denominations. The elimination of "dual administration" of mission was seen to have greater efficiency and economy. But the program impact of the decision was to produce negative repercussions. In an unpublished paper, Marian Derby, director of planning of the World Division, 1969–1971, charts a sharp decline in the numbers of single women serving as missionaries in both the Methodist and the EUB churches. Their numbers fell by more than 50 percent, from 578 in 1950 to 274 in 1970.[20]

The decline in missionary service by single women may have been an established trend before the actual merger of "women's work" within general denominational mission boards, but it had many correlative effects in mission programs. Derby cites research done by Dr. R. Pierce Beaver, the acknowledged "dean" of seminary mission professors. Beaver concluded that, among missionaries, single women had a stronger penchant than men or couples for relating to the women in another country directly rather than through church structures. This quality allowed single women to take a more experimental approach and assume greater risks. Consequently, with the demise of this missionary cadre, the mission lost its innovative and creative edge. Opportunities for working with women with "special talents and interests" were lost, which resulted in the loss of women's influence in the churches and the society as well. Mission churches and ecumenical agencies had fewer women serving as role models of strong leadership, so they further concentrated authority in the hands of men. Scholarship committees had fewer women on their committees and, in consequence, gave preferential treatment to male candidates. Educational opportunities and formal and informal leadership development programs were designed with male constituents in mind. The mission churches were losing their capacity to be strong advocates for women and to protect women's rights in public policy.

The Derby study offered strong motivation for a formal consultation by the Women's Division on the subject of "Single Women in Church and Society." The results of the consultation were strategically released to strengthen the role of the newly established COSROW. Its objective was to "further affirm that the visibility and participation of women in all areas of church life must be the goal of the total church." The consultation concluded that not only were women's voices in the church being suppressed but that single women were particularly vulnerable. It called upon the church to recognize "the need to affirm the validity and wholeness of singleness as a choice of life-style for clergy and laity, both women and men." With special reference to female clergy, the consultation summary aimed at the appointment-making authority of the bishops, calling upon them "to adhere to the mandate of the *Discipline* for guaranteed appointments for all ordained ministers." It identified the need for the church to examine carefully the issues of legal discrimination and to be better informed about matters of human sexuality. The Women's Division was urged to publish study materials for distribution to its members.[21]

The repercussions of the erosion of women's presence and their threatened loss of influence in mission did not escape the mission board itself. The Women's Division began a process of carefully documenting the devolution of policy and program control from women's leadership to male replacements at both the mission headquarters and the local agency levels. In its ten-year review of the General Conference action to divest it of its direct (independent) administrative authority for mission, the Women's Division engaged in a sharp dialogue with the National and World divisions about the role of women in staffing the U.S. headquarters of the Board of Global Ministries as well as local program units. The ten-year review also provoked detailed accounting for the use of funds the Women's Division allocated to the World and National divisions for the maintenance of programs for women and children. There was little satisfaction with the data received about the other divisions' handling of the women's mission legacy.

Gradually, the Women's Division began the process of tightening accountability for the use of its appropriations by other units of the Board. By 1990, the Women's Division had taken over the direct administration of support services, including the production of educational materials for United Methodist Women (UMW) and the distribution of all GBGM publications from the United Methodist Service Center in Cincinnati. By 1995, the Women's Division had also established joint committees of staff and directors (its administrative and policymaking arms) to guide funding decisions for all U.S. and international programs for women and children that were supported by Women's Division appropriations.

Autonomy in World Church Relationships

The global manifestation of Methodist mission successfully evolved from a missionary-centered church formation to the emergence of indigenous local church structures. With the rise of nationalism around the globe following the Second World War, indigenous church leaders and structures sought greater independence from the policies and dominance of their foreign mission-sending boards. Many will remember this period because of the provocative call for a "missionary moratorium." Missionary-established churches had produced talented young leaders who yearned for opportunities to lead and help sustain their churches within the cultures where they were planted. Continued dependence upon missionaries was an impediment.[22] Bishop Prince A. Taylor, Jr., a former Central Jurisdiction bishop assigned to preside over the Liberia Conference, summarized the case for the African Methodists:

> The course that Methodism might take in the days ahead must take into account the changing international character and climate, the impact of this change on the life of the Church. It is perhaps sufficient to point out that in Africa alone, in the last eight years, thirty-one or more colonies and territories have come into statehood, have elected their national leaders, have become members of international bodies, and have been admitted to the UN as equal with the former powers which held them in subjection. . . . Let me emphasize again that just as these countries no longer desire to be under the political domination of a foreign power, they will no longer accept foreign ecclesiastical control, whether by a bishop, a board, or a missionary. . . . They do not believe that persons living from three to seven thousand miles away, however erudite they may be, understand local needs as well as the national leaders themselves. . . . They want a structure that will make it possible for them to elect their own episcopal leadership and enough latitude to adapt the policies and program of their own peculiar needs.[23]

The polity of the denomination provided three alternatives for Methodist church bodies seeking greater independence: (1) autonomy, or structural independence from The UMC; (2) united churches, or mergers of Methodist bodies with other local churches, which then could request autonomy from the General Conference; and (3) central conference status, remaining within the organizational structure of The UMC. Autonomous and united churches could seek an "affiliated" status with The UMC. To those choosing the central conference option, General Conference would grant a measure of latitude to control their own affairs, especially in the drafting of their own *Book of Discipline*. This option permitted the churches to address contextual issues such as clergy recognition and membership in conferences, the structure of annual conferences, and the election of episcopal leaders via their central conferences.

The World Division began a series of Partnership in Mission consultations to redefine these relationships on the basis of the stronger self-determination sought by the former mission churches. Bishop Wicke, president of the Board of Missions in the 1969–1972 quadrennium, expressed the position of the Board as being "evenhanded" in saying to the churches: "The choice of the relationship is yours. Remain as a Central Conference and an organic member of the General Conference if you desire. Or, set up housekeeping for yourself and decide whether you wish to maintain a fraternal relationship with the 'founding brethren.' In either instance, our affection and loyal support are continuingly and evenhandedly yours. If you would wish that fraternal relationship to manifest itself in a Conference of Methodist Churches, we would be happy to discuss the possibility promptly."[24]

Wicke then questioned the prudence of maintaining this "lofty and insulated position of regal neutrality" and suggested the need to "share the wisdom [the Board] has gathered through its long history."[25]

By 1972, the issue had been settled with or without a clear directive from the Board of Missions or the General Conference. All the mission churches related to the former Methodist Church in Latin America and Asia had chosen autonomy, with the following exceptions. The United Methodist Church in Puerto Rico remained an annual conference of The UMC until 1992, when it was granted autonomy (with affiliated status) by the General Conference. The United Methodist Church in the Philippines remained in a central conference relationship, while the former EUB relationships in the Philippines, Ecuador, and the Dominican Republic chose the ecumenical alternative, becoming united churches locally but seeking affiliation with The UMC. The mission churches in Africa remained within the central conference structure. Even though the EUB mission in Sierra Leone first chose autonomy, it then reconsidered and became part of the West Africa Central Conference in 1972. After the church union in 1968, the United Methodist churches in Europe all remained in a central conference relationship.

Principles of autonomy were frequently summarized as self-direction, self-support, and self-propagation. While self-determination was a blessing for all the growing young churches, the failure of many countries to benefit from strong economic development has kept their governments and social institutions, including the churches, in a state of dependence. One of the negative considerations in seeking autonomy was the probability of reduced financial support from abroad. The African church leaders whose statement follows soberly addressed this reality in a consultation with representatives of the GBGM:

1. We support the maintenance of the Central Conference relationship. We believe that this is a better way toward genuine autonomy.

2. We feel that we must work hard to become true stewards of Jesus Christ so that we can shoulder our responsibilities in carrying out the mission of Jesus and his church in Africa with a greater degree of self-sufficiency.

3. We do not want to foster paternalism and we resent being called "product." We now want to produce as well in order to minimize or end the humiliation of being wretched beggars, and burdens on the World Division. When we strive toward relative selfhood of the churches in Africa, we will be able to serve the church with dignity, integrity, and self-response and thereby achieve true partnership in mission.

4. We ask that the African Churches be allowed larger freedom to plan and implement their own indigenous leadership in cooperation with persons in mission, that they use personnel and financial resources to their best judgment and adopt and implement policies without hindrance.[26]

In the early years of independence in various African countries, mission schools and hospitals were nationalized by heady governments, only to be returned within a few years for the churches to operate because of financial problems. Similar problems with managing church-based institutions were encountered by the small-membership autonomous Methodist bodies in Latin America. Whatever status the former mission churches may have chosen within the United Methodist family, most of them continued to look to the Board of Missions (renamed the Board of Global Ministries in 1972) for program and institutional support of the missionary work they inherited.

The family of churches that evolved from former Methodist and EUB missionary activity has maintained connectional relationships on a regional and international basis. The European churches have formed a European Council of Methodist Churches, which recently enlarged its membership to include the "mother church" of all Methodism in the United Kingdom. The presidents, bishops, and other heads of Methodist churches throughout Asia meet periodically to cultivate a fraternal relationship and to review the work of their respective churches. The most highly structured regional body is the Council of Evangelical Methodist Churches in Latin America (*Consejo de Iglesias Evangelicas Metodistas de America Latina*, or CIEMAL). It seeks to be a representative body of Methodism within the region, to contextualize the mission of the churches in Latin America, and to prioritize program responses for which funding is granted by cooperative mission boards, especially GBGM.

In the early dialogue over the future shape and direction of witness for a global Methodism, many looked to the World Methodist Council (WMC) to assume a stronger or more formal role. When the Commission on the Structure of Methodism Overseas (COSMOS) completed its work with a report to the 1972 General Conference, the WMC was expected to take the next step in creating a representative governance structure for Methodist bodies worldwide. Instead, the council remained a self-selected body of world Methodist church leaders, gathering out of a common Wesleyan heritage and acting on behalf of their churches without any binding authority. What the WMC does provide is a global connection allowing churches in the Methodist tradition to find occasional opportunities for fellowship and to undertake some work together. It welcomes the participation of all of the churches of Methodism, whether newly independent or continuing in a structural relationship to The UMC. But whether this informal structure adequately captures the vision of a global connection of independent Methodist churches — a vision that helped energize the movement toward local or national autonomy — has never been addressed, though the dialogue over the global nature of The UMC continues.[27]

Developing a Global Perspective

The expansive global reach of the missionary enterprise undertaken by mission boards of the predecessor denominations of The UMC was never in doubt. But when the general church structure for the new denomination was adopted in 1972, the word "global" inserted into the name of the agency to which mission administration was entrusted—the Board (later, General Board) of Global Ministries—had more than geographical implications. In an address to the newly organized Board of Global Ministries, the Reverend Emilio Castro of the autonomous Methodist Church in Uruguay helped to identify and define the aspects of being a global organization. From his Latin American perspective, "global" implied being in a responsible relationship to contemporary life-shaping forces, many of which were already having an impact on the mission of The UMC.

1. *Global* means the realization of a world interaction. . . . What happens in your mission to minorities or peace movements, etc., are inspirational helps or stumbling blocks to our mission in Latin America.

2. *Global* is a dimension that respects, enriches, but never suppresses or suffocates the local. Our global perspective should help the selfhood of the national church. That limits your freedom . . . but surely it gives you a new dimension of freedom that is called love.

3. *Global* is the willingness to listen to all voices in the Christian world. . . . The discussing processes should be enlarged. . . . This will complicate your working style but will add wisdom and responsibility to your mission.

4. We have a global Gospel for a global mission . . . a unity in itself . . . not a piecemeal approach but a call to *metanoia* [repentance]. This will mean that . . . seven divisions [of the Board of Global Ministries] will listen to each other and . . . share an understanding of the *humanum* [human race] that you want to serve.

5. *Global* means a pooling of your resources . . . for better missionary service. . . . It is also your opportunity to receive help from churches and people all over the world.

6. *Global* means to realize the global dimension of your nation's attitudes. A global mission means for you to act responsibly in relation to your nation's foreign policy, to the investment policy, to the behavior of big corporations, to the shaping of a sound public opinion.

7. *Global* is a big word. We need to be reminded of our littleness. We are not alone in the world. God works through many agents. We should not be messianic-minded but servant-minded.

8. *Global* means an attitude of openness towards the world. We cannot be provincial. It is to have an attitude of hope in relation to the future of mankind [*sic*] while we work with courage to fulfill our role in order to make that hope real.[28]

So, in addition to administering the global mission of the denomination, the Board of Global Ministries was again being challenged to take on the mission of modeling a new organizational behavior. As the work of the new Board progressed into its first quadrennium (1973–1976), Bishop Paul A. Washburn, the president, and the Reverend Dr. Tracey K. Jones, the general secretary, lamented the concerns or anxieties about this challenge expressed by mission constituencies in the church. These concerns provided much evidence of the tension between doing business as usual and accepting the increasingly global nature of the organization. The list included the following: lack of interdivisional cooperation within the Board; too much time spent on internal communications within The UMC at the expense of the mission task itself; a possibly waning concern for human liberation; weak theological grounding; and a complaint that "in our haste and commitment to help others, we dehumanize each other."[29]

Living with high expectations and suffering the criticisms of demanding mission constituencies became a way of life for the Board of Missions on the way to becoming a "new" Board of *Global* Ministries. Was the scope of its work too demanding and the diversity of its constituencies (served and supporting) too great to serve a common good? Or, was the Board awakening to the never-ending process of self-criticism and correction that is part and parcel of the culture of all social institutions caught in the dynamics of revolutionary change? Each constituency had its own analysis. Ethnic minorities saw evidences of racism; mission partners murmured about paternalism; women detected sexism; youth alleged ageism; theological conservatives found too much liberalism; and liberals complained about the conservatives' protection of traditional values. Denominational bureaucrats questioned the complexity of the Board's organization, which resulted in numerous appeals for greater efficiency through organizational restructure and even headquarters relocation. (See chapter 5 for a further discussion of these issues.)

Mission Themes: Reconciliation and Unity

There were strong responses by the Board of Global Ministries to its changing mission situation: some proposed pragmatic program activities, and some offered visionary, pathbreaking ideas, while others were inclined toward quite ponderous and generally theoretical discussions. The work of all The UMC's agencies, however, was to be guided by a quadrennial program theme of "Reconciliation," established by the 1968 General Conference. It was a timely theme, including a financial appeal, designed to address the brokenness of communities after the impact of the social crises of the 1960s.

Economic Development and Empowerment

The Board concluded that the root of the problem was powerlessness, and the response would be programs aimed at community development, with a goal of reconciliation. The National Division Committee on Policy and Program drafted a position paper rejecting separatism:

"The history of the American experiment reveals that most major minority groups have had to achieve a degree of social power in order to gain equality of opportunity. This opportunity, once realized, has provided a threshold from which such groups have achieved a wider participation in society. The current emphasis on empowerment and separatism may be seen as a temporary, but essential, element in facilitating further minority group participation. Separatism is not a goal in this instance, but a phase in a process of moving toward a fuller community. This background suggests a general goal of moving through separatism toward a new humanity or community."[30]

This policy base resonated with the program theme of "reconciliation." It also precluded any favorable response to the more militant black agenda expressed by James Forman and other advocates of reparations. The Reverend Dr. J. Edward Carothers, associate general secretary of the National Division, reminded Board members of the inadequacy of a response focused upon money alone. After all, $500 million distributed among twenty million African Americans would be small change, hardly enough to stimulate significant systemic change. Carothers concluded:

> It is clear . . . that all the churches in the nation do not have enough money to produce alone the changes our nation desperately needs in the realm of economic development. . . . What the nation needs now is a middle class that has a deep economic concern. It should be an important part of our aim in mission to get this movement going through the specific involvement of our people in a better understanding of national patterns. There are few indications right now that our church people have a real feeling for the plight of the poor. This is not because they are hardhearted. The reason is that people do not dare permit themselves to feel a burden that seems beyond their powers to deal with in some constructive way.[31]

Carothers had already led Board efforts to invest in the rebuilding of urban communities through investment in high-risk, minority-owned small businesses. The Mission Enterprise Loan and Investment Committee (MELIC) identified $3 million of the Board's general funds for management. For two and a half years, the committee reviewed applications and business plans from minority firms in poor U.S. communities and then recommended thirty-one loans totaling $887,000 directed to businesses located in seventeen cities and twelve states. In addition, two loans were made to organizations in other countries. Many of these investments leveraged other funding from local banks, government (the Small Business Administration), and foundations that shared the objectives of empowering local communities through economic development. The endeavors financed included two gas stations and a credit union, nursery school, radio station, furniture company, and consulting firm. In a report documenting the difficulties of administering a national loan program without sufficient staffing and technical services, the general treasurer of the Board reported a net loss of a quarter of a million dollars on the investments.[32]

Urban Strategies

The MELIC experiment was a highly practical response to the economic plight of minority urban communities. But Carothers's philosophy regarding the limitations of money was self-fulfilling. MELIC ended when the National Division had no more money to invest and the other two GBGM divisions chose not to participate. For Carothers, the next frontier for national mission was to capture the minds and hearts of church members. He believed that transforming attitudes regarding the causes of poverty could move church members from passively sitting in pews to joining local efforts at social change. The strategy he put forward was based on lay training and leadership development modeled by the National Division's creative response to the urban crisis: the Metropolitan Urban Service Training program (MUST). This organization, based in New York City, gave encouragement to pastoral and lay leadership in United Methodist churches in decaying urban neighborhoods.

Carothers proposed a new direction for MUST II. In an era when the church seemed to be held in "suburban captivity"—with denominational funds flowing out of urban neighborhoods into new church building in fast-growing suburbs—he wanted to liberate affluent suburban "captives" from a state of arrested Christian development, breaking down the economic barriers that insulated them from the poverty crisis next door and motivating them to invest their skills and resources in economic empowerment of the poor.

The crisis addressed by efforts at community or economic development was not to be interpreted as a "national crisis" but as a "crisis in the nations." The Board was challenged by its president, Wicke, to recognize that "urbanization is as much a problem in Cairo and Calcutta as in Chicago."[33] With that understanding, the Board moved on several fronts. A Boardwide Task Force on World Development was established with Theressa Hoover, associate general secretary for the Women's Division, as the chair. She saw the mandate from the Board as being not the creation of a new program but an internal focusing of existing Board strategies on the global or systemic nature of the crisis facing urban populations. The task force encouraged the Board to act more intentionally as a global entity, guided by the ecumenical WCC program theme of "Mission on Six Continents." It emphasized the principle of self-determination as a primary objective in all development work. It favored a good look at mission within the U.S. as putting "our own house in order" — but not to the neglect of cooperative mission "to the genuine needs of people wherever they are." It encouraged the Board to see itself as a missionary receiving — as well as sending — agency, placing a new emphasis on accepting personnel from mission partners around the world to help U.S. churches with the mission on their doorstep.[34]

The challenge to consider mission strategies for urban development on a global scale caused the World Division to rethink some of its assumptions about the arbitrary geographical definition of its work beyond the U.S. In a report to the Board, it acknowledged: "The crisis in black/white relations in the United States is part of a world crisis, which presses with utmost urgency upon the world community. It calls the Board of Missions and the World Division to a new recognition of the rights of oppressed peoples everywhere. . . . The World Division must press the urgent global claims of justice and focus any reformulation of priorities within a framework that takes full account of the oppressed communities of the world both within and beyond our own nation."[35]

In a controversial decision, the World Division concluded that it would "participate financially in a significant measure in whatever amount the Board of Missions may allocate to black community development in the United States."[36] But to be certain that its distinct global mission mandate be addressed, the division went on to formulate its own global urban-development agenda. Its urban program was headlined as "Twelve Cities in Twelve Nations."[37] In Africa, the cities selected were Salisbury, Rhodesia (now Harare, Zimbabwe); Lubumbashi, Democratic Republic of the Congo; and Freetown, Sierra Leone. Here the World Division emphasized the value of having MUST director Randolph Nugent and National Division executive Negail Riley available to serve as consultants on developing strategies and program structures for urban ministries. In Latin America, São Paulo, Brazil; Buenos Aires, Argentina; Lima, Peru; and Ciudad Juárez, México, were chosen. Partner churches, ecumenical outreach agencies, and personnel with which the division had experience in each setting were recommended channels for resources. MUST II was again engaged to assist, particularly with a consultative process in Juárez and El Paso, sister cities on the Río Grande. In Asia, the cities chosen were Calcutta, India; Seoul-Inchon, Korea; Manila, Philippines; the city state of Singapore; and major cities in Japan. In this region, significant working relationships on urban matters were already established with ecumenical bodies, including a regional umbrella structure in the Urban Industrial Committee of the East Asia Christian Council.

The "Twelve Cities" program represented a significant means of prioritizing the development and channelling of resources for a global mission strategy, particularly in urban and economic development. While the pattern of support for this new direction emphasized grant making, the funding addressed strategies for leadership training and development, community organizing, and modeling new forms of ministry, such as industrial missions. Nevertheless, the capacity for managing a continuing response left much to be desired. This global and regional program theme and focus may have been provoked by the Board's crisis-response mentality and did not survive into subsequent quadrennial planning.

Community Development

The Board Task Force on World Development was conscious of the degree of unpreparedness in the church at large for a mission program shift from traditional missionary activities to a more policy-oriented approach to development projects in Third World countries. It stressed the importance of interpretation with the church constituency, especially programs of development education designed to foster attitudes and strategies to reinforce needed social change. The Joint Committee on Education and

Cultivation responded with events entitled "Why Global?" Such workshops with mission leaders in United Methodist districts and conferences laid out the agenda for development, including the underlying causes of poverty and oppression in Third World countries.[38] As part of its Quadrennial Emphasis (1969–1972), the World Division funded the placement of journalists in Asia to do full-time reporting on development issues for readers of U.S. church publications. The World Division also helped to fund research centers that developed educational resources from a Christian perspective, emphasizing developmental values related to human dignity, quality of life, and social, racial, and economic justice.[39]

The Women's Division initiated a community-based model for development education. It funded the services of a group of activists in Baltimore to "develop and implement experiments in Third World Awareness and Action in selected communities of the East Coast and Midwest." The goal of the project was "to significantly alter the awareness of people to structures and forces which enslave and dehumanize people; to enable people to adopt a new [missional] life style characterized by corporate action aimed at restructuring society in the U.S. and aiding the liberation of Third World peoples."[40] The workshops in selected communities probed the local level of awareness of the sufferings and injustices facing Third World countries and the people's readiness to form or join local action groups addressing these issues. It was a one-year, small-budget project that provided insights into the models of development education that the Women's Division had already introduced through its mission education programs at the regional, conference, and district levels of women's organizations.

The principle of "self-determination" that guided the Board's efforts to undergird community development efforts with personnel and funding resources was most dramatically achieved by the ecumenical and secular organization known as IFCO (Interreligious Foundation for Community Organization). This was a broad-based organization of local community organizing or development groups in the U.S. It cultivated funding from church groups and foundations in order to make grants to its diverse membership. IFCO members, who represented every racial and ethnic group and who engaged in local community organizing around a host of social issues (such as housing, welfare, education, health care, militarism, racism, criminal justice, and the like), were present at every level of the organization and involved in all decisions, from organizational bylaws to distribution of grants. Church groups that were familiar with the complexity of ecumenical organizations had an appreciation for the purposes, and patience with the functioning, of this multifaceted body. IFCO's direct access to local community groups and to indigenous leaders involved in movements of social change made it a promising force for the changes that churches were eager to accomplish. IFCO was endorsed by Black Methodists for Church Renewal, which advocated strongly for Board of Missions funding for this organization. The United Methodist relationship to IFCO was managed principally by the National Division, which remained in a funding relationship to the organization through the 1970s and into the 1980s. By the end of the century, the organization had refocused its work several times. As it became more ideologically defined by Third World political forces, its mainline Protestant church support diminished. Still, it remained often a radical voice and strong advocate for causes of international justice and peace (for example, challenging the economic boycott of Cuba by shipping computer equipment for churches and other community groups there).

Rethinking New Church Development

Local church participation and leadership in the rebuilding of communities provoked a rethinking of the denomination's investment in "brick-and-mortar" strategies for congregational development. Following the Second World War, Protestant churches raced against one another to establish congregations in rapidly expanding suburban communities. For this purpose, a team of new church developers was recruited, trained, and hired by the Home Mission and Church Extension Board of The Methodist Church. Team members were individually assigned to conferences to organize new congregations and build church edifices in new housing developments. In most cases, they were placed at the disposal of annual conferences, but some were assigned by and directly accountable to the Home Mission Board. The Board supported their work with financial grants and construction loans. The technical services of Board architects and a team of fundraisers (Finance and Field Service) were also on call.

In the 1960s, this mobilization of church resources for new church development came under the scrutiny of those calling for ministries of community reconciliation and church renewal. In a popular book entitled *The Suburban Captivity of the Churches*, Gibson Winter, a professor of ethics and religion at the University of Chicago, compared the costly strategy for church expansion in suburbia to a voluntary abdication of ministry and service in critical urban communities. The prestigious Cathedral of St. John the Divine, located on the edge of New York City's Harlem community, made a symbolic and strategic move in postponing its $20 million building completion and redirecting its building funds to outreach programs in housing, education, and other social justice ministries. In 1968, *Renewal* magazine, a popular journal among inner-city church pastors and laity, called for a one-year moratorium on church construction and a redirection of church stewardship toward programs that contributed to world peace.

The debate over the apparently conflicting values of church building and mission outreach was summarized in articles in *New World Outlook* by *Renewal* editor Stephen C. Rose and Bonneau P. Murphy, the assistant general secretary for the Section on Church Extension of the Methodist Board of Missions. Rose took what he assumed to be the theological high ground, saying: "He [Jesus] was concerned to inform all men of a new reality which might require some buildings over the long haul, but which had more to do with getting out of buildings and into 'all the world.'"[41] Murphy countered with a firm defense of his own leadership of denominational efforts at extending the ministries of the institutional church. He argued for recognition of the sanctity of property: "We need a church-wide crusade to save our sanctuaries and provide homes for new units. We need to become aggressive and enthusiastic about building new churches. The 'no church building group' is contributing to the sense of complacency of our people."[42]

The enthusiasm and accomplishments of the postwar wave of new church development were not equaled again in the twentieth century. The ease with which local churches decided to relocate from racially changing city neighborhoods to "high-potential" suburban developments was countered by a new denominational policy: "The local church shall make every effort to remain in the neighborhood and develop effective ministries to those who are newcomers, whether of a cultural, economic, or ethnic group different from the original or present members."[43]

The rising property values of suburban land outstripped annual conference and National Division reserve funds for site purchases. Increased construction costs put a premium upon church loan funds. The urgent concern for energy conservation in the 1970s called for greater stewardship in more efficient design and construction of church buildings. With the exception of conferences in those sunbelt states that experienced record population growth, the number of United Methodist new church starts diminished annually. The trailing statistics alarmed the proponents of church growth, who alleged a failure of the church's evangelistic mission. Research studies have documented a strong correlation between new church development and membership growth in annual conferences. The findings encouraged some new church adherents among conference program officers. After all, new churches would add new contributing units to conference program budgets. Leaders of organized racial/ethnic groups in the church advocated the causes of both church revitalization and new church development in designing their national plans for ministry to growing populations. The general boards of Global Ministries and Discipleship collaborated in a Joint Committee on Congregational Development to create new resources and conduct annual training events for pastors and conference leaders in new church development assignments.

Though initiatives for congregational development throughout the church have been generally well-conceived and well-defined, funding for this capital-intensive activity has remained the missing ingredient. No proposal has been presented to a General Conference of The UMC for the establishment of a denominational fund for new church development. This activity has always been considered the primary domain of annual conferences, and only a few have garnered the resources needed to meet the challenges and inflated costs of land purchase and new church construction. GBGM administered the only churchwide loan fund for church development: the United Methodist Development Fund (UMDF). Yet its capital — more than $60 million in individual and institutional investments — is small compared to similar resources held by considerably smaller denominations that operate with a higher level of centralization in program and financial administration. Thus, while The UMC entered the twenty-first century with various levels of activity in its conferences, it lacked a strong connectional strategy for resourcing potential membership growth by developing new sites for local church ministries.

Vietnam War Resistance

Building bridges of reconciliation between communities and groups in conflict included a response to the growing national consensus that the U.S. involvement in the Vietnam War (1954–1975) not only was a mistake, but immoral. Churches and ad hoc religious groups were organized into a

At the Democratic National Convention in Chicago in 1968, police beat and imprisoned students and others protesting against the Vietnam War. *(Photo courtesy of AP/Wide World Photos. Used with permission.)*

variety of efforts to question and protest the U.S. involvement in the war. In 1969, the Board of Missions adopted a strong statement on Vietnam, which was prepared and recommended by the Women's Division. This statement recognized the devastating impact of the war in Vietnam and at home: "The Board of Missions of The United Methodist Church believes that . . . our nation has imposed immense suffering on the people of Vietnam and condoned poverty, racism, militarism, and the destruction of the environment at home. The United States has continued and expanded its participation in the Vietnam war for the last fifteen years, and a minimum of one million human beings, Vietnamese and American, have been killed."[44]

Given these facts, the Board supported active dissent against the U.S. Government policies.

Our relation to our government and its policies is shaped by a concern for life with meaning. While this usually takes the form of support for, and participation in, those governmental policies and programs that help [people] fulfill their potential to lead meaningful lives, we must also on occasion question and criticize particular government policies or programs that serve death rather than life. . . . When the policies of a government over a long period of time, and despite continued pleas for change, serve destruction rather than life, when the Church calls again and again for an end to destruction and a new affirmation of life but is ignored, at that point Christians must move from criticism to active opposition to those policies.[45]

Finally, the statement expressed solidarity with those groups and individuals that were engaged in protests and demonstrations to change the U.S. Government Vietnam policies. "The Board of Missions finds no justification for continued United States participation in the war in Vietnam and believes that further United States participation in the war is in profound violation of the Christian faith. We call not for a reduction in that war and a reduction in our participation, but for an immediate end to that war and an immediate end to our participation. In taking this position, we associate ourselves with those individuals and groups who are publicly demonstrating their commitment to ending the war in Vietnam and creating a just and humane society at home. We affirm our support for new initiatives and pledge our cooperation in the struggle to turn our nation away from death and toward life."[46]

The direct efforts made by the Board to implement its policy included the establishment of an Indochina Task Force to monitor government policymaking activities, the support of conscientious objectors to the war by offering alternative service opportunities in missionary programs, and the direct participation of the United Methodist Committee on Relief (UMCOR) in the Vietnam Christian Service program (VCS). This was a cooperative effort by development agencies to provide personnel to work in rebuilding the villages of Vietnam as soon as cessation of hostilities allowed them entry. The Board Joint Committee on Mission Personnel was charged with recruiting participants for this direct service, along with documenting conscientious objector status for young people seeking alternatives to military service. Board missionary programs were certified opportunities for conscientious objectors to the war.

As the Vietnam War dragged on, the Board became involved in antiwar activities, including ministries to those resisting the military draft. The World Division and other units of the Board of Global Ministries cooperated with the Board of Christian Social Concerns and some ecumenical organizations in planning, funding, and participating in international consultations — held in Japan, Paris, and Seoul — on peace priorities for the war in Indochina. Becoming an advocate for Amerasian children, most of whom had been fathered by U.S. military personnel serving in Vietnam, UMCOR urged the U.S. Government to assume a proactive role in assuring the placement of these children in the foster care of U.S. families.

In a resolution on the theme "Indochina: A Time for Healing," the Board advocated U.S. diplomatic recognition of the governments of North and South Vietnam, the promotion of cultural exchanges, and a lifting of the embargo against UNICEF use of U.S. Government funds for children's relief programs in Vietnam. Several divisions of the Board joined other agencies of the denomination in working on issues related to the young adult population disaffected as the result of U.S. involvement in the Indochina war. These agencies worked on amnesty for the 500,000 Vietnam-era veterans with less than honorable discharges and the additional thousands of resisters and deserters in exile. They participated in counseling programs for veterans who were incarcerated or who suffered emotional and mental health problems known as the "post-Vietnam syndrome." They supported counseling and legal aid for war resisters and military deserters in exile. They worked with organizations developing a support network for disaffected female veterans and wives or mothers of men who served or refused to serve in the war. And they advocated for the repatriation of Vietnamese families, especially children, desiring to return. The largest financial commitment was to the Fund for Reconstruction and Reconciliation in Indochina, a program of the WCC aimed at reconciliation with the estranged people of the region following the war. UMCOR contributed $1.1 million to this program and to direct relief activities of the WCC immediately after the war ended.[47]

Agency Transformation

The tumultuous era of revolt and rising expectations in the 1960s and 1970s presented numerous mission challenges to the institutions of the churches. Of all Protestant denominations, The UMC was the most diverse and thus most subject to the demands of active constituency groups. The mission board was the focal point of the struggle. It strived to achieve a posture of affirming diversity within a common mission purpose or direction.

Conflict Management

While some soon became beleaguered by the many confrontations that characterized the Board's business, the general secretary, Tracey K. Jones, offered a theological interpretation of events. He appealed to the Board to see "the impact of the life of Christ . . . in the tremendous revolutionary movements of our time and in the deep concern for the humanization of society. . . . [W]hether it is a time of recession or a time of advance, the critical issue is . . . to learn as much as possible [from] what is happening both in the secular and ecclesiastical worlds."[48] He urged a process of re-training for staff and directors to benefit from new learnings and to appropriate new directions in mission into the program philosophy and objectives of the Board.

Advocates for change came from within and beyond the membership of the church. Fortunately, many of the most articulate critics also exhibited great patience in interpreting new directions for the mission program and policies of the denomination. Gradually, the Board began to see the value of the guidance of leaders from its racial/ethnic mission constituencies. In a growing multicultural context in North America, and facing a newly independent postcolonial mission situation in most of the Third World countries it served, the Board needed leaders with racial/ethnic minority backgrounds to secure the future witness of the denomination. Their leadership would come to the Board only at a price, that is, a change in institutional patterns of behavior, especially those reflecting overt and covert forms of racism.

Racial Inclusiveness

One of the first demands of the Black Methodists for Church Renewal was for the Board to hire an ombudsman. The ombudsman concept originated in Scandinavia, where citizens and consumers lacked access and needed an agent to investigate their complaints against government or big business. The first Board ombudsman, Harry Gibson, assumed the position in 1971. He immediately took on the role of facilitator for incorporating the mission aims and aspirations of racial/ethnic constituencies into the programs and policies of the Board. He pledged to give special attention to the "alienated . . . who have something to say to an organization like ours" and to work "in a collaborative style to develop possible alternatives."[49]

An Inter-Ethnic Task Force was established to create a forum for addressing issues of racial/ethnic participation in program and policy development and staffing. In a major report to the directors, this task force identified areas of work (or deficiencies) in each of the program units of the Board. The report focused sharply on personnel issues, especially the need to increase missionary recruitment efforts in racial/ethnic communities and to develop an affirmative action plan for employment of Board executives and general staff. It also called for soliciting racial/ethnic perspectives in defining theological positions and for closer consultation with racial/ethnic leaders to increase sensitivity to offensive language used in interpreting mission in minority churches and communities. The Board agreed to forward the recommendations to each unit and established a subcommittee in its standing Committee on Research and Development to review all responses within a year. The subcommittee was also "empowered to seek solutions to the issues."[50] This action began an intentional long-term process of incorporating racial/ethnic perspectives into policymaking and of increasing the numbers of racial/ethnic personnel throughout the Board.

Elimination of Institutional Racism

In 1976, a more significant step was taken in authorizing the employment of a consultant group to address issues of institutional racism at the Board of Global Ministries. A small expert group — including one black woman, two black men, and one white man, all with professional and academic backgrounds in social work and church organization — was charged with developing a four-phase plan of action: (1) The discovery of indicators of institutional racism in the Board of Global Ministries. (2) The development of strategies and evaluative tools for action, including the formulation of an interorganizational task force within the Board to determine the courses of action. (3) The implementation of a plan of action intended to eradicate racism in the Board. (4) Reports to the Board after one year to assist it in permanently eliminating institutional racism.[51]

By 1977, the work of the consultants had created a Board Task Force on Institutional Racism and developed a definition: "Institutional Racism is the systematic perpetuation of the belief that whites are inherently superior and nonwhites inherently inferior, through structures, policies, and practices which exclude nonwhites from sources of real power, goods, and services, in order to maintain control by whites over the rewards of power and material resources."[52]

The Reverend Joe Agne, chair of the task force, reported that, in the first year of its work, no fewer than thirty indicators of racism were identified in Board policies and practices. He expressed hope that elimination of institutional racism would become a "top priority" of the Board.

The Task Force on Institutional Racism received annual extensions of its initial authorization so that its work could continue. In the 1981–1984 quadrennium, the work of the task force was assigned to a new standing committee of the Board: the Committee to Eliminate Institutional Racism (CEIR). By 1981, CEIR had formalized a set of twenty-five indicators for monitoring racism in various areas of Board work and life: Mission Development, Budget/Allocations, Personnel Policies/Practices, Decision-Making Power and Authority, and Ethos-Climate of Values/Attitudes. The indicators were referred to each unit of the Board, which then set up subcommittees on institutional racism to create action plans for the elimination of racist behaviors in their program activities and policies. The indicators were specific enough to raise the consciousness of Board members and staff, making them aware of incidents of racism in daily activities and decisions. With increasing frequency, individuals were emboldened to challenge actions that they found to bear the marks of racism. The indicators also provided a rational basis for discussing these actions and incidents.

The challenge of drafting successful plans to alter beliefs and eliminate behaviors that Agne described as "deeper than . . . intentions and woven into the fabric of life" became a constant struggle. Progress in the area of increased racial/ethnic representation on staff was often cited in the reports of the ombudsman: "In 1969, ethnics were 7.5 percent of the total executive staff. By 1976, ethnics represent 23.4 percent of the total executive staff. In 1969, only one division of the Board included an ethnic of color in its cabinet. . . . In 1976, no division is without such representation at cabinet level."[53]

The drafting of strong affirmative action plans within each unit established significant goals and provided guidelines for implementation. CEIR continued to monitor and report changes in staffing patterns. This committee's actions on behalf of increasing or maintaining high levels of racial inclusiveness were reinforced by monitoring groups from the General Commission on Religion and Race (GCORR). The commission often cited the progress within GBGM as an example for other United Methodist general agencies to emulate. GCORR also became a defender of the Board when racist attitudes surfaced in the general church, heard in the harsh voices of critics alleging problems of staff incompetence. Progress would not have been sustained without the vigilance of the CEIR. With each discussion of budget reductions or organizational restructure, the implications of the principle "last hired, first fired" had to be confronted.[54]

One of the areas of greatest disappointment was the difficulty of increasing the number of racial/ethnic persons in traditional missionary categories. A report indicated that between 1960 and 1977, while the percentage remained the same in a declining work force, the actual number of racial/ethnic missionaries in the ranks of the World Division declined from 48 (of 1,587, or 3.0 percent) to 22 (of 660, or 3.3 percent). Inflating the small numbers were nationals who married missionaries and therefore were not recruited as a result of Board efforts. Because the missionary community was a primary source from which the World Division could recruit executives to administer mission programs, there was little hope of achieving affirmative action goals without an infusion of executive personnel from elsewhere in the church. When turning to racial or ethnic groups within the church for candidates, the World Division encountered strong competition from other general agencies pursuing affirmative action goals. Gradually, however, the World Division's staff roster came to include the sons and daughters of parents who had grown up in the churches that missionaries helped to establish in Latin America, Africa, and Asia.

Lest the motivation for recruiting racial/ethnic persons into the ranks of the world missionary community be reduced to a numbers game, one African-American recruit offered an important correction.

> As a person of color from the U.S., I've had to face and deal with prejudice all my life. Many white missionaries have not dealt with their own racial prejudices before coming to the field. Their prejudices, both overt and latent, are not often dealt with on the field either. One of the ways this expresses itself is when the missionary describes the American experience and American churches to Africans. White missionaries leave out the black American experience and the black church. I've found that what Africans know about black America has come from sources other

than missionaries. I have also heard white missionaries make blatantly prejudicial statements about Africans. The Africans and I also would pick it up but the missionary would not realize the statement to be so racially prejudiced.[55]

In this view, the missionary experience and witness needed to reflect the mission and ministry of the whole church. It needed to value the particularities of cultural experiences in each racial/ethnic group.

To help with the recruitment of minorities for missionary service, Mission Personnel brought on a racial/ethnic staff member, who increased efforts at cultivating recruits from black colleges and churches and through direct approaches to other racial/ethnic organizations.[56] But there was more to the job than getting the message to new audiences. The Board had much to learn about making the missionary enterprise palatable to constituencies for whom it was a negative message. For racial/ethnic persons with a background in mission churches, memories of past racist actions and attitudes on the part of missionaries were a turnoff. Further discouragement came as carefully recruited racial/ethnic persons withdrew from missionary service, often citing lack of acceptance within the dominant white culture of the missionary community. The World Division persisted in efforts at retraining career missionaries in antiracist behavior, and Mission Personnel made raised consciousness about racism a part of the orientation and training of all candidates. Still, such efforts were only short-term in duration and were often insufficiently reinforced in places of assignment.

In 1976, the National Division directors set a goal of increasing racial/ethnic minority participation in mission service programs by 25 percent. Only the Community Developer and United Methodist Voluntary Service programs—aimed largely at racial/ethnic communities and financially supported by the denomination-wide Human Relations Day offerings—showed a high level of racial/ethnic minority participation.[57]

Each unit of the Board organized its own Committee on the Elimination of Institutional Racism. The committees were charged by the Board CEIR to develop and monitor action plans to eliminate institutional racism in their respective program areas. The process stimulated some movement by the units but soon became encrusted in a seemingly benign form of institutional racism. The submission of plans seemed to become a rhetorical exercise. Plans were proposed and revised but the results were seldom evaluated. The redundancy of the work and the overlapping membership of the Board CEIR and the unit committees were questioned in the restructure of the Board in 1996. The responsibility of the CEIR was then given to the Executive Committee of a GBGM reorganized into units by function, not geography.

Few organizations have invested as much effort in researching, documenting, and addressing institutional racism as has GBGM. The Board's indicators of institutional racism were used in training events in many Board-related programs and were shared with other projects, mission agencies, and connectional bodies of the church. These indicators were often requested for use by ecumenical and other national organizations, with appreciation for GBGM's pioneering efforts.

The Racial/Ethnic Missional Priority and Beyond

The UMC has received kudos from other denominations for efforts in cultivating racial/ethnic minority membership and program outreach. With the growing potential for extending United Methodist fellowship and service to new members and their communities, however, rising expectations can overwhelm even the most faithful efforts to respond.

In 1976, the General Conference established a missional priority on strengthening racial/ethnic minority local churches. In addition to new funding allocated by General Conference to GBGM (and to other participating general agencies), the Board prioritized $1 million of its World Service income for use by the National Division to work on church development, salary support, and outreach programs in black, Hispanic, Asian, and Native American churches. The funds were disbursed to the annual conferences that developed comprehensive plans for work with these U.S. minority groups. Initially, the missional priority addressed urban areas with large minority-group populations. As patterns of immigration and growing birth rates produced a greater geographic distribution of these populations, more conferences participated.

By the 1990s, the missional priority that treated all racial/ethnic minorities as one constituency was supplemented by national plans for ministry among each individual ethnic group. These separate plans reflected the growing influence and organizing initiatives of racial/ethnic groups that developed proposals and funding requests for General Conference action and then mobilized personnel and churches to participate.

An exception was the Korean-American proposal to the 1996 General

Conference, which sought to establish a nongeographical missionary conference. Disenchanted with the delaying tactics of many annual conferences in accepting into full membership pastors born and educated in Korea, the leadership of the Korean-American United Methodists saw the possibility of exercising self-determination in such matters through a missionary conference structure.

When the proposal was brought to the National Division of GBGM for endorsement, strong opposition arose from Korean-American female clergy. The women alleged that the male-dominant Korean-American clergy establishment already discriminated against them within annual conferences. They feared further setbacks within a closed missionary conference system. The National Division also expressed misgivings about structurally separating a vital membership group from the active life of the conferences and The UMC. The proposal was defeated initially by the National Division and ultimately by the General Conference.

Despite these votes, GBGM shared the frustration of the Korean-American church leaders. The growth of Korean-American local churches was widely recognized as the result of leadership and hard work by many first-generation immigrant pastors. When these pastors were refused membership standing in annual conferences, many turned for help to the Korean Methodist Church (KMC), their very evangelistic-minded parent church in Korea. The help came in the form of strong advocacy in several formal KMC consultations with GBGM leadership but also in a more aggressive KMC plan to establish its own mission conference in the U.S. to accommodate Korean-American clergy who were bypassed for membership in The UMC. The missionary activity of a partner church within the bounds of UMC annual conferences was a difficult concept for the affected conferences to accept. In some conferences, conflicts arose as Korean-American UMC congregations chose to leave the denomination for the KMC mission conference, taking with them properties and facilities purchased with UMC connectional assistance.

GBGM responded by creating a few regional mission structures composed primarily of Korean-American pastors and congregations that were still unrelated to the annual conferences of The UMC. A Korean-American superintendent who was willing to work with a GBGM and jurisdictional advisory committee was named for each of the missions. The arrangement provided for more frequent and formal communication with UMC leadership at jurisdictional and conference levels. But the progress on the annual conference membership issue was still not satisfactory to the Korean-American pastors.

When the Korean-American proposal to the 1996 General Conference failed to find support, GBGM provided an enhancement of the Korean-American mission-structure concept. A new provision admitted the mission pastors into missionary status with GBGM for a maximum period of three years. During that time, the Board would work with the pastors on a program to have their pastoral orders recognized by the annual conferences in which they were located. Limited salary support and related employment benefits from GBGM offered a level of financial security to the pastors. However, negotiating a process of recognition by conference officials still presented a considerable challenge.

Meanwhile, Korean-American UMC leaders decided to refocus their efforts on program rather than polity issues. They presented to the 2000 General Conference a proposal that had received the endorsement of GBGM. It addressed training and development resources for Korean-American UMC leadership in local churches and conferences. Particular attention was paid to cultivating the younger generations that no longer identified with the immigrant congregations. A high proportion of young second-generation Korean Americans was not attending any church, but significant numbers were choosing multicultural ministries. The proposal submitted in 2000 won the support of General Conference and is being implemented by Korean-American leadership with GBGM administrative support.

The Korean-American experience detailed above highlights the mission challenges encountered within an ethnically diverse and organizationally complex church. The UMC, sensing its opportunity to reach growing racial/ethnic minority populations in the U.S., established a program priority and set aside resources but refused to give up control. Thirty years after the decision to open the church to new racial/ethnic constituencies, Korean-American congregations and leaders are still excluded. The judicatory leaders — the conference boards of missions and boards of ordained ministry — have rejected the gift of Korean-American successes in church development among their immigrant populations. One of GBGM's indicators of racism describes this behavior as "the failure to recognize the contribution of ethnic-minority cultures, traditions, and leadership."[58]

Among the most frequently imposed barriers to acceptance of Korean

Americans were the enforcement of language requirements and educational standards for ministry, along with limited financial resources for nurturing mission congregations. Instead of mobilizing the energies and resources of a connectional church to embrace the evangelistic ministries of Korean-American Methodists in their midst, United Methodist leaders protected the established church. Opening membership to another culture meant extending the rights and privileges of participation, including leadership. The failure to extend a welcome diminished the effectiveness of the church's mission among Korean Americans and other immigrant populations. The challenge for the church to be faithful and productive in mission is to heal itself of the racism that remains "deeper than . . . intentions and woven into the fabric of life."

Conclusion

The mission board, now the General Board of Global Ministries, cannot be accused of sitting out a revolution. Neither can it be heralded for being at the forefront of social change. What can be said is that the mission agency of The United Methodist Church was a visible and resourceful target of forces bringing necessary social change to the institutions of society. The agency accommodated change by adroitly managing human and financial resources to achieve modest objectives of inclusiveness. In developing new programs to respond to alienated communities and constituencies and in reconstituting its staffing and directorate to assure broader representation of minorities, it served as a prototype for other agencies and conferences within the Methodist connection that undertook similar shifts in program and leadership. But neither the leaders of the forces of change nor the reactionary forces within the church found the changes initiated by GBGM to be satisfactory.

CHAPTER 2

A Survey of Latin America
and the Caribbean

$\mathcal{T}$HE TERM "Latin America" embraces México, Brazil, and all the Spanish-speaking nations of Central and South America. This region is geographically associated with the nearby islands of the Caribbean Sea, many of which have English as their official language. The mission context in Latin America has been the subject of much analysis and discussion within The United Methodist Church (UMC). The proximity of the Latin American countries to the United States, locus of United Methodism's principal membership and institutional base, heightens the intensity of Methodist family relationships in the Americas.

In the early years, the missionary movement created strong connectional ties between Methodists north and south of the Río Grande. At that time, faced with the general antagonism of Roman Catholic authorities toward Protestants in the region, Methodist missionaries and their growing number of followers were united in their efforts to witness to the gospel in Latin America. Though initially hindered in their ministries of evangelization and church development, which the dominant Catholic Church regarded as proselytism, they were successful in their development of social-service institutions to serve the general population.

Methodism in Latin America

By the mid-twentieth century, Latin American Methodists were forming and registering national churches in countries beset by enormous political and economic problems. U.S. business interests were looking for low labor costs and stable political environments for their investments in the region. Countries with idle work forces and strong military regimes

Legend for Church Relationship to UMC

Autonomous	A
Affiliated Autonomous	AA
Affiliated United	AU
Covenant UMC	Cov
Central Conference	CC
Concordat	Con
Cooperative Mission	CM
Ecumenical	Ecum
Independent	Ind
Mission	Msn

offered attractive opportunities, requiring only minimal doses of development assistance in return. Under such schemes, only the elite business partners of multinational firms and the ruling government leaders were enriched, while the general populations suffered from increasing poverty. Most analysts blamed the U.S. for this inequity, citing U.S. dominance and control of market conditions throughout the region, which led to an imposition of U.S. political will on Latin American governments.

Correcting the injustices inflicted upon the poor in Latin America became the cause of a group of priests and bishops of the Roman Catholic Church. At a gathering of all of the Latin American Catholic Church bishops in Medellín, Colombia, in 1968, those who were committed to the struggle for social change successfully drafted a conference statement that provoked the ire both of Rome and of the Latin American oligarchies. Negative public reactions to the statement were couched in Cold War rhetoric, alleging church complicity in the spread of Communism from Cuba to other countries in the region. The Catholic Church hierarchy developed a strategy for silencing their rebellious bishops and gradually removing those with liberation or revolutionary aspirations from positions of influence. These moves seemed to radicalize further those already committed to social justice — those who had identified with the poor through organizing local faith-based communities and engaging in movements aimed at political change. But the ongoing challenge from impoverished communities met strong resistance from Latin American governments that curried favor and military support from administrations in Washington, D.C.

In 1971, Methodist and other church leaders visited the annual meeting of the Board of Missions with an aim of interpreting the revolutionary context of Latin America. In a panel presentation on the subject "The Challenges and Opportunities We Face," a social agenda for the ministry of the churches was spelled out. Methodist church leaders chose this platform to announce that they were adopting the struggle to end human suffering and exploitation and were embracing the movement for self-determination by their people. "The possibility of neutrality does not exist," they said. "Either we are side by side with our people or we turn our backs to them." They appealed to the Board to recognize how quickly their constituencies were becoming politically polarized and to acknowledge the need for an "authentic autonomy of the Methodist churches in Latin America." The Methodist leaders reported seeing positive signs that some of their churches were ready to side with the forces in their respective countries that were working for freedom for their people. They admitted that some churches "are still searching their own way," pointing out that "some are too much engaged or afraid and they prefer to close their eyes to reality." Consequently, the leaders recognized the need for churches to join with other peoples' movements in building social structures that promised "a more just distribution of the fruit of their work."[1]

When the panel members moved on to discuss what their approach to mission in this changing context required from the Board of Missions, they crafted a new paradigm for church-to-church relations. While requesting continued partnership in support of the joint missionary enterprise with Methodist churches in the region, the Latin American church leaders asked the Board to become proactive in their national struggles: (1) To challenge the silence and the distancing of most of the North American public from the process taking place in Latin America through a program of "conscientization." Such a program would begin with a refocusing of the Board's mission education efforts among United Methodist congregations. (2) To stand in solidarity with the sufferings of those who were part of the movement for social change in Latin America. "Throw all your weight on the side of those who are being persecuted for the sake of justice," they demanded. "We prayerfully expect that this Board will do whatever it can to influence the American government in their favor, knowing that a word from Washington will be carefully heard in Latin America."

The mission partners were pleading for a shift in mission focus — from converting Latin Americans to the Christian way, to convincing North American church members to become politically engaged in the battle for a moral foreign policy toward Latin America. Just as some of the Latin American Methodist churches were ill-prepared for engaging in the liberation struggles their leaders were espousing, so also the North American church members — indoctrinated by Cold War propaganda regarding protecting the Western Hemisphere from further Communist invasion — were hard to reach with a message calling for a reduction of U.S. power and influence in the region.

A position paper on Latin America, prepared for the World Division of the Board of Missions in 1969, spoke of "illusions and reality" when it came to addressing concerns for justice in Latin America. The writers concluded that the American public had been "misled" into thinking that the U.S. Government was pressing for needed political reforms in Latin American countries; that U.S. foreign policy was supportive of the rights of people to self-determination; that U.S. military presence in Latin America was needed to protect against Communist aggression or subversion; that the "American way" of modernization was a benevolent contribution for which underdeveloped Latin American countries should be grateful; and that North American missionary activities in Latin America were free of the paternalism that marked other kinds of American influence in the region.[2]

The approach to the mission of "conscienticizing"[3] the church and mobilizing a public advocacy for social justice in Latin America would require a comprehensive strategy. The Latin America Committee of the National Council of the Churches of Christ in the U.S.A. (NCC) kept in touch with fast-moving events and provided analyses for member communions. A thorough treatment of issues required disclosing the clandestine military operations of the U.S. Government. Church leaders were outspoken about the assassination of Archbishop Oscar Romero in El Salvador, the disappearance of political activists in Argentina, and the U.S. involvement in the overthrow of the Salvador Allende government in Chile in 1973. The Sanctuary Movement organized church groups and institutions in the Southwest to aid political refugees from Guatemala, El Salvador, and Nicaragua. Nevertheless, these refugees became the target of heightened enforcement activities by the U.S. immigration authorities, and many of the sanctuary providers were arrested and subjected to trials in the federal court system. "Witness for Peace," a Christian direct-action group, recruited significant numbers of church members to travel to Central American countries to gain firsthand experience of the threat to civilians caused by heavy-handed military regimes and the rebel groups backed by U.S. Government policies and troops. All of this activity produced a strong and vocal constituency of church activists of every denomination in the U.S. — activists who were fully engaged in efforts to change government policies toward this conflicted region.[4]

A distinctive mission education program was developed and conducted by the Reverend Dow Kirkpatrick, a World Division missionary interpreter. Kirkpatrick — a veteran pastor of large and prominent churches in Atlanta, Georgia, and Evanston, Illinois — and his wife Marjorie were recruited as "missionaries in reverse," that is, missionaries from Latin America to North America. Their terms of service were equally divided between living and experiencing mission in the Latin American context and then itinerating in the North American churches, telling the story of churches engaged in struggles for human dignity and social justice. According to Rev. Kirkpatrick, the story from Latin American Christians held the promise of redemption for North American Christians. "God is speaking a special word among the poor and oppressed," he said. "The revitalization of our spiritual condition depends upon our hearing from them that word."[5]

Drawing on controversial elements of Latin American Liberation Theology, Kirkpatrick believed that interpreting the word from the poor required an analysis of the causes of poverty. He concluded: "Faithful preaching begins by asking why there are so many poor. For me to be rich, other 'sisters and brothers' must be poor. For the church to fail to tell me so, because Marx also says it, is a failure to define sin." He appealed to North American United Methodists, who might be inclined to resist the insights from Latin American communities of faith because of ideological leanings, to receive those insights as a spiritual gift. "They have learned from Jesus that the poor [in spirit] are the blessed ones. Their call to solidarity is an offering made by the poor of the earth to become one with them, those whose only expectancy is the Kingdom. . . . We need help to qualify ourselves for the benefits of the Beatitudes."[6]

The Kirkpatricks carefully documented their experiences and published reports to the North American churches that reflected the perspectives of those in the midst of the struggle. They developed a retreat format known as "Encuentros," offering a more rigorous approach to group study and interaction with the issues than missionary itineration patterns would normally provide. Their efforts often produced a corps of supporters for the Latin American liberation agenda within churches, districts, and conferences of The UMC.

Telling the mission story from the Latin American perspective did not always depend upon North American interpreters. In 1982, the General Board of Global Ministries (GBGM) sponsored an itineration of Methodist bishops and church presidents from Latin America to the five U.S. jurisdictions of The UMC. Bishop Paulo Ayres Mattos of Brazil, president of the Council of Evangelical Methodist Churches in Latin America and the Caribbean (*Consejo de Iglesias Evangélicas Metodistas en América Latin y el Caribe*, or CIEMAL), observed a "lack of knowledge about Latin America . . . a lot of misunderstanding and very strong prejudices."

Margarita Grassi, former president of the Methodist Church in Uruguay, noted the scarcity of youth in the U.S. groups she met. But she was impressed with the "great sensitiveness and openness" of these small groups, in which she discovered a strong commitment to social justice among some aging members. Ultimately, she saw the need for further education, dialogue, and encouragement among churches of the north and south: "We feel that the lack of knowledge of historical processes as well as the diversity of information, frequently contradictory, confuses many honest and concerned church members. Ministers have a social conscience but in many cases are apprehensive of a commitment, which could be costly. As we say this, we are conscious that this is also one of the situations faced in our own churches."[7]

"Democratization" became the popular political theme of the post–Cold War period. The tragic conflicts that had preoccupied most of the Central American countries finally yielded to tenuous political settlements, and the phenomenon of elected governments was experienced across the entire region. Yet the new governments were too weak to assure their citizens many benefits from new investments through regional trade agreements such as the North American Free Trade Agreement (NAFTA). There was no prosperity and plenty of corruption as the illegal drug trade and other forms of trafficking filled the void. A mission partnership in advocacy was still needed, but the intensity surrounding social justice issues mellowed in the 1990s. At that time, the churches turned to more traditional programs, including evangelization and church development.

Cooperative Mission Relationships

The formation in 1969 of CIEMAL provided an organized structure in which these churches could present a common vision and direction for ministry in the region. CIEMAL's membership comprised all Methodist churches in the Latin American region that traced their origins to the missionary movement of The UMC and its predecessor bodies. The council provided needed denominational recognition in the region for those churches that had recently chosen autonomy. According to Bishop Mattos, the newly independent churches felt isolated and were yearning for a sense of fraternity and cooperation with one another. CIEMAL would connect and unite churches that otherwise were religious minorities in their own countries. "It brings an end to the mission paternalism of the past and helps the churches feel like adults," Mattos said.[8]

To that end, CIEMAL sought to negotiate bilateral relationships with other members of the global Methodist family, including churches in Europe as well as the World Methodist Council. CIEMAL's formal organization offered an umbrella under which member churches could work together, while the individual churches continued to define their own programs. As president of CIEMAL, Bishop Isaias Gutíerrez declared: "We cannot do anything the national church doesn't ask for. . . . We work in mutual respect."[9]

CIEMAL was generally amenable to progressive leaders committed to their churches' involvement in social transformation. At the Sixth General Assembly meeting in Havana, Cuba, in 1993, delegates elected Rita Olíva Valdez of Cuba as their general secretary. Olíva was not only the first person from the Caribbean to hold that position but the first woman and layperson to do so. Conservative leaders of Methodist churches in the region tended to offer deference to the organization by participating in assemblies, though they were seldom entrusted with major leadership responsibilities. Bishop Aldo Etchegoyen of the Evangelical Methodist Church (EMC) in Argentina has provided a theological grounding and contextual perspective for the mission of CIEMAL in his fertile reflections upon the theme *conexionalidad a favor de la vida* (connectionality in favor of life). The dominance of the Latin American economic system over the political systems dealt so much death and destruction to the region's people that the churches witnessed together to God's incarnate strategy for bringing life. According to Bishop Nelson Campos Luiz Leite of Brazil, this required making "connectionality a living reality, not a theory. We are the body of Christ." The bishop went on to affirm: "It is not our own ministry. We are members of one another. We must build each other up in love for the purpose of the ministry. . . . We must come together to witness as Methodists, to live in connectional fashion, locally, regionally, nationally, internationally. The Reign of God for all is lived out in connectionality."[10]

Connectionality among Methodist churches in Latin America was also expressed in a strong commitment to ecumenism. The Latin American Council of Churches held its organizing assembly in November 1982. It immediately found its prophetic voice in addressing U.S. "acts of aggression" in Central America: "We have been moved once again by the many signs of violence evident in our countries. We have prayed to God for relief, and we now want to ask all of you to make a firm request to the government of the United States of America urgently to change its policy toward Central America, since this policy creates oppression, threatens imminent war, violates life, and leads to death."[11]

Bishop Frederico Pagura of the Evangelical Methodist Church in Argentina, honorary "dean" of Methodist bishops in Latin America and president of the Latin American Council of Churches, wrote to the NCC to denounce the U.S. not only for its activities of "de-stabilization in Nicaragua" but also for the "transformation of Honduras into a military fortress" and the support of "a corrupt and inhuman regime in El Salvador." In speaking to U.S. United Methodists in 1984, Bishop Pagura called for a "return" of the U.S. to a respect for justice and a realization of the American dream of hope and freedom for all. In an interview with journalist Tracy Early, Pagura said that "if people of this country had any love for the people of Latin America, now was the time to show it. And if they did not show it now, sending missionaries in the future would mean little."

CIEMAL also became involved in the effort to bring peace to Nicaragua. In the 1960s, the Sandinista National Liberation Front had been founded as a resistance movement to the thirty-five-year dictatorship of the Somoza family in that country. The new movement organized a guerrilla campaign that lasted seventeen years. Achieving power in 1979, the Sandinistas pursued policies of nationalizing the extensive land and industrial holdings of the Somozas. In 1981, however, the Reagan administration in the U.S., citing fears of Communist influence in the region, announced its aim of removing the Sandinistas from power by providing support for a dissident army of former national guardsmen led by Eden Pastora, a former guard commander and a deserter from the Sandinista government. Support for the counterrevolutionaries, or Contras, took the form of U.S. military training in neighboring Honduras and secret funding in violation of U.S. congressional prohibitions.

Finally, in 1987, the United Nations and the Organization of American States negotiated an end to external support for armed opposition groups in Nicaragua (the Esquipulas Accords). With this development, the CIEMAL Council of Bishops invited representatives of the Council of Bishops of The UMC to visit Nicaragua on a fact-finding mission. Thus in March 1989, fifteen bishops of The UMC joined fifteen of their

Latin American colleagues in a delegation to Nicaragua as "ministers of reconciliation and witnesses of peace." Under the critical eye of the church press, they conducted visits with religious leaders, journalists, government officials, aid workers, and local citizens. They gained a firsthand perspective on controversial issues involving economic hardship, the protection of human rights and individual freedoms under the Sandinista government, and the extent both of military cruelties and of suffering by the innocent. Bishop Elías G. Galván summarized his experience as one member of the visiting delegation: "I went to Managua with an honest desire to understand the Nicaraguan reality and willingness to put aside my own prejudices and stereotypes so that I could listen and learn. As a result, I have become convinced that the Nicaraguan people have a strong desire for a peace that respects their dignity and recognizes their rights to self-determination. It was clear to many of us that the Sandinista government is ready to negotiate for a just peace. . . . They have demonstrated their commitment to peace by their active participation in the Plan of Esquipulas and the glaring fact that Nicaragua is the only nation which has met most of the conditions agreed upon."[12]

The issue of peace in Central America had become so politicized in the U.S. that the messengers of peace—especially the United Methodist bishops—were subjected to greater criticism in some church quarters than was their message. War-weary Nicaraguans went to the polls in February 1990, believing that they were voting to end the war by electing opposition leader Violeta Chamorro to the presidency. But efforts by Chamorro's new government to accommodate a strong Sandinista political opposition provoked reaction in her own party and failed to stabilize her government. The disarming of the Contra military progressed slowly but failed to end the violence in the northern part of the country. Peace in the region would require progress in neighboring El Salvador and in Guatemala, as the Esquipulas Accords had envisioned.

CIEMAL became the representative voice of Methodism in the region. It consulted with the Latin American and Caribbean staff of GBGM regarding program strategies and funding. Since the scope of GBGM staff responsibilities included the Caribbean, the autonomous Methodist Church in the Caribbean and the Americas (MCCA) was encouraged to join the discussions and soon became a full member of CIEMAL. While CIEMAL received funding for the programs it sponsored on behalf of its member churches, the churches themselves continued to receive their respective program grants directly from GBGM.

CIEMAL functioned with a lightweight administrative structure. A single executive worked with the officers of the organization to carry out a variety of cooperative ventures with the funding partners and member churches. Coordinating relationships, not administering programs, enabled CIEMAL to fulfill a critical connectional service for ministry and mission in the region.

In March 1992, the World Division of GBGM approved the establishment of a permanent fund for Latin America, with Etchegoyen's theme of "Connectionality in Favor of Life." A goal of $2 million was established and a program developed to solicit major gifts within a three-year period. Interest earned on all contributions was to be returned to the fund until the goal was reached. Then the annual income would be invested in programs of leadership training, church development, and outreach, to be proposed by CIEMAL and implemented through the Methodist church connections throughout the region. Upon retirement from his ministry in the New York Annual Conference, the Reverend Wilson Boots, a former missionary in Bolivia, was returned to part-time missionary status to organize the promotion of the fund under a new identity, "Encounter with Christ in Latin America." Most permanent funds administered through GBGM were created with restrictions limiting them to specific institutions and projects in individual countries. By contrast, the new fund established a precedent for serving regional interests and being cooperatively administered by GBGM with a regional partner.

By 2000, CIEMAL's partnership with The UMC extended beyond the mission agency. CIEMAL shared in developing the National Plan for Hispanic Ministry and was a companion to *Metodistas Associados Representando la Causa de Hispano-Americanos*, the Methodist Association Representing the Cause of Hispanic-Americans (MARCHA), the United Methodist caucus of Hispanic Americans. The General Board of Discipleship has collaborated with CIEMAL in developing Christian education program materials that have been utilized in both the U.S. and Latin America. The Latin American College of Bishops functioned as an entity within CIEMAL and frequently interacted with the United Methodist Council of Bishops. CIEMAL was also the acknowledged channel for Methodist cooperation with other Protestant churches in the region and beyond. It is represented in the council of churches for Latin America. It cultivated a funding relationship with the United Church of Canada, the Methodist Church in Great Britain, and the mission board of the Germany Central Conference of The UMC. A major exception was the

World Methodist Council (WMC), which did not recognize CIEMAL because it was a regional church body and the WMC charter restricted membership to individual churches.

When a rebellion of indigenous peoples erupted in southern México in the late 1990s, CIEMAL extended its hand to the Roman Catholic archbishop and hierarchy, who worked tirelessly to bring about reconciliation in the state of Chiapas. This produced a reciprocal gesture from the Catholic Church when the CIEMAL assembly convened in México in 1998. That meeting was the first occasion on record at which a high-level cooperation was nurtured between Methodism and the dominant Roman Catholic Church in the region.

Latin American Church Programs

Methodism in Latin America and beyond has been enriched by cooperative initiatives from the region. In the difficult years of military governments, the churches offered encouragement to one another. With the lifting of political oppression, many of the churches refocused their energies upon church development and leadership training. Though the numerical strength of the Methodist churches in the region has been weak, the passion for mission by the church leaders and the resources for mission remained strong.

Cuba

Though located in a Caribbean republic, the Methodist Church in Cuba was considered part of the Latin American region because of its mission history, associations, and cultural ties. It was the first among many Methodist mission-established churches to declare its autonomy in the 1960s. The hostile political situation it faced under the revolutionary Communist government of Fidel Castro required the Cuban church to distance itself from a missionary heritage associated with the U.S. During the revolution, the Methodist missionaries in Cuba returned to the U.S., and many of the Cuban pastors joined them. With autonomy, the previous episcopal supervision from the Florida (United Methodist) Episcopal Area came to an end. Now the church had to focus on the Cuban realities and on its ministry, especially its effort to help people find meaning in their daily lives. In the process, the Cuban Methodist Church achieved

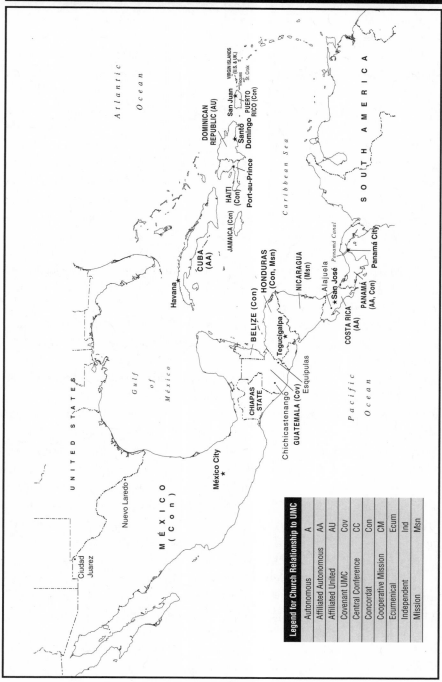

Atlantic Ocean

VIRGIN ISLANDS (U.S. & UK.)
Vieques
St. Croix

DOMINICAN REPUBLIC (AU)
San Juan
PUERTO RICO (Con)
Santo Domingo

Caribbean Sea

SOUTH AMERICA

HAITI (Con)
Port-au-Prince

JAMAICA (Con)

CUBA (AA)

HONDURAS (Con, Msn)

NICARAGUA (Msn)

Alajuela
Panamá Canal

Havana

BELIZE (Con)

Tegucigalpa

San José

PANAMÁ (AA, Con)
Panamá City

COSTA RICA (AA)

Esquipulas

Gulf of México

CHIAPAS STATE

Chichicastenango
GUATEMALA (Cov)

Pacific Ocean

UNITED STATES

México City

MÉXICO (Con)

Nuevo Laredo

Ciudad Juarez

Legend for Church Relationship to UMC	
Autonomous	A
Affiliated Autonomous	AA
Affiliated United	AU
Covenant UMC	Cov
Central Conference	CC
Concordat	Con
Cooperative Mission	CM
Ecumenical	Ecum
Independent	Ind
Mission	Msn

complete self-support for its program, including pastoral support and clergy development.

For years, the Cuban churches and the government leaders experienced strained relations, but in 1976 the new constitution included a guarantee of freedom of religion. The hard line of the official Communist policy of atheism softened considerably. According to Joyce Hill, then an executive secretary for Latin America in the World Division and a former missionary to Cuba: "One of Cuba's leading government officials recently affirmed that Christ is not an adversary of the Cuban Revolution. He added that the churches are free to participate in the life of Cuba in any way they want since both churches and the Revolution are concerned with the dignity of human life." Upon the celebration of the centennial of the Methodist Church in Cuba, Hill affirmed that the Cuban Methodists had "an absolute trust that the Lord of the Church is also the Lord of History, [a faith] which is open to respond to the challenges and opportunities before it, which is willing to pay the price of Christian discipleship, and which is filled with the joy that comes through witness and service."[13]

Perhaps the strongest evangelization activities in the Latin American region have occurred in Cuba. In 1990, after a dialogue initiated with the government by the Cuban Ecumenical Council, President Fidel Castro lifted restrictions against Christian worship and Christians' participation in public life. The response to new initiatives by the churches was overwhelming. By the end of the decade, the membership of the church had quadrupled to more than 40,000. According to a 1993 report by United Methodist missionary Phil Wingeier-Rayo, the 108 church buildings remaining from the missionary period were "insufficient to accommodate the demand of the church. While five years ago, pastors struggled to maintain congregations of twenty members, today those same sanctuaries are packed with standing room only for latecomers."[14] Not satisfied with serving only in historic locations, the Cuban Methodist leaders planted more than 250 house churches in new neighborhoods.

By the century's end, Cuban Methodist churches were serving a growing segment of the population — those looking beyond revolutionary slogans and national programs for more sustaining personal or spiritual values. With the gradual shift toward an unofficial U.S. dollar economy, many living in communities dependent on local markets experienced hardships. There were few opportunities for church members and workers to find gainful employment, and the church faced severe economic challenges. Reaching out to assist, GBGM approved major funding for such basic items as the repair and redevelopment of existing church buildings, the training of pastoral candidates for the new congregations, and salary support and benefits for all pastors. A relationship was restored between Methodists in Cuba and United Methodists in Florida. Before autonomy, the United Methodist bishop in Florida provided supervisory support for the Cuba mission. In the 1990s, pastors and laity were able to take part in mutual exchange visits, dialogue on critical issues of U.S. policy toward Cuba, work on volunteer projects together, and the creation of church-to-church partnerships in mission.

The Cuban church continued to respond to new opportunities for ministry, including work in hospitals, prisons, and homes for the aged. In 1998, GBGM participated in a joint building venture with the Methodist Church in Cuba—a project that received Cuban government permission for the construction and administration of a new housing project for the elderly. In an uncharacteristic move, the government also permitted the resumption of United Methodist missionary assignments to Cuba, allowing U.S. missionaries to accompany the Cuban church and to help with the deployment of a limited number of United Methodist volunteers visiting Cuba to assist the church with various building projects.

Brazil

The first Methodist church in Latin America to gain its autonomy was the Methodist Church in Brazil, which became independent in 1930. With about half a million members, the Brazilian church was the largest of the Latin American Methodist churches. In August 1996, in Rio de Janeiro, it also became the first national church in Latin America to host the World Methodist Conference. The Brazilian church demonstrated vitality in a diversified ministry that embraced both charismatic and progressive models. In a churchwide plan for ministry adopted in the 1980s, called the Plan for Life and Mission of the Church, Brazilian Methodists emphasized the gifts for ministry that each member could offer to the church and to the world. The plan called upon the church to become a servant church in the life of the world, stating that "mission happens when the Church gets out of itself, involves itself with the community, and becomes an instrument of the newness of the Kingdom of God."[15]

This commitment of the Brazilian church to extending its own missionary calling has resulted in the establishment of new missionary conferences in the northeast and northwest. By the end of the twentieth century, the church was wrestling with how to welcome more Brazilians of African heritage into its membership and leadership ranks. Afro-Brazilians made up more than 50 percent of the country's total population, giving Brazil the largest population of African ancestry outside Africa. In response, the Methodist Church in Brazil, where Portuguese is the official language, has opened its doors to Portuguese-speaking mission partners in Angola and Mozambique as well as Portugal. It especially welcomed candidates for ministry who sought the excellent educational opportunities in the Portuguese language offered by Methodist seminaries in Brazil. Brazilian Methodist missionaries were also being sent to start churches among Brazil's own diaspora in the U.S., with congregations established in the New York and Boston metropolitan areas and in Florida.

México

Methodism in México began in 1871 with a missionary overture by the West Texas Conference of the Methodist Episcopal Church, South. Alejo Hernández, a Mexican convert, started a ministry in the border city of Nuevo Laredo and prompted the purchase of property and the development of the first Methodist place of worship there in 1873. The Methodist Episcopal Church in the northern U.S. began its own Mexican mission in 1872 with the assignment of Dr. William Butler, a career missionary who had pioneered Methodist mission in India. In 1930, by action of the respective General Conferences of the founding churches, the two branches of Methodism in México were united in the autonomous Methodist Church of México. The 1976 General Conference approved a concordat relationship between The UMC and the Methodist Church of México that granted voting privileges for two representatives of each church at their respective General Conferences.

A strong cooperative mission relationship developed between Methodists on both the U.S. and the México sides of the Río Grande. This relationship, once based upon the formal assignment and receiving of missionary personnel, has evolved into a direct sharing between local congregations through joint sponsorship of mission volunteer projects. Volunteers of all ages from United Methodist churches, working side by side with Methodists in México, have built churches and other mission buildings and helped with the ministries of the various social outreach projects of the Methodist Church of México. Educators from United Methodist colleges and seminaries devoted their vacation time and sabbaticals to teaching in the schools, colleges, and seminaries of the Mexican church. Church clinics have attracted medical personnel from United Methodist congregations to make a similar dedication of time and professional skills to further the outreach of the Mexican church among underserved populations.

Crossing the border between México and the U.S. came to be viewed by poverty-stricken Mexicans as holding the promise of opportunity and security, while the immigration policies of the U.S. Government have remained hostile. The hostility is symbolized by the razor-wire fence erected by U.S. immigration authorities along the entire border to discourage Mexicans from entering the U.S. illegally. While many U.S. households and businesses benefit from the hiring of Mexican "illegals," the road to permanent citizenship for Mexican immigrants was obstructed with official roadblocks.

In the 1970s and 1980s, a Southwest Border Consultation process was developed by both U.S. and Mexican Methodists to help churches and agencies on both sides of the border deal with the mounting immigration crisis. United Methodist community centers, schools, and hospitals practiced an open admissions policy but were overwhelmed by the demand for services from immigrant families with few or no economic resources. Mexicans were drawn in large numbers to employment in assembly plants called *maquiladoras* opened by U.S. firms along the Mexican side of the border to exploit low-wage workers. Cities like Cuidad Juárez, facing rapid population growth from these transitory workers, had few resources available to improve their infrastructure and soon acquiesced in the development of shantytowns. All the problems associated with urban poverty —environmental degradation, poor health, juvenile delinquency, crime, drug addiction, and drug trafficking—consumed the attention of Mexican Methodists, whose family members were counted among the abused. The border consultation process sponsored training of personnel from both U.S. and México United Methodist/Methodist churches in providing and administering needed social services. It also provoked the leaders in both churches to lift their voices in advocacy for stronger government regulation of the *maquiladora* industries and for the protection of human rights in the writing and administering of immigration policies.

The Methodist Church of México, with 150,000 members, was at the end of the century organized into six conferences with more than 400 churches. It served the vast geographic reach of the country, including indigenous peoples of the Tarahumara Mountains in the north, the urbane citizens of the world's largest city—México City—in the central region, and the marginalized Indian communities of the south. In each region it has developed a significant number of programs of mission outreach. While welcoming financial assistance to maintain the network of schools, social centers, and other mission projects within its conferences, the Methodist Church of México remains committed to recruiting and developing leadership from within its own ranks.

Guatemala

The 1992 General Conference of The UMC received into covenant relationship the Primitive Methodist Church in Guatemala. The Guatemalan church had begun under missionaries from a conservative denomination based in the U.S., having its spiritual roots in the Wesleyan movement. When the indigenous church leaders broke ranks with the missionaries and organized an independent church, they sought out stronger ties—first with Latin American Methodism, through contacts with CIEMAL, and then with The UMC.

The church members, drawn from indigenous tribal communities residing in the mountainous rural interior of Guatemala, were deeply affected by frequent government military forays and counterattacks by private rebel armies that vied for the loyalties of the people. At a Sunday morning worship service in Chichicastenango in 1993, a visiting delegation of World Division directors was greeted by a congregation made up primarily of widows and orphans who had lost their husbands and fathers to the insidious warfare between the Guatemalan government and its own people. In the absence of their pastor, a lay leader provided a new understanding of what the connectional relationship in the Methodist family was meant to accomplish. "What we are looking for," she said, "is that there will be no more martyrs in our country. We suffer because we are poor, women, and indigenous. What we are struggling for is not that one would have more, but rather for the good of all. . . . Unfortunately for many of us, we do not have enough life in us to finish our mission. But if we lose our life for justice, we know we are part of the church. So I ask you not for money, but for solidarity."[16]

Maintaining solidarity with these relatively new Guatemalan Methodists required an understanding of their ancestral roots and a sensitivity to the impact on them of years of persecution and suffering. More than 40 percent of the church members traced their history to ancient Mayan communities. Despite their history as a people under siege—first by Spanish conquistadors, then by Guatemalan troops and rebel armies — they maintained their way of life and clung to their cultural traditions. They considered the Spanish language to be a foreign tongue. Most Mayan families could count loved ones among the casualties of military conflicts or among the populations confined to military encampments or lingering in refugee camps throughout the region. The pastors of the church, most of whom had a Spanish heritage, sought ways to help these long-oppressed people in the struggle to rebuild their communities. This effort required redeveloping an economic base for devastated localities. When Christian aid funds were available, they were invested in small grants to sustain individual families and to begin collective programs in agricultural production on church-owned land. The Primitive Methodist Church in Guatemala also developed health and education programs for mothers and children, including the large number of orphans. Though, for all practical purposes, the church was starting life from scratch, its ministries set ambitious goals. In the words of the Reverend Marcos García Hernández, president of the church: "We try to teach [our members] to go high in their lives, to make something of themselves. . . . People have confidence in us [because] they know who we are and what we are trying to achieve."[17]

Since the Primitive Methodist Church identified with the Methodist church family in the region and in the U.S., significant partnerships were developed to assist with rebuilding local communities and strengthening the witness of the Guatemalan church. Methodists in México have sponsored exchange visits with youth groups, pastors, and church leaders. A missionary couple from México was sent to work with the church on theological education and nutritional health programs. Leading a conference visitation team to Guatemala, Bishop Elías Galván of The UMC Desert Southwest Conference was inspired by the ministry of Florida León López, a twenty-nine-year-old widow whose husband was among those who "disappeared" at the hands of the military. She traveled every Monday morning by bus and finally on foot to San Sebastian Lemoa, a mission outpost of the church. There she taught other widows of the disappeared who were enrolled in programs of nutrition, animal husbandry, and arts and crafts creation. Her ministry demonstrated the high calling of a church of the poor whose mission is among the poor. According to Rev. García (cited above), "Our work, as we understand it, is to go to the communities that have nothing, to work with the people who have been forgotten, to support those who have suffered the most."

Bolivia

Autonomy for the Evangelical Methodist Church in Bolivia came in 1969. At its first General Assembly in Cochabamba, the Reverend Mortimer Arias, a Uruguayan pastor serving in Bolivia, was elected bishop. Arias led the Bolivian church to assume a prophetic posture in the unstable political situation that characterized much of Latin America at the time. Bolivian authorities had cooperated with the U.S. troops who had successfully tracked down Cuban revolutionary Ernesto ("Ché") Guevara in the Andes in 1967. The statement from the church, written by Arias, was entitled a "Manifesto to the Nation" and warned of the country's "drift toward military fascism." It questioned the partial suppression of the constitution, the placing of military men in key government posts, and the lack of participation in government by the people. It described the suffering of the people caused by economic exploitation on the part of wealthy countries. But it also rejoiced in hopeful "signs of humanization" in "some new measures and reform" of the present revolutionary government. And it called upon the church to participate with other groups working for the "conscientization and liberation of our people,"[18] *conscientization* referring to education on sociopolitical-economic issues. The church would continue to struggle to find its life and witness among threats and counterthreats by political and military rulers for much of the 1970s.

The Bolivian church's primary ministry to society was directed through Methodist social service institutions: a hospital in La Paz and several schools in major cities. These institutions remained the most visible legacies of the missionary movement in Bolivia. But while they have given the church both a source of social influence and an economic base for its ministry, they also shaped a church characterized as largely urban and middle class. As leadership of the church passed into the hands of indigenous leaders, the focus of its mission and witness has become the rural areas where traditional Aymara and Quechua peoples were in the majority. In 1983, Bishop Rolando Villena spoke of a church in transition. "The Methodists must begin to see the situation that they are in as Bolivians," he said. "Can we really be part of or with the people when the church creates expectations among the people because it has large institutions, such as hospitals. . . ? We want to create something that is in communion with the poor. This is what we have in the altiplano [high plateau].

Response magazine, the journal of United Methodist Women, continually called attention to women around the world in its articles and photos. This cover showing Lake Titicaca in Bolivia conveyed the dignity of an indigenous woman. *(Photo courtesy of UM Archives and History)*

We must also work on changing our own mentality. . . . [When I was] talking about this problem with a pastor, he told me that it was unjust for a pastor to receive a monthly salary of 25,000 pesos [$60] when one considers that many people live with 10,000 pesos [$25] a month. These are questions that must be answered."[19]

Bishop Eugenio Poma, the first bishop elected from among the Aymara membership, brought to the church a heightened sense of how to carry out evangelization among his people. "The church has been part of the systematically organized massive intervention of Western culture," he said, "exterminating our cultural values, encouraging our children not to see themselves as Indians anymore. . . . This process of evangelization conflicts with the self-esteem of indigenous peoples, who believe that their culture has something of value to contribute."[20]

With this new emphasis, the church demonstrated remarkable growth, reaching more than 14,000 members and 30,000 constituents, the majority being from the Aymara and Quechua indigenous communities. Bishop

Poma recognized the need for a trained leadership for a growing church. He instituted the development of an indigenous "Andean theology" based on the cultural and historical values of the people native to the Andes Mountains. It called for the empowerment of indigenous theologians who were devoted to reflection upon a Christian tradition from an Andean perspective. Poma's vision held the promise of creating a strong church, representative of indigenous cultural values and leadership. Unfortunately, the influence of bishops upon the Bolivian church seemed to be as short-lived as their single-term tenure. The struggles against the dominance of middle-class institutions and the influence of the Western cultural values they imposed were overwhelmed by a continued economic dependence, complicated by ethnic tensions and factionalism within the church. More is said about the Bolivian church in chapter 5.

The Bolivian church has shared in partnership arrangements with several conferences of The UMC in the U.S. The long-term relationship with the California-Nevada Conference has endured in spite of various shifts in leadership and program direction. Commenting on this partner relationship, Bishop Villena said: "The enrichment is mutual. We receive more in economic terms, of course, but we share with [our partners] new methods for evangelization and our experience of the Word of God among the people."[21]

Perú

The Methodist Church of Perú became autonomous in January 1970. The Reverend Dr. Wenceslao Bahamonde of Lima was elected bishop of this church of 2,753 members. Methodists in Perú remained a small fraction of the Christian population there, but Methodism was growing among Perú's indigenous populations by the end of the century. This increase has produced a shift in the balance of the church from dominance by members of mestizo (mixed Spanish and American Indian) ancestry, who are based in affluent communities along the coast, to a larger indigenous Indian population living in extreme poverty on the altiplano (high plateau). Episcopal leadership and the most successful initiatives of evangelization have passed into the hands of pastors and laity among the traditional Andean communities. The issues confronting the church leaders in 2000 concerned the need to reappropriate resources and create opportunities for leadership to honor the new membership equation and make an impact on the future directions of the church. The Methodist missionary presence in Perú has been limited to occasional faculty appointments at the theological center, where the number of Methodist graduates in recent years has been too small to keep pace with church growth. The training of indigenous pastors who have been recruited from among a largely illiterate population will in the future require new strategies for leadership formation.

Methodist churches in Perú benefit from strong connectional ties to annual conferences in the U.S., especially the North Carolina Conference. This partnership produced a rich sharing of experiences, including leadership exchanges and the development of resources for the discipline and training of local church leaders.

Uruguay

In 1968, the principle of self-determination for Methodists in Uruguay received a strong and unprecedented embrace by the United Methodist missionaries serving the church there. They voluntarily chose to leave their appointments and to return to the U.S. in order to allow Uruguayan church leaders the freedom to chart the future of their church without outside influence or control. The following year, the small church became autonomous, adopted its own constitution, and elected its own leaders. The Reverend Dr. Emilio Castro, a noted ecumenist and social action leader, was elected bishop (later president) of the Methodist Church in Uruguay.

The institutional challenge of replacing the financial support lost with the departure of the missionaries was aggravated by the demise of the country's economic and political security. An urban guerrilla movement, the Tupamaros, gained support among the masses of the oppressed poor, which provoked a military junta to take control of the government. On one occasion, Central United Methodist Church in Montevideo was taken over by the Tupamaros. Also, Uruguayan police detained Rev. Castro and other religious leaders for several days for seeking to mediate the release of prisoners kidnapped by Tupamaros rebels. According to church President Beatriz Ferrari, when some sense of national equilibrium was regained, the church members found they were "polarized and dispersed." By the close of the twentieth century, church membership had dwindled to 1,193, with only eleven ordained pastors and four lay ministers. But the church sought to remain "present and active in the intellectual and social life of the country," largely through cooperative efforts with other Protestant groups.[22]

Chile

In 1970, the Socialist government of Salvador Allende was voted into office by popular election. President Allende proceeded to act on his mandate to address the economic deterioration of Chile by nationalizing the copper industry and the banking institutions. Angry business leaders conspired with displaced politicians, the Chilean military, and the Pentagon in the U.S. to depose the president with a violent military coup in September 1973. With signs of mounting disarray in the country, pastors of the autonomous Methodist Church of Chile issued a strong statement from the site of their annual Pastors' Institute at El Vergel. They declared their "recognition and respect for the democratically elected and constitutional government." They rejected the prospects of civil war and the "climate of violence in all its forms." And they called attention to "past exploitation and oppression of the poor in rural areas and in the cities" as the cause of the current political problems.[23]

Depite the overwhelming defeat of Chile's brief dream of realizing social justice through political reform, the churches maintained a strong witness to liberty during the dictatorial rule of General Augusto Pinochet of the army. The ecumenical Committee for Cooperation and Peace in Chile kept a strong public profile, actively advocating for human rights. For example, the committee provided a legal defense and safe extradition for more than 30,000 Chileans arrested by the military regime because of their allegedly liberal leanings. Among them were Methodists, including the Reverend Dr. Samuel Araya, a pastor and professor of Old Testament at the Evangelical Theological Community in Santiago. Rev. Araya was taken to a makeshift prison camp called the "House of Peril," where he was incarcerated for a short time along with "all sorts of people . . . concerned with building up a new society . . . where a new sense of justice came into being." During his imprisonment, Araya offered a pastoral ministry to other inmates, many of them recovering from incidents of torture and abuse. One inmate, whose body was black and blue and whose fingernails had been pulled out, told Araya: "In the midst of my despair, one thing told me never to give up, and that was the knowledge that a group of Christians were praying for me."[24] Because of Araya's international reputation and his outspoken advocates in The UMC in the U.S., he was released on the condition that he would leave Chile in seventy-two hours. Then, along with other Chilean church and national leaders, he began a period of exile in the U.S.

During the dictatorship of Augusto Pinochet, Chile suffered thousands of deaths of innocent civilians, and its traditional democracy was repressed. This honor guard marching outside Pinochet's presidential palace in 1987 symbolized the harshness of the regime. *(Photo by Charles Cole, courtesy of GBGM)*

Unfortunately, the confusion introduced by the coup and the military government succeeded in silencing the leadership of the Methodist Church of Chile. In December 1974, Bishop Jan Vasquez signed a published statement expressing support for the military government. While acknowledging certain excesses of the government in the treatment of political prisoners, he criticized the "distorted image" of the junta created by Chilean refugees, including members of his own church.[25] With growing international pressure on the Pinochet regime and the increasing threat of civil unrest, the dictatorship yielded to the return of a constitutional government via national elections in 1989. The return of democratic rule brought new freedom to the church to exercise its ministry, noted for its many Methodist institutions dedicated to education and to social and health ministries throughout the country.

Argentina

The distinguished leadership of Bishop Frederico Pagura has marked the ministry of the Evangelical Methodist Church (EMC) in Argentina. As a local pastor in Mendoza, Pagura experienced the 1976 fall of the Juan

Those protesting the *desparacidos* (disappeared) in Argentina during the military dictatorship of the 1970s and 1980s chalked this image on a sidewalk in Buenos Aires in 1987. *(Photo by Charles Cole, courtesy of GBGM)*

Perón government and the military coup that brought a suspension of civil liberties and a campaign of terror against citizens through kidnappings, torture, and murder of opponents. Pagura allied himself with human rights groups that denounced the activities of the government and that drew up a list of more than 7,000 "missing persons." When few were speaking out against this "dirty war," he joined a group of grandmothers who conducted silent vigils in the Plaza de Mayo in Buenos Aires after the denial of their demand for information about their missing loved ones. He also endured reactions to his courageous witness, including the bombing of his Mendoza church. The General Assembly of the church in Argentina elected him bishop in 1977. This was the second time he had been elected to the office of bishop, having served a term in Costa Rica and Panamá from 1968 to 1972.

With Argentina's return to democracy in 1983, the church was showing signs of revitalization. Bishop Pagura commented: "Now that we are just beginning to get a taste of a new democracy after a long period of repressive military dictatorships, our people are beginning to hope, but there is still a great deal of disorientation and pain over the past and many insecurities still haunt our people in the present. Our church is faced with a great opportunity and responsibility to communicate a message of consolation, courage, and hope to many persons who are confronting a future full of uncertainties and difficulties."[26]

Young people had returned to Argentina's churches. Three women were named superintendents in 1985, including the Reverend Nelída ("Nelly") Ritchie, who became one of the seven presidents of the World Council of Churches and was elected in 2000 to succeed Bishop Aldo Etchegoyan as bishop of the Argentine EMC. While continuing to focus its ministry upon issues of human rights, the Argentine EMC has shown a special concern for communities of the poor. Argentina's failing economy and enormous foreign debt have produced a growing population living in poverty. Programs of health, education, and community development were carried out in barrios and among the Toba and Mapuche peoples in the northeastern and southern regions of the country. The Argentine EMC has also joined discussions with the Methodist Church in Uruguay and with other denominations about strengthening Protestant witness and presence in the region through a possible union.

Panamá

The intervention in Panamá by the U.S. military in December 1989, resulting in the capture of Panamanian General Manuel Noriega and the termination of his dictatorial rule, became the occasion for a constructive church partnership of Methodists in Panamá and the U.S. The military campaign was concentrated in Panamá City, and the destruction from the bombing and the fires that followed leveled the sprawling neighborhood of Chorrillo. Most houses in Chorrillo were deteriorating wooden structures originally built for Panamá Canal construction workers, but they had served as homes for thousands of Panamá City's poorest citizens, who were largely of African descent. After the destruction, more than 18,000 survivors took up residence in overcrowded refugee camps. It took almost two years for government authorities and the U.S. Agency for International Development to administer resettlement grants—and then only with much evidence of corruption.

The situation prompted Donald Stewart—a United Methodist layperson, a practicing attorney, and a former U.S. senator from Alabama—to investigate. He proposed that GBGM enable Methodist churches in Panamá and United Methodist churches in the U.S. to cooperate in the rebuilding of a portion of the destroyed homes. After meetings with Methodist leadership in Panamá (representatives of the Evangelical Methodist Church of Panamá and the Panamá District of the Methodist Church of the Caribbean and the Americas, or MCCA), negotiations with the housing minister of the Panamanian government produced a building site and approval for government funding. Thanks to the volunteer labor—from both Methodist churches in Panamá, The UMC, and local Chorrillo refugee families—that supplemented the small government grants, the resources were stretched further to produce many homes of quality construction.

The volunteer effort also helped the church members better understand the plight of their neighbors. According to Bishop Secundio Morales: "We've always worried more about the internal affairs of the church, attending to the needs of our own congregations. Working with the poor is a big challenge for us. The frustrations of the relationship force us to wrestle with the reasons for their poverty and marginalization." The Reverend Mario Nicolas, superintendent of the MCCA, also credited the project with changing the attitudes of church members: "They were afraid of the unknown and thus were hesitant," he explained. "Yet once they met people face to face, it was impossible for most not to respond to the needs of their sisters and brothers."[27]

Early in the 1970s, the two branches of Methodism in Panamá discussed the possibility of a merger but never progressed to a serious proposal. In 1989, however, the response to the plight of the victims of the invasion brought the two churches together in mission. Two lots in the middle of the subdivision of new homes were left vacant. The residents asked that a Methodist church be built there.

Costa Rica

The Evangelical Methodist Church (EMC) of Costa Rica has focused its attention upon evangelizing efforts that would extend its witness to a variety of settings—from poor squatter towns in the central region and on the southern border with Panamá to mountain communities of the north, some prosperous and some poor. The outreach program was initiated under the leadership of Bishop Roberto Díaz (1988–1993), who believed that a declining church membership warranted a new approach. "In the last ten years," he said, "we realized that our congregations were very small and that a lot of people left. We lost a lot of laymen and parishioners, so we kind of adopted a liberty of expression, charismatic expression." He described worship in the rural churches as having a "Pentecostal flavor" where people "dance in the spirit."[28]

Bishop Díaz understood the need to develop pastoral leaders for the new churches and proposed the development of a "seminary," or Bible college, in Alajuela. There, student pastors from rural areas could receive specialized training suited for their primary task of church growth and development in rural areas. Díaz critiqued the preparation of pastors provided by the established Latin American Biblical Seminary based in Costa Rica: "[Pastors] leave the seminary prepared with a lot of theology," he admitted. "But if we say, 'You are going to Santa Rosa,' they would say: 'Just a minute, I'm a city pastor. I would like to go to another country to a workshop.' While they are traveling, the people leave. The church loses a lot of money, a lot of time, and in the end loses the worker."[29]

The leadership of Díaz and his shift toward conservative evangelical theology provoked a few leading pastors to part company with the church. But the aggressive evangelization campaign caught the attention of the independent Mission Society for United Methodists (MSUM). In Costa Rica, MSUM seemed to find a "case study" for its own raison d'être: a return to a priority on evangelism for revitalizing Methodist missions. So MSUM recruited volunteers to assist Díaz in church-building programs and in the development of the Alajuela seminary. Missionaries from MSUM were assigned to teach and provide other services to the Costa Rican church. New resources were generated to accomplish the bishop's aims.

The engagement of MSUM in Costa Rica was accompanied by criticism of the policies and practices of the official mission agency of the church, GBGM. (This issue is discussed further in chapter 5.) Because of GBGM's commitment to funding the Latin American Biblical Seminary in San José, the development of a second seminary was not greeted with much enthusiasm. Moreover, Díaz had given public expression to his fears that the seminary was a bad influence on Methodist students. "They have become educated at seminary, have read a lot of Marxist theory," he said. "They have escalated in the political sense, and all that they have seen has made them consider that liberation theology is an option through which the people of Latin America can be liberated. . . . Liberation theology creates a warlike spirit in people. They will become angry about injustices and soon they will be using violence as justification."

The director of the seminary was Mortimer Arias, a distinguished Latin American Methodist and former bishop of the Evangelical Methodist Church in Bolivia. Reacting to the criticism, Arias declared: "There are people who put labels on us, but we do not need to accept labels. What we really believe in is Latin American commitment, Latin American theology, and Latin American belief in the Scriptures from Latin American realities." He further defined Latin American theology as done by those "who are in a particular situation in society. In this case it is Latin American society . . . a situation of marginalization and oppression."[30]

Although the church press was tempted to sensationalize the conflicts internal to both the Evangelical Methodist Church of Costa Rica and The UMC, the mission proceeded unabated among a people who welcomed the good news in their own hearing, unembellished by politicized interpretations. In 1993, Luis F. Palomo, a former president of the Costa Rican EMC, was elected to succeed Díaz. He has given leadership to the church's evangelistic witness, with a strong emphasis upon the development and training of pastors and laity. His administration has strengthened the church's relationship to the prestigious Methodist High School and has cultivated support for new institutions, including the Bible institute, retreat center, and Methodist Book Store in Alajuela.

The Caribbean Region

The mission connection of The UMC to most of the Caribbean has been the autonomous MCCA. The church was founded by British Methodist missionaries, who were quite successful in establishing churches in most of the British colonies on Caribbean islands as well as in Guyana and the Central American countries of Belize, Honduras, Costa Rica, and Panamá.

The Methodist Church in the Caribbean and the Americas

Expatriate British citizens were a ready constituency for the MCCA ministry, but the outreach to the indigenous populations through education and social development programs quickened with the emancipation of these peoples from slavery in 1834. The recruitment and training of leaders was approached in a systematic fashion, eventuating in the founding of the United Theological College of the West Indies in Jamaica. The training efforts produced a solid corps of pastoral leaders with a strong affinity for the British formalities of worship and a great devotion to the Wesleyan hymnody. Until they gained autonomy in 1967, the island churches were organically related to the Methodist Church in Great Britain through individual district structures. The new structure brought the districts and churches into a general or "conexional" conference that meets every three years to make policy and provide a program or denominational structure for its members' common ministry.

Several forces brought the autonomous MCCA into a closer relationship with The UMC. Proximity to the U.S. was the most obvious. The Caribbean islands were vulnerable to frequent devastating storms and related natural disasters, to which the churches in the U.S. were quick to make a neighborly response. The appeals of the United Methodist Committee on Relief (UMCOR) were generously supported and became an avenue of greater communication between The UMC and the MCCA. Associations developed further with the growth of the volunteer movement in the United Methodist churches, especially in the Southeastern Jurisdiction of the U.S. Volunteers were readily recruited for the short jaunt to one of the islands to serve on work teams, helping to rebuild storm-wrecked properties or to assist with other projects.

Haiti

UMCOR made the island country of Haiti, which shares Hispaniola with the Dominican Republic, a major focus of its attention and resources. Haiti's status as the poorest nation in the Western Hemisphere provided major opportunities for development activity. A number of programs of the Haiti District of the MCCA benefitted from the partnership with UMCOR. The district school system was strengthened by the addition of facilities and a publishing house for its curriculum development program. The women's leadership development program received grants for community health and economic development initiatives. The constant companionship of volunteer teams gave encouragement to church leaders and members in their struggle to maintain human dignity in the face of poverty and political repression.

GBGM followed political developments in Haiti with a keen interest in the protection of human rights.[31] Among those who escaped the oppressive dictatorial regimes of Papa Doc and Baby Doc Duvalier were Methodist Church leaders, many of whom were embraced by the Florida Conference of the United Methodist connection. The hundreds and thousands of Haitians departing for the U.S. in unsafe vessels brought national attention to the desperate conditions on Haiti's end of the island. UMCOR supported Church World Service advocacy and repatriation programs for Haitian refugees.

The Duvalier regimes ended with Haiti's first democratic elections in December 1990; but the newly elected president, Jean-Bertrand Aristide, was overthrown by a military coup less than a year later. In 1994, U.S. troops restored Aristide to power and a UN peacekeeping force remained in Haiti for three years, but these actions failed to address the political and social divisions in the country. GBGM responded to the Haitian crises by sponsoring or participating in several bilateral (Methodist/ United Methodist) and ecumenical delegations.

Challenges for the MCCA

Many of the conferences of The UMC that served changing urban communities in the U.S. faced a shortage of pastors available to serve their churches, especially in racially changing neighborhoods. People of color had not been recruited in sufficient numbers to respond to requests by transitional congregations for pastors with whom new arrivals could identify racially or culturally. So conference officials went "shopping" and were attracted to the supply of well-educated (and English-speaking) clergy in the MCCA. Offers were extended and transfers made until the leaders of the MCCA legitimately protested this "brain drain." They made appeals for some forms of intervention that would protect the MCCA's diminished ranks of pastoral leadership.

The British Methodist Board of Foreign Missions entered into a process of reassessing the content and style of its relationship to the mission churches it had established around the globe. Favoring full autonomy as the ultimate aim of its missionary activity, the British board began reducing financial subsidies for many churches it believed could function at a higher level of independence. In 1967, the MCCA was eligible for such recognition and action. Unfortunately, as the appropriations from the British church declined, the churches of the MCCA could not replace this support by their own stewardship. So new fraternal and supportive relationships were sought, and The UMC was potentially an attractive mission partner.

Consultations with GBGM and its Division on Ecumenical and Interreligious Concerns resulted in a petition to the 1976 General Conference in which The UMC and MCCA agreed to enter a concordat relationship. This kind of disciplinary relationship carries with it a high-level recognition between the churches involved, namely, guaranteed representation in their respective policymaking bodies. The UMC concordat relationships in 2000 were limited to the British Methodist Church, the Methodist Church of México, and the MCCA.[32]

The MCCA faced many challenges in its mission and ministry. It struggled to find a suitable structure that recognized both the independence needed by each district and the appropriate level of authority required to maintain denominational or connectional life in the larger region. The diversity of the population in the region required sensitivity to the cultural needs of people of African, Carib or other Native American, and European descent. The depletion of the ministerial ranks continued, with the transfer of clergy members to other conferences in the U.S. or Great Britain. The church was dependent upon a strong deaconess movement and trained local lay pastors to fill its many pastoral appointments. The economy of the region had fallen on hard times, with most islands dependent upon a fickle tourism industry or a foreign-controlled agricultural commodity market of bananas and sugar. The islands were also vulnerable to increasing penetration by the international drug trade, accompanied by social problems such as violence and addiction. And they were forced to cope with seasonal storms that regularly destroyed homes, churches, schools, and other mission institutions.

Puerto Rico

The mission relationships of The UMC to Puerto Rico were structurally defined by political boundaries. Because Puerto Rico is a self-governing island commonwealth in union with the U.S., and since its people have U.S. citizenship (island residents have no voting rights; Puerto Ricans on the U.S. mainland can vote), the Puerto Rico Annual Conference had a judicatory relationship to The UMC Northeast Jurisdiction. The National Division was assigned administrative responsibility for the program and funding relationships of the church on the main island of Puerto Rico and the adjacent islands of Vieques (part of Puerto Rico) and St. Croix (in the U.S. Virgin Islands).

In the 1970s, the National Division entered into dialogue with the Puerto Rico Conference about the island's controversial political status and the future standing of the church. Open discussion of a political issue within the church was a difficult task, but considering alternatives to operating as an appendage of a North American church structure was more appealing. National Division participants in the dialogues with the Puerto Rico Conference leaders concluded that most of those favoring a political status of independence for the island wanted to maintain the current church status as an annual conference of The UMC. Conversely, those most vocally supporting U.S. statehood or Puerto Rico's U.S. commonwealth status were interested in exploring church autonomy.

In 1991, the World Division endorsed independence for Puerto Rico.

Noting the island's subjugation to foreign powers for more than 500 years, the division welcomed a decision of the UN Committee on Decolonization stating that Puerto Rico was indeed a colonial subject of the U.S. and affirming its right to self-determination and independence. The division expressed its "total support and solidarity with the people of Puerto Rico and its right to self-determination" and called upon the United States to "facilitate a process of decolonization."[33]

Like the MCCA, the Puerto Rico Annual Conference sent many of its pastors to conferences on the mainland U.S., where Hispanic congregations were in development. All the while, the conference maintained a well-educated and experienced pastoral membership to tend to its own churches and to conference programs. Scholarship assistance—from the Crusade Scholars program of GBGM and from HANA (Hispanic and Native American) scholarships administered by the General Board of Higher Education and Ministry—helped the conference keep many of its brightest and best students closely related to the church and in church vocations.

With only limited real estate available on the small island, acquiring properties for church development became the focus of the Puerto Rico Conference leaders. This, along with maintaining and expanding existing church buildings, presented a financial challenge to the conference and the congregations. Small grants and a favorable loan rate from the National Division made the task manageable. However, an onerous exception to indigenous leaders' proud accomplishments in church extension has been the failure to obtain the rights of property ownership to most of the church building sites. With few exceptions, GBGM held the titles. Legal complications, high transfer taxes, and the costs of maintaining insurance on the developed properties have thwarted several attempts at transferring titles.

In 1992, GBGM joined the Puerto Rico Annual Conference in petitioning the General Conference to grant autonomy to the church. A new and visionary leadership team had successfully convinced the Puerto Rican conference of the wisdom of local accountability, including the selection of a bishop from within its own membership. A plan for increasing the membership through aggressive church development activities and a promise to engage in active mission relationships with the larger Caribbean region were readily endorsed by GBGM. Major contingencies included continuing current levels of financial support by GBGM for eight years, representation on the Council of Bishops, and participation in The UMC pension plan for pastors and church workers. The General Conference of 1992 gave its blessing to the Puerto Rican church and the conference became the autonomous Methodist Church of Puerto Rico. The 2004 General Conference of The UMC approved a concordat relationship between the autonomous Methodist Church of Puerto Rico and The UMC. The concordat recognizes the voting rights of delegations from each General Conference to the other.

Other Relationships

In addition to MCCA and the Puerto Rico Methodist Church, The UMC related to the Dominican Evangelical Church and the United Evangelical Church in Puerto Rico. These two churches had been in mission relationships with the Evangelical United Brethren Church, in cooperation with other sponsoring North American denominational mission boards. Both of these churches offered vital programs and boasted indigenous leadership. They had modest church structures and sought to function with their primary financial support coming from their membership. Pastors and other church leaders usually found additional employment to supplement their small income from church sources. The Dominican Evangelical Church and the United Evangelical Church in Puerto Rico provided an alternative model to the customary one of denominationally sponsored and structured mission churches.

CHAPTER 3

Mission Personnel and
Leadership Development

*The Great Commission is addressed and responded to
by churches in every place. Missionary sending and receiving
will flow reciprocally across the face of the earth through the
channel of God's grace. All churches will be enriched in faith
and renewed in understanding and commitment by the
witness from sending and receiving.*[1]

*H*OW ARE THEY to believe in one of whom they have never heard?
And how are they to hear without someone to proclaim him? . . . As
it is written, 'How beautiful are the feet of those who bring good news!'
. . . So faith comes from what is heard, and what is heard comes through
the word of Christ" (Romans 10:14–17, NRSV). The biblical basis for the
mission strategy of sending personnel to live and share the gospel of
Christ does not change. Even so, dynamic forces outside the church and
changing realities within it shape the experiences of sending and receiving
those who are called.

In the context of postcolonial realities and in the aftermath of the social
revolution of the 1960s, the philosophy of leadership became the crucial
issue in United Methodist mission. A reexamination of the expectations
for the presence of missionaries in so many critical places for ministry was
a primary occupation. In reviewing the literature of this time, it is all too
easy to focus only upon the disappointments and the need for reforms.
Perhaps too much energy has been devoted to critique. But there is more
to the story.

In the period from 1968 to 2000, The United Methodist Church

(UMC) moved from a narrowly conceived vision of the missionary calling to recognition of the missionary nature of the world church. Partner churches, that is, former "mission churches," claimed their rightful calling to lead their churches and take the gospel to their communities and beyond their borders. Young leaders from within the churches offered themselves for training and service both in the church and in other helping professions and forms of national service. Through official denominational channels or by means of direct migration, pastors and laity of mission churches that once received the missionaries of The UMC themselves enthusiastically began to take up ministry and mission within the former "sending" conferences in the United States. Racial/ethnic churches in communities beset by civil unrest and beleaguered by systemic injustices demanded a role for their leaders in rebuilding their communities and congregations. Members of the laity across the denomination were mobilized into cadres of volunteers performing missionary service at home and abroad.

In these ways, the missionary era was not ending but changing. Even though fewer individuals may be recruited and commissioned by the church for traditional forms of missionary service, the response to new forms of missionary calling has resulted in a dramatic growth in the number of people and the value of resources invested in United Methodist mission. Not all mission activity of members and member churches can be counted, or counted upon, by the denomination's mission administrators or policymakers. The sacrificial service of short-term volunteers today parallels the crosscultural missionary service of earlier generations who were called into lifetime vocations. But the work of the volunteers often lies beyond the reach of the church's oversight or vision. A failure to acknowledge these new developments ignores significant testimony about ways in which the Christian faith is being shared with those who have never before heard or heeded the gospel message. The following narrative attempts to tell the story of how the call to mission is being received and increasingly embraced by the whole church.

Missionaries

The most widely understood and supported mission activity of the church is the recruitment and sending of mission personnel. The New Testament church sent and supported the apostles in their witness to

Christ in Jerusalem, Judea, and the larger gentile world. Paul's missionary journeys defined the proselytizing nature of the Christian faith. This outreach would not be confined to a single culture or place but would grow and be enriched by the contributions of new believers in a variety of social contexts.

The history of the church has been written as a missionary movement — following Christianity's momentum from the Middle East to the cultural and political strongholds of Europe; spreading from Europe to the expanding western frontiers of North America; and flowing from the Northern Hemisphere to the lands south of the equator. In 1963, the World Council of Churches (WCC) acknowledged the broad scope of missionary activity in adopting the program theme: "Mission to and from Six Continents." Some found an implication in this theme that the geographic expansion of the church was an indication that the missionary task was now complete.

A Changing Missionary Role

Most missionary-sending agencies had to contend with a changing role for missionaries. Vociferous leaders of the mission churches were challenging their continued dependence on missionary direction. With postcolonial independence for new nations came a surge of self-determination and control in social and religious life as well as in political institutions. The revolutionary and chauvinistic spirit that sent colonial authorities packing for home also found expression in the churches through a call for a "missionary moratorium." Such a call originated with an action of the All Africa Conference of Churches in 1974. The backers believed that only a disciplined interruption of the systems of outside funding and expatriate personnel would bring an end to foreign domination of their churches. Many traditional patterns of missionary influence had already been challenged and changed; but now leaders wanted fuller independence, especially "an opportunity to work with their own resources to find their own selfhood and identity."[2]

The rhetoric of the moratorium expressed in Africa found resonance within the regional meetings of church councils in Asia and Latin America. The moratorium's purpose and significance required much interpretation in missionary communities, mission agencies, and supporting churches. In 1968, Bishop Lloyd Wicke, president of the United Methodist Board of Missions, had already asked the question: "Just what is the nature of the vocation of the missionary in a world community pluralistic in almost every dimension of its existence?"[3] He reported that the Methodist missionaries in Uruguay had given notice of their decision to return home, "not because of disenchantment with the Gospel or its validity, but because of their certainty that the Church will only come to itself when its life is totally controlled by the indigenous leadership." A Methodist missionary, Frederick Dale Bruner, writing in *The Christian Century* a few months earlier on his perception of the missionary presence in the Philippines, concluded that it had "become a hindrance. It has overstayed its usefulness," he said, "And in overstaying, it has perhaps harmed itself."[4] Bishop Wicke pleaded with the Board to have empathy for the missionaries: "The missionary is a 'caught' person in many ways, seeking freedom for the friend yet not knowing how to free himself. He is impaled between the expectations of the sending agency and its constituency and the demands made upon him by those to whom he is sent. He is torn between the inner compulsion which motivates him and the outer restraints which time and circumstances place upon him. The older absolutes which provided clear beacons for his predecessors are fading and the newer ones too often appear as institutional relativities or authoritarian irrelevancies."[5]

But Wicke also prepared the Board for some tough questioning of the traditional role and work of the missionary and urged Board members to begin "experimenting" with alternative forms of service.

One "alternative" surfaced among church renewalists; they advocated greater attention to domestic issues raised by the civil rights movement and the struggle for justice by other marginalized groups within the North American context. The leaders of the Black Methodists for Church Renewal (BMCR) called upon the Board of Missions to withdraw all of its "overseas" missionary personnel—more than 1,400—for retraining and redeployment among "the alienated poor in America." In a critique of the Board's seeming fixation upon missionary activities abroad, BMCR said this move would "represent a serious effort to cease the imperialist domination of other cultures and would make possible the necessary process of indigenization and self-determination of all Third World citizens."[6]

The Board would examine new opportunities for mission service in crisis spots in the U.S., but the impending changes forecast for the management of its large and conspicuous "overseas" missionary enterprise claimed its immediate attention. Responses were needed on several fronts.

The criticism of the missionary complicity with the dehumanizing forces of colonialism was most compelling when voiced by leaders of national churches. Ezekiel Makunike, a United Methodist journalist and communications specialist in the newly independent Zimbabwe government, complained of the complacency of the very missionaries to whom he was indebted for his introduction to Christianity. "Before the 1950s," he wrote, "I do not remember ever hearing a missionary utter the words 'racial justice' or 'equal rights,' to say nothing of 'political independence!' Politics was clearly outside the sphere of awareness and the vocabulary of mission-trained pupils like us. . . . Consciously or unconsciously, missionaries were part of the imperialistic design and facilitators of the purposes of the colonizing powers."[7]

Because there were few forums available in the church for open debate about the politics or ideology of the missionary enterprise, indigenous criticism seldom reached the larger church constituency. The attention of supporting mission constituencies was more readily drawn to the fruits of the missionary enterprise, such as new generations of church-educated leaders who were taking government positions in the newly independent countries.[8] The anticipated decline in the number of missionary personnel recruited and sent to places of assignment brought criticism from the evangelical ranks of the church. The call by national churches for a missionary moratorium increased the sensitivity of Board staff to the kinds of missionary placements these churches would accept. Even without the influence of the moratorium, national church leaders were already reserving internal church administrative positions and most pastoral appointments for their own personnel. This left primarily social development and technical service assignments open to Western expatriates. The evangelical critics of the Board saw this situation as a major retrenchment, especially from the work of evangelism and church growth that they insisted was far from over. Influential critics, including former missionary personnel, formed an ad hoc Evangelical Missions Council (EMC) to air their concerns more effectively. They sought to develop a strategy for extensive dialogue with the Board of Missions on issues of missionary philosophy and program.

The active missionaries were caught in a dilemma and needed the Board's attention. As stated by Malcom J. McVeigh, a United Methodist missionary serving in Angola: "We recognize there is a great deal of confusion about the role of the missionary in our world. We are united in our commitment to Jesus Christ, but we are not of one mind as to what that means for our service throughout the world. There is an urgent need for redefining the missionary task in our day and for closer communication among the Board of Missions, the missionaries, and the national churches as to what a missionary is and should be."[9]

The Reverend Dr. Eugene Stockwell, a Latin American missionary who had returned to the Board in an executive capacity in 1962, was an obvious choice to promote missionary morale. He produced a paper — "What Does It Mean to Be a Missionary?" — for wide distribution and dialogue in the missionary community. While noting the revolutionary changes and forces of secularization that had either destabilized or diminished the direct influence of missionaries, Stockwell devoted most of his attention to the loss of missionary self-esteem. Whether in relationship to the growing independence of the "receiving" churches or to the supervisory authority of a Board readily distracted by global crises, the missionaries felt undervalued. Published responses from representatives of the missionary community dwelled on work-related issues, especially lack of services from the Board.[10] But a call for a more thoroughgoing analysis of the missionary vocation in the context of the changing international situation found support among the Board's directors.

A Review of Missionary Policies

In October 1971, the report of an International Task Force for the Study of Continued Involvement of Missionaries Overseas (SCIMO) was presented to the Board of Missions. This task force addressed the issues raised by the call for a missionary moratorium but without any abdication of the missionary function and purpose. The task force report immediately endorsed self-determination by the national churches and the need for corrective policies and procedures to limit the excesses of missionary power: "We recognize the right of each national church to say at this time whether or not it desires missionaries from the U.S.A. and the conditions under which such missionaries will serve; however, we stress that the general welfare of the missionaries is the joint responsibility of the two churches involved in mission. We recognize further the serious problems which have at times arisen for missionaries because of lack of directives concerning channels of accountability."[11]

The SCIMO report gave increased attention to the involvement of national churches in the placement process and recommended heightened expectations and requirements for missionary recruitment and training. Candidates for missionary service were to demonstrate previous service outside their own countries and to be "selected carefully with an eye to their racial attitudes as well as to their political sensitivity, experience, diplomacy, and willingness to be 'involved.'" The report embraced the ongoing national struggles for justice and the role of the churches in revolutionary changes taking place. It recommended "increased attention to furlough retraining in order that missionaries have experiences which will help them to become aware of those systems which militate against the liberation process."

Such changes in the approach to missionary activity in the receiving nations also implied changes in strategy by the sending organization. The World Division of the General Board of Global Ministries (GBGM) committed itself to foreign policy advocacy in Washington and to constituency education regarding "U.S. international relations, specifically U.S. economic, military, and cultural imperialism." Moreover, in countries with despotic governments, the World Division pledged cooperation "with programs that will support the people who are suffering injustices and political oppression."

Finally, the SCIMO report endorsed the concept of "internationalization" of the missionary community. It recognized the importance of indigenous church personnel by approving a funding relationship for national persons in mission to replace departing expatriate personnel. It also recognized the U.S. as a major "world mission field" and pledged the World Division to efforts to recruit personnel from churches around the globe and seek placements for them in the U.S. among churches, seminaries, connectional bodies, and unofficial groups, especially minority caucuses of the denomination.

Preparations for Missionary Training

The Board was carefully maneuvering around monumental challenges to its primary activity of deploying missionaries in the churches around the world. From the Board's administrative perspective, its efforts avoided a shutdown of the North American missionary enterprise and even enlightened the larger church concerning the increasing role of missionaries from national churches — a sign of the fulfillment of the church-planting activity of the missionary movement. But criticism surfaced around the Board's adoption of the world's social, political, and economic agendas for

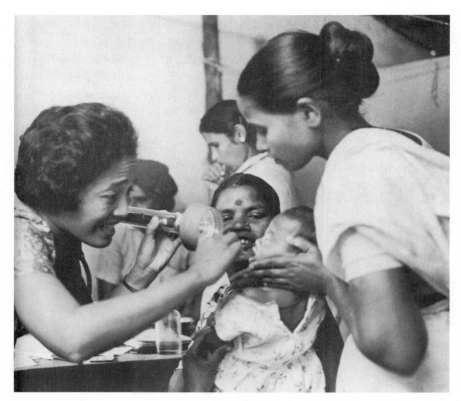

Dr. Esther Mabry typified the dedication and spirit of sacrifice of the traditional missionary who traveled from the U.S. to another country to minister
to those in poverty. Here she examined a child at the Sheriff's Garden Clinic
in Bangalore, India, in 1970. Mabry's work was not restricted to medicine:
she developed economic self-help for landless women, including setting up a
grain cooperative through which participants were able to buy and raise animals and make enough money to send their children to school. *(Photo by Toge
Fujihira, courtesy of UM Archives and History)*

future missionary activity at the expense of the traditional mission mandate to proclaim the gospel and make believers. This critique was the
main theme of the denomination's unofficial EMC as its representatives
met with Board officers and senior executives on many occasions for dialogue, discussion, and (usually) disagreement.

The EMC reverted to various tactics to make its point that the Board
had abandoned its evangelistic mission in favor of social and political development. It administered a survey of all World Division missionary per-

sonnel and published a short list of those who met its litmus test of adherence to sound conservative biblical and theological principles. In distributing its list, the EMC suggested that only these missionaries deserved the support of evangelically inclined United Methodist churches. The council frequently accused the Board's missionary recruitment policies of having a liberal theological bias. As evidence, the EMC produced case studies of missionary applicants with evangelical beliefs who had been turned down by the Board. It further cited statistical data from conservative mission agencies identifying "people groups" around the world who had yet to hear the gospel preached to them in their own language. The EMC questioned whether these peoples would ever be reached without evangelistic missionaries and the resources of Western sending agencies, implying the reluctance or limitations of mission churches in effectively taking up this task. The critics gave scant attention to the fact that most of this "unreached" population was located in countries and cultures strongly influenced and shaped by other major religions, especially Islam. Interfaith relations were not a part of the EMC strategy for mission, while any notion of pluralism was unacceptable.

The Board's policies and administrative guidelines on international missionary sending were to be influenced in dialogue with the national church leaders. Messages sent by the churches and their leaders did not ease the dilemma. Unwittingly, the issue of missionary economics prompted and then discouraged the resolve of those who supported the call for a missionary (and financial) moratorium. Participating in a regional ecumenical forum, the Reverend Dr. Emerito Nacpil, then dean of Union Theological Seminary in Manila, used the simple questions: "Whom does the missionary serve? And what does [the missionary] do?" Thus he raised the difficult issue of dominance: an assumption of cultural superiority guided by Western economic values: "[The missionary] was supported by the faithfulness, stewardship, and tradition of his sending church, with the complex machinery and financial resources of a missions society or a board of missions, complete with an 'ambassador plenipotentiary' — the field representative or treasurer. This support was further undergirded by the 'superiority' of the missionary's culture and by the imperialistic ethos of a colonial or neo-colonial era."[12]

Nacpil called upon the churches to depart from this system and to recognize the potential of emerging churches to define their own mission and develop their work within the capacity of their own resources. He said,

"The selfhood of the church means that a church is fully responsible for managing its own life, for discerning the nature and demands of its own mission to the peoples in the midst of which it lives as a Christian community, for the sustaining of this mission with its own faithfulness and sacrifice and joy, and for evolving a form and style of life which expresses its own identity as God's people in a particular sector of the world. . . . The work that it [any future missionary endeavor] entails is to be determined as a necessary and urgent expression of the mission of the inviting church and it must be supported primarily by the faithfulness and stewardship resources of that church."

Though self-determination was the mantra for mission churches in the postcolonial period, too few have been able to attain a level of self-sufficiency. In 1981—seven years after his organization had declared a moratorium on receiving missionary and financial aid—Maxime Rafransoa, the newly elected general secretary of the All Africa Conference of Churches, told its gathered assembly: "Obviously the idea of a moratorium has died and has been duly buried." But the underlying goal of greater self-reliance remained alive. "We want to be helped to be ourselves," he stated in a follow-up interview. "Our raw materials are still pilfered or sold at low prices, our labor force is always cheap to profit capitalism, and our brains are still drained towards [other] countries by better pay."[13] The economic dominance of nations of the Northern Hemisphere overlooked the problems of overwhelming indebtedness facing the developing nations of the Southern Hemisphere. The demand of international lending bodies for debt repayment drained national budgets for local development priorities. The borrowing nations suffered from poor standards of living and little capacity for building a stable economic base that would even hold out the promise of developing local support of an organized church. In these contexts, missionaries still provided the only source of external investment through funds raised for meager stipends for church workers and other locals working in church-sponsored development projects. Until local economies were adequately stimulated and developed, the missionary presence had to provide the principal economic activity and opportunity. Thus patterns of dependence upon outside resources and influence continue unabated in the developing world.

This is not to suggest that indigenous churches had given up on the goal of self-support. They were still seeking to achieve it, but their capacity to instill incentives for self-development was diminished among members who saw little improvement in their lot in life. Few mission churches have been able to establish any form of apportionment giving to connectional or central church structures. These churches required grants in mission aid to maintain their infrastructure as well as their mission projects.

This context may explain the moderation in the voices of the African United Methodist bishops in their statement to the Board of Global Ministries regarding future missionary deployment: "We acknowledge that God is calling us to a greater responsibility, sensitivity, and stewardship in the ever-widening challenges and needs of our time," they said. "God is calling us to witness more effectively and to engage all the resources [that God] has placed at our command; and God is also calling us to work together as one people, sharing in relationships."[14] The African bishops asked the World Division "to continue to seek and send persons in mission as needed and requested by the churches." Reflecting some of the concerns of the call for a moratorium, they urged recalling ineffective missionaries who "no longer cooperate with the national leadership and who have outgrown their usefulness." All missionaries, they pointed out, were to "be accountable to the African church." The bishops further urged the World Division to change the cultivation patterns for missionary support—from designated giving to the missionary, to promoting the "program of the churches in Africa." "The ongoingness of the program," they said, "must be ensured or maintained, whether missionary 'X' or national 'Y' is serving."

A delegation from Latin American churches reviewed the SCIMO report in 1971 and proceeded to develop implementation criteria, all of which heightened the role of the national churches in assisting the World Division with missionary training and placement. Chief among the churches' concerns was a thorough introduction to Latin American cultural realities, which they believed could be more adequately addressed by a time of residence in a study center such as those in Cuernavaca, México, or Costa Rica. Perhaps the most compelling recommendation was to institute a three-year trial period for each newly appointed missionary, after which the national church would determine whether the missionary was "contributing positively to the life and mission of the autonomous church."[15] If the national church were to decide upon a missionary's discontinuation, "the reasons for such a decision [would be] made perfectly clear to the missionary." On matters of economics, the task force expressed its concern about the disparity between missionary salaries and those of local church workers and recommended allowing national church leaders to establish all salaries. It also discouraged perpetuation of donor support for individual missionaries rather than direct support for the programs and projects of the churches those missionaries served.

Veteran Latin American missionary Raymond K. DeHainaut offered an insightful perspective on the changing role of "foreign" mission personnel. He was present when Methodist missionary colleagues in Uruguay decided to return home, claiming they were a "hindrance to the progress of the church in that country." He celebrated the emergence of strong leaders in the autonomous national church in Argentina, who had assumed the many leadership posts previously filled by missionaries like himself. He asked: "What am I doing here? Did God really call me to be a missionary in present-day Argentina?" His regional superintendent, the Reverend Hugo Urcola, told him: "Yes, it is true that we have reached a certain degree of self-sufficiency, but Argentina is a big country with many problems (the increasing burden of national debt, unemployment, social alienation, the dissolution of the family, discrimination against our aborigines, secularization, etc.). And we have invited you missionaries to help us in areas where we are short-handed."

After consulting other church leaders and local pastors — all of whom manifested a strong interest in their church's receiving missionaries who had a loyalty to the Argentine church and a willingness to work under its authority, a comprehension of the historical and cultural context of the country, and a commitment to interpreting Latin American realities to North American churches — DeHainaut concluded: "I have come to realize more than ever before that foreign mission is a two-way street. I have been greatly enriched by my years of service in several Latin American countries. I came back to Argentina for the second time because I need to be here."[16]

The Board of Global Ministries strategy of preserving the missionary-sending function — by acknowledging and "fixing" what was broken — would produce mixed results. The decline in the numbers of missionaries assigned to international service — from more than 1,400 in 1968 to slightly more than 400 by the year 2000 — was inevitable. Nevertheless, critics attributed this decrease to a reduced commitment to evangelizing efforts and the failure to see greater opportunities for missionary service beyond those defined by partner churches. The World Division often interpreted the decline as an economic problem caused by rising costs of missionary deployment in an inflationary cycle of the emerging global economy. In spite of special promotional efforts, there was little or no increase in apportioned or special giving for missionary support from local churches.[17] But neither the effort at interpreting the changing realities of mission nor the pace of redefining, creating, and implementing new mission policies or programs satisfied critics.

By 1984, GBGM advocacy for church participation in movements for social change and its new policies for missionary deployment had reached a crescendo. Riding on a wind of confidence, GBGM's adversaries established an independent missionary-sending society, which they called the Mission Society for United Methodists (MSUM). The MSUM was committed to providing an alternative channel that personnel and churches could use to support the traditional missionary agenda of the church. The new agency did not seek either official recognition from or accountability to the United Methodist General Conference. Still, its supporters often submitted petitions encouraging that official governing body of the church to revise legislation in ways that would make it easier for local churches to participate in MSUM's financial support. These efforts were successful only in provoking the General Conferences of 1984 and 1988 to give official recognition to only one missionary-sending agency, GBGM.

The legislative process yielded one crumb to proponents of MSUM by mandating dialogue on mission issues between leaders of the new society and GBGM. These dialogues, presided over by the Council of Bishops, occurred for two quadrennia without a meeting of minds. Some of the denomination's partner churches were more than casual observers, since the conflict within the North American UMC would certainly be exported to their churches through missionaries deployed from two different agencies within one sister church.

MSUM established an office in Decatur, Georgia, for its executive secretary and a handful of program and administrative staff. Its promotional appeals to churches found a hearing among those conservative pastors and congregations that wanted to support missionaries who would emphasize personal evangelism and church growth. MSUM's official strategy focused on opening work in new areas, thus avoiding complicated protocol matters of existing church relationships. Its recruitment of missionaries was generally successful, but the full salary support of missionaries often required the personnel to contract with at least one other sending agency. By 2000, the society reported a roster of more than 400 persons and a multimillion-dollar operations budget. A few missionary assignments were made to sympathetic sectors within partner churches of The UMC (and GBGM)—most notably Costa Rica, the Philippines, Russia, and a mission from Brazil to Paraguay—but most MSUM personnel would choose to work through independent missionary-receiving organizations in various countries.

Confusion and conflict over the identities and purposes of the unofficial MSUM and the official GBGM occurred from moment to moment in the organizational life of The UMC and among partner church leaders. Some United Methodist bishops were asked to appoint clergy members of their annual conferences to missionary status with the unofficial mission society. Reasoning that an episcopal appointment would be tantamount to official recognition of the new society, the bishops denied such appointments, whereupon the clergy members took leaves of absence in order to follow their missionary calling. Leaders of MSUM, who pressed their debate with the bishops in public statements, did not abandon their cause.

Leaders of national churches, who saw problems in the growing dependence upon missionary leadership, did not welcome the activities of the unofficial United Methodist sending agency. After all, they had worked closely with GBGM to address many of the deficiencies in the recruitment, training, and assigning of missionaries. Most indigenous church leaders understood the dynamics of the organizational and theological conflict within The UMC that had prompted the development of an "alternative" mission society. But they did not want to see the conflict exported to their churches by the deployment of missionaries.

By the end of the twentieth century, a choice existed, even though the official standing of GBGM was well established. As a GBGM official, the author once visited an African United Methodist church partner. Upon meeting a bright young scholarship prospect of the conference, he was asked: "Are you with the Board in Atlanta or the one in New York?" Location, not denominational legitimacy, seemed to be the means of identifying the nature of a relationship with United Methodist mission. More is given on MSUM in chapter 5.

Missionary Preparation and Training

The most significant benefit from deliberations over the changing missionary role came with increased attention and resources spent in missionary preparation and training. To help train missionaries for the changing realities of their global placements, an interdenominational Mission Orientation Center was established in 1959 at Stony Point, New York. However successful the organizing effort, by 1972 the sponsoring denominations had lost interest in providing the financing and administrative support this cooperative effort required, and mission boards created their own training programs. The United Methodist Board first substituted a six-week orientation program, but this brief training was widely recognized as inadequate for preparing new personnel for their mission appointments. Finally, in 1986, the Mission Personnel unit of GBGM was charged with developing a new, residentially based, comprehensive program. The task force of GBGM directors inheriting this assignment identified biblical and theological studies as key ingredients in the curriculum. Consequently, they urged that the new training program be located on the campus of a United Methodist theological school. After a search that involved most of the twelve denominational seminaries, a contract was signed with the schools in Atlanta — Candler School of Theology and the Interdenominational Theological Consortium, of which United Methodist Gammon Theological Seminary was a part.[18]

The Mission Resource Center opened in Atlanta in 1989, and a formal six-month training program was inaugurated. All candidates took up occupancy in seminary housing and were enrolled in foundation courses at the schools. An important component of the curriculum was the establishment of mutual learning objectives. After several weeks of participation in the program, candidates were asked to review their expectations with staff members, who offered counsel to the candidates and to GBGM regarding their continuation in the program. If additional course work were required or longer exposure to the training recommended, candidates would not proceed to commissioned status. If they chose to withdraw, that option was pursued. The GBGM, the receiving churches, and the candidates were much more intentionally involved in the preparation and placement process than before.

Over time, all training programs for GBGM mission personnel began to take place at the Mission Resource Center or under its auspices. These

These US-2s, short-term missionaries, engaged in a protest march in Washington, D.C., in 1983. The US-2 experience served to introduce many young people to the rigors and joys of mission service, and many went on to become professionals in mission and leaders in the church. *(Photo by John Goodwin, courtesy of UM Archives and History)*

programs included orientation for national personnel recruited for service as church and community workers, as US-2s (in a two-year, young adult, mission service program), and as mission interns (in a three-year, young adult international and U.S. mission exposure program). The center also extended its training services to partner churches. The Korean Methodist Church (KMC) sought help in formalizing its training and supervision of the hundreds of missionaries that local Korean churches were recruiting and supporting in mission service in as many as fifty-two countries. A few of the candidates and staff of the KMC Board of Mission and Evangelism were sent to Atlanta to participate in the training modules as trainees and potential trainers of their missionaries. Other partner churches and conferences of The UMC sent leaders to the Resource Center to take up periods of residence as international mentors and consultants.

The Mission Resource Center also became home to the Missionary Wellness Program. The World Division introduced this comprehensive health care initiative for all its mission personnel. The services of Atlanta-based medical institutions, physicians, and counselors were at the disposal of the Wellness Program for diagnosis, treatment, and instruction on preventive health maintenance. Services included thorough examinations prior to commissioning and immediately upon return from each term of service. For many personnel, this program provided a continuing relationship with a professional team in health services when such care was not available in their home communities or places of assignment. It also assured the World Division of a higher level of health maintenance for its mission personnel and held the prospect of cost reductions in insured-risk coverage.

New Missionary Programs

Innovations in missionary deployment developed during the period 1968–2000 were designed to address the critique of traditional missionary behavior from partner churches and conferences abroad and the judgment of key constituencies among United Methodist churches in the U.S. The development of placements in which missionaries would be under local church authority would require considerable dialogue and adjustments within receiving churches. Addressing cultural insensitivity that impaired the effectiveness of existing personnel and removing barriers that excluded people of color from the ranks of "foreign" missionaries required long-term training and recruitment strategies.

Nevertheless, in 1976, the World Division initiated special short-term programs to introduce members of North American racial/ethnic minorities to international ministries, programs, and projects.[19] With a theme of "Mission Interaction," the division recruited racial/ethnic minority candidates for exposure to and involvement in mission situations for three months to three years. Special funding was set aside within the division's missionary budget to finance the program. Racial/ethnic groups within United Methodist churches were the primary source of candidates recruited to serve in this program. The program successfully introduced people of color into traditional missionary placements for work among constituencies that had previously experienced only Caucasian missionaries. Given the experience and expertise of the new racial/ethnic recruits, placements and tasks were created that had never before been considered for missionary deployment, such as work among Korean minorities in Japan and among the African diaspora in Latin America. A reciprocal program was later devised in which persons from partner churches and conferences abroad could be sent to North America, where they would take up residence and leadership in programs related to racial/ethnic constituencies of The UMC. Known as "Inter-ethnic Interaction," the program recognized the increasingly global nature of the church's mission. In particular, it focused on connecting dispersed peoples who shared a common ancestry and culture.

Out of a growing awareness of the need to internationalize mission personnel in a global church, the World Division took steps to formalize the concept of Persons in Mission (PIM). This process involved recognizing the fact that the missionary calling was not limited to churches in the Northern Hemisphere. Ecumenical discussions had advanced the understanding that faithful disciples of all churches are called into missionary service and are a significant part of the shared resources of the universal Christian church. A specific program to accommodate this gift of leadership across The UMC—the PIM program—was developed in 1974.[20] While the term "Persons in Mission" was once proposed as a collective category for all missionaries, the terminology found a more limited application to the mission personnel in partner churches serving in their own or other countries. More specifically, a PIM served in a position funded with an appropriation from the World Division. The funding was designated for the position, not the individual. The funded positions were determined in consultation between the World Division and the partner church or conference.

An immediate objective of the PIM program was to help the larger church experience the diversity of the global missionary community. To that end, the World Division aimed its resources at creating positions in the U.S. conferences of The UMC in which representatives of partner churches and conferences could serve. It was believed that these colleagues in mission serving at this level in the denomination would have the greatest connectional impact. U.S. conferences were informed that their local PIM was not a representative of the Board of Global Ministries but a missionary of a partner church or conference. Thus their congregations had the opportunity to "receive" (as well as "send") missionaries. As a result, some U.S. United Methodists heard the gospel from a new perspective and were able to celebrate the gifts for ministry that these partner personnel brought to them from other cultures.

In 1973, the South Indiana Conference invited the Reverend Satish Gyan of the Methodist Church in India to serve as a missionary "with" their churches. The conference paid his salary and gave him this assignment: "Interpret Third World concerns to the church and community." His message was that "the comforts and conveniences of people in the First World—North America and Europe—are at the expense of the comfort and convenience of the Third World. . . . This is wrong. Christians especially can't afford to live in a spirit of self-satisfaction." Rev. Gyan got a mixed response to this message, but he concluded: "People are beginning to see the other side of the coin: that people living in different cultures, traditions, political and economic environments have significant contributions to make in the life of the church."[21]

The PIM program also provided funding for mission personnel of the partner churches and conferences to serve in countries other than their own or the U.S. It supported evangelists from the African churches who moved across national boundaries to establish new churches, allowed trainers in church development in Latin America to work regionally, enabled Indian pastors to work among the Indian diaspora in Fiji, and underwrote training and the sharing of pastoral support among Methodists in Brazil and United Methodists in Angola and Mozambique, all of whom shared a common language: Portuguese. In effect, the PIM program supported the cutting edge of the expanding contemporary mission movement. By 2000, missionary personnel were on the increase among the growing churches of the Southern Hemisphere. In most cases, they were already equipped with the required language skills and cultural sensitivities in which an outsider would have to be trained.

The longer-term purpose of the PIM program was to institutionalize positions in the leadership structure of the partner churches and conferences themselves. Funding from the World Division was particularly designated for positions that advanced "pioneer" or "special" ministries. The priority was not on existing positions in church or conference structures but on creating an evangelistic focus "for the development of churches and other Christian communities." The request for proposals asked participating churches and conferences to identify how they would develop support to sustain the ministry beyond the term of World Division financing. The declining economic conditions in many countries eventually dictated priorities, however, so many of the PIM positions were associated with administrative functions of the churches and conferences, not their most creative ministries. In the 1990s, the Women's Division stimulated a renewed consideration of the original purposes of the PIM program by strictly designating its appropriation for personnel to work in specialized ministries with women and children.

Another innovation in the United Methodist mission personnel program addressed the U.S. mission context. The Community Developers Program was initiated in 1968 in response to challenges from black leadership in the church (including Black Methodists for Church Renewal).

These leaders called on the Board of Missions to direct more mission program resources to minority communities in the U.S. Funding came first from the denominational "Fund for Reconciliation," and later the program became part of The UMC Human Relations Day offering. The inspiration for the program was provided by the Reverend Negail R. Riley, a doctoral candidate at Boston University School of Theology. Rev. Riley was a local United Methodist pastor and a professor at Philander Smith College in Little Rock, Arkansas. His doctoral thesis boldly declared that "in God's world, no person is an outcast," and he applied this concept to the missionary program of the Board of Missions when he became an assistant general secretary of the National Division in 1969.[22] The Black Community Developers Program that Riley designed opened the door to a new style of missionary leadership—a style coming from community activists with instincts and skills for mobilizing communities to address racism and the conditions of powerlessness it produces. "All of a sudden there started appearing strange-looking folks with Afros and dashikis working in the churches with this new program," commented the Reverend William T. Robinson, a supervising pastor in Detroit. But his final assessment was that "they brought the message as well as the clout of the church to the streets."[23]

In 1970, the Community Developers Program established a component for developers from other U.S. minority groups (Asian, Native American, and Hispanic). Personnel were identified and recruited by local church pastors and leaders from their memberships and neighborhoods. The community developers were recognized (not commissioned) and trained by the National Division, but they remained employees of the local churches or programs. Funding from the division went to the local churches, not directly to the individuals. The developers worked on organizing minority neighborhoods with the goal of developing solutions to such protracted problems as inadequate education, housing, economic opportunities, and political representation. Because these developers did not compromise their church identity, churches were sometimes drawn into the conflicts, but the churches also reaped the benefits of successful program outreach. A good number of the developers opted for full-time work in the church, including careers in pastoral ministry and church administration.[24]

Deaconesses have enjoyed a particular status in The UMC, being recognized as filling a special office in the church's missionary structure. In the former Methodist Church, the office of deaconess — not open to married women until 1959 — was the approved channel of career service for laywomen of the church. Deaconess service had its origins in German conferences of the immediate predecessor denominations of The UMC: The Methodist Church and the Evangelical United Brethren Church. It was strongly associated with the expansion of these denominations' mission outreach. Under the administration of the Woman's Division of the Board of Missions of The Methodist Church, deaconesses pioneered the development of many national mission projects and institutions in the U.S. They provided a continuity of service and commitment that stabilized their ongoing work in impoverished communities.

In 1956, the General Conference of The Methodist Church voted to open the way for women to enter the ordained ministry of the church. This new option for laywomen was followed by a restructure of the Board of Missions by the General Conference in 1964. As part of this restructure, the Woman's Division had to give up its mission personnel and programs. The Commission on Deaconess Work was dismantled, and the deaconess program was moved to the National Division. These changes — the opening of ordained ministry to women and the transfer of the deaconess program — resulted in a reduced capacity on the part of the Board of Missions to promote the recruitment of young women for deaconess service. Both factors contributed to a declining emphasis on the office of deaconess.

In the 1970s and 1980s, the future of deaconess service became embroiled in study processes approved by General Conference that were aimed at sorting out all categories of authorized ministry within the denomination. In a statement issued by the 1988 Convocation of the National Association of Deaconesses and Home Missionaries, the deaconesses expressed disappointment that proposals emerging from the study process were not focused on the issue of "lifetime commitment to mission at the national level." When the starting point for the study became annual conference salary and benefit requirements, the proposals considered by General Conference inevitably ignored critical areas of service among "multicultural and ethnic communities, isolated rural areas, inner cities, and the church of the poor."[25]

By action of the 1992 General Conference, deaconesses who were commissioned for missionary service by GBGM were also given the option of seeking ordination within the nonitinerant diaconal ministry of the

Josephine Pablo, a Filipina, illustrates the serving ministry of the deaconess movement. Deaconesses comprise a laywoman's movement that has gained new strength in recent years and has succeeded in recruiting young women like Pablo, who eventually emigrated to the U.S. *(Photo courtesy of UM Archives and History)*

church. The decision was left to the individual, and the diaconal choice proved to be attractive to many serving within program entities of annual conferences. Meanwhile, to distinguish the deaconess program, which was still under GBGM administration, from the diaconal alternative administered by the annual conferences, recruitment emphasized the missionary nature and history of the office of deaconess. This office's linkage with deaconesses in partner churches and ecumenical agencies around the world made candidates part of a global community of women in mission — the World Federation of Diakonia: Diaconal Association and Sisterhood. With these emphases, the deaconess program began to experience a resurgence of interest and enrollment. In 2000, the office of deaconess remained the only United Methodist missionary category solely dedicated to maintaining laywomen in mission service.

Leadership Development

Mission discourse throughout the last quarter of the twentieth century was often marked by contrition over the legacy of an earlier era. The missionary movement from the West to the East and Southern Hemisphere in the eighteenth and nineteenth centuries was too closely linked to the colonial powers of the time. It brought with it exploitation of local cultures and abuse of indigenous peoples. But there were also moments when the good work of earlier missionaries received the recognition and affirmation the movement deserved. One such moment was remembered as a highlight of the eighth assembly of the World Council of Churches (WCC) in Harare, Zimbabwe, in December 1998. President Nelson Mandela of South Africa was invited to the platform to address the assembly just after President Robert Mugabe of Zimbabwe had finished his remarks, which included an indictment of missionaries for a history of colonial complicity. Mandela saw the historical pendulum swinging in another direction: "As we were coming here, I told President Mugabe that he is a younger man than myself, and I said perhaps the experiences I have had he did not have during his time. But I said my generation is the product of church education. Without the missionaries and other religious organizations, I would not have been here today. The government of those days took no interest whatsoever in the education of Africans, Coloreds, and Indians. The churches bought the land, built the schools, equipped them, appointed and employed people. Therefore when I say we are the products of missionary education, I recognize that I will never have sufficient words to thank the missionaries for what they did for us."[26]

The development of leaders for church and society was an essential mission strategy, producing long-term benefits. In many countries, education was the opening wedge for establishing a missionary presence. Majority religious antipathies and government restrictions on evangelistic ministries were circumvented through the establishment of mission schools serving the general population. The women's missionary movement focused uniquely upon educational opportunities for young women, who were generally ignored by government and private educational institutions, including the church.

When churches were successfully established and leaders chosen, most were products of missionary education. The posting of missionaries to positions of church leadership diminished with the rising numbers of trained leaders from the local membership ranks. This indicator of mission growth and development is often slighted by those who judge the "success" of missionary efforts by counting the numbers of missionaries assigned. Indigenous leaders offer an effective role model for future generations. They are usually the strongest advocates of local or national values in shaping institutions and generating support.

Scholarships

The mission program most frequently credited with developing Methodist leaders worldwide is Crusade Scholarships. Begun as a post-World War II assistance program, Crusade Scholarships helped students from war-ravaged countries in Europe complete their education in other places. The General Conference soon broadened the program's scope. In fact, when the program celebrated its fiftieth anniversary in 1994, it identified more than 7,000 recipients of scholarships and fellowships in more than 50 countries.[27] The primary objective of the Crusade Scholarships was to prepare individuals "for more effective service in their countries."[28] To this end, the program made available block grants for churches to allocate to promising students enrolled in educational institutions in their own countries. It also directly administered scholarships to individuals recommended by the churches for professional or graduate-level study abroad. The scholarships covered round-trip travel, tuition, fees, room, meals, textbook allowance, and monthly incidentals; but successful candidates usually had additional financial support from other sources.

Selection criteria for Crusade Scholars required each candidate to demonstrate "a commitment to return to his/her own country or region upon completion of the Crusade program."[29] The experience of the Reverend Finaue Dyer Tu'uholoaki of Fiji exemplified the purpose of the program. In 1979, this soft-spoken and smiling Methodist pastor was chosen to take up studies at Perkins School of Theology in Dallas, Texas. He characterized his selection as an acknowledgment of a social responsibility. "I am able to study in the States as an individual," he wrote. "But the importance is not my individuality but my part in the society. I have seen myself as part of that whole which is the church in Fiji and in the South Pacific." He returned to Fiji in 1981 with permission to present a new mission statement to the annual meeting of the Methodist Church conference. The paper challenged the church to draft a new constitution by elaborating a mission of reconciliation to resolve various social and politi-

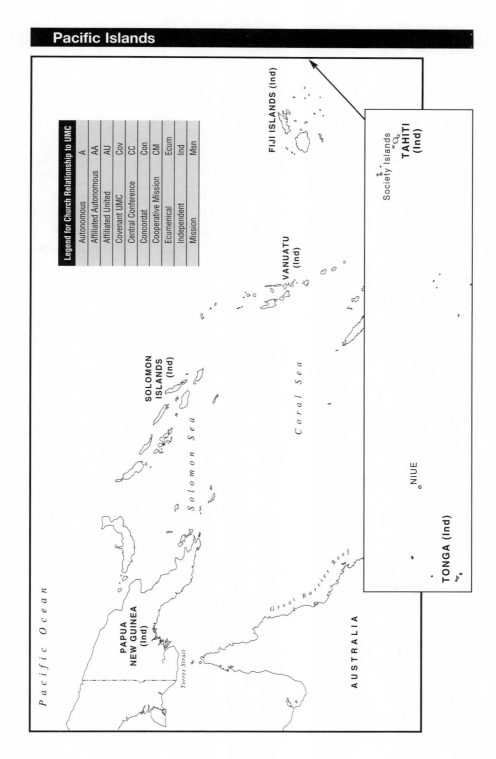

Legend for Church Relationship to UMC

Autonomous	A
Affiliated Autonomous	AA
Affiliated United	AU
Covenant UMC	Cov
Central Conference	CC
Concordat	Con
Cooperative Mission	CM
Ecumenical	Ecum
Independent	Ind
Mission	Msn

Pacific Ocean

PAPUA
NEW GUINEA
(Ind)

Torres Strait

SOLOMON
ISLANDS
(Ind)

Solomon Sea

VANUATU
(Ind)

Coral Sea

FIJI ISLANDS (Ind)

Society Islands

TAHITI
(Ind)

NIUE

TONGA (Ind)

AUSTRALIA

Great Barrier Reef

cal conflicts on the island. "What should reconciliation mean to individuals, clans, tribes, races, churches, and the whole nation?" he asked. "Reconciliation would be a complete or thorough change, a transformation of relations from an attitude of hostility, enmity, [and] division to one of friendship, communion, and unity."[30]

The primary support for the Crusade Scholarships program was raised from the annual churchwide World Communion offering. The funding has been generously supplemented by grants from the Women's Division, which help to sharpen the selection criteria to include women among the candidates for professional career training. Over the years, the rising costs of graduate-level education and the relatively stable amounts raised through the churchwide offering have limited the effectiveness of the program. Fewer individual scholarships were given, and the block grants diminished in value at a time when there was rising competition in the churches for the use of scholarship funds.

Crusade Scholarships, which began as an international program, soon developed a significant U.S. component. By 1955, 30 percent of its scholarship allotment was directed to minorities in the U.S. In 1971, this amount was increased to 35 percent and in 1975, to 50 percent. The rationale for the increase was based upon the demand for leadership development and minority empowerment in the church and society. A significant growth in the number of minorities seeking graduate training created a need for help with the rising costs of their education at a time of declining commitment from federal and state governments. With a limited source of available funding, the increasing percentages of U.S. scholarships could be offset only by a reduction in scholarships awarded for students abroad. But supporters of this shift toward serving more racial/ethnic constituents in the U.S. emphasized that "empowering of the local church base is essential in effective world-community witnessing."[31] While other churchwide scholarship programs were created to address the expanding requirements of minority population groups in the church, the screening of applicants for Crusade Scholarships has increasingly focused more on the distinctive calling to mission service in the church or society.

The Kendall Fund Program, administered by the Health and Welfare Division (later the Health and Relief Program Area) directed financial assistance for persons of African-American heritage pursuing graduate or professional degrees in health professions. The income from the generous estate of Harry F. Kendall—founder of an insurance company that survived the Great Depression by selling policies in primarily black neighborhoods—provided the scholarship funds.[32] The grants were for relatively small amounts, totaling $30,000 per year for all recipients. When the division received the corpus of the estate, it too became available for distribution. GBGM then decided to go beyond grant making and fulfill the purpose of the fund with a large capital donation to a black college, United Methodist-related Philander Smith College in Little Rock, Arkansas. This donation was to be used to establish a training program and facility for black students pursuing careers in medicine. A new building at the center honored the Reverend Dr. Randolph Nugent, the first black elected general secretary of GBGM and the longest-serving general secretary in the agency's history.

Academic Institutions

In addition to providing scholarships to individual students of partner churches and conferences, another leadership development strategy was to seize opportunities for strengthening church-related academic institutions in various world regions, especially Asia, Africa, and Latin America. The World Division leadership development grants were distributed with a preference given to students enrolled in such schools. There was a far greater return on investment in building up enrollment in these schools by providing quality educational opportunities than in continuing the well-worn practice of sending the brightest and best off to universities in Europe or North America. More students could attend schools in their regional settings at much lower costs. And strengthening these schools also created teaching opportunities for educators from the churches in the region.

The mission schools, which played a critical role in cultivating academic ambitions among each generation of church members, were also the "feeder" academies for institutions of higher education. Their fate, however, ebbed and flowed with the rising aspirations but declining economic conditions of newly independent governments. In Africa, some schools were taken over for government administration, only later to be returned to the churches in a state of disrepair. The churches managed to keep the schools running when governments could not, thanks to the faithfulness of educators among their membership who were willing to endure hardship without complaint. In Latin America and Asia, the mission schools survived by securing a place in a competitive, private education market.

They generally served a clientele that came from higher economic levels than their church members, but this often allowed the churches to receive a subsidy in higher tuition. In some instances, however, the importance of deriving income superseded the mission of promoting quality education.

Mission schools and colleges founded in the U.S. provided opportunities for minority students from poor communities to receive a formal elementary and secondary education with strong elements of cultural affirmation. The Navajo Methodist Mission School (later United Methodist Center) in New Mexico, the Holding Institute in Texas, and the Tampa Methodist Mission School in Florida specialized in educating Native American and Hispanic students whose special needs were not being addressed by public schools. The Allen High School in Asheville, North Carolina, served poor black students from within and beyond its local constituency. As a residential institution, it once enrolled and supported students, recruited by African-American United Methodist churches in urban areas of the North, who required an educational alternative to troubled neighborhood public schools in their inner cities. The mission colleges (Paine College in Georgia and Bennett College in North Carolina) served youth from rural black communities who had little access to colleges with more competitive admission policies. These colleges have remained close to their moorings in GBGM while seeking guidance from the General Board of Higher Education and Ministry for negotiating their way into new academic programs, mastering financial management, and pursuing future development options.

Women in Higher Education

The historic role of the Women's Division in promoting educational opportunities for women was dramatized in the division centennial observance during the 1987–1990 quadrennium. Singling out critical needs of African women, centennial goal number three declared: "By 1990, with direction from women of Africa, the Women's Division shall implement plans regarding higher education for women in Africa."[33] Staff and director teams were selected for visits to Africa for consultation and dialogue with African women leaders to assess concerns about limited opportunities for women in higher education in church-related schools. These teams found that the earlier Western missionary influence had defined a domestic but economically crucial role for women in the home that limited the access of female students to any advanced levels of formal education. The teams' first conclusion was to redefine the aim of higher education as it was used in the centennial goal. For women in the African context, the goal had to include a more immediate objective, namely, a level of education "which was higher than the women had." The teams' report to the division documented many areas of needed change of policy or specific improvements in basic levels of education provided by church schools. These areas included library services (upgrading books, equipment, and facilities), boarding facilities (hostels) for girls, current textbooks and supplies, and science/math lab supplies and equipment. The report also recommended the designation of one-half of the Centennial Fund, the whole of which totaled $835,000, for scholarships for African women seeking higher education in Africa, the U.S., or other countries.

A Symposium on African Women and Higher Education, held in April 1994, concluded the implementation of the Centennial Goal. The site of the symposium — the campus of the newly established United Methodist Africa University, located in Zimbabwe — was strategically selected to have an impact on the church's emerging higher education objectives for Africa. The event brought together women educators from Africa and from institutions of women's higher education sponsored by the Women's Division in Korea and the Philippines. Platform presentations featured African women who had risen to high offices in governmental and church life. Young women on their way to leadership in the African churches were in attendance. The issues of gender discrimination in education were addressed head-on. Vocational choices and leadership opportunities for African women were promoted. A strong dialogue and advocacy was fueled, and women in Africa were befriended, encouraged, and empowered in their ongoing struggle toward equality.

Student Christian Movements

In the early decades of the twentieth century, the student movement was a primary force in mobilizing the churches in North America and Europe for engagement in world mission. The Student Volunteer Movement for Foreign Mission (SVM) was formed under the auspices of the YWCA and YMCA, the major unit for campus ministry in North American colleges and universities. This movement's sole purpose was the recruitment of young people into missionary careers. Under the inspirational leadership of the influential Methodist layman John R. Mott, hundreds of chapters were formed. Using the popular theme of "Evangelization of the World in This Generation," the SVM interpreted the Great Commission of Matthew 28:19 ("Go . . . and make disciples of all nations") as the obligation of every Christian. Thousands of young adults were recruited and presented themselves for service in the ranks of denominational mission boards.

Mott's mission vision was strongly evangelistic but was also influenced by the Social Gospel. The fulfillment of the gospel was the realization of the reign of God. Mott worked energetically and traveled extensively to recruit a global missionary community that was committed to social service and social justice. As the first general secretary of the World Student Christian Federation (WSCF), he developed the prototype for a worldwide ecumenical organization that would keep its membership engaged in significant dialogue, witness, and service through quadrennial meetings and program activities.

The student movement thrived in both national and international contexts before the development of modern forms of transportation and communication technologies. The agendas for meetings evolved from a focus on internal matters of spiritual development, missionary activity, and vocational opportunity in the life of the church to a confronting of issues from within mission contexts, including empowerment of indigenous church leadership, militarism and pacifism, racism, and support for national struggles for independence. Early in its development, the WSCF took pains to shake off its dependence on North American and European stimulus by encouraging the organization of regional units and by structuring roles for indigenous church leadership. The student movement was shaping new ecumenical expectations and influencing the formation of other ecumenical structures.

In the 1960s, the focus of the young adult or university movement turned from the mission God entrusted to the church to God's mission in the world.[34] The movement called upon the church to join God's renewing and redeeming activity manifested in the forces of social change. An emphasis on full-time engagement of the concerns of the laity in the secular world replaced church or missionary vocations as a strategy for having an impact on the world with the good news of the gospel. In 1961, the WSCF adopted a creative proposal from Margaret Flory and her Presbyterian Commission on Mission and Ecumenical Relations. It offered two-year internships to students from the U.S. and other countries for service on the social "frontiers" that the WSCF 1959 Quadrennial Conference had identified for study and response. In the first decade of the program of "Frontier Interns," 139 young adults were selected and placed in international settings with organizations (universities and other agencies) working on issues of social change such as nationalism, urbanization, economic development, rural revolution, industrialization, educational reform, and women's issues. All worked at subsistence levels of financial support, modeling a new form of missionary obedience.

As the Frontier Interns program matured, students from the Third World were favored in the recruiting process. As a result, some of the supporting mission boards in North America wanted their own constituents to have more opportunities for participation. In 1977, the World Division of GBGM initiated its own Mission Intern Program. Ruth Harris, executive secretary for Youth and Young Adult Ministries, designed and directed the program for college graduates who were seeking short-term nontraditional forms of missionary service or experience. The resulting program's three-year terms were divided equally between placements outside and within the U.S. Placements were created or selected in accordance with a program theme selected for each three-year class. This theme, as in the ecumenical Frontier Internship program, addressed issues of social justice. Upon completion of their terms, many United Methodist mission interns entered regular missionary service, opening the ranks of missionaries to creative youthful energies and perspectives.

After completing the U.S. part of his assignment, Philip Wingeier, a mission intern who had first served in Nicaragua, became the first United Methodist missionary to return to Cuba under the Fidel Castro government. His Christian formation and calling to missionary service was shaped by the profound witness of Nicaraguans who were suffering from the brutality of the guerrilla war between the Sandinistas and the U.S.-backed contras. Wingeier wrote:

"I underwent a conversion experience in which the lesson of the poor allowed me to see my vocation in a new light. . . . The words and actions of the Nicaraguan people speak the truth. Their example has become so much a part of me that, since coming home, I have seen injustices and inequalities that I had not been able to see before. Although I had been commissioned to 'carry the Gospel into the world,' the people of Nicaragua gave me new eyes with which to read it."[35]

The social and political upheavals taking place in the U.S. shaped the response of the student Christian movement within the country. The struggles to reform racial injustices, correct growing economic inequalities, and end military atrocities in Vietnam consumed the energies of the student movement leaders. Their commitment to seeking justice exceeded their abilities to nurture the student organizations they led. So the University Christian Movement, created in 1966, disbanded in 1969. The North American regional unit of the WSCF (covering the U.S. and Canada) perished in spite of several attempts by denominational mission boards to help it continue as a vital ecumenical entity. Efforts at re-energizing denominational campus ministries and chaplaincies were attempted but were not as singularly focused on missional issues or international programs as the earlier student movements had been. North American denominational mission boards supported and participated in the quadrennial meetings of the WSCF, but a strong and viable base in their respective membership bodies was lacking. While the role of the WSCF diminished within the North American student ministry programs, student leaders from Asia, Africa, and Latin America made the WSCF a useful arena for networking and dialogue within the world ecumenical context. The organization provided a platform for their voices to be heard by churches within their own regions and in the assemblies and forums of the WCC.

An enduring contribution of the student movement to the history of the world ecumenical movement and its member bodies has been its capacity for leadership development. The student exchange programs and regional conferences of the WSCF, for instance, provided young adult participants from a host of countries with opportunities for exposure and service. The distinguished ecumenist D. T. Niles, a Methodist from Ceylon, served as president of the WSCF from 1952 to 1960. Phillip Potter, a Methodist from the Caribbean, succeeded Niles and later served as general secretary of the WCC from 1972 to 1984. In 1976, Mercy Ododuye, a Methodist theologian from Ghana, became the first woman elected president of the WSCF. She then continued to serve in ecumenical offices, including associate general secretary of the WCC. Rena Karefa-Smart, an Evangelical United Brethren African American married to a Sierra Leonean, was vice chair of the WSCF from 1956 to 1960. Lydi Nacpil, a United Methodist from the Philippines, was elected vice chair of the federation at the General Assembly in 1981.

In his reflections on the 1995 centennial observance of the organization at its General Assembly in Yamoussoukro, Côte d'Ivoire, Jean-François

Delteil, cosecretary general of the WSCF, drew upon strong biblical and theological foundations for interpreting its history and charting its future: "What holds this community together is at least three-fold: firstly, it is the common awareness of the need for more Justice and Grace in human relations, in other words ethics and commitments; then, it is the common biblical memory of the active liberating presence of God in human history, a presence which continues to be manifest in the life of the churches, the ecumenical movement, and the WSCF; but what would all these be if not for the hope that projects us into the future, the common hope, for ourselves and for the world, that we have because of the life, death and resurrection of Jesus of Nazareth."[36]

Mission Volunteers

We have examined in this chapter the changing roles of leadership in mission, from the traditional missionaries to indigenous church leaders and from conventional church workers to creative community development and social justice vocations. In most of these arenas of service, the personnel are working in an employed or professional relationship to the church or the mission agency. Another development that deserves special mention is the emergence of the mission volunteer movement. Volunteers in mission is a concept that has grown in popularity, especially among local churches, where laity are increasingly anxious to make a direct (or in-kind) contribution of labor to mission projects, whether in the U.S. or abroad.

The first efforts to appropriate this volunteer resource for work at the national or denominational level were initiated by the United Methodist Committee on Relief (UMCOR) in 1968. At that time, the Reverend Dr. Harry Haines, associate general secretary for UMCOR, met Michael Watson, a medical doctor and active United Methodist from South Carolina. Watson and a pastoral colleague from the South Carolina Annual Conference had been promoting the use of lay volunteers for short-term mission projects within the conference and beyond. Watson's activities earned him a nomination to the governing board of the National Council of the Churches of Christ (NCC), where he met Haines. Haines assured Watson there were places for laity to serve in the extended mission of the church. Watson soon received a call from James Thomas of UMCOR, inviting him to assist with the delivery of health services in the tiny Caribbean island of Anguilla. He found a typical Third World situation: a lack of professional medical services and adequate health-care facilities. Watson immediately promised to organize teams of medical personnel to visit the island over the course of the next twelve months to conduct examinations, administer inoculations, and perform surgeries.[37]

Subsequently, UMCOR invited Watson to go to Haiti. There, in the region of Jeremie, Watson found a dearth of medical services and medicines and discovered that 20 percent of the babies were dying from neonatal tetanus. Upon returning home, he organized follow-up volunteer medical teams to administer tetanus inoculations. As Watson described it: "We sent down three teams. They gave 45,000 immunizations to the people. It was quite an experience for those who went. In one place the people crowded and crushed in on them so badly that the police had to be called. In another place they broke in the wall of a church trying to get to the team."[38] Watson became an enthusiastic participant, interpreter, and leader in a movement that soon spread beyond the borders of his annual conference, extending throughout the Southeastern Jurisdiction and across the whole church. Not only health-care workers, but building teams, educators, children and youth, and adult volunteers with a host of other skills and services to offer were enlisted for projects that reached well beyond the neighboring churches in the Caribbean to Central and South America, Africa, Asia, and Europe.

The principle of the movement was "voluntary" service, meaning that participants covered their own expenses. But Watson also saw a hidden potential benefit for the church in opening a channel for mission involvement to members who otherwise might have been disaffected by signs of political polarization in the church. "In my area," he said, "there is criticism of the Church today as being too liberal. I say that part of the greatness of The United Methodist Church is its breadth. It is broad enough to have people of very liberal persuasion and people like myself who are very conservative. No one can expect the Church to narrow down around one position because then it would lose something."[39]

While UMCOR was quick to pick up on the mobilization of volunteers for services in various relief and development projects, other divisions of the Board of Global Ministries had some difficulty fitting this form of mission service into their organizational life. UMCOR had a well-established practice of deploying consultants and other troubleshooters to engage in crisis assessments. These volunteer physicians, engineers, builders, and other professionals and practitioners helped to round

Mission volunteer Ron Jack-
man, New York City, handed
an adobe brick to Benigno
Garcia Rodríguez, lay pastor in
Portillo del Norte, Honduras,
as the two helped to rebuild a
house destroyed by Hurricane
Mitch in 1998. *(Christie R.
House photo, courtesy of GBGM)*

out the UMCOR stable of experts. The National Division had some previous experience working with programs such as United Methodist Voluntary Services, facilitating referrals of short-term volunteers, especially
young adults, to established host programs in local communities. National
(U.S.) mission institutions, founded by the former Woman's Division and
administered by the National Division, organized great numbers of volunteer work teams for exposure to their *national* mission contexts long before and after volunteering for *global* mission became the major focus of
other organizing efforts. But there was little capacity for responding to
the dynamism and independent initiatives of volunteer groups surfacing
from within the greater United Methodist constituency. The World Division, operating primarily with personnel and policies to accommodate
traditional full-time missionaries, labored over a host of issues introduced
by volunteer workers. Securing an invitation from a church or agency,
providing proper orientation to the volunteer at both sending and receiving sides, committing sufficient volunteer time to complete the project,
and assuring church leaders that volunteers would work under their authority and would not displace local workers—these were some of the
matters addressed by the World Division in a policy statement issued in
1974.[40]

The volunteer movement, thriving on inspiration rather than organization, would not be regulated by national church authorities. In an age of

jet travel and instant worldwide communications, connections were made between willing workers and local projects in various settings. Teams of volunteers from local churches, districts, conferences, church colleges, and other church-related venues were crossing national and cultural boundaries with greater rapidity than all the missionaries deployed by the mission board. Volunteers returned home telling moving stories of human need, evidencing a great sense of satisfaction from their work, and inspiring others to follow in their footsteps. The Southeast Jurisdiction capitalized on the energy and enthusiasm for volunteerism and created a steering committee to formulate a program response for the region. After consultation and dialogue with units of the Board of Global Ministries, the World Division assigned a missionary couple to help it develop the volunteer concept. David and Mary Sue Lowery of Chile spent one year in the New York office in 1974–1975, attempting to understand this phenomenon, to interpret it to the division, and to define an appropriate role for the Board to play in the future development of volunteer mission. One year was insufficient time in which to complete such a task, but funding for a "volunteer coordinating" role was maintained.

In 1976, the Reverend Tom and Margaret Curtis — missionaries returning from assignments in Rhodesia — were invited to continue the development of a mission volunteer program for the Board.[41] The pace of program development in the Southeast Jurisdiction was greater than that assumed by the Board, so the Board placed the Curtises at the disposal of the jurisdictional steering committee. They became active coordinators of volunteer efforts of churches, districts, conferences, and finally the entire jurisdiction, which gradually assumed primary financial support for Tom. In this way, Tom Curtis became the first full-time director of the United Methodist Volunteers In Mission (UMVIM) of the Southeastern Jurisdiction. Tom's pioneering efforts were beneficial to other jurisdictions experiencing a similar program thrust behind volunteer mission activities. Soon the Board was asked to provide financial support for coordinators in other regions, especially the South Central and North Central jurisdictions.

The General Conference of 1980 approved an amendment to the 1400 paragraphs of the *Book of Discipline*, which defined the responsibilities of GBGM by adding "coordination of volunteers in mission." The petition to amend was sponsored by the Southeast Jurisdiction Steering Committee for Volunteers In Mission. The same General Conference also authorized the restructure of the GBGM during the 1981–1984 quadrennium.

This aroused new hope within the mission volunteer movement for a strong response from the Board. When the dust settled, the new organizational structure placed mission volunteers under the Mission Personnel Resources Program Department. Funding was provided for staffing three positions to work on "coordination" of volunteer programs of the conferences and jurisdictions. At this late stage in the development of this program in the life of the church, "coordination" may have been the only option. Conferences and jurisdictions were more than adequately managing their programs. They welcomed additional resources, especially financial contributions for their staffing purposes. Assistance with administrative tasks, such as developing training materials or setting up a database for available projects and volunteers, was also well received. But programs remained autonomous at the jurisdictional and conference levels, while GBGM sought channels of cooperation.

In addition to the jurisdictional coordination of volunteers, GBGM now related to several U.S. annual conference–initiated partnership programs with churches or conferences in other countries. One of the earliest such programs was Operation Classroom, a project of the Indiana Area conferences with the Liberia and Sierra Leone annual conferences. Operation Classroom focused on strengthening the United Methodist mission schools in these West African nations. Schoolteachers, administrators, construction workers, and others were recruited and sent by the Indiana conferences to participate in teacher training, curriculum development, and classroom repairs or upgrading.

The World Division placed an Indiana pastor and his wife, the Reverend Joe and Carolyn Wagner, on the missionary payroll so that they could give part-time service to the oversight and supervision of area church members participating in the program. The Wagners helped to develop creative methods for local church involvement in Operation Classroom. Church members began collecting school supplies and classroom furnishings for shipment, raising scholarship funds to encourage African students to pursue higher or professional education, and hosting African students or educators attending U.S. schools or leadership development seminars. The Wagners even developed a church school curriculum for use in local churches in Indiana and West Africa to introduce children in each place to the others' cultural values and traditions, thereby enriching the Christian experience of both.

In addition to short-term volunteers, the conferences recruited their own missionaries for GBGM to send for a full three-year term of service. Operation Classroom became a model for focusing the attention of one or more conferences on a particular mission in a systematic and holistic manner. This partnership has endured more than a decade of testing and has even survived protracted civil conflicts in both Liberia and Sierra Leone. It has also mobilized other conferences to participate in or develop similar programs.

Volunteerism functioning at this high level developed into a GBGM program strategy known as In Mission Together. Board staffing and resources were packaged to support conferences and other mission units desiring to make a substantial long-term commitment to mission development with a partner church or conference. Many conferences in the U.S. already cultivated some form of partnership with conferences abroad, but they were encountering project overlap and other difficulties in communication and continuity of effort.

In Mission Together assisted the Mozambique Initiative in coordinating the relationships of several U.S. conferences with the conference program staff in East Africa. Two of the annual conferences working in partnership with Mozambique, East and West Missouri, took the lead in proposing missionary support for a "coordinator." They enlisted other conferences in their vision for a united response to a comprehensive strategy for church development in Mozambique. Representatives participated in consultations in Mozambique, and a master plan was developed for implementation. The Missouri conferences took responsibility for pastoral support. More than 400 churches in the conferences were enlisted in underwriting the basic salary of the 140 pastors assigned to the growing churches in Mozambique. Computer technology enabled communication between the churches, helping the participants realize the benefits of connectionalism, over and above their financial support.

Conference partnerships that featured volunteers engaging in mission activities or projects are too numerous to mention. While personnel exchange visits were the most prominent activity, the development of a covenant understanding of the special relationship of partner conferences within the global Methodist connection was the most lasting value. The partnerships, based on a mutual commitment by the conferences to aid one another in fulfilling their goals of ministry, provided for mutual enrichment and learning. Not giving but learning to receive gifts from others was the most difficult lesson for affluent Christians. The intentional sharing of the experiences of the participants with other members of their local churches extended the benefits of learning from the individual to the larger church community. Then the spirit of a true connectional partnership was realized.

The impact of volunteer engagement in mission requires a variety of assessments. From the perspective of many volunteers and local churches participating in the program, there are testimonies of spiritual renewal and fulfillment through acts of goodwill toward others. There are also questions regarding the stewardship of sending uninitiated volunteers thousands of miles for brief intervals of direct service. Host churches and projects express gratitude for the additional resources the volunteers bring directly to their communities. But questions are raised about the impact of imported free labor on local projects needing to cultivate an enterprising spirit of self-development.[42] Some missionaries look upon volunteers as second-class servants of the church, while others are quite effective in organizing the volunteers to support and further the work to which they are assigned. Cultural sensitivities have been offended when visiting teams fail to be inclusive or are unaffirming of local values or customs.[43] The denominational mission agency could only admit to its own lack of ingenuity in channelling this strong energy within the church constituencies to more harmonious and productive purposes. Not until GBGM initiated church development in Russia following the collapse of the Communist system were volunteers entrusted with major program responsibilities for the Board. (Chapter 9 develops this story further.) The outpouring of interest in bridge building with Russia after the Cold War resulted in the Board's cultivating unprecedented financial support for and personal involvement in a GBGM mission activity.

In the 1996 restructure of GBGM, Mission Volunteers became a discrete program entity within the organizational structure. The program moved from channelling small amounts of financial support to five jurisdictional programs in the U.S. to sponsoring its own programs for youth, young adults, retired people, and other population or interest groups in the church. The Global Justice Volunteers program provided two- to three-month volunteer opportunities for youth and young adults in Third World settings. "Primetimers" was a new initiative to serve the travel/study/service interests of older people by offering service venues in the U.S. and other countries. The Mission Volunteers unit also offered training for volunteers in partner churches and conferences as well as for those in the U.S. Training sessions were held in Liberia and Bolivia. More than 54,000 United Methodists, it was estimated, participated in volunteer program activity annually, contributing 16 million hours of volunteer labor.[44]

Conclusion

The events of the period of history between 1968 and 2000 help develop an important distinction between mission calling and mission sending or receiving. The *calling* of an individual into the mission of the church is admittedly God's business. The "mission," after all, is God's business. The *sending* of a missionary as the agent of God's mission is the church's business. The place and nature of the service rendered is defined after some form of consultation with the one called and the hosts. The calling to participate in God's redeeming and reconciling mission in the world is the same apostolic mission to which Christ invited the first twelve followers. And it remains the same for the variety of forms of missionary service negotiated between the church's senders and receivers. As the apostle Paul taught, though individual members of the body have different functions, it is the functioning of the whole body (the church) that these parts serve.

The missionary movement is not an institution. Even if there is a temptation to create such structures of permanence in the life of the church, the missionary movement needs to be scrutinized and tested for its relevance to the changing needs of the church and humankind. To that end, the challenges to missionary service in the last quarter of the twentieth century generate a greater vitality and effectiveness for the ministry of those who will take the church to new frontiers of witness and service in the twenty-first century.

The missionary movement is becoming an international movement, witnessing to the universality of Christ's church. In extending this witness, churches around the globe are both sending and receiving missionaries. Giving up the notion of being the home base, or "headquarters," for the church's mission is a challenge for The United Methodist Church. It is accustomed to being the dominant partner or element in mission relationships. If it is serious about discovering its global nature, an immediate indication will be its readiness to become a "mission field." It still has much to learn about welcoming others whose obedience to the gospel commends their witness from many cultures and contexts.

CHAPTER 4

A Survey of Africa

*H*ISTORY HAS NOT BEEN fair to Africa. Two externally imposed experiences—the slave trade and colonialism—interrupted the process of indigenous state formation and development of great empires across the continent and introduced artificially imposed systems of administration and production. Forgotten is the trans-Atlantic slave trade that robbed Africa of about twelve million of its able-bodied men and women. Forgotten is the colonialism that followed the slave trade and introduced a system of exploitation of Africa's resources to feed the industries of the Northern Hemisphere. Forgotten is the Berlin West African Conference of 1884–1885 that crudely balkanized and divided Africa into geographic regions controlled by the West with scant regard to ethnic boundaries of backgrounds. Forgotten, so soon, is the Cold War's geopolitical struggle for spheres of influence, Africa becoming the focal point for the ideological conflict and the arms contributing to the havoc today in countries like the Democratic Republic of the Congo (DRC), Burundi, and Angola. Even the struggles for independence that brought self-rule and self-determination to many African nations were unable to counter the long-term effects of history. The liberation movements could not reverse the character of Africa's state systems that resulted from the arbitrary forging of nations from disparate tribes and groups. This context sets the stage for the many conflicts on the continent today.

On the economic front, the foreign exploitation of the continent's rich natural resources was unrelenting. The total wealth of Africa, with twice the population of the U.S., was only a little more than that of Belgium. While there was some economic improvement in the 1960s and 1970s, it was not maintained. Per capita incomes fell in the 1990s. It was estimated that more than half of the population in Africa south of the Sahara was living in absolute poverty. Despite its capacity to feed itself, Africa was the only region to produce less food per capita in the 1990s than in the previous decade.

The social challenges were enormous. Some statistics from the United Nations make the point. The maternal mortality rate in sub-Sahara Africa at 700 per 100,000 was the highest in the world. The average years of schooling at 1.6 in 1992 were the lowest in the world. Life expectancy at birth was 51 years in 1992, the lowest in the world. The number of chronically undernourished children in Africa continued to increase, from 100 million in 1969 to 168 million 1990. If there were an indicator of the proportion of population upset by war, the continent of Africa would rank number one.

Ending Apartheid and New Beginnings

At the beginning of the twenty-first century there was still too much desperation, destruction, and death marking daily life on the African continent, but there were significant achievements to celebrate. The final victory of South Africans over apartheid and the establishment of a free democratic state were recognized worldwide as monumental achievements. The struggle against apartheid was a moral battle in which the churches were engaged. Beginning in 1968, the World Council of Churches (WCC) and the National Council of the Churches of Christ in the U.S.A. (NCC) urged their members to examine their institutional investments in companies doing business in South Africa. In 1972, the General Conference of The United Methodist Church (UMC) adopted a resolution urging church bodies to "seek from all United States corporations doing business in Southern Africa the facts of their involvement including the history of such involvement, as relations with workers and with the governments and ask that these facts be public."[1]

With the help of the Interfaith Center for Corporate Responsibility (ICCR), a subsidiary of the NCC, the Women's Division and the World Division of the Board of Global Ministries filed stockholder resolutions demanding disclosure statements from companies such as Eastman Kodak, Texaco, and Caterpillar concerning their operations in South Africa. In a report to the Board, staff member Isaac Bivens summarized the actions: "We are saying as clearly as we can that the Church cannot ignore

Black leader Steve Biko's remains were carried through a crowd of mourners on Sept. 25, 1977, to a sports stadium in King Williams Town, South Africa, where about 20,000 attended an open air rally in his memory. Biko had died thirteen days earlier while in the custody of South African government security police. (*AP Photo/Tomkins, used with permission of AP/Wide World Photos*)

the source of its profits when they come from its investments in societies where they are clearly traceable to the unjust exploitation of other humans."[2] Many firms complied with the request, but the data showed only minimal adjustments in their discriminatory hiring and personnel policies.

In 1985, the ecumenical campaign against apartheid escalated to a strategy of divestment. The Board requested official statements from twelve companies demanding the dismantling of apartheid and threatening withdrawal of their business interests from South Africa if the government did not comply. And the Board approved a divestment policy of its own, voting "not to do business with or invest in banks or financial institutions that make loans to the government of South Africa or its agencies." It further provided for the divestment of Board investment in all U.S. corporations whose products or services were used by South African military or police.[3]

While the anti-apartheid strategies of the churches and other organizations involving economic sanctions were met with considerable resistance and were strongly criticized by industrial giants and governments for exacting more pain on the suffering population than the companies at which they were directed, they were ultimately credited with delivering the decisive and final blow to the weakened South African regime. In 1993, after Nelson Mandela became president in the first multiracial national election, the World and Women's divisions of the General Board of Global Ministries (GBGM) rescinded their policies restricting investments in South Africa. The building of a new South Africa would require significant infusions of economic support from the world community. The South African Council of Churches established a "Code of Conduct" promoting responsible patterns of reinvestment which the divisions heartily endorsed.[4]

The popularity and prominence of the democratically elected government offered great hope and promise for neighboring states in southern Africa. The unrest and warfare in Mozambique, for example, was given a reprieve, and the beginnings of a stable political and economic context began developing. President Mandela used his personal and official influence to bring warring factions to the table in the DRC and to mediate other regional conflicts like Burundi. A free South Africa gave encouragement to free elections and development of stronger self-governance in other African countries. At least twenty-four countries, according to the UN, conducted national elections and established representative governments in the 1990s.

Church Programs

Emilio J. M. de Carvalho, presiding bishop of the West Angola Annual Conference, reflecting upon the devastation of two decades of postindependence warfare in his country, looked to the church to "reclaim its role of peacemaker": "It seems to me that in spite of ideological and religious confusion, the church has not yet lost its prophetic calling to work for the restoration of human beings. The church must uncover new ways of extending its witness and mission and *be* the church to the suffering peoples of our world by sharing its resources, its spiritual life, and its love with them. These are new times. We must simply refuse to drink old wine from old wineskins."[5]

Emilio J. M. de Carvalho was imprisoned by the Portuguese colonial authorities during the struggle for Angolan independence. In 1972, while he was serving as president of the Union Theological Seminary at Dondi, he was elected bishop and presided over the West Angola Annual Conference. *(Photo courtesy of UM Archives and History)*

Even though major initiatives had to be taken by the international community to respond to the critical problems of the continent, African churches were leading the way to a brighter future. Where government services were nonexistent or unreliable, the institutions of the churches, e.g., schools, hostels, clinics, hospitals, and development programs, were serving the needs of the people. While suffering from severe food shortages and overcrowding conditions, African churches cared for their own displaced persons as well as housing large numbers of refugees from neighboring countries. Students were in need of school fees. Schools were in need of books and supplies. Hospitals were in urgent and constant need of medicines, beds, mattresses, linens, bandages, and other essential materials.

If the mission of the churches in Africa were to succeed, there also needed to be a stronger advocacy from Christians worldwide. United Methodist Bishop Arthur Kulah of Liberia once told the Council of

Bishops, "Speak for us or we'll never be heard around the world. Help us have peace because our peace is your peace." A public recognition of a genuine interdependence of God's people required a strong prophetic voice in an age of excessive accumulation of wealth and concentration of power in one nation of the world. The churches, whose mission programs had made such a great investment of personnel, money, and material resources in Africa, had considerable leverage in getting the attention of policymakers directed to the most neglected continent. A cooperative strategy for mobilizing missionaries and church leaders to make their voices heard in corridors of power was — and still is — needed. Effective advocacy can produce humane policies with long-term results that will make all of the sacrificial ministries of African churches as well as the project funding and partner church relationships worthwhile.

The following is a brief reprise of the journeys of United Methodist–related African churches during the turbulent years of the middle- to late-twentieth century.

Southern Africa

Zimbabwe

Many United Methodists kept a close watch on events of the liberation struggle in the British colony of Southern Rhodesia because of the involvement of Abel Muzorewa. In 1963, Muzorewa returned to his homeland from studies in the U.S. British pressure to hand over rule to African leaders was strongly resisted by the colonial ruler Ian Smith. In defiance of the British direction, Smith declared a Unilateral Declaration of Independence for Rhodesia in 1965. The move was met by the institution of economic sanctions by the UN and isolation in the world community, save the apartheid regime in neighboring South Africa. Muzorewa was quick to join other countrymen in the struggle for human rights and African rule. While addressing social issues, his career as a pastor took him from a local pastorate to a national office (youth secretary) in the Christian Council of Rhodesia. In 1968, the Africa Central Conference elected Muzorewa to succeed the popular but exiled missionary bishop, Ralph E. Dodge.

Muzorewa became associated with the United Africa National Congress (UANC), a national political party. In 1971, he was selected to represent the African perspective on a proposal on constitutional reform from Prime Minister Smith. With each move into the public spotlight, authorities responded with both personal harassment and new religious restrictions upon the church. But the major object of government repression was the growing African resistance movement. When pursuing a "bush war" with armed rivals in the Patriotic Front became too costly, Smith began to look for a political settlement. In 1978, Smith signed an "internal agreement" with Muzorewa and other African leaders opposed to the militant Patriotic Front. It called for national elections and the installation of African leadership, but the white minority protected its economic interests through a legislative veto.

In the national elections of 1979, Muzorewa became the first African prime minister of the country and renamed it Zimbabwe-Rhodesia. His leadership role was brief and came with little acclamation. The internal agreements that brought him to power were criticized by many, including a resolution adopted by the Women's Division of GBGM. His promise to

Abel Muzowera was elected bishop by the Africa Central Conference in 1968 and in 1979 became the first African prime minister of his newly independent country, which he named Zimbabwe-Rhodesia. His tenure lasted only until 1980, when Robert Mugabe became prime minister. *(Photo courtesy of UM Archives and History)*

bring warring factions into a peace process failed. The military position of the Patriotic Front became more urgent, causing an intervention by Britain and African allies. Under an arranged cease-fire, the British sponsored new elections in February 1980. Robert Mugabe's Zimbabwe African National Union party handily defeated all opposition. Muzorewa's UANC came away with a disappointing three seats in Parliament, dwarfed even by Smith's guaranteed thirty-five-seat white minority block.

During his political forays, Muzorewa yielded the leadership of the church to his predecessor, Bishop Dodge. Like other missionary-established churches, The UMC in Zimbabwe was both rural and conservative. The prominence of a church leader in the political life of the country was a difficult concept for the church to embrace before, during, and after Muzorewa's term in office. Muzorewa remained an outspoken critic of his rival, Prime Minister Robert Mugabe. He decried restrictions upon religious freedom as he found government agents following him on his administrative duties. On one occasion his complaints prompted his arrest and deportation. For much of his tenure, the church did not benefit from his personal oversight and lived in the shadow of his notoriety. In reflection upon his decision to become engaged in politics and to lead his church into the liberation struggle in his country, Muzorewa commented: "I'm sure of one thing, that it was the will of God at that particular time that I should be in the midst of it all. And along with my Christian brothers and sisters, I have taken it that it's the business of the church to bring relief to our society and to live for freedom. . . . The Church is witnessing in the situation where it is law that black and white cannot mix in their residential area, that they cannot live or stay in each other's house on the other side of the fence. The United Methodist Church (and other churches) have witnessed in this situation, have stood firm, and have talked the best they can against the regime and sided with the revolution."[6]

With independence came the opportunity to cultivate new places of witness and service within the country. The migration of the African population from rural to urban areas resulted in the establishment of new congregations in key cities. Christopher Jokomo, bishop of the Zimbabwe Area in the 1990s, assessed the implications for the church: "Because of continued growth and expansion the church is always short of adequately trained pastors. . . . Membership continues to grow as there are more areas which must still be reached by the Gospel."[7]

DJIBOUTI

SOMALIA

ETHIOPIA

KENYA
(A, CC)
★ Nairobi

Arua
UGANDA
(CC)
Jinja •Busia

RWANDA
Goma•
Bukavu★
Bujumbura★
Uvira•
BURUNDI (CC)
•Kigoma

Gitega
Arusha
Dar es Salaam

TANZANIA (CC)

*Mozambique
Channel*

MOZAMBIQUE
(CC)

MADAGASCAR

Chicuque

SWAZILAND
•Maputo

LESOTHO

Indian   Ocean

CENTRAL
AFRICAN REPUBLIC

DEMOCRATIC
REPUBLIC
OF THE CONGO
(CC)

Lubumbashi

MALAWI

Kitwe•
Ndola•

ZAMBIA (CC)
Lusaka ★

Harare ★
Mutare•
ZIMBABWE
(CC)

•Maun

BOTSWANA
(Msn)
Gaborone ★

Pretoria
★
Johannesburg

SOUTH AFRICA
(A, CC)

Cape Town

REPUBLIC
OF THE
CONGO.

CAMEROON
(Msn)

GABON
(Msn)

EQUATORIAL GUINEA
Libreville•

ANGOLA (CC)

Luanda•

•Quessua

•Dondi

NAMIBIA (A)

Windhoek
★

South   Atlantic   Ocean

Benue River

NIGERIA
(CC, Cov)

N. Banyam
Jalingo

Niger River

Ibadan
Lagos

BURKINA
FASO

BENIN

GHANA
(A)
Kumasi
Accra

TOGO

CÔTE
D'IVOIRE (CC)
Yamoussoukro
Abidjan

GUINEA
BISSAU

GUINEA
Conakry•
Freetown•
Rotifunk★
Moyamba•

SIERRA
LEONE
(CC, A)

LIBERIA (CC)
Monrovia•

Legend for Church Relationship to UMC

Autonomous	A
Affiliated Autonomous	AA
Affiliated United	AU
Covenant UMC	Cov
Central Conference	CC
Concordat	Con
Cooperative Mission	CM
Ecumenical	Ecum
Independent	Ind
Mission	Msn

The importance of social ministries through the establishment and maintenance of first-rate educational and health-related institutions brought national recognition to the church. While the 1980 General Conference was probably persuaded by the prospects of relative political stability in the country to select Zimbabwe as the site of the first church university to serve the entire continent of Africa, the decision was also recognition of the conference as an able host.

The missionary outreach of the church took it into neighboring countries. The first venture was Botswana. In 1968, the Africa Central Conference met in Gaberone, the capital city of Botswana. The delegates heard a report of the exploratory investigations of Rhodesian missionary Marshall Murphree into a cooperative mission in the isolated and semi-arid northwest region of the country.[8] A cabinet minister of the newly independent government of Botswana issued a plea for help in serving the vast educational and health needs in the area. A representative of the United Congregational Church of Southern Africa (UCCSA) also addressed the body. The UCCSA was already at work in the city of Maun and issued a warm invitation for cooperation from the Methodists. The central conference members from the DRC, Angola, Mozambique, and Rhodesia answered the call. But the response came from Rhodesia. A Botswana Committee was established and recommended a strategy for United Methodist involvement. Since the church in Maun was already handled by the Congregational mission, it was agreed that United Methodists should focus first on education. Existing government secondary schools in western Botswana were able to enroll only one-fifth of the eligible primary school graduates. The Rhodesian Annual Conference adopted the plan, and the United Methodist Board of Missions helped with the funding. Bishop Muzorewa assigned the missionary architect and builder John Schevenius to draw the plans and Philemon Machiri, an African building foreman, to begin construction. The Maun Secondary School has been in continuous existence ever since. Its construction was followed by the building of a clinic with a specialization in women's health and maternity center. The mission is under joint administration of the Zimbabwe UMC and the UCCSA.[9]

United Methodist pastors were assigned as missionaries to local communities in Malawi and South Africa. In both locations, initial contacts were made with exile groups from the colonial governance of Rhodesia. In each setting, the pastors have started church schools both to subsidize the work and reach young families with information. A district structure with a superintendent has been created in both locations.

Mozambique

Independence came to Mozambique in 1975 after a fifteen-year struggle against Portuguese colonizers. It brought to power the Front for the Liberation of Mozambique (FRELIMO), a movement with leaders with roots in Methodist mission. The founder and first president of the front, Dr. Eduardo Chivambo Mondlane, received his elementary schooling at the Cambine Methodist Boys School and his secondary education in South Africa. He was the first African from Mozambique to study at the University of Lisbon. There he came in contact with other African students from Portuguese-controlled countries and engaged in conversations about forming national liberation movements. Mondlane was honored with a Crusade Scholarship and pursued studies in the U.S. at Oberlin College and earned a Ph.D. in anthropology at Northwestern University. For a brief period he served on the faculty of Syracuse University and as a research officer at the UN.

Mondlane returned to Mozambique to organize his liberation movement, but resistance from the Portuguese forced him into exile in Dar es Salaam, Tanzania, in 1964. There he established a FRELIMO headquarters and founded the Mozambique Institute, where many Mozambicans — anticipating the liberation of their homeland — came to study for future careers in medicine and education. As president of FRELIMO and chief architect of his country's liberation struggle, Mondlane was a visible target for Portuguese resistance. In February 1969, he fell to an assassin's plot when he opened a letter bomb that was delivered to his home.[10]

The war came to a sudden conclusion in April of 1974 when the successor to the dictatorial Salazar regime in Portugal was deposed by his own military. A transition government under the victorious FRELIMO forces was established with Samora Moises Machal, Mondlane's successor, as the first president. At the time of the celebration of independence in 1975, the United Methodist Bishop Escrivâo Zunguze rejoiced in the manner in which the new FRELIMO government had developed a nationwide structure to rebuild the country. While the FRELIMO philosophy of governance was influenced by Marxist principles, the bishop reported that "most" of the leaders "are Christian people" presenting the church with a "wonderful opportunity to win non-Christians."[11]

Among the leaders was Graca Simbini Machal, another Methodist Crusade Scholar and minister of culture and education in the government of her husband, President Samora Machal. The new government's policy of nationalization of education responded to an 85 percent national illiteracy rate. The United Methodist mission schools cooperated with the government in correcting the abuses of colonial rule. Strategies for non-formal education that were clandestinely developed and administered by the women of the church under colonial government restrictions were given a new burst of energy in the post-independence period. Margaret Mujongue, president of the Women's Society of Christian Service, noted the excitement for learning among Mozambican women: "Now everybody is going to school, even old ladies. . . . Some people can't see, but they say, 'Teach me, I can hear.' "[12]

An independent Mozambique was perceived to be a threat to the apartheid regime in neighboring South Africa. It gave support to the remnants of the defeated fighters of the Salazar Colonial Army reorganized under the banner of the National Resistance Movement (RENAMO). It conducted a reign of terror across the country for more than fifteen years, attacking centers of economy and pillaging rural villages. In order to gain support from a wider world community, the FRELIMO government gradually shifted away from its Marxist ideology to establish a "mixed economy." It attracted new foreign investments to address the growing national debt and produced the leverage needed to bring RENAMO to the negotiating table. The peace talks sponsored by Italy were protracted but produced an agreement for a UN-monitored cease fire along with the recognition of RENAMO as a political party. Multiparty elections were scheduled for 1994. The FRELIMO party was victorious with the re-election of President Joaquim Chissano.

The government recognized The UMC in Mozambique as a partner in social development projects such as Chicuque United Methodist mission hospital. Though the hospital was administered as part of the government's national health program, the church provided trained personnel, including doctors, nurses, and administrators to operate the hospital. The church, once confined primarily to a few rural areas. has expanded into all of the provinces of the country. In 1989, it dedicated a striking new edifice in the capital city of Maputo to accommodate the growing Chamoncula United Methodist congregation. The conference strategy for church development included the opening of schools in many locations with the blessing of the government. This reflected the values of its episcopal leaders, especially Bishop Almeida Penicela, one of the few Africans permitted by colonial authorities to pursue a career in higher education. His successor, Bishop João Somane Machado, has placed a strong emphasis upon training for the clergy of the conference and extending local church ministries through elementary education.

The mission of the Mozambique church extended to South Africa, where a pastor was assigned to minister in Soweto with Mozambican migrant laborers. This ministry supported the faith of thousands of men who left family and homes to find employment in South African gold mines. In addition to spiritual nurture, the ministry included a health clinic and offered literacy classes to enable workers to communicate with their family members in Mozambique.

Angola

Portugal, the least beneficent of the European colonizers in Africa, was also the last to relinquish political control over its colonies. This policy prompted the formation of the Popular Movement for the Liberation of Angola (MPLA) in 1956 to put pressure on the Portuguese to recognize the right of self-determination. A leader of the movement was Dr. Agostinho Neto, son of a United Methodist pastor, a former Crusade Scholar, and a medical doctor in Luanda. Neto's support for national independence provoked his arrest and detention in Lisbon both during his student days and after his formation of the MPLA. For his own safety and the effective functioning of the party, he directed the movement from Leopoldville in neighboring Belgian Congo. The movement was systematically structured around military and civilian strategies for self-rule. Local community leaders were trained and ready to take over the administration of those areas controlled by the liberation forces. The vision for a new and free Angola would spread from village to village.

In 1961, a group of MPLA militants demonstrated in the city of Luanda, rampaging through the prisons and other strategic centers. While the action served as a "manifesto" for the liberation movements in Angola and other countries, it was successfully put down by the military force of the Portuguese. It resulted in the loss of life of many Angolans, including United Methodists, and the detention of thousands in overcrowded prisons. Among the imprisoned were many United Methodists, including Emilio de Carvalho, a pastor and future bishop of the church.

From 1960 until 1972, The Methodist/United Methodist Church in Angola was headed by a Norwegian, Bishop Harry Peter Andreassen, who used the heightened tensions at the end of the colonial period to run the church under his sole authority. Programs, policies, and financial matters were controlled by his office. His growing unpopularity provoked the early election of his replacement on the third round of balloting at the 1972 central conference session. De Carvalho, dean of the Union Theological Seminary at Dondi, was elected and immediately set about the tasks of empowering Angolan pastors and laity for leadership in the church. Among his first appointments was that of Engracia Dias Cardoso to the position of field treasurer, the first African woman to hold the position in all of Africa. She had the unenviable task of sorting out church finances and property matters, including the rightful ownership of the episcopal residence built and claimed by Bishop Andreassen as personal property.[13]

With the overthrow of the government of Antonio de Oliveira Salazar in Lisbon in 1974, the African colonies of Portugal were given their independence. Self-rule in Angola began under the Alvor Accords of January 1975. The agreement set a date for self-rule in November and named three competing liberation parties to share responsibility for establishing a government. Meeting in its regular annual conference session in August, the 45,000-member United Methodist Church in Angola took account of its losses—thousands killed, maimed, imprisoned, or made homeless by war. It issued a formal declaration of support for "the total and complete independence of Angola" and rejoiced in the freedom of the political prisoners and their return home. The statement also acknowledged the "valuable action developed by the liberation movements" and urged them to drop their "out of date" differences and form a "democratic government . . . truly free and independent."[14]

Unfortunately, lasting political and ideological differences were exploited by continuing Cold War interests in controlling the resources in the region. The war for independence was soon converted into a civil war among political factions. The National Front for Liberation (FLNA), assisted by U.S. intelligence agents, received military support from Zaire. The Union for the Total Independence for Angola (UNITA) had backing from South Africa and Portuguese settlers. The MPLA was aligned with socialist countries in Eastern Europe and eventually aided by military and civilian support from Cuba. As the armed conflict heated up, the MPLA defended its base in the capital city of Luanda and on the agreed-upon date for independence unilaterally declared Angola's sovereignty.

Recognition of the MPLA government by the UN in 1976 helped establish its legitimacy, but the rebuilding of Angola proved to be a daunting task. Rich in resources, especially oil, the economy was in ruins. The physical destruction left by the war for independence was extensive. Efforts to establish a stable government and reliable infrastructure of civilian services were undermined by the unrest caused by the ongoing military activities. But life continued in Angola, and so did the determination of The UMC to participate in the rebuilding. Luanda had become a city of refugees from war-torn rural villages. Among them were a great number of orphans, amputees, and other war casualties. Marlina de Carvalho mobilized women of the church to establish nurseries and other childcare programs in their churches. Clinics were opened with the assistance of international aid organizations. Reserve funds that were safely protected in World Division accounts during the years of liberation struggle were released for the rebuilding of churches, salaries for pastors and church leaders, and programs and projects. The Norwegian United Methodist Mission Board maintained its alliance with the Angolan church throughout the conflict, assigning mission personnel and sending financial resources. The Norwegians were instrumental in directing their government grants in aid to the Angola church projects focused on the health and educational needs of the population.

With the demise of the Cold War in late 1980s, the East/West competition over client states in southern Africa dissipated. The ascendancy of the anti-apartheid forces in South Africa prompted new consideration by that government of its aggressive policies toward neighboring countries under African rule. Support for client military groups in Angola dried up, and serious peace talks began with UN brokerage. Agreements of 1989 resulted in a decommissioning of military combatants and included general elections in which all parties participated in 1992. The MPLA party and its president Jose Eduardo dos Santos handily won the election, which was immediately rejected by Jonas Savimbi, leader of the opposing UNITA party. He promptly returned to a military strategy to gain power, a pursuit that did not end until his assassination in 2001.

The military conflict fueled ethnic and regional differences within The UMC in Angola. The leadership of the church in East Angola where the historic Quessua Mission compound was located resisted the pastoral and administrative leadership of the episcopal area in Luanda. In 1988, General Conference gave its approval for a second episcopal area in Malanje, and Moises Fernandez was elected by the Africa Central Conference to oversee it. This action did not succeed in addressing all of the conflicts with local churches, and the presence of military forces in the area created additional tensions. Even the security of Bishop Fernandez's residence was breached on one occasion by armed insurgents, an encounter that forced him to escape by jumping from a second-story window and breaking both legs in the fall to the ground.

The UMC in Angola maintained a strong presence in the country through its efforts at church development and social outreach. Its clinics and childcare programs addressed the vast numbers left homeless and maimed in the civil war. GBGM and other international aid organizations have focused on the removal of land mines left behind by warring factions. (See chapter 9 for a further discussion.) Meanwhile the witness of the church extended beyond its borders with pastoral appointments to ministries among expatriate Angolans residing in South Africa, Namibia, and Portugal.

Central Africa

Zaire/Democratic Republic of the Congo (DRC)

Strong tribal and regional identities in Zaire and the DRC have long frustrated efforts at achieving national unity. The goal of independence realized in 1960 was soon jeopardized by the breakaway of the North Katanga province and the assassination of its first prime minister, Patrice Lumumba. A persistent civil war plagued the nation until army commander Joseph Mobutu was chosen by international financial stakeholders and Western governments to depose weak political leaders and then empowered by them to become their "strongman" president.

Mobutu introduced his own brand of nationalism under his doctrine of "African authenticity." He changed the name of the country to Zaire, assumed a new African name for himself (Mobutu Seso Seiko), and decreed the end of European cultural influence symbolized by the giving up of all Christian baptized names given to Zairian citizens. While making new claims upon African legitimacy distracted the population, Mobutu was able to nationalize the country's major industries for his personal gain and to benefit his bureaucratic cronies. He provided the U.S. with outposts for

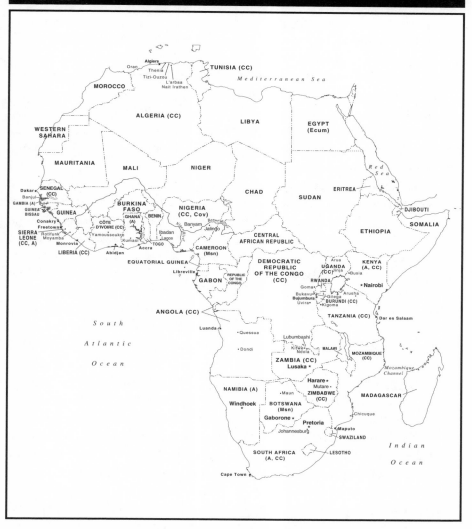

Legend for Church Relationship to UMC	
Autonomous	A
Affiliated Autonomous	AA
Affiliated United	AU
Covenant UMC	Cov
Central Conference	CC
Concordat	Con
Cooperative Mission	CM
Ecumenical	Ecum
Independent	Ind
Mission	Msn

gathering military intelligence throughout the region, and as a cover for the U.S.-supported FLNA of Angola, engaged in counterrevolutionary activities in neighboring Angola.

Church life was influenced by Mobutu's policies of Africanization and nationalization. The churches received government support for the operation of their schools. They did not want to interrupt that important source of revenue, which often was used for more than teachers' salaries. Likewise, the government's health program helped supply church clinics with medical supplies and limited funding. But the government was tired of dealing with so many branches of Protestantism existing in the country. The churches proposed the formation of an ecumenical structure known as the "Church of Christ in Congo." It would be the sole legal representative of the churches to the government. While this idea was supported by many of the thirty-eight denominations or religious groups operating in the country, The UMC resisted it. Bishop John Wesley Shungu withdrew the 80,000-member church from the plan for church union, citing the issue of losing legal representation. Onlookers attributed his action to a loss of personal standing and authority to another prominent leader of another denomination who was chosen as the "general secretary" of the Church of Christ.[15]

In 1972, the Africa Central Conference elected Bishop Onema Fama to succeed Shungu. In the context of African authenticity, Onema graciously assumed the mantle of African cultural authority reserved for tribal chieftains. Mobutu recognized him with the government's highest honor — the Order of the Leopard. At the conclusion of the first annual conference session following his election, Onema was given a "new" name, Ulami a Koi, "Guardian of the Leopard." In addition to his sensitivity to the delicate relationship between church and state, the new bishop saw the value of ecumenical cooperation and served in the elected leadership of the umbrella Church of Christ.[16]

The rapid growth of the church in Zaire and sensitivity to distinct tribal or regional interests required the creation of additional administrative structures. New episcopal areas were created in 1976 for the Southern Conference and in 1980 for the North Shaba Conference. Bishops Katembo Kainda and Ngoy Wakadillo were elected to preside over the new areas, while Onema remained as bishop of the central conference. The UMC in Zaire placed a high value upon trained pastoral and lay leadership. It not only administered elementary and secondary schools but

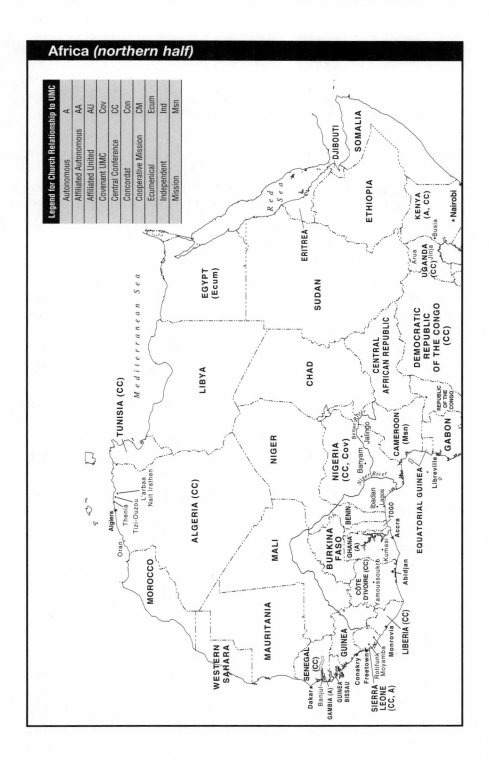

Legend for Church Relationship to UMC

Autonomous	A
Affiliated Autonomous	AA
Affiliated United	AU
Covenant UMC	Cov
Central Conference	CC
Concordat	Con
Cooperative Mission	CM
Ecumenical	Ecum
Independent	Ind
Mission	Msn

SOMALIA

DJIBOUTI

ETHIOPIA

KENYA
(A, CC)

*Nairobi

*Busia

UGANDA
(CC) Jinja

Arua

Red Sea

ERITREA

EGYPT
(Ecum)

SUDAN

Mediterranean Sea

LIBYA

CHAD

CENTRAL
AFRICAN REPUBLIC

DEMOCRATIC
REPUBLIC
OF THE CONGO
(CC)

TUNISIA (CC)

NIGER

NIGERIA
(CC, Cov)

CAMEROON
(Msn)

GABON

REPUBLIC
OF THE
CONGO

Benue River

Jalingo

Banyam

Libreville

Algiers★
Thenia
Tizi-Ouzou
L'arbaa
Nait Irathen

Oran

ALGERIA (CC)

MALI

Niger River

Ibadan
Lagos
Accra

TOGO

EQUATORIAL GUINEA

MOROCCO

BURKINA
FASO

GHANA
(A)

Kumasi

CÔTE
D'IVOIRE (CC)

Yamoussoukro

Abidjan

MAURITANIA

WESTERN
SAHARA

SENEGAL
(CC)

GUINEA

LIBERIA (CC)

Monrovia

GUINEA★
BISSAU

Conakry

Rotifunk

Moyamba

SIERRA
LEONE
(CC, A)

Freetown★

Dakar★
Banjul

GAMBIA (A)

[141]

two major universities. Mulinguishi University served the Southern and North Shaba conferences with programs ranging from elementary classes to postgraduate degrees. Patrice Lumumba University, located in the Wembo Nyama mission in Central Congo Province, provided similar curricular opportunities for students. A remarkable number of United Methodist scholars from Zaire have pursued higher educational opportunities in Belgium, France, Canada, and the U.S. In addition to satisfying its own need for professional leaders, The UMC in Zaire and the succeeding DRC has contributed more than its share of leaders for the larger society and the international community.

The Congolese have survived on one of the lowest per capita annual incomes in all of Africa ($130 in 1996). Mobutu treated the wealth of the country as a private domain. So long as the U.S. needed Zaire and its resources (copper and other strategic minerals for weapons development), Mobutu had resources needed to placate the population and enrich himself. As the Cold War waned, so did his usefulness. The deficiencies and corruption of his government came under closer scrutiny. Anticipating the rise of democratic reforms, he declared an end to one-party rule but lacked a plan for dealing with the upsurge in political self-expression that hit the country. He reverted to methods of military control, but the failing economic system of Zaire presented new difficulties. He was often unable to meet government payrolls, including that of the military. His solution was to give the soldiers permission to pillage the meager possessions of local villagers. Zaire was soon caught up in a cycle of internal unrest and violence.

In 1996, Zaire played host to refugees from the ethnic genocide in neighboring Rwanda. The camps became havens for escaping Hutu soldiers who — supported by the Zairian military — continued their ethnic cleansing attacks against Tutsi tribes living in enclaves in eastern Zaire. Veteran guerrilla leader Laurent Kabila organized a network of local militia and, with material support from Uganda, made quick work of defeating Mobutu's military and forcing his abdication from power. Kabila promptly renamed the country the Democratic Republic of Congo. His government was self-appointed, excluding legitimate political leaders and ignoring international protocol. He soon faced military threats from rebel groups within the country, and the armies of Uganda, Rwanda, Angola, and Zimbabwe sent forces to reinforce the government military. The combatants ignored international efforts at peacemaking like the Lusaka

Onema Fama was elected a bishop by the Africa Central Conference in 1972. He recognized the value of ecumenical cooperation and served in the elected leadership of the umbrella Church of Christ. *(Photo courtesy of UM Archives and History)*

Accords. The human cost of the continuing conflict in the DRC weighed heavily on the minds and hearts of religious leaders. A coalition of major religious groups organized by the All Africa Conference of Churches initiated a peace process in 1999 with the participation of each of the rebel groups and the government. The process laid the foundation for more conclusive talks led by the South African government.

All three conferences of The UMC in the DRC have initiated mission thrusts in new contexts. Central Congo has assumed responsibility for mission with the pygmy populations. Its pastors and health workers provided hospitality and aid to refugees fleeing ethnic assaults in neighboring Rwanda. (See chapter 9 for a further discussion of the impact of this migration on United Methodist mission in East Africa.) The Southern Conference established a new district in neighboring Zambia, where Congolese refugees have frequently found hospitality. The North Shaba Conference (Katanga Province) established a district in Tanzania (Kigoma Province). When many would submit to discouragement over the travails of unrelenting warfare, corruption, and poverty that have consumed the country, United Methodists continued to find new opportunities for witness and mission.

West Africa

Liberia

Methodism in Africa began in Liberia with African Americans from the U.S. going to Liberia in the 1820s. Founded as a colony for freed slaves from North America, Liberia never quite lived up to the former slave aspirations of a "homeland." The native populations were reluctant to receive those of similar skin color who spoke a different language and had a foreign religion. The mission to Liberia would therefore be more complicated than the first missionaries imagined.[17]

The roots of United Methodism were firmly established in the Libero-American population. The church nurtured strong connections to the government. President William V. S. Tubman, who served from 1943 until his death in 1971, was a life-long Methodist, having served as a local pastor and delegate to the 1928 General Conference of the Methodist Episcopal Church. Tubman's presidency was credited with such progressive programs as women's suffrage and extension of full rights of citizenship to indigenous people. When William Tolbert, his vice president, succeeded Tubman, United Methodist Bishop Bennie Warner became the country's new vice president.

In 1979, Liberia experienced political unrest over the rising price of rice. The following year, army Sergeant Samuel K. Doe led a successful coup d'état that resulted in the execution of Tolbert and other cabinet members. The life of Warner was spared because he was attending a meeting of the Council of Bishops in the U.S. at the time. Since he was unable to return to Liberia, the central conference was compelled to elect a new bishop. Arthur F. Kulah, a pastor and theological educator with seminary training in United Methodist schools in the U.S., was elected to the post in 1981. He was the first bishop to serve the Liberian church under a government that was hostile to churches.

Doe, the first president to come from the indigenous population, secured financial backing from the U.S. in return for the protection of vast financial holdings and military installations in the country. He was elected in 1987 in an election that banned the participation of significant opposition forces. In 1989, rebel leader Charles Taylor led an incursion from neighboring Guinea and consolidated support among ethnic groups that were antipathetic to Doe's Krahn tribal roots. Other rebel groups organized, and soon the country was in the throes of a civil war that created a refugee population of nearly one million and cost the lives of 150,000 Liberians.

The civil war created a terrible burden for the churches. Members were lost and church buildings destroyed. Kulah's efforts to lead the religious community into the role of peacemaking was interpreted as an opposition threat by Doe and provoked retaliation. In Kulah's own words: "On July 2, 1990, he sent some soldiers to my house to kill me. My sister-in-law had heard through a friend who works in security that they were coming. I managed to escape before they arrived. The soldiers came right after I left, surrounded my house, and began firing at it. They took everything we had in the house. Later, the soldiers came back, set the house on fire, and burned it to the ground."[18]

Kulah was frequently forced into hiding. He literally walked between the lines of the fighting forces in pursuit of his episcopal and pastoral duties. Prior to the General Conference in 1996, he had not been heard from for several weeks. During the conference session his colleagues in the Council of Bishops were notified that he had safely walked out of the country, crossed into neighboring Côte d'Ivoire, and headed for Denver, the site of the conference. When he appeared at a conference plenary session during the second week, he was greeted with a thunderous ovation, to which he responded with tears, saying, "Please don't forget Liberia."

In 1997, Charles Taylor won presidential and parliamentary elections and took control of the country from the interim government. Hoping that his election would bring peace and security to Liberia, the people have seen Taylor produce little or nothing. He has focused instead on plundering resources of the country as well as neighboring Sierra Leone, keeping the whole region in turmoil. United Methodists in Liberia have not lost hope. With help from other United Methodists offering volunteer labor and financial support, churches, homes, and schools are gradually being rebuilt, farm plots replanted, animals rebred, and children who were recruited as soldiers welcomed back to their communities and schools through programs of counseling and support. The ministry and mission of the church in Liberia is "not giving up."

Sierra Leone

In preparation for union in The UMC, the Board of Missions of the Evangelical United Brethren Church (EUB) advised its mission-related churches to embrace local autonomy through relationship to united

Randolph Nugent, center, general secretary of GBGM, joined mission leaders in Liberia in 1983 at a memorial service for Melville Cox, the early Methodist missionary to Liberia who urged, "Let a thousand fall before Africa be given up." *(New World Outlook photo courtesy of UM Archives and History)*

churches locally or as autonomous United Methodist churches. In either case, they could maintain an affiliation with The UMC. The United Methodist Church of Sierra Leone experienced twelve years of autonomy and then reconsidered its status. Upon invitation of the General Conference Commission on Central Conference Affairs in 1980, Sierra Leone United Methodists chose "reunion" with The UMC. The decision at its own general conference in February 1981 was not greeted with encouragement from its Bishop Emeritus Benjamin A. Carew: "Is there any good reason to sacrifice autonomy at this point? We have, in all areas of church life, made considerable progress since autonomy. . . . Autonomy has helped us tremendously because we have got relationships that we did not have before. We have cordial partnerships in mission with the Swedish, German and Canadian churches. All these show that God is with us. Why should we retract when our flowers are blooming and everything going fine?"[19]

The mission of the EUB Church in Sierra Leone emphasized education. The Albert Academy for boys in Freetown and the Harford School for Girls in Moyamba produced many of the country's first leaders at the time of its independence in 1961. The same schools produced trained leaders for the growing church that comprised 275 congregations serving a constituency in excess of 75,000.[20]

As in other newly independent African countries, church schools and hospitals came under governmental plans for nationalization. The obvious decline of the schools and the state-of-the-art hospital at Rotifunk, created through strong mission relationships to the EUB Church, became a grave concern for church leaders and supporters. A structural relationship to The UMC was perceived to be of a material benefit to the church in regaining its influence and channelling support for these institutional ministries.

While most local economies in poor countries can generally be counted upon to support the ministries of local churches, even the sacrificial stewardship of the members is unable to produce sufficient income to support the connectional infrastructure at the church judicatory levels. Membership in the central conference configuration of The UMC provides financial support for the episcopal office and offers more frequent access to the mission stewardship of conferences, districts, and local churches through itineration of its leaders. In choosing a structural relationship to The UMC, Sierra Leone found new opportunities to undergird its ministries. Bishop Thomas Bangura became adept at communicating the mission needs of his church to former EUB Churches and many former Methodist congregations that generously responded.

The General Conference approval of the Sierra Leone petition to return to the structures of The UMC included permission to create a new West Africa Central Conference for Liberia and Sierra Leone United Methodist conferences. It was hoped that both conferences would find a fraternal fellowship and accountability in providing a United Methodist witness in the region. While ecclesial structures have assured continuity in administrative oversight for the conferences, national histories have not been conducive to the enrichment of a common community. Instead, internal civil conflicts have engulfed Sierra Leone and Liberia, creating only opportunities for each to provide hospitality for one another's refugees.

To some extent the conflict in Sierra Leone was a "spillover" from Liberia. The failure of Sierra Leone governments to provide for the welfare of its citizens cannot be excused, but the rebel forces that brought so

much instability and cruelty to the citizens of the country found sanctuary and financial support from Liberia. A government imposed by a military coup in 1992 was not successful in holding off the advances of guerrilla forces in the diamond-rich eastern part of the country. Interventions
by the British and the occupying forces of the Economic Community of
West Africa only prolonged the fighting that advanced into the heart of
the capital city of Freetown in 1995. After a cease-fire and peacemaking
efforts of the British and the UN, an elected government was returned to
power in 1996. The leader of the rebel Revolutionary United Front was
detained, but his party was recognized as a strategy for neutralizing the
military activities. Elections in 2001 seemed to have returned the country
to democratic rule.

The fighting, especially in the rural areas of the country, interrupted
the ministry and services of The UMC in Sierra Leone. Bishop Joseph
Humper participated in interfaith efforts that have brought about the
negotiated settlement and the transition into a democratically elected
government.

Nigeria

The United Methodist mission in Nigeria began in 1906 with the missionary journey and subsequent ministries established by the Reverend C.
W. Guinter of the Evangelical Church. After the Second World War, the
British Methodist Church had difficulty supporting the mission it had established in the region south of the Benue River, and it was merged with
the mission in 1946, which by that time was part of the EUB mission.

The local administration of the mission shifted to indigenous control
with the creation of the Muri Regional Church Council in 1954. Nigerian
church leaders headed the council, and it ordained Nigerian pastors and
appointed Nigerian superintendents to oversee the work of the districts
on each side of the Benue River. By 1968, the council was more focused
upon the mission and outreach of the church in Nigeria than upon the
church union that occupied the attention of the sponsoring EUB Church.
When tensions over constitutional revisions surfaced in the Muri Regional Church Council in the 1970s, a new interest in a direct relationship
to The UMC emerged in council discussions. Representatives were sent
to the 1980 General Conference in Indianapolis and to the Liberia Annual
Conference and brought back encouraging reports. The 1980 General
Conference approved the petition from the church council to become the
Muri Provisional Conference and relate to the newly formed West Africa

Central Conference. Bishop Kulah was assigned to oversee the development of the provisional conference into a full annual conference. He brought leaders to study UMC doctrine and polity in Liberia. In 1992 the conference qualified to become a full annual conference, and the West Africa Central Conference meeting that year elected Done Peter Dabale the first resident bishop of the church.

The United Methodist Church in Nigeria developed a strong program of evangelism that accounted for its rapid growth and development. While it still struggled with regional tensions within the church, the major focus was upon training pastors and laity for service in the churches. In 1989, the church established its own seminary at Banyam but also supported the Theological College of Northern Nigeria (TCNN) in Bukuru, where its students received bachelor of theology degrees. In 1994, the church reported a membership of 95,000 in 570 congregations organized into 15 districts.[21]

The cultural context in which this church developed was marked by religious hostilities. The population was equally divided between Muslims (North) and Christians (South), making governance a delicate piece of diplomacy. Unfortunately, Nigeria had only limited experience with democratic rule, but even the military governments had to pay deference to this tenuous balance. Divisions within both major faith groups precluded serious efforts at interfaith dialogue. Instead, authorities had to deal with frequent conflicts between local groups of believers that sometimes manifested themselves in the form of church/mosque burnings and violent street altercations. A constructive response from the Christian community was found in a stronger emphasis upon interfaith issues in the curriculum of schools for pastors and church leaders, like the TCNN.[22]

The social outreach ministry of The UMC in Nigeria by 2000 continued a mission of social development and outreach to the general population. Though the mission schools and hospitals were operated by the state, the church had established nonformal education programs for rural areas promoting literacy, maternal health, job training (tailoring), forestry services, and community health (drilling water wells). It had established its own church primary and secondary school at the new church headquarters in Jalingo. The historic Guinter Hospital remained one of the finest facilities in the region.

(See chapter 9 for mission initiatives of GBGM in Senegal, Burundi, Uganda, Kenya, and Tanzania.)

Africa Methodist Partners

Mission programs and relationships in Africa at the end of the millennium were not confined to the United Methodist organizational connection. The churches begun by missionaries of the Methodist Church in Great Britain were a part of the mission funding and other program efforts of United Methodists. United Methodist General Conferences have granted "covenant" relationships to Methodist churches in Ghana, Côte d'Ivoire, Sierra Leone, Kenya, and Nigeria.[23] In addition, GBGM had program relationships with Methodist churches in Gambia, Namibia, and South Africa. Aggressive programs of evangelization by United Methodist conferences have tested relationships to some of these churches. African United Methodist evangelists occasionally reached into the Methodist church domains in neighboring countries. Most often, the established Methodist church in the country was not serving the groups reached by United Methodist evangelists. Tribal and language differences defined the boundaries of church life in Africa, not the civil (or former colonial) divides which were conveniently adopted by church or mission judicatories.

All of the Methodist (including United Methodist) bodies were united by an ecumenical commitment to the All Africa Conference of Churches (AACC). In this ecumenical organization, Methodist churches are in strong fellowship with other mission-founded as well as independent African churches. The AACC had become a strong voice for the churches on the continent, speaking both to the world community and to Africans. Like many organizations on the continent, this too was a fragile structure but one of the few which transcended political and economic self-interests and could focus on the future and well-being of Africans. The leadership of the AACC was securely in the hands of African church leaders. Jose Chipenda, in his term in executive leadership of the organization, worked assiduously at recruiting young Africans for posts in the organization. In reflecting on the generational transition in leadership and the enormous challenges facing the church in Africa, he acknowledged: "We who are leaders must shoulder the blame. We have responsibility in which we must not fail, and that is to enable our successors to succeed."[24]

CHAPTER 5

The Corporate Dimensions of Grace

United Methodism in mission today:
A life changed by grace; a church formed
by grace; and a world transformed by grace.[1]

$\mathcal{F}$OR MORE THAN a century and a half, invoking the "Great Commission" (Matthew 28:18–20) provided sufficient motivation for engaging the people called Methodist in Christian mission. A deep sense of the spiritual (eschatological) urgency of making disciples/believers in all nations prompted individuals to consider giving their lives to the missionary calling. A pervasive loyalty led local churches to support the denominational mission board that sent them to places of service far beyond their homes.

The missionary movement of the nineteenth and early twentieth centuries was indeed a powerful force and—for the churches—a visible sign of the power of God working for the redemption of the whole world. This movement generated within The Methodist Church (1939–1968) one of the largest and most resourceful mission programs of all mainline Protestant churches. But it also fostered an image of missionary dominance and control by the sending church/mission board that became the focus of strong controversy over the purpose and objectives of the church's mission(ary) program.

By mid-twentieth century, indigenous church leaders, tasting the newly won freedom and independence from colonial forces, were boldly presenting the urgent needs, extensive human suffering, and gross injustices which the missionary movement had overlooked or failed to address. Missionaries began to play a diminished role in indigenous churches as these churches requested and received direct support for their own efforts to proclaim the gospel and strengthen their communities.

The turmoil in the streets of major cities and on university campuses in the United States in the 1960s aroused a hail of criticism of the churches and their complicity in the racism that produced devastating conditions of poverty and inequality for persons of color across the country. Leaders of ethnic minority groups in the life of The United Methodist Church (UMC) appealed to the church to see and support a mission at its doorstep while it was taking stock of the status of its witness worldwide.

These dynamics and conditions set the stage for a critical reexamination of the mission foundations and directions of the denomination. The Board of Missions found itself on the horns of a dilemma. Any reduction in the strength of its missionary deployment would be criticized by an "evangelical" constituency in the church for stepping back from the obedience to the "Great Commission." Failing to allocate new or additional resources to programs aimed at overcoming oppressive forces within communities of the U.S. as well as abroad, would disappoint and discourage leaders among sensitive minority constituencies that represented potential growth for The UMC.

Responding to the Historical Moment

By the end of the decade of the 1960s, each of the meetings of the Board of Missions became an occasion for intentional analysis, reflection, and program planning. General Secretary Tracey K. Jones, in a report to the newly elected Board members in September 1968, urged them to transcend the controversial character of the issues they would be addressing and seize the historical moment as "one of the great creative periods in missionary history. . . . Never before in the history of the Christian faith has the name of Christ been more widespread. Furthermore, the impact of the life of Christ has been seen in the tremendous revolutionary movements of our time and in the deep concern for the humanization of society."

In response to the revolutionary changes taking place in the world community, Jones announced the formation of four administrative or staff task forces to provide the Board with mission program directions for the 1970s. The first task force would address the issues of theology, in particular those mission questions that were summarized in the theme "Salvation Today" selected for the forthcoming 1972 Conference of the World

Hunger was a global concern of the Board in the 1970s, but it would soon emerge as a U.S. concern as well. Faye Fannin helped to feed the homeless at this ministry at Crossroads Center/Harwood Crossing in Dallas. The ministry was sponsored by First United Methodist Church and First Presbyterian Church in Dallas. *(Photo by Joan LeBarr for UM News Service)*

Council of Churches (WCC). Through ecumenical dialogue, the familiar boundaries of the debate between personal and social understanding of salvation would be given a larger context in a series of regional conferences involving Orthodox, Protestants, Evangelicals, and Roman Catholics. Jones said the objective would be to gain a new understanding of the missionary task that would require an examination of issues presented by a study of anthropology and world religions. And further, the task force would engage the timely question of how institutions become either agents for change or forces that thwart the Kingdom of God.

A second task force would focus on planning for the future of the mission program of the Board. Jones said, "The fantastic changes of the past eight years have been exciting, exhausting, and sobering. The realization that the decade ahead will be much more of the same is hardly a sedative to our nerves. On the national and world scene the question is, can we discern the shape of what this decade might be? . . . We can only lead if we know where we are going." Issues anticipated for address included racism,

increasing secularity, a deepening generation gap, a widening gap between poverty and affluence, and the influence of intellectuals.

A third task force would address world hunger and development. Programs of social action and sustainable community development were making greater claims upon the resources of the Board. The rationale for this
shift away from church-based and institutional programs needed to be
clarified and the growing number of programs coordinated. A major challenge would be to offer a reasonable interpretation for such programs
fitting into the mission of the church for a general church constituency
that was still enamored with more traditional activities of the missionaries.

A fourth task force would deal with ecumenical issues. The UMC was
the largest contributor to the program and administrative budgets of
the National Council of Churches (NCC) and the WCC. In 1968, the
Board of Missions allocated more than $2 million to these ecumenical
agencies, believing strongly in the necessity or principle of working with
other Christians engaged in programs of mission witness and service globally. But these councils were being subjected to considerable criticism for
their "liberal" perspectives and agendas. With an unwavering conviction
about the importance of organic unity to the mission of the church, Jones
conjectured, "We have every reason to believe that in the next decade
the relationship between the Roman Catholic Church and the World and
National Councils of Churches will become much more intimate. The
growing relationship between the Orthodox churches and the Protestant
churches is equally significant. One can only hope that, in the next decade,
there will also be a much closer relationship between the conservative
Evangelicals and the mainline Protestant churches."[2]

While evidence of the productivity of each of the task forces is difficult
to chart, the importance of the assigned themes would grow with each new
quadrennium. The task of laying firm biblical and theological foundations
for mission produced long discussions and debates at Board meetings. It
required interpretation of the emerging theologies from the churches in
the Southern Hemisphere that found empathy for their struggles toward
self-determination in the motif of liberation-oriented ideologies. It meant
responding to the criticisms of the organized evangelical leadership of
the denomination, who accused the Board of divesting itself of recognized
biblical authority to pursue a social agenda. The dialogue and debate
helped produce a formal statement of mission theology adopted by the
Board in 1987, which neither satisfied the critics nor covered much new
ground.

The emphasis upon defining mission directions through formal planning processes, or developing programs for management by program objectives, strategies, and outcomes, found a continuing strong resonance within the Board. As this exercise shaped the budget and policymaking duties of the Board, it brought considerable influence to the committees, such as the Research and Development Committee and its successor the Mission Development Committee, where the function was lodged. To a great extent, these committees ultimately absorbed the conceptual aspects of the subject matter assigned to the other three task forces (theology, world development, and ecumenism).

The world hunger and development programs evolved and remained well protected within the divisions of the Board that funded them. Only the administration of world hunger programs eventually came under the scrutiny of a Boardwide staff task force. This overview was the result of General Conference designation of the issue as a churchwide missional priority. All units of the Board were called upon to examine their specific program mandates and activities for correlative strategies for a campaign to end hunger. The program design involved more than project funding. Educating the church constituency to patterns of reduced food consumption brought Health and Welfare and Mission Education units to the table. Addressing agricultural or environmental public policy issues required a uniform approach from all units. The United Methodist Committee on Relief (UMCOR) provided general oversight of the coordinated Board response to the denominational priority. But the crisis response specialization of UMCOR did not lend its services and resources to supporting longer-term issues of community economic development. More pathbreaking model development work, like the National Division's Mission Enterprise Loan and Investment Committee, was the sole domain of the sponsoring divisions. A Boardwide strategy for developing programs involving systemic economic or political change was still needed.

Ecumenical strategy development and coordination within the Board remained a vision, but not a reality. Even with the addition of the Commission on Ecumenical Affairs to the organizational structure of the Board in 1972, the ecumenical/organizational links to the individual funding divisions remained unaffected. The assumptions regarding the importance of ecumenical cooperation were generally unchallenged within the Board. Nevertheless, the unfavorable reporting in 1986 by the *Reader's Digest* and a follow-up broadcast by *60 Minutes* on CBS-TV accusing the church councils of supporting liberation movements and guerrilla armies caused an official review by the Council of Bishops of how much influence ecumenical councils should have over United Methodist mission directions. Gradually, the nurturing of ecumenical programs via funding and staffing began to diminish. By the end of the century, The UMC was no longer the major denominational funder of the church councils. Other program delivery channels were created, including a nongovernmental organizational entity within UMCOR which brokered government funding for international development projects—a role to which The UMC had historically looked to Church World Service of the NCC to fulfill. Likewise, other ecumenical relationships became more complicated to negotiate, administrative costs more expensive, and defense against criticism more time-consuming. While the official commitment to a common witness of the world Christian community remained unchanged, the resolve of The UMC to actualize and fund it waned.

The most significant clues to changing mission program directions during the last three decades of the twentieth century are found in the reports of the Board's planning processes. Following union of the EUB and Methodist mission entities, the newly organized World Division began a process of discerning the major mission thrusts of the new quadrennium. Even though the partner churches around the world were consulted on the matter, the four areas selected for program concentration were fairly predictable and reflected subjects which often dominated Board plenaries: "urbanization, hunger and national development, peace and preparation of the laity for its mission."[3] In defining the work and implementing new strategies, the World Division involved representatives of other units of the Board, principally, the Women's Division, National Division, and Education and Cultivation.

While some in the church were calling upon the World Division to redirect substantial resources to address the urban crisis in the U.S., the division employed its constituted authority for leading the church in mission beyond the U.S. by identifying no fewer than twelve major world cities for strategic investment of program and personnel resources.[4] The program was soon expanded "Beyond the Twelve Cities" to incorporate funding for grassroots efforts at rural organizing and agricultural development. Funding for many of the agricultural projects corresponded to the Board's goal to address issues of world hunger.

Development *education* was the focus given to the World Division's approach to national development. Rather than fund material efforts at building new communities, the division sought out groups that were working on the critical issues of self-esteem, human dignity, quality of life, and social justice. Grants were provided to enlarge their efforts by including the values of theological reflection and conceptual understanding to the otherwise secular or nationalistic undertakings of many groups organizing around social change.

Perhaps the commitment to work on peaceful resolution of military and social conflicts represented the division's greatest risk-taking in new program directions. The division designated resources for program grants to a variety of peacemaking endeavors. The war in Indochina received the most attention, with grants going to groups (including the Board of Christian Social Concerns) participating in building international alliances to increase political pressure to end the war. A small grant was made to the Canadian Council of Churches to assist with its ministry to U.S. draft-age immigrants. Church partners in Brazil, Philippines, and Japan were also given grants to enable their participation in movements to resolve regional conflicts or to sponsor/attend conferences, workshops, and training events.

Interpretation and Implementation

The World Division leadership saw the quadrennial emphases as a legitimate extension of their program mandates, but the staff member managing the effort acknowledged difficulties in communicating this perspective: "In our enthusiasm . . . we still have not communicated fully that [these emphases] represent our concern for total mission, the mission of a community of those who have made a decision for discipleship to Jesus Christ. Where our communication has been unclear, there are those at home and abroad who ask whether we have forgotten the primary purpose of the Church. But where our concerns about urbanization, hunger and national development, peace and preparation of laity for its mission are understood in their total context, the response has been heartening."[5]

In referring to new and changing program directions for the 1970s, Dr. John Schaefer, the associate general secretary of the World Division, 1968–1973, told the directors that they should be prepared to participate in a process of "reconstruction" that would "prove to be a difficult, a painful and a frustrating task." Nineteenth-century goals and objectives of mission were inadequate, he said, for even the "more conservative mission boards and agencies that claim to have remained more faithful to our Christian traditions." In place of a church-centered expansion agenda, he commended ecumenical reformulations of mission that are cognizant of a "worldwide struggle for meaning, dignity, freedom and love." According to Schaefer, the new formulation "emphasizes the vulnerability of humanity embraced in the incarnation and ultimately transformed by the resurrection power of God in Jesus Christ. It affirms total salvation in both personal and social dimensions of life. It promises a new humanity and bids the church to be engaged in the crying needs of people for world peace, justice, development, the very concerns we are stressing this quadrennium."[6]

Not only theological foundations, but also but an analysis of social, political, and economic considerations undergirded the new program directions. A strong stimulus was offered for partners to engage in new and experimental approaches to addressing critical needs, and these values were reflected in the criteria established for program and project funding:

1. Is the project community based?

2. Does it seek to enable the poor and powerless to shape the decisions that affect their lives?

3. Is it anti-paternalistic; that is, does it make man [sic] the subject rather than the object of development?

4. Is it ecumenical in character?

5. Is it presently under, or seriously working toward, national leadership? Or, is it heavily dependent upon expatriate direction?

6. Is it moving seriously toward local support?

7. Can it be expected to have multiplier potential for other areas with similar problems?

8. How comprehensive does it seek to be in terms of the larger framework of development in the nation as a whole?[7]

By 1973, the Board Research and Development Committee had formulated eleven "indicators" of overall program effectiveness. The indicators would help measure the fulfillment of the mission of the church, which the committee chose to define on behalf of the whole church and without any hesitancy of embracing a liberation perspective: "The church is called to proclaim, in action as well as worship, the Lordship of Jesus Christ, who liberates persons, calls them into community, and transforms persons and systems. The Board of Global Ministries struggles to witness to God's purpose and action in a pluralistic world. The work of the Board must be judged by the following indicators."[8]

The indicators of effectiveness touched on several themes and aimed to resonate with various constituencies:

1. Biblical and theological groundings would find an anchor in the mission statement itself, which is inclined toward a progressive view of realizing the Kingdom of God through acts of social as well as personal liberation from sin and all forms of oppression.

2. Ecumenical or cooperative approaches to mission engagement were favored, but "oneness and mutuality in religious and ideological witness" were the ultimate values in a world fraught with conflicts.[9]

3. Awareness of global responsibility introduced the concept of pluralism, or affirming cultural values beyond one's own, and stressed the importance of contributing to a growing global self-consciousness of the denomination (UMC) itself.

4. Strengthening local congregations in achieving their mission implied evidence of strong accountability by local churches to the immediate communities they served as well as cognizance of the global church of which they were a part.

5. Participatory planning—especially in United Methodist connectional relationships—opened the door to involvement or representation by the communities of persons served in the development of programs and projects.

6. Personal empowerment—especially of women, the elderly, youth, and racial/ethnic persons—called for identification with the poor and the powerless.

7. Systemic change aimed at humanization and justice provided an emphasis upon long-term structural changes in society and its institutions.

8. and 9. Elimination of racism and sexism raised the issue of inclusiveness, especially within the churches, and called for intentional commitment to combatting inequalities.

10. Direct services to unserved or underserved constituencies focused new and additional resources upon populations and services in relation to needs, not traditional programming.

11. Rigorous program evaluation was emphasized as a system or style of work rather than a function of program administration.

The new program directions were "process oriented," favoring "accountability" and requiring additional levels of organizational review and supervision. The more relaxed but outmoded patterns that led to missionary dominance of program and policy matters could no longer be trusted. The program development process was created to emphasize and protect emerging values, such as inclusiveness, global thinking and actions, participatory decision making, liberation and empowerment of oppressed groups, affirmation of cultures, and sensitivity to other Christian traditions and religious ideologies. There was no expressed intention of replacing more traditional program values, which favored well-established relationships, just a heightened emphasis upon the more rational procedures of setting goals, objectives, strategies, and indicators of achievement.

Communications

Mission giving is a corollary of both strong mission education and effective communication. Church members respond financially when they are adequately informed about mission needs. In an age of advanced communication technologies, mission in The UMC has been challenged to find a direct benefit from the strong motivational impact that the media makes upon its members.

The most direct channel of communication with the membership at the time of denominational merger in 1968 was a monthly general subscription magazine, *Together*. The mission agency published its own monthly journals — *New World Outlook* for subscribers interested in denominational and ecumenical mission issues and programs, and *Response*, a membership journal with information and program resources for United Methodist Women (UMW). *Together* became an early casualty of revolutions in the media that also consumed other general subject periodicals, even such popular organs as *Life* and *The Saturday Evening Post*. *The Interpreter*, a monthly publication of program helps for leaders in local churches, and *Circuit Rider*, a journal for pastors, reached key constituencies in local churches. Both magazines carried occasional feature articles on mission issues or programs, but the most reliable channels for in-depth reporting on mission information were *New World Outlook* and *Response*. Unfortunately, *New World Outlook*, a high-quality publication, suffered from a declining readership (to about 10,000 subscribers by 2000), required an annual budget subsidy, and was reduced to a bimonthly schedule.

Ezekiel Makunike worked as a journalist for the government in Zimbabwe but became proficient in communications with the Methodist church there. His work demonstrated the professionalism of many indigenous leaders in Africa. *(Photo courtesy of UM Archives and History)*

The principal print media publication available to communicate current mission news and information to the broadest constituency of United Methodists was *The United Methodist Reporter (UMR)*. It was an independently owned publication based in Dallas, Texas. It was begun by a group of enterprising United Methodists to address communication needs of annual conferences and local churches. They offered editorial and publishing services for weekly, biweekly, or monthly editions of a newspaper-style publication, with their conference or local church headlines and stories on the front page and denominational and other church news on subsequent pages. *UMR* grew rapidly in popularity and soon replaced most conference-published newspapers and found a substantial market for its services among large membership churches. The denomination was experiencing a new phenomenon in church communications — an "unofficial" denominational press. While *UMR* reported denominational activities and developments on a timely basis to a growing constituency, The UMC had no control of the content nor influence over editorial policy. Sensationalism sells news, and *UMR* often focused on conflicts and controversy within the church that denominational officials would rather have ignored. So, while *UMR* offered a direct channel to hundreds of thousands of United Methodists, the stories about Christian mission selected by its editors were often short of the inspiration or information for which mission leaders hoped.

Mission interpretation efforts of the General Board of Global Ministries (GBGM) featured a variety of events sponsored with the mission "linkage" personnel in annual conferences. Global ministries secretaries of the annual conferences were occasionally brought to the New York offices for training and informational meetings to prepare them for sharing mission stories. "Mission Saturation" events sponsored in the annual conferences brought missionaries, Board program staff, and project personnel into districts for a week at a time. After a district rally, they were assigned to local churches, where they preached, taught church school classes, led prayer meetings, and met with informal groups to create a new level of interest and support for mission programs close to home or on another continent. "High-level dialogues" were scheduled for bishops and conference officers who wanted to receive firsthand briefings on critical mission issues or policy developments from the general secretary and senior staff of the Board.

Changes in audiovisual techniques brought new opportunities for developing a heightened awareness of contexts served by the mission outreach of the church. Filmstrips and slide presentations gave way to video productions, the most extensive of which was the *Mission Magazine*. Produced jointly by Education and Cultivation and United Methodist Communications, half-hour videos were produced and distributed for conference mission leaders and pastors for mission interpretation. After their use in local churches, church leaders were encouraged to present them to local television stations for airing during program time devoted to religious broadcasting. Taped interviews with mission project personnel and church leaders from various countries were sent to radio stations for broadcast.

With the developments in telecommunications that produced the internet and its world wide web came an opportunity to communicate with a global constituency. Experimentation with this medium as a tool for enhancing mission information is described in chapter 9.

Mission communications was more than a tool for promotion among supporting congregations. It provided technical assistance to mission partners who were making use of the public media for publishing and broadcasting the Christian message. Missionaries with expertise in religious journalism and broadcasting were instrumental in training mission church personnel in strategies and techniques for sharing the gospel via print and broadcast media. They specialized in evangelistic programs directed to those who had not yet heard the gospel as well as programs aimed at nurturing special constituent groups, such as youth, young adults, and the elderly. Interpretation of current events from the perspective of informed leaders of the Christian church created opportunities to promote understanding, dialogue, and discussion in interfaith or multicultural contexts. Soon the social justice questions that the mission of the church confronted in other sectors became an obvious focus in its media mission.

The ecumenically supported World Association of Christian Communication (WACC) cultivated a significant network of communication specialists in the developing world. WACC challenged the lack of access to public media experienced by people in poor communities worldwide. High technology equipment and training that successfully transmitted messages from affluent cultures in the Northern Hemisphere remained out of reach for communicators of the Southern Hemisphere. WACC developed mission programs that successfully introduced church and community leaders to leading information technologies. It confronted cultural discrimination that often prevented young people and women from seeking careers in the industry by creating community-controlled ventures that welcomed them. Such ventures also affirmed the value of local programming and reduced dependencies upon imported signals from dominant European and North American broadcasting companies that ignored local sensitivities and talent.

Organizational Context

The program directions of the Board were changing, and mission programs ventured into new areas of work. Meanwhile the planning process, by which changes were introduced, was being institutionalized.

Planning for Mission

The new denominational structure adopted by the 1972 General Conference reflected the growing popularity of megastructure management, consolidating the work of some smaller units (Division of Ecumenical and Interreligious Concerns and the Board of Hospital and Homes) into one large GBGM. The Board subsequently focused on managing increasingly diverse program responsibilities by introducing standing committees on program development (like Research and Development) and evaluation. All of the units of the Board were engaged in a rational process of identifying program objectives, strategies, and processes for evaluation. Consultants were employed to develop a system and methods for overall program evaluation.

While the Board initiated these disciplines in response to a changing global mission context, changing church institutional realities also became a driving force. The 1972 general church restructure adopted a vestige of the EUB Church structure and created a program coordinating unit in the General Council on Ministries (GCOM). Its major function was to establish systems of accountability for the work of general church program agencies. The council bought into the prevailing organizational theories that supported management by objectives and required all of the program boards and agencies to submit program plans and budgets for review and recommendation on a quadrennial basis.

Many among the mission constituencies found it difficult (or even offensive) to participate in the assignment of programs and program dollars to particular objectives and strategies in the comprehensive mission plan or to line items in organizational budgets. While they cited conflicts with local cultural values which had little appreciation for databased systems, underneath was a resentment of church organizations taking on the characteristics of corporate structures. The hired staff, who may have held similar values or attitudes, were often chastised for implementing the process. But organizational systems prevailed in the church, and the mission relationships learned to acquiesce.

Establishing and articulating Board program goals evolved over the years with a consensus developing around four functional areas of work, namely, evangelization, church development and renewal, alleviation of human suffering, and advocacy of justice and systems change.[10] Program planners could subsume all of the program activities of the Board under these major headings. Changes in the actual language of these mission goals were occasionally introduced. For instance, a specific goal entitled "liberation" of oppressed peoples was consolidated in a goal emphasizing the establishment of justice and peace, and the controversial noun deleted. Perhaps the most substantive amendment occurred in the goal defining evangelization. The first approved goal in 1973 emphasized "communication" of the gospel "to all persons and in all places and to invite them to obedience in Christian discipleship."[11] In the 1985–1988 quadrennium, the toll of dialogue with the evangelical mission leaders within the denomination influenced the planning process that offered more precision around the function of making new disciples. The goal was changed to a more proactive: "Witness to the Gospel for an initial decision to follow Christ."

Institutional Racism

A significant area in which the Board initiated an aggressive program direction was the elimination of institutional racism. There was a growing recognition about the subtlety with which church organizations tolerate racist behaviors, but until an organization became proactive in identifying and correcting those attitudes and actions, it would not be open to or benefit from the full participation of persons of color. With the employment of an ombudsman, restyled as the more inclusive ombudsperson, the Board soon began to hear more clearly and embrace those who were helping it witness to the gospel through its programs and projects in a variety of mission contexts, especially among the poor and the powerless. Leaders from these contexts were recruited to fill vacant staff positions, and others were brought into membership on the board of directors, often through an at-large membership category when they were not nominated and elected through regular membership channels.

A critical mass of racial/ethnic constituents needed to gain formal recognition in the Board of Global Ministries (and other general program agencies of the church) was gradually established, but the ethos of institutional racism had yet to be penetrated. The Board established a committee and enlisted a team of consultants to engage in further research on the issues of racism and develop action plans for the Board to implement. During the 1977–1980 quadrennium, the team compiled a list of indicators of institutional racism and invited the membership of the Board to begin a process of monitoring the behaviors and activities of its member units. Through testing, the language of the indicators was refined, edited, and adopted by the Board. The development of indicators successfully helped the Board enter into formal dialogue about the evidences and implications of racist behavior. The indicators provided a training tool for staff and classes entering or returning to missionary service. A Boardwide committee was established to assure their use within the organization. Each unit of the Board was required to develop action plans for how an an antiracist commitment would have an impact on its programs and policies. Finally, the publication of the indicators brought recognition by other national and international organizations working toward the same goal.

Mission Theology

There was a general shift in thought and reflection upon the theological foundations for mission engagement in the Methodist tradition. The influence of the ecumenical movement was running strong in most Protestant churches in the 1960s and early 1970s. The World Conference on Salvation Today sponsored by the WCC Commission on World Mission and Evangelism in Bangkok, Thailand, in 1973 tried to set the tone for the churches' response to revolutionary changes taking place in the global context.

The conference called for a "renewal in mission" through the recognition of the "mature relationships" now existing between the churches. The old missionary situation rooted in the sole authority of mission agencies to administer funds and personnel had created a set of "power relationships" which were "alien to the church." Needed was a "mutual commitment to participate in Christ's mission in the world." This new relationship was to be based upon "an acknowledgment of interdependence within the world Christian fellowship." "No particular church can claim full autonomy . . . but each church must be free to be itself within its own national or cultural milieu and to respond fully to the movement of the Holy Spirit within that milieu."[12]

The visionary direction seemed commendable, but the major implication of adopting this working relationship of mutuality meant dropping the established bilateral mission relationships (i.e., direct administration of resources between an individual "sending" agency and an individual "receiving" church) that defined most transactions of denominational or independent mission agencies. This pattern of controlling interest prompted the churches' call for a moratorium on sending funds and personnel. While the conference stopped short of endorsing its universal application, the moratorium was encouraged in some situations to help churches define their own "authentic selves in mission to their own milieu."

No specific model or alternative structure was proposed for achieving mutuality in mission administration, but the creation of local, national, or regional church structures to interact with any or all of the mission agencies was discussed. The formation of regional councils of churches had already led to the development of networks for churches and agencies to increase dialogue and consultation on mission strategies and seek to avoid unilateral program activities. But the primary task was a spiritual or theological matter, not a policy or administrative issue. The emphasis was upon the discovery of the "liberating power of the Gospel" which moved the churches to a stronger affirmation of their own cultural values and the development of distinct indigenous theologies, while the agencies were left wondering how to appropriate and interpret this new contextual reality.

In a panel presentation to an Education and Cultivation plenary, senior Board staff and a missionary representative reflected upon the theological basis of mission. The Bangkok formulation of salvation as a liberating experience found endorsement and rejection. World Division staff member Eugene Stockwell argued for oneness to new expressions of spiritual experience that embraced a social as well as personal context: "We can affirm the purposive ways and varying styles in which people seek the liberation of themselves and the communities in which they participate." Africa missionary Marvin Wolford, reporting on his experience in itinerating in local churches, said, "new theologies and philosophies which come to the constituency leave them rather cold. . . . There is a lack of interest until a personal contact with a need is established." He argued that the missionary is still the agent that personalizes human need and provides the connection for the church to respond. Theressa Hoover, associate general secretary of the Women's Division, acknowledged that the church "was in the era of being afraid of using the word liberation." But "the concept of liberation assumes in its central function God's saving action, human response and social analysis." Hoover directed her listeners' attention to the dynamics of the socializing process and the hard lessons therein for Christian missiology:

"Every civilization has a center and a periphery. As the center matures, it is the periphery that becomes worthy of our attention. That is where the new forms of social organization are born, usually out of the struggle of an oppressed people against those who dominate. . . . Perhaps we should rejoice in bringing home an increasing number of missionaries, understanding that there is also an increasing number of indigenous leaders in countries which missionaries from North America leave. Perhaps our theology of mission needs to help us re-focus geographically." [13]

The debate over the theological center and program focus of United Methodist mission theology was just beginning. The tensions were often characterized by various polarities. In addition to Hoover's center-versus-periphery dialectic, some of the more stereotypical categories were liberal versus conservative, liberation versus evangelical, and traditional versus radical. Ira Gallaway, the associate general secretary of the Division of Evangelism at the General Board of Discipleship (GBOD) and later a dominant figure in the formation of the independent Mission Society for United Methodists, addressed the Board in March 1973. He appealed for a "centrist" theological position for the denomination's mission program with a single focus on the Great Commission's evangelizing mandate: "We need to know where the people are who make up the church on the local level. The majority still believe in the central traditional beliefs of the church. They feel that the task of the church is reaching beyond itself and winning others to Jesus Christ."[14]

The leaders of the Board of Global Ministries stood by the ecumenical formulation of salvation at the Bangkok conference, which readily incorporated evidences of social forces for change into the contemporary and transforming power of the Holy Spirit. The liberating qualities of the search for identity for individuals and communities of faith within their individual cultures were affirmed in Board program goals and statements. But doctrinal emphases upon the uniqueness and centrality of Christ's saving activity, not the influence of culture or contribution of ethnic heritage to Christian identity, occupied the attention of the traditionalists in the denomination.

Dialogue on Philosophy/Practice of Mission

The Evangelical Missions Council (EMC) was organized to provide a "corrective" to some of the social forces influencing the mission directions and policies of the Board of Global Ministries. The leadership comprised pastors of large membership churches and some former missionaries who shared a conservative evangelical theological perspective. Similar groups had formed in other mainline denominations looking for answers to the general membership decline that had begun to plague the Protestant witness in North America. While denominations were adapting to many changes taking place in the society, critical attention was directed to the denominational mission programs. Mission work enjoyed the reputation for successfully promoting programs and generating strong constituent loyalties. Mission boards were conspicuous for administering considerable financial resources and were seen as pivotal agencies for institutional revival. But, according to the "reformers," their agenda and leadership would need redirection.

The effectiveness of the EMC in making its criticism public and thus creating doubt or uncertainty about the direction of the denomination's mission agency won it a hearing by the Board. The leaders of the EMC met with officers of the Board of Global Ministries on several occasions. Critics of the Board from among its mission constituencies, especially racial/ethnic and youth/young adult groups, were always included among the invited guests and made formal presentations to meetings of the Board. The dialogues with the EMC were generally private and only sometimes reported to the Board, since EMC leaders made liberal use of their own public relations channels. The discussions revealed a unanimous agreement on the importance of a strong mission program within the church but generated considerable disagreement over how to achieve it. There was a consensus on the importance of sound biblical theological foundations as a basis for developing the denomination's mission program but disagreement on the starting points and content of a mission theology. There was, however, a momentary and perhaps misplaced unanimity of opinion on the capacity of mission theology to reform and unite the church behind its mission program. While the dialogues stimulated considerable interest on the part of the Board and eventually the General Conference in drafting mission theology statements, neither effort would satisfy the critics of the denomination's mission program.

The formal dialogues with the EMC began about 1968 and continued until the formation of the Mission Society for United Methodists (MSUM) in 1984. In 1984, General Conference mandated dialogue meetings between the GBGM and MSUM under the direction of the Council of Bishops. In 1988, General Conference ordered continuation of the dialogues but dismissed the bishops from participation.

Drafting a Mission Theology Statement

During the 1981–1984 quadrennium, GBGM, under the leadership of its new General Secretary Randolph Nugent, carried out a restructure of its organization. The centerpiece of the restructure was always to have been a theologically grounded mission statement. But the work went to the 1984 General Conference missing that statement. That General

Conference adopted a petition from a group of seminary professors to commission the drafting of an official denominational mission statement. The professors shared a similar hope that a rationale for mission would be a unifying force for the growing distance between mission-oriented constituencies and leaders in the church.[15] A commission was named to produce a statement for the 1988 General Conference to consider. Meanwhile, GBGM appointed its own committee to complete the mission theology statement promised to accompany its restructure. Three non-returning members of the of the Board from the previous quadrennium were appointed to serve on the new committee. One of the three, C. Rex Bevins, who chaired the Board's influential Research and Development Committee, was named to preside over this important work.

Knowing that the production of such a statement would get close scrutiny, the Board decided upon an open process. A series of mission theology consultations were scheduled in various U.S. locations for participants selected by their conferences. A common resource was chosen for the consultations, namely, *Mission Evangelism—An Ecumenical Affirmation*, a popular position paper the WCC produced in consultation and input from its critics among "evangelicals" and independent mission groups. Each event was designed to allow sufficient time for small groups to react to the content of the study document. Their responses were recorded and informed the writing of the Board's mission statement. Likewise, similar consultations were held with global mission partners in Africa, Asia, Latin America, and Europe.

The drafting and editing process was tedious, with the committee presenting material to Board plenaries for reactions, suggestions and then rewrites. The drafters depended heavily upon guidance from the Wesleyan theological heritage. While emerging theologies were referred to, the controversial Liberation Theology received no commendation. The concept of *Missio Dei*—the sending nature of God revealed in both Old and New Testaments—was featured, along with a strong call to full participation in partnership with God and other missionary churches, congregations, and leaders in a holistic and global missionary enterprise.

The finished statement, "Theology of Mission Statement: Partnership in God's Mission," was completed and introduced to the church in a celebratory "global gathering" in Louisville, Kentucky, in March 1987. The event was organized around the major themes of the document. Translations were produced in major languages of the global mission constituencies. The document was published in pamphlet form and widely distributed. It was used for mission interpretation, devotional reading, and program rationale.[16]

Meanwhile, the commission with the mandate from the general church to write a mission statement kept tabs on the Board's project. The commission membership contained fewer professors of theology than the original sponsors of the petition may have anticipated or desired. Nevertheless, the final product was a substantive document drawing heavily upon Wesley's theology, especially the doctrine of grace. The drafters studied Wesley's sermons for evidences of his mission foundations. They discovered that Wesley had never preached a sermon on the text from Matthew popularly referred to as the "Great Commission." His messages were aimed at stirring a human response to initiatives of God's grace in their lives and within their world. Gratitude for God's loving and forgiving grace, not a mandate, command, or even a commission, prompted Methodists toward mission engagement. Methodism in the New World functioned as a mission long before it took on ecclesiastical form. It was a mission to the frontiers for which itinerate preachers were called and sent on horseback to conduct revivals. When the church was securely planted, Methodists still understood themselves as a people formed by grace, within a church reformed by grace, and in a world to be transformed by grace.[17]

The completed document was sent to the General Conference of 1988, which did not adopt it but recommended its publication and distribution to the church for study. The same General Conference produced major rewrites of the historic disciplinary documents on "Doctrinal Standards" and "Our Theological Task." The framers wanted to be certain that there would be no competition or confusion of these primary works with any other official statement. So *Grace upon Grace — The Mission Statement of The United Methodist Church* was reduced to a study document and probably undervalued as a defining perspective on Christian mission from a United Methodist perspective.

With the drafting of these documents in the decade of the 1980s, the theological pendulum had clearly swung back from its position of ecumenical solidarity with the experience and leading of the churches among the world's newly liberated countries to the more traditional, though not generally familiar, moorings of Wesleyan thought and practice. The goal seemed to be creating a stronger Methodist identity or tone for understanding, interpreting, and guiding United Methodist mission involvement. Some argued that a stronger emphasis upon distinctive denominational thought and history would contribute to a richer ecumenical dialogue and witness. Others alleged a diminution of a commitment to cooperative witness in mission and the realization of the visible unity of the church.

Financing Mission

Support for the missionary outreach of The UMC is well grounded in its connectional organizational philosophy. The primary costs of the mission programs of the general church are apportioned to the conferences and local churches as a part of a general church fund known as World Service. As the title suggests, the monies contributed to this fund enable the denomination to support a worldwide program of witness and service. Initially, the burden of such an extension of the ministry of the church fell upon its mission agency, and the largest claims made upon the fund came from the Board of Missions of The Methodist Church and its successor, GBGM. As the General Conference of the church established new denominational programs including missional priorities, this mainline channel for connectional support of mission was affected. The new programs required special funding and absorbed the increases in apportioned giving that were generally anticipated for the World Service fund. Then, as other general agencies created programs of global outreach, they made increasing claims upon the quadrennial distribution of the World Service fund. The mission agency's dominance began to shrink and by the last decade of the twentieth century had decreased to less than 50 percent.[18]

Financing United Methodist mission required more than the funding generated through the channel of general church or apportioned giving. United Methodist Women (UMW), the most active local promoter and supporter of mission in the church, directed significant funding to mission programs and projects through its national organization, the Women's Division of GBGM. The division administered funds received from local units that make an annual "Pledge for Mission"—undesignated giving for U.S. and global mission programs with women, children, and youth; contributed to special offerings with program themes selected by the division; and made supplemental gifts designated for specific projects. In addition, the Women's Division managed generous endowment and reserve funds established by individuals and organizations for various mission programs or individual projects.[19]

Unlike provisions for other general agencies, a special fund-raising license was given to the mission agency. A channel of "second mile giving" (beyond the apportionment) was created in 1948 with the establishment of the "Advance for Christ and His Church." Each quadrennium, a list of mission projects for direct promotion among the churches was created by GBGM and approved by GCOM. These projects reflected critical "second mile" needs of the churches and conferences, programs that are beyond the level of support provided by regular grants made through the budget of the Board. The promotion of Advance projects among contributing churches assumed that they would meet in full the "first mile" apportioned giving to the World Service general fund before committing to the additional mission support. Thanks to the efforts of regional staff employed by GBGM for promotional work directly with conferences and churches, the annual contributions for mission through the Advance averaged more than $28 million per year over the last quarter of the twentieth century. That amount equals the income level of World Service for the Board's mission programs. Unlike World Service however, no Advance funds could be used for administrative expenses. One hundred percent of every Advance gift was transmitted directly to the designated project.

The most visible promotional activity on behalf of United Methodist mission continued to be the scheduled visits of missionaries to their supporting churches. Missionary support remained the largest single program budget commitment of GBGM. Even though the full support of every missionary sent by the Board was assured before the missionary was commissioned and assigned, direct participation of local churches in the support of missionary personnel was encouraged through "covenant" relationships. The covenant implied financial support through the Advance designated for selected missionaries, participation in a prayer fellowship on behalf of the missionaries and their ministries, and a regular exchange of communications via a missionary letter, e-mail, and visits. Missionaries on home assignment (furloughs or intervals between contracted years of service in mission settings) itinerated among the churches that accepted "covenant" support and solicited new covenanting congregations. The funds contributed by covenanting congregations supplemented the regular missionary budget generously underwritten by income from apportioned funds from the general church World Service fund and from the Women's Division.

Missionaries have historically created the financial support required for most of the institutions and projects they have helped create. In addition to missionary salary support, they have actively promoted the needs of the constituencies they served so that these needs could be included in the General Advance program. They also have an impressive track record of presenting opportunities for special mission stewardship for generous gifts by affluent church members and other individuals. Missionaries have successfully encouraged family members and friends to include their programs in their wills and estates. GBGM managed most of these bequests through its investment portfolio and then distributed the interest earned as specifically directed by the donors to the beneficiary programs on an annual basis. In the 1970s, the Board developed a current and deferred gifts program as a means of institutionalizing this creativity of the missionaries. A small staff trained in financial planning offered assistance to individuals interested in leaving a portion of their financial assets to Board or other mission programs. By 1997, the program reported more than $108 million of income for mission programs.

Mission Education

The benefits of mission education far exceeded the often-anticipated results in financial promotion. The distinctive content of mission education was a primary body of knowledge grounded in the church's reflections and learnings from its study of the historical and contemporary activities of a missionary God and a people called to witness and service in the name of God. The value of mission education was its vitality in shaping a relevant witness for the church at every level. It sought to inform all of the ministries of the church, especially how it shared the gospel through proclamation and witness; cultivated its spiritual life through worship and prayer; created new communities of faith in various cultures; defended those who suffered from systems and acts of injustice; interpreted its faith in interreligious and secular dialogues; and brought healing and reconciliation among individuals, groups, and nations.

But defining and developing a curriculum for teaching these essential components of contemporary Christian mission remained an elusive goal. The value of introducing children and youth to Christian mission has been recognized by church school curriculum designers at GBOD, who were charged by the *Book of Discipline* to consult with GBGM in developing that emphasis. There was, however, no basic structure in local churches like the traditional Sunday school that provided a ready-made forum for systematic mission education. Opportunities for adult education had to be created locally, and Christian mission was seldom a subject for study and reflection. To that end, some mission education efforts of GBGM focused upon the pastor as "mission educator."

In 1973, the Education and Cultivation Development (ECD) unit of the Board began an intentional effort at developing educational modules for pastors. The division arranged for a series of consultations with pastors that would identify the needs and opportunities presented by their ministries for introducing mission education in local churches. From this data, models of mission education for pastors were designed, created, and conducted in the jurisdictions and conferences of The UMC.[20]

ECD also focused on mission education for pastoral formation in United Methodist seminaries. Few of the denominational schools maintained full-time faculty positions for missiology or offered significant course selections in the field of Christian mission. Special mission "teach-ins" were scheduled with some cooperating seminaries. Teams of Board staff and mission personnel invested a week on seminary campuses conducting mission seminars, leading chapel worship services and promoting missionary careers. In order to personalize world mission on its campus, the Methodist Theological School of Ohio entered into a contractual agreement with the World Division to provide annually a teaching position for a missionary with appropriate academic credentials. As the phenomenon of globalization affected education, other seminaries turned to the Board for assistance with their curriculum enrichment that included encounters and exchanges with students and faculties of Methodist seminaries on other continents.

The most formidable effort in mission education for United Methodists was the Schools of Christian Mission sponsored annually by the Women's Division. The curriculum included three studies based on a theme — one on a designated country of particular concern to Christian mission, one on a contemporary issue for mission, and another on spirituality. These themes were traditionally selected at an ecumenical table (sponsored by the Division of Christian Education of the NCC). When the interest and support of other denominations diminished in the early

Schools of Christian Mission of the Women's Division became the para-mount method for educating leaders throughout the connection on mission. The division carefully prepared volunteers for leadership of sessions. *(Photo courtesy of UM Archives and History)*

1990s, the Women's Division urged GBGM to maintain the function. A crossfunctional team of mission executives recommended study themes, selected authors for the curriculum, and developed the resources for the annual regional and conference schools that attracted United Methodists in the tens of thousands. Schools of Christian Mission remained the one forum in the church that offered substantive discussion and dimensioning of the complexities of mission engagement. Mission leaders looked to the schools as a recruitment and training ground for interpreters and advo-cates of Christian mission in United Methodist and ecumenical settings.

The Women's Division aim of equipping laywomen for mission leader-ship took on a significant institutional form when the division acquired the campus of Scarritt College in Nashville. In the 1980s, Scarritt's spe-cialization in training personnel for professions in church and mission leadership could no longer be sustained. The Women's Division decided to pursue its rights to ownership of the property and developed a unique center for personal development with a focus on the gifts of women in leadership in church and community. After a considerable financial investment in remodeling existing buildings, the Scarritt-Bennett Center opened with an independent board of directors. The board was accountable to the Women's Division, which continued to underwrite much of its program. According to its mission statement, "Scarritt-Bennett Center is a place of hospitality, education for Christian ministries of justice and equality, reconciliation and renewal, cooperation and interaction within an ecumenical and global context. Rooted in mission, the Center has a strong commitment to eradication of racism, empowerment of women, education of laity, and spiritual formation."[21]

To fulfill its program mandate, the center scheduled opportunities for laypersons to pursue certified courses "to enhance their theological knowledge and deepen their personal growth." It sponsored workshops and retreats with a variety of themes for personal development. Special worship services were planned to celebrate liturgical festivals and community events. A multicultural consciousness pervaded the planning for all curricular and social events on the campus as well as the design for intentional dialogues on diversity held among a larger constituency throughout the southeast region and beyond.

While formal patterns of education and training for mission leadership could not be replaced, informal experiential learning opportunities were definitely in the ascendancy.

The growing popularity of voluntary service and mission travel seminars caused mission educators to find ways to infuse these experiences with intentional reflection, understanding, and growth. The Mission Education and Mission Volunteer program units of the Board developed study materials aimed at increasing participants' sensitivity to the context in which they visited or worked. Identifying cultural characteristics of the host church/community to enhance personal relationships developed through sharing work or hospitality was a significant contribution to a successful experience. It also helped visitors evaluate the influence of culture upon their own behavior and thus more effectively interpret their experiences when they returned home. While the Board was not able to keep pace with the vast numbers of groups experiencing "hands on" mission opportunities, it saw great potential in adding quality to the engagement for those who sought it.

The Impact of an Independent Mission Agency

The Theology of Mission Statement and the rewriting by General Conference of basic statements on theology offered a refuge for the mission program from the continuing theological and cultural conflicts within the church. The Mission Society for United Methodists (MSUM), created by a coterie of pastors and leaders from the increasingly vocal and successfully organized "evangelical" spectrum of church membership, was on a quest for wider recognition of its cause. To establish its organizational context and enlarge the constituency base for its new venture, MSUM made frequent allegations about the mission philosophy and practices of GBGM. The Mission Society alleged the Board was not responding to requests for missionaries from partner churches around the world, turning away applicants for missionary service because of their evangelical theological persuasion. MSUM would recruit and send missionaries with an evangelical persuasion. It alleged that GBGM and many mission partners/conferences/churches were not taking evangelistic initiatives in new areas or winning new converts to the gospel. MSUM would assist the churches with this work and send missionaries to begin new work where The UMC and mission partners were not presently engaged in this mission activity. It alleged that the GBGM emphasis on ecumenical cooperation and social development programs was not well understood and was distracting potential United Methodist support from programs of evangelism and church development. MSUM would provide an alternative channel for United Methodist donations to mission fields for evangelistic mission that would otherwise be lost to independent mission organizations or activities.

While coveting the status of an "independent" organization, the leaders of MSUM wanted their organization to be identified with The UMC. They did not ask the general church for permission to organize their mission society but incorporated the brand name "United Methodist(s)" into their title. Use of this name would give the society access to the churches and generous resources of the denominational membership without accepting the patterns of accountability of its connectional system. When the General Conference of 1988 and succeeding conferences re-affirmed GBGM as the official mission agency of the church, MSUM exploited the decision for its promotional purposes among the evangelical faction of the denomination, which was growing increasingly restless with general church policies and practices. It reacted when bishops decided not to appoint clergy members of their conferences to MSUM for missionary or

staff positions, and it gradually found sympathy from a handful of episcopal leaders who disagreed with their colleagues' interpretation/enforce-
ment of the general church's position.

The independent or alternative status of the new mission society was
more than a juridical problem within the denomination. It introduced
confusion and conflict among global mission partners who looked to the
GBGM as the sole administrator of United Methodist mission program
and policies. Methodist church leaders in Latin America were the most
vocal in describing the negative impact of MSUM unilateral missionary
activities in their countries. They sent a delegation to the meeting of
GBGM in April 1989 citing divisive actions of MSUM personnel in
Colombia, Paraguay, and Costa Rica. They viewed the existence of
MSUM as a further manifestation of a growing internal conflict within
The UMC that threatened the unity of the church not only in the U.S.
but throughout its global mission relationships. They therefore pleaded
with "The United Methodist Church . . . to clarify its position in relationship to this situation caused by its conflicts and to determine with
clarity which is the official organ responsible for establishing relationships on its behalf, as well as where and with what authority the Mission
Society for United Methodists can operate among the churches in Latin
America."[22]

Similar complaints were heard from leaders in other mission venues,
but not with the persistence of the churches in Latin America. Their geographic proximity to and informal networking within the churches of the
denomination in North America opened doors to both individual and
organized mission efforts from among constituencies newly energized by
the MSUM as well as the growing mission volunteer movement within
the denomination. Neither group really recognized the authority of
GBGM, nor the general church, in establishing its mission relationships.
Similar to MSUM, local church mission leaders worked directly with
individuals and institutions in neighboring countries of Latin America
(later elsewhere) to establish their mission projects and continuing mission relationships. They accepted and offered support without discrimination, whether it came through official connectional channels of The
UMC, MSUM, or any other agency or individual. Church officials in
host countries, as well as executives in GBGM, were often the last to
know about these local mission initiatives. Mission partners who looked
to the Board or the denomination to "control" this activity failed to recognize the nature of origin, strength of ownership, and scope of these

self-directed mission activities. MSUM was the organized and most identifiable manifestation of the popularization of mission and its devolution from denominational control to local initiative.

The phenomenon of self-directed and "hands on" mission experience by the local church constituencies generated a host of costs and benefits. The collaboration between the official mission agency and church leaders in mission contexts was complicated by a variety of third-party activities. Resources generated by local church initiatives and the MSUM were delivered directly to programs and projects without passing through a sending or receiving denominational agency. Hopes for any equitable distribution of mission funds according to a rational or comprehensive plan were eluded. Strategies for deployment and accountability of missionary personnel (or volunteers) to a common (receiving or sending) church were thwarted. Communications through a single administrative office of the official denominational mission agency grew increasingly irrelevant as the number of new locally or independently initiated projects grew exponentially. But local churches with direct (especially global) mission programs found rising levels of excitement and interest in their entire church program. They became growing churches. Their members participating in mission outreach programs or supporting an independent agency critically focused on a specific (or "new or innovative") person, place, or project found a greater sense of satisfaction from their efforts than channelling their support via a denominational agency. Firsthand exposure through personal and group visits to project sites afforded an understanding and appreciation for mission far beyond the capacity of a missionary to interpret in letters and an occasional home itineration visit.

This new passion for mission outdistanced the response of both MSUM and GBGM. The former was singularly focused on recruitment and placement of full-term missionaries. GBGM did not know how to relate to a program initiative that it could not fully own and operate. Both groups were distracted by focusing on their differences. The 1984 General Conference had hopes for resolving their differences through a mandatory dialogue hosted by the Council of Bishops. With little or no progress to report to the 1988 General Conference, continuation of the dialogues was encouraged but the conference excused the Council of Bishops from further participation.

The Board acknowledged the will of the General Conference for continued dialogue but intentionally shifted the ground from theological issues to more practical matters like complaints. GBGM wanted to focus on two subjects: "The use of criticisms of the Board for fund raising, and reported conflicts in mission field involvements."[23] As long as GBGM was perceived to be a legitimate target, MSUM had opportunities to exploit the newsworthiness of each conflict or contact with the Board for the promotion of its "alternative" channel for mission giving. MSUM had an expanding capacity to generate conflicts with increased support for a growing number of deployed missionaries. So the Board voted to establish a terminus to dialogues: "If after the next series of discussions there is not evidence of measurable progress toward a resolution of our differences with the Mission Society for United Methodists the dialogue will be discontinued."

Two controversies in Latin America were pivotal in the rise and fall of MSUM influence within the mission program of the denomination. In Costa Rica, MSUM was successful in making the newly elected Bishop Roberto Díaz beholden to them for financial support and building a popular base for his leadership within the Evangelical Methodist Church. Díaz, without benefit of a formal theological education himself, publicly criticized GBGM for its support of an ecumenical seminary in his country. The seminary enjoyed academic accreditation and recruited students from all of Latin America. The bishop accused the seminary of aiding and abetting the influence of Liberation Theology. This attack prompted MSUM to offer him help in establishing a Methodist seminary (Bible college) to train Methodist pastors in an evangelical context with a major focus upon reaching new followers. Díaz's criticisms of GBGM found a sympathetic hearing via frequent articles devoted to the matter in the *United Methodist Reporter*, which characterized the bishop's conflict with GBGM as a kind of David and Goliath contest. MSUM made the matter its *cause célèbre* and sent missionaries and funds to establish the school as well as their own organizational "stake" in the regional context. GBGM was left interpreting the internal dimensions of the conflict within the Costa Rican church and receiving appeals from aggrieved pastors within that church and leaders of Methodists church across the region who saw foreboding signs of a growing church schism. In dialogue with MSUM, GBGM and church leaders in the region offered this conflict as a case study on the divisive impact of having an "alternative" mission agency within the United Methodist mission program.

The second controversy also involved the manipulation of a leadership choice of a partner church. Carlos Huacani, a lay pastor of the Evangelical Methodist Church in Bolivia, was elected bishop of his church in a contested election in 1994. More than his predecessors, Huacani saw his election as an opportunity for controlling the patrimony of his church for partisan and personal interests. Not only did he proceed to appoint persons of his own political persuasion to offices in the church, but he quietly began mortgaging church-owned properties for personal gain. Dissatisfaction with his leadership quickly mounted within the church. A special church assembly was called to reverse Huacani's election and conduct a new election. Zacarias Mamani, who had previously served in the office, was elected. Huacani refused to live by the decision of the church and continued to portray himself as the bishop and Mamani as the leader of an unofficial faction. Huacani enjoyed a following among his Aymara-speaking constituency, primarily in the altiplano region. He rallied their support to influence government officials to recognize him as the legitimate bishop. Because the titles of many of the properties attached financially by Huacani were still held in the name of GBGM, the Board was asked by Mamani and his officers to intervene legally and administratively. Meanwhile, MSUM had concluded that the Board's role was questionable and defended Huacani. The society published a statement in the local Bolivian press in which it implied representation of itself as an official mission representative of The UMC that was in full support of Huacani. This tactic not only complicated matters within the church, but since such public notices in Bolivia have legal implications, it jeopardized the Board's legitimate claims to property ownership in the courts. After months of controversy which included public demonstrations, arrests, and rounds of costly litigation, the Bolivian courts found Huacani guilty of embezzling church funds. He was sentenced to prison and incarcerated. Only then did MSUM's support for him become mute in order to avoid embarrassment. The GBGM was left with a substantial price tag for its involvement in legal representation and provision of additional streams of funding for church programs and institutions in Bolivia which were threatened during the conflict.

Though the events in Bolivia also received extensive coverage by the church press, the attention span and interest among mission supporters began to decline. MSUM had already cultivated a loyal constituency to undergird its programs. A political consensus seemed to be emerging among leadership in the denomination to refrain from public treatment of the society as a pariah while still withholding any official status. GBGM had begun to reduce its vulnerability to criticism by taking a number of key program decisions, in particular creating a stronger profile for its work in mission evangelism.

Mission Evangelism

One of the major learnings from the conflicts over mission theology and program administration experienced in the 1970s and 1980s was how engagement in institutional defensiveness ignored the growing passion for mission developing in The UMC. Instead of offering a considerate and compassionate response and channel for participation by individuals and groups at the edges of the organizational mission structures of the church, the denominational mission program administered by GBGM presented the image of resistance, criticism, and judgment. If it did not change its posture, the cleavage in the denomination would only grow.

The leadership of GBGM persuaded the Board members in the 1985–1988 quadrennium to appropriate this learning and to initiate a new program and structural thrust aimed at addressing one of the most critical issues on the evangelical mission agenda. The keystone of the evangelical criticism of the mission program of the GBGM was the subordination of evangelistic mission to developmental and advocacy programs. The Board had maintained that its approach to evangelism was through effective cooperation and support of its mission partners, many of whom were reporting record growth in membership and outreach in their communities. The force and accuracy of this position was seldom heard over the high-decibel criticism leveled at the Board by its detractors. There was, nevertheless, a growing awareness within the Board that even the perception of a general default in a primary program area had to be treated as fact.

In a report on the status of the dialogues with MSUM, General Secretary Randolph Nugent presented a proposal to the meeting of GBGM in March 1987. It called for the creation of a new Mission Evangelism Program Department to respond to growing opportunities for proclamation of the gospel. He cited a growing world population with strong concentrations of migrants in major urban areas and large populations living in remote rural areas out of reach of development who have "lost hope and see no promise in life." He called upon the Board to invite into partnership other individuals and groups in the church to benefit from their experience and expertise in direct evangelism with the aim of lifting the whole church to "higher levels of faithfulness in sharing the good news."[24]

Any notions held by Board members to speak against an increased emphasis on evangelism were quickly dismissed, but the idea of a new department was not greeted with much enthusiasm. The proposal was amended with more structurally innocuous language, and then the idea of creating some kind of "programmatic structure" was referred for further study. The proposal was taken up again at the annual meeting in October 1987 and was adopted with the following language:

> A new programmatic structure on mission and evangelism be considered for addition to GBGM. Its purpose shall be to enable the Board in fulfilling its responsibility for proclaiming the Gospel in areas where it has not been heard. Its function will be to assist the Board through the World and National Divisions, and other units with such matters as:
>
> 1) Locating and identifying places and groups of people with a Christian witness or where the witness has not penetrated the culture;
>
> 2) Developing strategies for initiating ministries within and among these places and groups in consultation with mission partners, taking ecumenical relationships into account;
>
> 3) Nurturing newly gathered communities of Christians leading to the establishment of United Methodist congregations, enabling them to be linked to The United Methodist Church through missionary outreach of the GBGM;
>
> 4) Providing advice to the missionary selecting, training and placement processes of the Board with particular attention to the functions of evangelism and proclamation.[25]

Implementing the proposal presented a stronger challenge than introducing it. In amending the Board bylaws to accommodate the new "programmatic structure," organizational issues of staffing, authority, and budgeting all came to the fore. A new executive secretary with cabinet-level standing would be hired to oversee the work but without any direct supervisory authority over other executives with program responsibilities. (The cabinet comprised the general secretary, some administrative staff, and elected staff who were chief executives of the divisions and departments.) A new committee of directors was approved to make policy recommendations to the Board on the functions of the office. When the committee was formed at the beginning of the 1989–1992 quadrennium, influential directors were assigned to the committee, but they struggled to achieve an effective role among the longer-term vested interests within the Board organization. Their reports to the Board were always challenged as exceeding the limited authority granted to them in the bylaws. An executive was hired, never fully empowered to work with the program entities of the Board, and then perceived to be acting independently.

The major achievement of the Mission Evangelism Committee of the GBGM in its first years of existence was the facilitation of a new mission initiative in Senegal. At the urging of the committee, the program divisions of the Board were invited to identify places were there was then no Methodist witness and to undertake a feasibility study for beginning new work. General Secretary Nugent commended Senegal, where he believed the World Division could successfully build upon the effective agricultural development efforts funded by UMCOR. A task force including directors, staff, and an African church representative was organized and a process initiated to study, conduct interviews with ecumenical partners, make country visits, secure a formal invitation from governmental representatives, and then assign missionary personnel. The missionary deployment in Senegal was team-oriented, with persons recruited from both the North American and French-speaking African United Methodist churches. The major issue in this context remained exercising high-level sensitivity to interfaith relationships, since Senegal was 98 percent Muslim. While the expectations for growth of United Methodism had to be modified by this contextual reality, churches were organized and outreach ministries established in a manner that represented the fullest expression of the denomination's spiritual heritage of holistic ministry. The origins of this work were clearly rooted in the Board's decision to organize its resources to stimulate new efforts at evangelization.

In 1993, S T Kimbrough was hired to fill the vacant position of executive secretary for Mission Evangelism. He brought the rich background of theological studies and teaching combined with musical composition and performance. He immediately embraced the basic mandates of the committee by putting an emphasis upon "interpretation" of the spiritual development and evangelizing thrusts of the church's global mission partners. He networked with church musicians around the world and published a series of "Global Praise" hymns, songs, and worship resources with enrichment from the spiritual life of churches around the world. Other publications informed the church of the Board's evangelistic initiatives, such as developments in Russia and the Baltic states where the historic Methodist witness was being revived. A team composed of staff from GBGM and GBOD coordinated the development of educational resources to nurture new Christians and Methodists in several emerging churches in Asia, Europe, and Latin America. Renewed contacts were established with professors of mission and evangelism in United Methodist seminaries.

When Kimbrough had effectively demonstrated the value of his contributions to the Board's ongoing program thrusts, his leadership in developing new program ventures in evangelistic outreach was readily accepted. He undertook the research and made the initial probes that reopened Methodist churches in Lithuania and helped establish a Methodist witness in Cambodia and Nepal along with other Methodist churches in the region and in Switzerland. In each context he worked with emerging church leaders to identify and affirm their cultural gifts that would enrich Methodist Christian worship with indigenous hymns and liturgies.

How the gospel is shared among people of other living faiths became a critical issue in regions where Christianity was a small minority presence or was encountering vigorous activities of other faith groups. With the growth of Islam in the Southern Hemisphere and the rising frequency of encounters between Christians and Muslims in some contexts like Nigeria, a commitment to working with church leaders and missionary personnel in developing resources and promoting an understanding of the common roots and distinctive practices of these two great living faith groups was essential. Southeast Asia, where Methodism had more than a century of interaction with the Islamic faith and culture, was chosen as the venue for a trial dialogue.

Methodist leaders from the Philippines, Singapore, Malaysia, and Indonesia were invited to two dialogues, the first in July 1995 and the second in September 1997. Through small group dialogue, considerable data was produced on existing relationships between Christians and Muslims in their regional context. The United Methodist witness in this context was admittedly that of a religious minority, but its emphasis upon scriptural and social holiness offered a bridge to the larger society, including Muslim populations, through ministries of compassion and service. It was agreed that Methodism could promote harmony among people of these faith traditions. Leaders expressed the need for educational resources to help their members overcome their fear of the Muslim influence and authority so that they could act upon the strong values of their Wesleyan tradition. A resource prepared for the consultations by GBGM missionary Robert Hunt entitled *Islam in Southeast Asia* was highly valued by participants in the seminars and requested for publication and distribution in their churches. The value and importance of this initial dialogue commended the process for replication in other contexts.[26]

Organizational Context for Mission—Restructures

Many historical streams of church life and mission involvement flowed into the organized structure responsible for administering the mission programs of The UMC. The existence of various continuing corporations with origins in predecessor denominations was one indicator of the multiple legacies given legal protection within GBGM. Prior to church union in 1968, The Methodist Church owned the distinction of managing the most far-reaching mission organization of any Protestant denomination.

Implementation of 1964 Agreements

Until 1964, the administration of the program was divided by sources of funding. The Woman's Division of the Board of Missions cultivated strong support for the programs of national and world mission it operated. The National and World divisions of the Board of Missions received direct funding from the World Service fund of the denomination for their programs. This came to be considered by many denominational leaders (overwhelmingly male at that time in history) as an expensive form of "parallel administration" of mission programs belonging to The Methodist Church. The 1964 Agreements, entered into by representatives of the Council of Bishops and the Board of Missions (but never ratified by the Woman's Division), folded the program administration of the Woman's Division into the management units of the National and World divisions and the Committee on Education and Cultivation. The Woman's Division, which had made a formidable investment in the mission program of the denomination, was left charting a new course. Resisting devolution into a fund-raising unit for other units of mission, the leadership worked tirelessly at infusing the Board's administrative and policymaking functions with their historic program values in serving the needs of women and children and channelling their financial resources to accomplish the same.

As part of its monitoring of the implementation of the 1964 Agreements, the Women's Division called for a major review at ten years into the "new" administration of their historic work by other units of the Board. Common themes in their assessment of the status of their program interests in the Board were: appropriate levels of women staffing in Board units and in related projects; continuation of mission education programs for children, youth, and university students; adequacy of patterns of property maintenance and improvement; frequency and effectiveness of training and measures of accountability for project supervisory personnel on administrative relationships to the divisions; participation of women in consultations with mission agency partners on program directions or policy development; and interpretation and enforcement of guidelines for use of designated funds from the Women's Division.[27]

Never satisfied that its vital program interests were effectively transferable to other units of the Board, the Women's Division gradually introduced more direct measures for influencing the administration of the mission programs it continued to fund. The greatest vulnerability was felt to be its loss of direct funding and communication channels with its program constituencies of women and youth in churches and projects around the world and the agencies and institutions it founded in regions of the U.S. The division sought to address this deficiency in the 1993–1996 quadrennium, when "joint committees" were structured for administering the budgeted and other program resources of the Women's Division for national and international ministries with women, children, and youth. Executives from the division's staff cabinet were assigned to manage corresponding (National Ministries and International Ministries) staff teams from the three divisions (World, National, and Women's) that made funding recommendations directly to the appropriate committees.

The Women's Division also resumed direct management of its own publications and promotional materials. A division staff member was appointed to direct the work of the Service Center in Cincinnati, Ohio. The editor of *Response* magazine was returned to the division staff from Education and Cultivation. A new emphasis on marketing emerged with the realization that changing social and demographic patterns of the constituency required more creative approaches to attract new membership and increased support. While introducing these internal changes with no small impact on other units of the Board, the Women's Division remained involved but generally unaffected by structural changes of the general board.

Health and Welfare

The general restructure of the denomination adopted at the 1972 General Conference brought new program entities into the Board of Global Ministries. The Board of Health and Welfare Ministries (previously Board of Hospitals and Homes) was reconstituted as one of seven divisions of the new Board of Global Ministries.[28] Its offices were located in Evanston, Illinois. The initial reluctance of this unit to give up its independence may have been reflected in the lengthy process of closing out its offices and moving staff to the new headquarters in New York. While the goal of the framers of the new structure was to provide a holistic vision and approach to the delivery of health services through the mission agency of the church, there was considerable confusion within the Board over existing program mandates and functional boundaries of Health and Welfare, National Division, World Division, and the Women's Division.

The National Division approached health matters from its theoretical and practical mission base in community empowerment with particular attention to participation of racial/ethnic and impoverished populations and service to them. The World Division had responsibility for administering medical mission personnel and resourcing clinics and hospitals of the mission churches globally. The Women's Division maintained funding for and owned the property and facilities of health institutions in the U.S. and other countries. Each unit engaged in advocacy for public policies that advanced health services. The new Health and Welfare Division brought into the Board its service and credentialing relationships to a variety of institutions managed by the U.S. annual conferences serving children, youth, and aging populations.

These health-related program responsibilities were assigned to the divisions by the *Book of Discipline*, and the leadership of each understood them to be an exclusive domain. Integrating these independent functions into a common mission strategy or management structure was never fully achieved, but agreements, or accommodations, were reached between divisions. The National Division accepted the professional services of a staff member of the Health and Welfare Division in fulfilling its administrative responsibilities for mission health agencies in its portfolio. The World

Division staff member providing missionary health services and consultant services to mission hospitals was transferred to the Health and Welfare Division but also maintained an office in the World Division. To implement these agreements, the National and World divisions transferred to the Health and Welfare Division an appropriate amount of their World Service (apportionment) funding.

The reception of the Health and Welfare Division into the Board of Global Ministries was made more complicated by a heated labor dispute at one of its hospitals. The Pikeville Hospital in Kentucky, in the throes of a strike by its organized workers, appealed to the division for intervention. The division entered the fray on the side of the hospital management, only to find National Division sympathies and support for the workers. This action prompted many to question whether the division could accept the mission perspective of the other divisions which operated with an increasingly popular preferential option for the poor and the oppressed. When the Health and Welfare Division broadened its program reach beyond institutional ministries to address such issues as women's health, preventive health care (adopting the international health community emphasis upon Health for All by the Year 2000), ministries with persons with handicapping conditions, parish nurse (congregational health ministries) programs, and the AIDS pandemic, the questions of the more assertive mission-minded constituencies were addressed, but the more traditional clients, especially institutional administrators, became restless.

The tensions reached a crescendo when a lawsuit was filed against Pacific Homes, Inc., a California retirement center related to the Pacific and Southwest Conference of The UMC. This agency had issued lifetime care contracts to its clients without providing and protecting sufficient reserve funding to guarantee its performance. The suit, brought by residents of the home, named as defendants the local agency, the annual conference, The UMC, and the Health and Welfare Division of the Board of Global Ministries as the "certifying" agency of the denomination. Plaintiffs sought millions of dollars in damages. Attorneys representing the Board spent months and years in costly litigation efforts. World Service funds of the Board had to be set aside for attorneys' fees and ultimately damages when the case was lost. Risk protection from potentially massive liabilities related to Health and Welfare's certification of United Methodist–related service institutions became a prominent mission issue. The certification process had to be redefined but without abdicating a responsible mission and ministry to populations served. Ultimately, the Health and Welfare Association, an organized network of agency administrators and directors, dropped its affiliation with GBGM and took on the task of issuing accreditation as an independent agency for its membership comprising United Methodist service institutions.

Throughout the trials, Health and Welfare remained a vital program ministry within GBGM. It provided professional counsel for the management of mission medical institutions, offered leadership development grants, initiated new program directions (mentioned above), and participated in Boardwide program developments like the Russia Initiative. It demonstrated the lasting nature of the relationship of healing ministries to the outreach mission programs of the denomination.

Ecumenical and Interreligious Concerns (EIC)

The small (single executive), relatively young (three years), and independent agency of the denomination working on issues of Christian unity and interfaith relations was destined to find new lodging in the restructure of 1972. The program affinity between Christian unity and mission commended it for inclusion in the mission agency. The fact that it was given status as a division in spite of its lightweight staffing and organizational components was a testimony to the significance of the denomination's commitment to ecumenical cooperation. But even with increased staffing, the organizational demands and expectations of the complex organizational structure of the Board of Global Ministries were often more than the new division could handle. It nevertheless made a valiant effort.

The infusion of a witness to the visible unity of the church into the mission strategy and programs of the denomination may have been too visionary. Board policies and administrative practices were strongly influenced by the bilateral nature (direct relationships between organic bodies of the same denomination) of historic missionary relationships. Developing joint denominational funding for missionary positions in countries where two or more denominational mission boards were represented was sometimes attempted but was not a common practice. Cooperation in areas of new program development was often more successful than achieving it in traditional or established program activities. Joint efforts with other denominations in church development efforts, like the planned community in Columbia, Maryland, were accomplished with a singular intentionality. Such Board ventures would probably have been carried out without the presence of the EIC. But even the thought of monitoring the thousands of project relationships of the Board of Global Ministries for discovering ecumenical opportunities was simply beyond the capacity of the new division. Asking the other divisions for accountability through reporting was often interpreted as busy work.

Major program funding for the programs of the NCC and the WCC resided securely in the budgets of the World, National, and Women's divisions. Even though the Council on Finance and Administration of the denomination looked to the EIC for administrative authority for the Interdenominational Cooperation Fund (an apportionment levied upon churches for the administrative costs of these church councils), no thought was given to transferring responsibility for the Board's program funding of the councils to the EIC. Neither was there any strong interest given to a coordinating role. Division executives selected to serve on the boards of ecumenical organizations would often meet their counterparts from other divisions of the Board at the meeting tables of the councils without an appreciation of the cumulative effect of their units' individual commitments.

Unlike other units of the Board, the EIC did not have a strong linkage within conferences and local churches. A section on "Studies and Interpretation" was created within the division to "develop a network of ecumenically concerned United Methodists" to help with building a membership base for pursuing the mission of Christian unity.[29] The division published materials for distribution to the connectional units of the church. In its previous life, the EIC had cultivated a close working relationship with the Council of Bishops, who were given ultimate responsibility for ecumenical representation. The council probably provided a stronger interpretive voice and better sounding board for many aspects of its work than either ecumenical advocates in the conferences or the mission agency. The bishops were quicker in their appreciation for the full ecclesiastical implications of the denomination's participation in the Consultation on Church Union than GBGM. Formal dialogues with other denominational or faith traditions frequently required an episcopal presence to match the presence of hierarchy in other delegations. Bishops needed to be involved in reviewing drafts of significant ecumenical study documents like *Baptism, Eucharist and Ministry* before they were released for distribution to the churches for response. The council was mandated by the *Book of Discipline* to consider any concordat agreements with other church bodies before they were presented to the General Conference for adoption.[30]

The "interreligious concerns" function of EIC had considerable coherence with the need of the mission agency to understand and relate its program strategies to changing mission contexts. The division was a strong proponent of interfaith dialogue based on conversations initiated by Christian study centers around the world. Dialogue represented a shift in mission strategy away from mission *to* persons of other faiths to discovery of a shared responsibility *for* the future of all humanity. In the words of the Reverend Robert L. Turnipseed, an EIC executive, "This shift suggests a recognition of a new historical situation where Christians must find ways to live together with persons of other faiths and ways to solve the fundamental human problems which threaten the survival of humanity itself."[31] The consequences of failing to grasp opportunities to understand persons of different cultures, faiths, and ideologies were becoming evident in all societies. The fundamental problems to which Turnipseed referred included questions such as: How do Christians function responsibly in contexts of growing pluralism; in the multireligious communities of Asia; in North Africa countries affected by the growth of Islam; among base communities in Latin America embracing revolutionary ideologies in the struggle against economic and political oppression; in technologically oriented communities in the West showing signs of new quests for spirituality; and in communities polarized by conflicting ideologies of Cold War politics? The urgency and practicality of dialogue had been overshadowed by the resurgence of racism, new claims of cultural superiority, and expressions of a strongly organized militant fundamentalism in most major religions. In The UMC, the still small voice of the EIC went largely unheeded, and its witness to the importance of building true *oikoumene* or world community was diminished.

In 1978, the EIC officially informed the Board that it was entertaining questions about where it should be located. The directors had considered a number of options but were studying two, namely: "to continue as a division of the Board of Global Ministries; or to become a Standing Commission, such as the Commission on the Status and Role of Women."[32] The latter option prevailed, and a petition for separation and independent commission status was prepared and adopted by the 1980 General Conference. The new Commission on Ecumenical Concerns and Interreligious Affairs continued to reside in its New York location and to benefit from GBGM support services.

1984 Restructure of GBGM

After a decade of trying to make the 1972 restructure of the mission agency work, including much wrangling over correcting denominational mission objectives for sensitivity to racial/ethnic inclusiveness, encouraging mutuality in mission development with global and national partners, accommodating emerging theological and cultural critiques, and balancing intense mission perspectives of supporting constituencies, the 1980 General Conference mandated another restructure of GBGM. The resolution gave authority to the Board to complete the process and begin implementation ad interim (between sessions of the General Conference), but it had to be done with the guidance and assistance of GCOM.

A high-level Board committee was appointed to undertake the task. The Committee of Ten worked quite independently and reported directly to the Board. Through dialogue with a similar group of directors and staff appointed by GCOM, every effort was made to hear and discern the input from both antagonists and protagonists of GBGM. Some of the voices called for creating a strong missionary unit within the Board, others wanted a unit on mission volunteers, and there were also calls for a unit on mission evangelism. In anticipation of the task, the Board Research and Development Committee had begun a study of all the functions and services of the Board and the constituencies they served to determine where, if any, overlap or duplication of program existed.[33] And a random sampling of church leaders with a variety of experience within its connectional life offered some clues as to how this constituency understood and valued the Board's mission administration and services.

With all of the data at its command, the Committee of Ten concluded that the major issues were of a management nature and set out developing a plan to achieve what it called "administrative flexibility" with only minor structural implications. The plan sought to strengthen the central management structure of the Board on both policymaking and administrative levels of the organization. The authority of the Board Committee on Personnel was strengthened, making it, rather than division committees, responsible for filling all elected staff positions upon recommendation of the general secretary. The general secretary was also given authority for recommending the distribution of the World Service funding to the funded divisions (exceptions were the Women's Division and UMCOR) and the allocation of all general contingency funds for program. These changes reduced some of the autonomy of the units of the Board and gave the chief operating officer of the organization a greater capacity to implement the program directions he presented to the Board.

The plan for administrative flexibility tried to influence program development and coordination, which had become pretty unwieldy in no less than seven supposedly equal centers of program initiation and direction. It empowered only three units of the Board as "divisions." The Women's Division would function as the policymaking body for the membership of UMW. World and National were identified as "program divisions" where major contextual program directions would be established and managed. The remaining four units (Mission Personnel, Mission Education and Cultivation, United Methodist Committee on Relief, and Health and Welfare Ministries) were classified as "program departments," which would use their program resources to complement the work of the divisions in their specific areas of specialization.

Directors elected to the Board were to be oriented to their primary membership at the Board organizational level. Here they would set the policy direction based upon the work of its standing committees. Standing committees were charged with general oversight of the Board's primary functions of making policies and setting program direction. A comprehensive plan for mission developed by the Research and Development Committee, an appropriations budget proposed by the Finance Committee, and an elected staff leadership cadre nominated by the Personnel Committee were approved in Board plenary for all of the units of the Board. Once these actions were taken, the directors were then to carry the direction from the Board to their unit assignments, first to one of two program divisions (World or National) and then either to a program department or to a standing committee. The members were also to serve an integrating function and promote Board unity as they crossed over these organizational lines, but most found loyalties to the individual units hard to resist. The staff also found it difficult to develop an appreciation for distinctions between divisions and departments to which they were assigned. But the ascending role of the general secretary within the Board was easily recognized. The position moved from a leveling influence among the three major divisions of the Board to a central authority in key matters of personnel, program planning, and budgeting.

1996 Restructure of GBGM

The final restructure of the century was provoked by two actions of the 1992 General Conference. The first was the decision, by a small majority vote, to approve a study that would recommend a new headquarters location (other than New York) for GBGM. The second was to give encouragement to the Council of Bishops to further its study of the implications for restructuring the denomination to reflect the increasingly global characteristics of the church. The missional implications of both of these issues will be addressed further but are noted here because they symbolize a continuing dissatisfaction with the administration of mission of The UMC.

The most telling action was the matter of the mission headquarters location. Critics of GBGM, who had tried unsuccessfully to introduce their reforms through previously mandated restructures, began demanding relocation of the headquarters. Many arguments were advanced, especially financial savings from moving to an area with a lower cost of living, but the unspoken motivation was probably to achieve a wholesale restaffing of the organization. This was seen as the only sure method of realizing a change in program direction.

Relocation of GBGM had been discussed at previous General Conferences, but it became the "hot button" issue in Louisville at the 1992 General Conference, which showed little empathy for continuing business as usual by any of the general church agencies. This attitude engendered some support for the call for a total restructuring of the denomination around its increasing vision for becoming a truly global organization, but it was expressed with a certain venom in the debate and vote on Board relocation.

When the directors elected to GBGM met at the first meeting of the new quadrennium in 1992, a small leadership group requested plenary time to reflect on the meaning of General Conference actions. After lengthy table conversations several issues were identified. There was a consensus on two points. First, that GBGM was too large and complex to function with efficiency the denomination expected. Second, that the Board needed to become more responsive to the wishes (mission objectives) of the leadership and membership of the annual conferences of the church. To address these concerns, a proposal from the Research and Development Committee was adopted to "hold Annual Conference dialogue groups focused on United Methodist missional concerns." The committee hoped that such dialogues would open doors to cooperation and contribute to the "development and replication of mission models to connect local church mission initiatives with the GBGM." And finally, it called for the "examination of governance and management issues as well as internal structures and functions for a more effective and efficient operation of mission."[34]

Dialogues were scheduled and conducted with the leadership of all of the annual conferences in the U.S. and with the central conferences. They were completed in a timely fashion to feed information into the Board's legislative process for the 1996 General Conference. While the content of the dialogues was instructive, the forcefulness of the schedule kept the Board dealing with constituency concerns on an ongoing basis. The listening process influenced both program development, which became much more collaborative with the conferences, and the Board's efforts to develop a responsive organizational structure. There was a growing awareness that if the Board did not take action on a major reorganization, it would face a strong reaction from the 1996 General Conference.

The Board named an official committee to steer its reorganization efforts. It also appointed representatives to sit on the general church committee on headquarters relocation. All the while, it had to keep alert to the work of the general church commission on restructuring for a global church. The first issue was the size of the Board. With no little struggle over the matter, the directors voted to cut the membership of the Board nearly in half, from 191 to 89. This action was taken with many factors in mind, including proportionate representation from central conferences and former missionary — now ethnic language — conferences in the U.S., and the Women's Division (in order to remain consistent with guarantees of representation in the 1964 Agreements).

The second major objective was to reduce the complexity of the Board structure. The committee keyed in on the separate corporate identities of the major divisions and other units which had generated a host of committees and crossover relationships which complicated the task of nominations and burdened individual directors with numerous assignments that the Board meeting schedule often failed to accommodate. It took on the daunting task of proposing the elimination of divisions and departments and of completely reorganizing around broad-based program responsibilities or functions. The only exceptions were the Women's

Division and UMCOR, whose program and constituency responsibilities as well as fiscal mandates required a continuing autonomy within the Board. A similar exception was granted to Health and Welfare Ministries to address legal requirements of an estate producing considerable financial benefits to its program.

The axiom of globality permeated every consideration of this restructure. In a global context, any division of labor around the concept of geographic boundaries seemed to be a contradiction. So the historic standing of the National and World divisions was moot. All programs and program resources of the Board were to be at the disposal of realizing a global mission mandate. Functions became the organizing principle and defined the new program/administrative structure. A program area on Evangelization and Church Growth accommodated church development activities of the former divisions and facilitated the work with conferences in new congregational development initiatives globally. A program area on Church and Community Ministries gave lodging to programs of urban ministries, town and country ministries, community development, and economic development. Mission Contexts and Relationships would provide oversight of both strategy development and administration of global mission relationships to conferences, partner churches, ecumenical bodies, and programs of leadership development. Mission Education focused on developing a curricular approach to preparing the church constituency to understand and interpret the mission directions of the church. Health and Relief incorporated the work of Health and Welfare and UMCOR into a single administration. Mission Personnel administered missionary services, including recruitment, selection, training, placement, and supervision. Mission Volunteers responded to the growing demand for direct involvement of constituent groups in opportunities for mission engagement beyond their communities.

Governance in the new Board structure was to become a function of the whole body of directors meeting in plenaries. The major standing committees of the Board, the general secretary, and the cabinet—rather than the program areas—would present proposals for action. The program areas had directors assigned and met at Board meetings to review and plan for the administration of mission programs but could only recommend new policy initiatives to standing committees for development and presentation to the Board. New proposals were to be global in vision and Boardwide in scope, not the single agenda of one of the units. To that

Bishop Joel N. Martínez became the first Hispanic to be elected head of a general program agency when he was named president of GBGM in 2000. *(Photo courtesy of UM Archives and History)*

end the Finance Committee presented one comprehensive budget, rather than having each unit offer its own. The Mission Development Committee developed a comprehensive plan for mission to address all of the program responsibilities and evaluated individual programs on the basis of their contribution to a holistic mission. The Personnel Committee established and enforced employment policies across the Board. The Committee on Bylaws and Legislation rolled up the organizational guidelines and requirements of all the units into a single Boardwide document. It developed one packet legislation for the Board to consider sending to General Conference.

To enhance further organizational unity and global vision, staffing assignments to various program portfolios were to be augmented by appointments to various crossfunctional teams. In teams the staff members would contribute their program expertise and experience to developing projects or exploring issues of both an urgent and developmental nature. They were to be accountable to the Board cabinet, sponsored by assigned cabinet members, and managed by elected staff.[35] While staff teams were not an entirely new development, the concept was to be given more general application throughout the Board with a more far-reaching recruitment of personnel. Persons with abilities that exceeded the requirements of their organizational posting were given opportunities to make greater contributions to the mission development process of the Board.

This Board reorganization, more than any previous attempt, stimulated positive behavioral change. This resulted from Board ownership of the decision, in part because it chose to move ahead with restructure to avoid consequences of actions anticipated by the next General Conference. Moreover, the pervasive trend toward direct involvement in mission by constituent groups in conferences and local churches had proven that the mission of the church was no longer dependent upon the initiation and management by a general church agency. There was plenty of creativity and interest abroad in the church and seemingly expandable resources for accomplishing mission when the local membership was involved. The attitude of the Board was changing from "What do you want from us?" to "How can we help you accomplish that?" The Board's response to the latter question was not fully spelled out in its structural recommendations but became apparent in the number of new program initiatives that began developing (discussed in chapter 6).

The 1996 General Conference received the reorganization of GBGM with neither resistance nor any acclamation. The delegates were more interested in the recommendation of the GBGM Headquarters Relocation Committee. After investing more than a million dollars and utilizing the services of a professional real estate management firm to research alternatives, the committee's recommendation was a site in Reston, Virginia (suburban Washington, D.C.). Among the finalists were Atlanta, Chicago, Dallas, and Denver, reflecting the regional distribution of church membership in the U.S. While the final recommendation may have satisfied the internal politics of the committee, it was not acceptable to General Conference. The reactive judgment repeated by more than one delegate was: "If there is one location worse than New York, it is Washington." Other delegates from the Southeast Jurisdiction got on the bandwagon of an alternative petition by supporting a location in the Atlanta vicinity. Neither the report of the committee nor any alternative was supported by the General Conference. The Board headquarters remained in New York, and the Board began making preparations for its new life in familiar but newly renovated offices.

Conclusion

The search for common ground in developing the mission of The UMC has been a major but disappointing enterprise. Throughout this struggle, the church probably learned more about its differences than it expected. Like other institutions, the cultural forces of a growing pluralism engaged the denomination in North America, awakening it to the political claims from others for self-determination, national independence, and then the perplexing realities of the emerging economic globalization. Defensive postures and self-preservation equally matched bold and revolutionary rhetoric. The denomination survived into the twenty-first century with scrapes and bruises from internal skirmishes, but still intact. As much as conflicting philosophies of mission unravelled the fabric of church unity, the church's strong heart for mission impelled it onward. The UMC had not squandered the vision of the Wesleys for a ministry to the whole person, addressing both personal and social holiness. Too much of the church's time, attention, and resources had been directed to the conflict over varying approaches to realizing this mission, but its continuing presence in critical contexts for mission during the last quarter century was seldom interrupted. The structures, leaders, directions, and purposes of its mission had been questioned, even while the effectiveness of its ministry through a global connectional commitment intensified. No organization or unit of The UMC needed to shrink from the heat of criticism and self-examination when the process yielded a greater appreciation for the redeeming activity of a God in the world to which the church was called to faithful witness and service.

CHAPTER 6

A Survey of Asia

*T*HE VASTNESS and complexity of Asia require that it be treated in re-gional contexts. The history and culture, including the history of Christian mission, in each region varies considerably.

Context Northeast Asia

Missiological researcher David Barrett has noted: "Before 1980, most Western Christians regarded the Far East as hostile to the Christian faith. . . . Today there is in place in East Asia a massive Christian Colossus of 80 million Christians, mostly Chinese, Korean, and Japanese."[1] In 1980 he estimated the number of Christians in the region at 16 million, making the rate of growth an impressive 550 percent.

China

In the twentieth century, the missionary movement in China experi-enced remarkable growth. According to Tracey K. Jones, former China missionary: "In 1949 there were thousands of Christian churches, dozens of denominations, three hundred Christian hospitals, thirteen Christian universities, more than a thousand Christian high schools, and several thousand Christian elementary schools." Following the successful revolu-tion of the forces of Mao Zedong, church properties were confiscated and the institutions run by the government. In the late 1960s, "everything was gone except for the Christ centered faithfulness of thousands upon thou-sands of Chinese Christians."

Christianity had always been considered a foreign religion as long as it existed in China, something that the revolution readily exploited. Ac-cording to Jones, only when all evidences of Christianity were officially

K. H. Ting had served in the ecumenical student movement before returning to China and eventually becoming head of the China Christian Council. He presided over an extraordinary growth in non-Roman Catholic Christian churches in China, despite the totalitarian government. *(Photo courtesy of UM Archives and History)*

banned in the 1960s and 1970s did the attitude of the Chinese people begin to change. Because Christians were not spared the excesses of the revolutionary fervor, the Chinese public began to accept its religion as rooted in Chinese history and values. Christians used the long hard years of criticism, ridicule, and forced labor to exercise spiritual disciplines of self-reflection. They were open to learning from past mistakes. With the death of Mao in 1976 and the changes in government, there was a gradual lifting of restrictions on religion. Surviving Chinese Christians found the "courage and patience to argue their case before the highest authorities that Christians deserved to be recognized as a religious community that was both Chinese and Christian."[2]

In 1982, the new constitution of the People's Republic of China (PRC) included a provision recognizing Christianity as one of the religions of China. The China Christian Council (CCC) became the official government-recognized structure for the promulgation of Protestant Christianity in the PRC. The formation of the council was the beginning of the "postdenominational period" in China, which embraced the historic cultural principles of the "three-self movement"—self-governance, self-support, and self-propagation. All cooperation with the CCC objective of self-determination would be developed on a nondenominational or ecumenical basis and in harmony with its purpose of creating a distinctively Chinese expression of the Christian faith.

The changes in mainland China prompted denominations to rethink further their own mission policies and program strategies. The United Methodist Church (UMC) had already established in its Board of Global Ministries a China program that maintained a liaison with Christian leaders in China and published educational materials for the large number of constituents interested in following developments in what had been one of its major mission fields. This work was funded by earned interest from reserve funds that had to be frozen because of the break in United States political relations with China and the demise of mission projects and institutions under Communist rule. In 1971, the mainline Communist government won sufficient support to replace Taiwan on the Security Council of the United Nations. There were further signs of liberalization of Communist rule within the country and increased acceptance of the role of the PRC in the world economic community. But U.S. anti-Communist foreign policy and its military involvement in southeast Asia during the 1970s heightened attitudes of U.S. hostility toward Communist China. Even though the National Council of the Churches of Christ in the U.S.A. (NCC) had earlier advocated full political recognition of the PRC, the position of The UMC remained in support of an ambiguous "one China" policy.

The 1984 General Conference of The UMC considered and adopted a twofold resolution that reflected changes in both the China church and political realities. It acknowledged responsibility for past mission policies that lacked cultural sensitivity and a commitment to Christian unity: "We are aware of historic links between the missionary movement and imperialism, and the movement's identification with economic and political forces which have been detrimental to its witness to Christ. . . . As the church renews its covenant of witness, ministry, and mission, it does so with deep repentance and humility, accepting God's forgiveness and seeking the forgiveness of those it has wronged."

In response, the China program of The UMC accelerated the pace of its work but through a collaborative relationship with other denominations. The NCC became the primary channel for denominations in the

U.S. to support those programs of the China Christian Council for which it turned to the world church community for assistance. A major task was the development of clergy and lay leadership for its expanding church membership. Humanitarian aid was channelled through the Amity Foundation, a subsidiary of the CCC that effectively developed many non-sectarian social programs and provided institutional services. Amity also operated a strong educational program for which it placed foreign personnel in schools and universities around China. The China program coordinated the recruitment of United Methodist personnel for the English-language instruction component of the program.

The 1984 General Conference also went on record affirming the "establishment of full diplomatic relations between the U.S. and the People's Republic of China." It recognized the importance of creating strong ties between the two countries for influencing "peace and stability of the Asia region." In particular, it called for a "peaceful approach to ending the long-standing conflict between the governments in the People's Republic of China and in Taiwan," but it recognized that "the resolution of the status of Taiwan is a matter for the Chinese people themselves."[3]

The immediate effects of the official PRC recognition of Christianity were quite dramatic. Church properties that had been taken over for warehouses and factories were returned and renovated by the CCC. The churches were soon filled to capacity for Sunday services of worship. More than twelve million Protestants were members of 15,000 churches related to the CCC by the early 1990s. Unofficial house churches added substantially to that number. A publishing house, Amity Press, was established near Nanjing, and more than thirteen million Bibles were printed and distributed in China. Seventeen Protestant seminaries trained young people for ministry. The Roman Catholic Church in China followed a similar trajectory of development, though it was divided between the Catholic Patriotic Association, which is government recognized, and the traditional Catholic church with ties to Rome.

In 1989, university students who resisted many restrictive academic and economic policies of the government radicalized the movement for democracy in the PRC. Demonstrations in Tiananmen Square in Beijing reached a point of confrontation with military units. At the height of the encounter, and before the demonstrators were crushed by military force, Bishop K. H. Ting, president of the CCC, communicated with mission agencies of the world Christian community. The General Board of Global

Ministries (GBGM) received a fax message with the text from Amos: "Let justice roll down like waters, and righteousness like a mighty stream." And a brief commentary: "We are with our people in this time of suffering and uncertainty." The CCC was living into its pastoral and prophetic role within the constraints of a changing but mercurial political context.

While the postmissionary struggles of the church in China have been focused upon raising up a truly Chinese church, a new generation of church leaders was looking forward to renew fellowship in the world church community. The Reverend Gao Ying, a young pastor and representative of the China Christian Council wrote: "There was a time when the selfhood of the church became for the church in China almost the one central truth of the Gospel. Today, we still maintain that it is important for the church in China or anywhere else to possess its own identity. . . . But we are glad that the pendulum has swung back to a point where we can see that we should not talk exclusively about the selfhood of our church. It is not enough . . . to be preoccupied constantly and narrowly with its selfhood. I am pleased to see the Chinese church rebuilding its friendship with the international church community. The church in China seeks both the unity of all Christians in our country and solidarity with all Christians abroad."[4]

In 1997, the city of Hong Kong was returned to the Chinese people by the British government. This historic event was observed by the CCC as part of a formal celebration of the 150th anniversary of the arrival of the first Methodist missionaries in Foochow (modern Fuzhou). A delegation accompanied by Jones went to Hong Kong to mark the arrival of Moses and Isabel White in 1847, and then went on to Foochow, where Methodism in China first took root. Jones said: "They would never have dreamed . . . or expected that the handful of Chinese Christians in China at that time would become through their suffering and faithfulness a hundred and fifty years later a truly Chinese self governing, self supporting, self propagating church number in the many millions. Such is the way that the mysterious power of God . . . has been at work."[5]

Since the return of Hong Kong, church relationships have been experiencing a redefinition. In 2000, the historic mission relationships to the Hong Kong churches established by missionaries of the former Methodist and Evangelical United Brethren churches remained unchanged. A new generation of leadership may need to emerge before unity with the mainland Christian community can be experienced. Taiwan's future was more uncertain. The political distance between Beijing and Taiwan was growing. The Presbyterian Church has been most vocal among the churches in pursuing independence for the people of Taiwan. The remarkable development of commercial and technological skills by the Taiwanese seemed to increase its potential for exploiting connections to the world community for support.

Korea

The most celebrated mission story of Korea is church growth and social witness. The thirty years that closed the twentieth century were characterized by the same assertive evangelization efforts of the missionaries who introduced Christianity during the Japan occupation (1905–1945) and the gifted converts who successfully established the church in the post–World War II and Korean War periods. In 2000, more than 30 percent of the population of South Korea was Christian, comprising 15 million persons, the largest penetration of any Asian country save the Philippines.[6]

Missionary endeavors in Korea drew successfully upon the strong spiritual foundations that are a part of the culture. Some of the shamanistic spiritual values, e.g., wealth, health, respect, family, and welfare, have given shape to the Christian witness in the Korean context.[7] Likewise, Koreans have found a certain resonance between the many incidents of suffering from political and social repression in their history and the biblical stories of the journeys of the people of God. The remarkable discipline of discipleship practiced by Korean Christians has made it a formidable force in world Christianity. The Korean Methodist Church (KMC), by setting annual membership growth goals, has become the second-largest in the world Methodist family with more than one million members.

Church development in Korea began under government control but by the end of the twentieth century many of the world's largest Christian churches, including Methodists, were to be found in Korea. Churches like Kwan Lim Methodist Church, founded by the Reverend Sundo Kim in Seoul, became one of several churches with memberships of more than 10,000. Such megachurches were capable of functioning independently of denominational influence. Their holdings included broadcasting and publishing facilities, mission and evangelization agencies, and educational institutions. While much attention was given to their strategies for church growth, there were also hundreds of small membership churches struggling to survive in rural areas.

In 1976, Dr. Lee Tai Young, a prominent Methodist lawyer and leader in the women's legal rights movement, was arrested in South Korea with others for observing Korean Patriots Day. She became a symbol of the struggle for human rights in South Korea and the church's support of the movement. *(Photo courtesy of UM Archives and History)*

In celebrating the strong institutional development of the churches in Korea, the prophetic witness of church leaders during this period must not be overlooked. In 1972, with an allusion to the heightening of tensions between Communist Democratic Republic of Korea (North Korea) and the Republic of Korea (South Korea), the Seoul government forcibly imposed a new constitution under the declared state of martial law. The conditions prohibited any discussion of issues that would normally prevail under the rule of civil law. Protestors, including pastors and church leaders, were arrested and subjected to military tribunals and lengthy prison terms. In 1974, the Board of Global Ministries endorsed a resolution of support for the church leaders and called upon the Korean government to rescind its state of emergency and for the U.S. Government to intervene to protect human rights.

In 1976, Dr. Lee Tai Young, a prominent Methodist lawyer and leader in the women's legal rights movement, was arrested along with nineteen other men and women, including the president of Church Women United in Korea. The occasion was their participation in the public observance of an historic day of March 1, 1919, when Korean Patriots—including many

Christians — staged an unsuccessful uprising against the occupying forces of Japan. The demonstrators focused their protest upon the many human rights violations of the current ruling military dictatorship. They were arrested for their efforts and were charged with attempting to overthrow the government of South Korea. Such was the deteriorating condition of civil liberties in South Korea.

In a joint endeavor with other denominations, The UMC became a strong advocate for restoring human rights in Korea. Through the Board of Global Ministries and the NCC, efforts were made to strengthen the voices of leaders of the movement for democracy in Korea. Among these leaders was Kim Dae Jung, a Roman Catholic layman and fierce leader of the political opposition who was imprisoned for his views. Kim's vision for a new Korea was soundly grounded in the principles of democracy and social justice. His movement, supported by the National Council of Churches in Korea, called for the immediate end of the emergency decrees, the restoration of parliamentary politics, and the creation of an independent judiciary. The long-term view included sound economic development to benefit national development, not just the corporate interests. The protestors called for an all-out effort at reunifying Korea (North and South).[8]

The division of the Korean peninsula was an unsatisfactory compromise accepted by the Panmunjom peace process begun in 1953. While it provided for a cease-fire, the two nations continued to prepare for war by amassing large armies supported by huge military expenditures from home and abroad. In 1984, as the KMC prepared to celebrate the centennial of Protestant mission (and the bicentennial of Roman Catholic mission), the executive committee of its board of missions offered a prophetic witness regarding the repressive nature of the military state: "The unjust powers of tyranny in our land must go no further in trampling upon dignity of human beings who have been created in the image of God." GBGM joined in recognition of the suffering of Koreans in both the South and the North. It recognized the perilous nature of civil life in Korea so long as the peninsula remained the focus of an ideological struggle between the U.S. and the Soviet Union.[9]

As early as 1988, reunification became a strategic objective of the churches. The World Council of Churches (WCC) brought Christian leaders from North and South Korea to Geneva. Plans were laid for a Jubilee celebration in 1995 for the reunification of Korea. It fell on the fiftieth anniversary of the liberation of Korea from Japan and the division of Korea by the two superpowers. All Korean churches on the peninsula and among the worldwide Korean diaspora celebrated a Common Day of Prayer for Korean Peace and Reunification on or before August 15, 1995.[10]

With the collapse of the Soviet Union in 1989, the agenda of reunification became more prominent in church consultations. Conversations between church leaders of the North and South were more frequent. Korean Christians in diaspora, especially those living in the U.S., became more vocal. Church groups and social organizations provided support for visits between family members (North and South) under terms permitted by the two governments. Dr. James Laney, former United Methodist missionary to Korea and president of Emory University, was named U. S. ambassador to Seoul in 1992. A friend of former President Jimmy Carter, Laney arranged for private talks between Carter and President Kim Il Sung of North Korea in 1993. That breakthrough helped the U.S. State Department find an opening for rescuing North Korea from the dangers of its policy of self-imposed political isolation by initiating formal talks with North Korea and the adoption of the 1994 Agreed Framework on nuclear development by both governments.

A drought and massive failure of the economy in North Korea in 1995–1997 accelerated contacts and initiated assistance programs with the people and governments of South Korea and the United States. Food and medical supplies were sent to P'yongyang through ecumenical channels. Korean-American churches raised substantial funding for food and food production in North Korea. The United Methodist Committee on Relief (UMCOR) became licensed as a broker for government and church-funded assistance and arranged for five shipments of foodstuffs totaling $8 million. One shipment was developed in partnership with a local church, First United Methodist Church in Houston. A high-level delegation from GBGM visited North Korea in 1999 to follow the food shipments and to meet with church and government leaders.

Church-to-church relationships between the KMC and The UMC in the period of 1968–2000 were filled by expectation and disappointment. In 1968 a major consultation was conducted at Onyang without common agreement on its purpose. Both churches recognized the rising influence of autonomy and self-determination in the decision-making authority of the KMC. The representatives from the World Division expected the KMC participants to focus on defining the church's future program directions of mission and ministry in the changing Korean context. The representatives from the KMC wanted an opportunity to perfect structural arrangements and policies for administering decisions regarding World Division project funding, property ownership, and institutional relationships in Korea.

While the KMC agenda prevailed during discussions at the meeting table, the World Division was not prepared to implement the recommendations. A recommendation regarding direct disbursement of project funds from the World Division to the KMC treasurer was not carried out. The World Division maintained a treasurer in Seoul who received funds from New York and sent them on to the projects. A recommendation to consolidate the legal holding bodies for property ownership and management into one that incorporated KMC representation was not implemented. Separate holding bodies under missionary management prevailed. Finally, little deference was given to a recommendation that a study be made of the social institutions organized by missionaries to clarify the relationship of each to the KMC. The institutions maintained their autonomy from the KMC and in many cases the World Division and Women's Division transferred property ownership rights to the boards of the institutions, not the KMC legal holding body.[11]

The failure of the Onyang consultation remains unforgotten by leadership of the KMC. It became a prominent part of the KMC recital of a conflicted history of the ties between the two churches during this period. Of equal importance, but mentioned with less candor, was division within the ranks of leadership in the KMC. A younger and somewhat militant group with a more aggressive agenda was contending for recognition by conservative church leaders. There was no diplomatic strategy of the mission board of the parent church that could avoid the criticism of either group. The preferred option of partnership was ruled out, and the World Division chose an independent course for its missionary and project relationships in the country that became formally recognized as the United Methodist Mission in Korea.

Follow-up attempts at renewing the relationship between the KMC and UMC were tried in 1983 and again in 1991. The growing constituency of Korean Americans in The UMC was a force for accomplishing discussion and dialogue on a series of issues, not the least of which was Korean church development in the U.S.[12] The 1991 consultation in Stony Point, New York, produced a new covenant agreement, the Joint Mission

Strategy Development, for work together on issues. The mission issues were defined in three areas: within Korea, within the U.S., and shared mission opportunities in world mission (beyond Korea and the U.S. where mission societies of the KMC churches were sending a large number of missionaries). Participation in the joint committee charged with continuing consultation on these matters included representation from the councils of bishops, the mission boards, the women's organizations, and youth of both churches. The joint committee had a struggle establishing itself as a long-term mission structure. Key leadership changed too often with the re-election of KMC bishops every two years and GBGM directors every four years. The committee lacked formal authority to make policy for either of the churches and its members were not prepared to implement or enforce any of its decisions. It explored areas of cooperation such as hosting KMC missionary candidates in the GBGM training program in Atlanta and clarifying the status of KMC mission personnel who had become coopted into the ministry of the Russia United Methodist Mission.

The two largest churches of world Methodism (i.e., The UMC and the KMC) nurture a strong family affinity but remain largely unsuccessful at official attempts to enter into a covenant for sharing strategies or resources for ministry. While the KMC benefits from strong spiritual directions focused on church growth and missionary expansion around the world, it has yet to perfect an organizational structure to sustain it. Much of its mission is developed by individual churches and pastors and remains beyond the capacity of the organized church to direct. On the other hand, the missionary zeal of The UMC ebbs and flows with its organizational prowess. Connectionalism was conceived as a missional structure well suited for extending the witness of the church to the frontiers of a new nation in North America and then other nations around the world. The connectional structures of The UMC are admired but appear all too foreboding to the Korean Methodists, who can mobilize mission resources without the accouterments of apportionments and make decisions without delegating their implementation to national church structures. The UMC admires the enthusiasm of the KMC but often questions the seeming absence of accountability through representative church structures. The KMC admires the vast resources of its parent church but often questions its sincerity when the urgency of issues is lost in slow-moving processes of organizational decision making.

Japan

Its post–World War II achievements in economic and technological development have kept Japan at the forefront of the world community. In spite of this embrace of globalization, many sectors of Japanese culture remain fairly impervious to the invasion of Western values, including religion. Christianity has yet to penetrate more than a fraction of 1 percent of the total population. Rather than become discouraged over the signs of rejection, missionaries have become even stronger advocates for mission boards to maintain a continuing missionary presence. The small Christian community, they argue, must not become isolated within Japanese society nor cut off from world Christendom. Their appeals have been honored with a highly disproportionate ratio of missionaries to converts.

The most formidable presence of the Christian church in Japan is found in the historic educational institutions established by missionaries. These schools maintain their Christian identity largely because North American mission partners of the established Protestant Church (the United Church of Christ in Japan, or Kyodan) are still sending missionaries to fill a few teaching posts. Some of these positions are dedicated to religious (i.e., Christian) instruction, but most missionary requests respond to the growing demand for teaching English as a second language. This traditional posting of missionaries continues because of two factors. The Kyodan has not developed the capacity to recruit personnel from within its own membership to assume these duties, and the institutions gain certain academic recognition when their faculties boast an international profile.

In 1972, ten mission boards working in cooperation with the United Church of Christ in Japan constituted the Japan–North American Commission on Cooperative Mission (JNAC).[13] The action represented a step forward in mission strategy development from the initiative resting solely with the sending mission boards in North America. It also opened a reciprocal process that included facilitating the desire of the Japanese church partners to be more significantly involved in their mission at home and to North America. Requests for posting of missionaries in Japan were prioritized by the Kyodan and a Council on Cooperative Mission and responded to by the participating mission boards in North America. The churches in North America opened their doors to receive a small number of mission personnel of the Kyodan who were sent to organize ministries

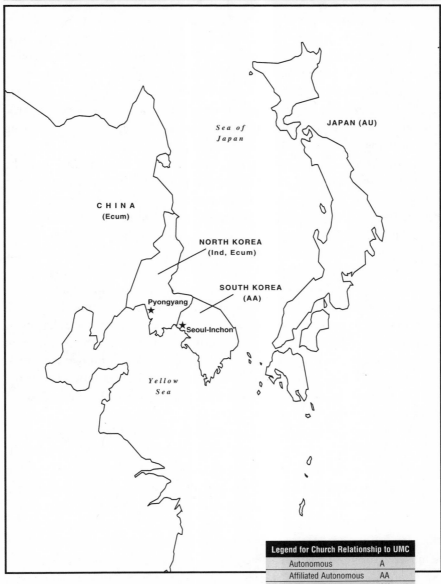

Legend for Church Relationship to UMC

Autonomous	A
Affiliated Autonomous	AA
Affiliated United	AU
Covenant UMC	Cov
Central Conference	CC
Concordat	Con
Cooperative Mission	CM
Ecumenical	Ecum
Independent	Ind
Mission	Msn

among the increasing numbers of expatriate Japanese living and working in many major metropolitan areas. In addition, the North American mission boards began receiving an annual financial grant from the Kyodan to re-invest in mission on its behalf elsewhere in the world. Since the amount each board received was prorated on its investment in missionary deployment to Japan, it was largely interpreted as a reimbursement for the growing cost of maintaining personnel in Japan, given the accelerating cost of living experienced by North Americans in Japan.

While the major activity in cooperative mission relationships with the United Church of Christ in Japan was providing North American mission boards an orderly process for posting mission personnel, there were other dimensions of the partnership. Though a small minority of the population, Japanese Christians discovered a catalytic role lifting a prophetic witness on various social issues. The church strongly resisted xenophobic legislation requiring all residents of Japan to carry identity cards. It embraced the rights of the minority Korean population in Japan and brought the Korean Christian Church in Japan into the membership of the JNAC. It supported Japan's constitutional provisions for freedom of religion by challenging public sentiments for a return of a role for the emperor in Japan's governmental system. And the church offered a ministry of healing and reconciliation by establishing a peace institute at Hiroshima, the site of the national memorial for Japanese lives lost in the atomic devastation that ended the Second World War.

The experiment in cooperative mission relationships has been both voluntary and coerced. The church structure in Japan was the pre–World War II creation of its government, whose motive was to control foreign influence as it prepared for war. Placing all Christian mission institutions and churches under a single authority forced the churches into subservience to the government but introduced a higher level of cooperation by the denominations and missionaries than they might otherwise have achieved. Cooperative efforts like JNAC sought to build upon this experience, but the dominance of government control and threat of possible interference seemed to overshadow attempts to liberalize the ministry of the churches beyond traditional missionary-based programs.

The government structure placed missionaries in charge of the property assets of their denominations in Japan. The churches had been good stewards of investments, which greatly appreciated when the Japan economy was strong, but the resources remained fixed in real estate holdings or in protected accounts for property maintenance. To liquidate these assets for anything other than re-investment in missionary housing or related mission activities within Japan met with strong resistance from the missionary community, the Kyodan leadership, and JNAC officers. Audits by governmental agencies gave attention to international fund transfers. Any increase in fund repatriation to mission boards in the U.S. might have exposed the Japan church and mission to greater scrutiny and complicated their ministry. So substantial financial resources were virtually frozen in Japan, representing "sunk costs" in maintaining a ministry that had yet to respond to new challenges.

By 2000, a growing aging population in Japan raised on the empty values of materialism should be reachable with holistic Christian ministries. Leadership development in the churches can benefit from the learnings of large numbers of youth and young adults enrolled in church schools and universities. These students have been introduced to the Christian way and should find nurture and support in the churches. They have been taught the Christian ethic and are capable of critiquing Western economic and cultural influences to which their culture has been introduced. They are prepared for leadership in the reshaping of national values. Not enough have been recruited into the teaching profession and assumed faculty positions held by Western missionaries. Such challenges are not routinely brought to the table for development of creative programs of cooperative ministry aimed at growing the church and deepening its relevance in Japanese society. So the nature and extent of cooperative mission in Japan is facing a challenge. Is it a structural problem or a leadership issue? Mission practitioners of the twenty-first century are likely to discover the answer as partners confront expanding opportunities for Christian mission in a variety of venues. Cooperative mission should enable Japan Christians to experience and participate in genuine church renewal and revitalization of mission.

Context Southern Asia

Density and diversity are the key characteristics of the population of this region, which extends from east of Iran through the subcontinent of India to Indonesia and the Philippines. Three of every five new births (happening every two seconds) occur in this part of the world. This region contains 30 percent of the population of the world and only 7 percent of the landmass of the globe. Southern Asia presents a profound concentration of humanity. India alone has more people than all the nations of Africa, Central America, and South America combined.

An indicator of the diversity of these peoples is the more than three thousand ethnic languages they speak. Adherents of all of the major religions of the world can be found in the region. Social tensions accompany diversity of this magnitude. Though most of the nations of the region have emerged from colonialism with new forms of self-governance, multiparty conflicts and ineffective leadership have frequently produced instability and authoritarian rule. The economies have rapidly converted from agricultural to industrial development, drawing rural populations to the already large urban centers for employment and a significant segment of poverty populations into foreign domestic employment or bonded service. Social inequalities are stark, with residents in Bangladesh — the poorest country in the region — surviving on U.S. $260 share of the annual gross national product while Singaporeans — the wealthiest population in the region — benefitting from U.S. $30,500.

The Philippines

The Philippines is the only country in the region in which Christians are the majority. While Roman Catholicism is the dominant branch of the Christian church, thanks to the colonial legacy of Spain, Protestant mission thrived following the conquest of the U.S. in the Spanish-American War at the beginning of the twentieth century. The Catholic Church became a strong force for political freedom under the dictatorship of President Ferdinand Marcos. It denounced fraud in the manipulation of a 1976 referendum endorsing the president's imposition of martial law. It supported trade unions and political parties that boycotted the 1981 elections that Marcos attempted to use to stay in power. Following the assassination of opposition leader Benigno Aquino upon his return from exile, Cardinal Hymie Sin lent the support of the church to the massive "People's Power" movement that won the allegiance and protection of the country's military and ultimately forced the unpopular Marcos into exile. In 1986 Cory Aquino was elected president, and a new constitution was approved by a national plebescite in 1987.

The Protestant witness throughout this period of political struggle was expressed through the leadership of the National Council of Churches in the Philippines. The leadership remained in dialogue with the opposition

Pacific Ocean

South China Sea

Cabanatuan

Mount Pinatubo

★**Manila**

Cavite

PHILIPPINES (CC, AA, AU)

Mindanao Gulf

Sulu Sea

MINDANAO

Davao

Kudat

Moro Gulf   Kidipawan

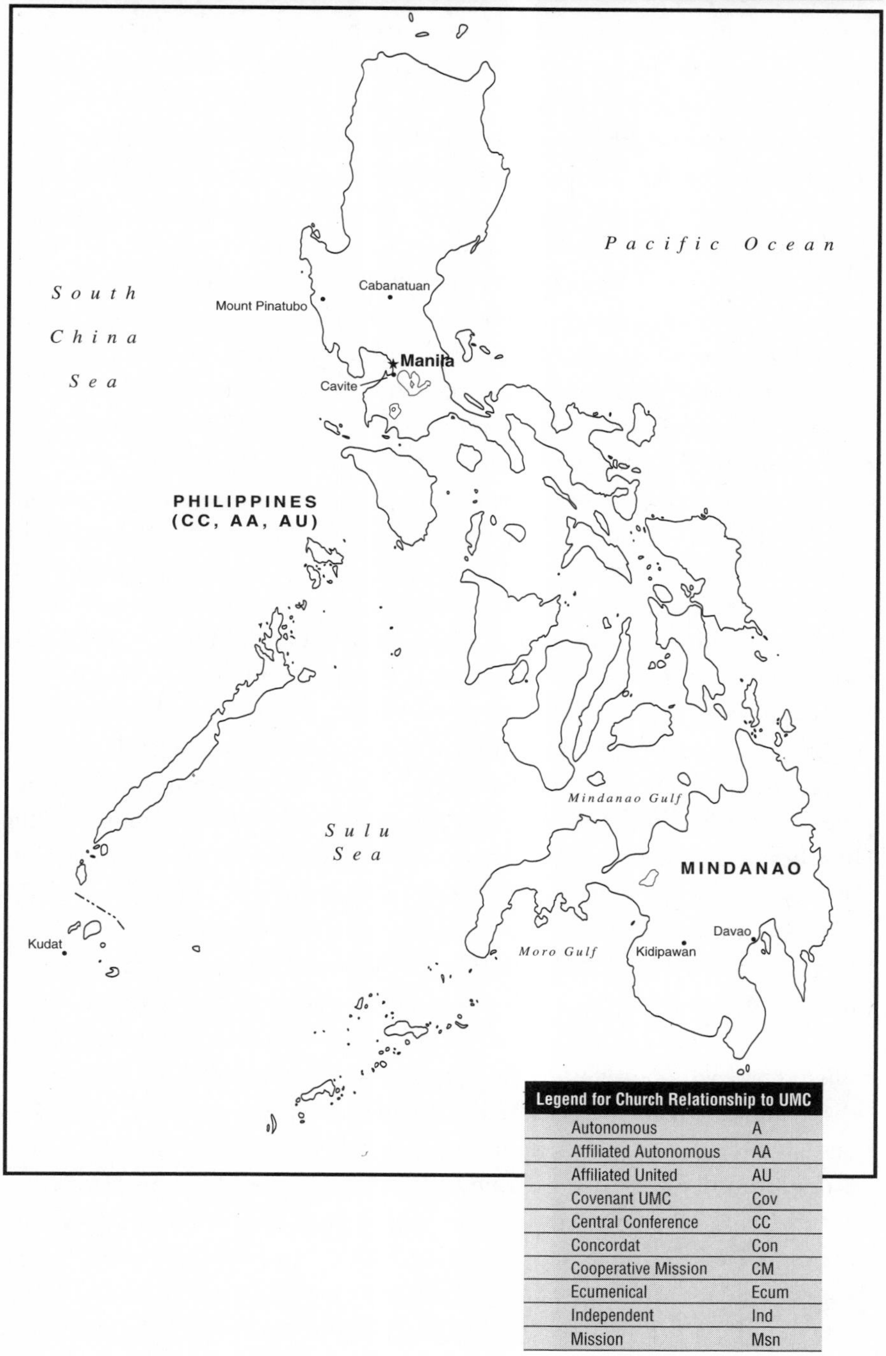

Legend for Church Relationship to UMC	
Autonomous	A
Affiliated Autonomous	AA
Affiliated United	AU
Covenant UMC	Cov
Central Conference	CC
Concordat	Con
Cooperative Mission	CM
Ecumenical	Ecum
Independent	Ind
Mission	Msn

parties and urged a strong commitment to the protection of human rights and the social development of the people of the republic. In May 1992, Fidel Ramos, an active member of the United Church of Christ in the Philippines (UCCP) and minister of defense in the Aquino government, was elected president. Ramos was respected for his leadership of the military to abandon its support for the Marcos regime. He was the first Protestant president of the country.

The mission of The UMC in the Philippines embraced both the autonomous United Church of Christ (established by missionaries of the United Brethren branch of the Evangelical United Brethren Church, along with colleagues from the Presbyterian, Disciples of Christ, Congregational, and Reformed Churches in the U.S.) and the Central Conference of The United Methodist Church in the Philippines. The two churches were very independent but remain linked through an ecumenical commitment and a continuous incorporation of institutions that shared a common mission heritage. The latter relationship was marked by serious conflicts over issues of leadership selection and policy development by the boards of Philippine Christian University and Union Theological Seminary in metropolitan Manila (Cavite). In the decade of the 1990s, The UMC chose to focus more of its resources on developing a separate institution for the training of its pastors at the expanding Wesleyan University in Cabanatuan. The United Methodist missionary presence in the Philippines diminished with the rise of a very capable leadership from within the churches. The few remaining by 2000 related primarily to educational institutions in administrative or teaching positions.

Under the leadership of Bishop Emerito Nacpil of the Manila Area, the mission of The UMC in the Philippines became church growth. Nacpil urged the pastors of his conference to become church developers. They were to lead their congregations in exploring the possibilities of establishing new congregations in neighborhoods without a United Methodist Church. Teams of local church members were specially trained to conduct needs assessments by listening to neighbors describe their vision of a community enriched by a new church presence. This process led to church-based efforts in community organizing, economic development, opening of educational opportunities, and development of other social programs in addition to a commitment to Bible study and spiritual development. These probes have produced dramatic results in the formation of new churches, creating a corresponding need for the organization of new districts and annual conferences.

The UMC mission in the southern Philippines (Mindanao) has also been marked by church growth with accompanying development of connectional structures. Bishop Jose Gamboa of the Davao Area emphasized the importance of leadership development for the future of the church in the region. The region was affected by the presence of Muslim and Communist-inspired rebel armies, making it very difficult to establish formal institutions for learning. Gamboa's methodology featured nonformal education that began with the basic needs of the indigenous leaders the church was calling into its ministry. It produced a strong corps of pastor educators whose dedication expanded the witness of the church in spite of hostile forces. Gamboa was frequently invited by ecumenical groups in the region and beyond to share his model for replication in similar contexts. In the decade of the 1990s, the church established a conference center at the mission station in rural Kidipawan. A Methodist University of the Southern Philippines was built to serve the region and to accommodate the first seminary or Bible college for formal theological studies. Under the interim episcopal leadership of retired Bishop Paul Granadosin, the construction of an episcopal residence and area office was completed at Kidipawan.

In 1998, The UMC in the Philippines celebrated its centennial with a week of planned events and a public witness in Manila. The future, not the past, of Methodism in the Philippines preoccupied the hearts and minds of the participants. Nacpil, a leader in the Council of Bishops dialogue on the global nature of The UMC, had inspired leaders of the central conference to think globally. The concept seemed to give equal recognition to all structures of a global denomination, but the benefits of such a standing within the regional and local contexts of the denominations like those in the Philippines were not so evident in the organizational prescriptions being proposed. A strong contingent of leaders favoring the alternative of church autonomy for United Methodists in the Philippines was highly active and visible in the church. These leaders succeeded in electing Daniel Arichea bishop in the 1993 central conference and re-electing him in 1997. He became an articulate advocate for a church structure that is Methodist in tradition and connectional in organization but locally accountable in leadership and style. In 2001, the central conference elected three new episcopal leaders with similar views. The move toward autonomy seemed to be gaining strength within The UMC in the Philippines. If successful, the church would join all of the other former Methodist mission churches in the Asia region in choosing independence from the United Methodist connection. And the case for a global UMC would lose considerable credibility without an organizational connection in the populous and influential Asia region.

The autonomous UCCP was an active participant in global mission relationships. It was active in national, regional, and world ecumenical bodies. It became a member of the European-based United Evangelical Mission Council, an organization that recruited member church relationships in developing countries. The UCCP adopted a policy for receiving missionary personnel that required expatriate workers to be reimbursed at the same salary level as their colleague church workers in the Philippine context. While respecting the values represented in such a policy, GBGM did not aggressively recruit candidates for service with the UCCP. Meanwhile, the missionary commitment to The UMC in the Philippines gradually diminished as local leadership generally replaced returning or retiring missionaries.

The Philippines has been vulnerable to harsh acts of nature. In 1991, the volcanic ash of Mount Pinatubo destructively fell on the landscape, claiming the lives of seventy Filipinos, crushing villages and causing the relocation of hundreds of thousands of citizens. The UMC, in cooperation with missionaries and students of Union Theological Seminary, responded with a community recovery and church development program. Led by missionaries Richard and Caring Shwenck, teams of workers made frequent visits to the affected area to help with ecological and agricultural development. They also nurtured leadership among the ethnic tribal groups among whom United Methodist ministries were formed and leadership was recruited.

The Philippine population has had to learn to accommodate the seasonal storms and typhoons that destroy homes and businesses. UMCOR responded with financial assistance and sponsored disaster-response training for conference and district leaders of the churches that were present and serving at every catastrophic occurrence. In addition, unjust and unstable political conditions under President Marcos produced disruptive economic crises. According to estimates, there were 1.2 million homeless people in the Philippines in 1990, many of them becoming squatters in urban areas.[14] Garbage dumps became settlements and provided scavengers with modest incomes from recycling of discarded plastics and glass. "Smokey Mountain," the name given to a continuously burning garbage dump outside Manila that sustained a community of thousands of permanent residents, was chosen as a site for ministry and church development by The UMC and assisted by missionary personnel. Until its removal late in the decade of the 1990s, it was a symbol of the desperate nature and persistent spirit of the poorest of the poor of the country.

India

The 1980 General Conference of The UMC recognized the Methodist Church in India as an affiliated autonomous Methodist Church. In spite of the prevailing tone of national independence growing out of Mahatma Gandhi's commitment to self-reliance and a popular foreign policy of political nonalliance, the decision for autonomy by the Indian church leaders (whose church was a branch of the former Southern Asia Central Conference) was marked by ambiguity. Other regional churches within United Methodist mission connections had already chosen independence when the Indian church councils were mulling over the issues. Some were uneasy about breaking ties to the parent church. Others demanded assurances of continued financial support after independence. One alternative that received much consideration and even a tentative vote of approval was incorporating the Methodist connection into the ecumenical United Church of North India. It was ultimately decided to avoid legal complexities of a union and the regional issues that would certainly rise with such a direction and to maintain the church's Methodist identity in a declaration of autonomy.

The newly organized Methodist Church in India (MCI) served a broadly disbursed constituency with a membership of more than 500,000. While clearly intended to be a national church, it yielded authority to the several regional conferences where ministries were carried out with greatest sensitivity to local cultural and political/civil realities. While English was used for official communications in church meetings, members and representatives came from more than twenty local language groups and often faced difficulties in interpretation. Church leaders were frequently first-generation converts to Christianity. Many had origins in poor rural villages and received their formal education in Methodist missionary schools generously distributed across the country. In the multifaith context of the country, Indian Methodists, whether first or successive generations, were Christian by choice. Though a minority presence in their own country, their association with a major denomination within the world Christian community assured them a recognizable identity.

The organization of the Methodist Church in India is a clone of The UMC in the U.S. Its *Discipline* was a carbon copy of the *1976 Book of Discipline* of The UMC. The practice of traditional Methodist connectionalism in program and administration, however, remained a foreign concept. While most of the local churches were financially independent and contributed to the beneficent programs of the regional church bodies, the functioning of the regional and national church bodies remained dependent upon the patrimony of church institutions and foreign mission contributions. "Head taxes" levied on the enrollment of students at Methodist Church schools and income from "gains on foreign currency exchange"[15] subsidized denominational budgets and salaries of elected officials. These techniques were a creation of the missionaries and helped the church survive in difficult economic times.

The largess of the missionary era in India remained the many hospitals, clinics, schools, dormitories/hostels, colleges, and other Christian service institutions that missionaries established. Following national independence and with the autonomy of the church, property titles and management of these institutions were transferred to the MCI. A strict condition was placed upon the transfer of titles of properties formerly owned by the Women's Division of GBGM. Any recommendation for the disposition or change in use of such property was to have the consent of the women's organization of the church (or regional body) and approval of the Women's Division. This provision was only casually enforced and almost forgotten until consultations between the division and women's units of the MCI brought the matter to light. Liquidating property assets by church leaders had become a convenient means of balancing judicatory budgets. Empowering women in the church to claim their rights to participate in the stewardship of these mission resources needed to be elevated to a higher level of priority.

National independence and church autonomy for India brought a declining role for missionaries. The government addressed the tense interfaith context of the country with official restrictions on the propagation of the Christian faith. New missionary visas were not granted; thus, retiring missionaries were not replaced. Indian church leaders were anxious to step in and were well prepared to assume new leadership responsibilities and opportunities in mission institutions. This transition in leadership and management of mission institutions had various byproducts, the first of which was decreased financial support. Minus the fund-raising capacity of the missionaries, many institutional budgets were stretched. Some barely survived on limited income, and others enjoyed considerable local prestige and the support of generous endowments. Graduates of mission schools now living and working in the U.S. on occasion visited their alma maters and found many of them in an embarrassing state of disrepair. With mixed experiences of success, they organized fund-raising campaigns to benefit their rehabilitation. In the late 1990s, GBGM invited the leadership of the MCI to consider a partnership in the rebuilding of its mission hospitals. The Health and Relief Program Area of the Board took general leadership and received endorsement from the Women's Division for a specific project aimed at renewing the historic Clara Swain Hospital in Bareilly. It was understood that the effort would be undertaken in a mutual partnership with the MCI. By the turn of the century, nothing but the expressed will to engage in such a major undertaking had been accomplished. Missionaries would not have left such an important challenge in such a state of uncertainty.

A second byproduct was a rather precarious relationship between the institutions and the leadership of the autonomous MCI. The mission institutions were all deferent to the authority of the MCI. The presiding bishop in each region became an influential member of the board of every institution. Institutions formerly related to the Women's Division operated with a high priority placed upon selecting women for positions of leadership. While the institutions operated with the expertise and dedication of a corps of deaconesses (under the appointment authority of bishops), most of the leadership positions were occupied by men. The Women's Division of GBGM explored ways to resource this cadre of women leaders whose service to the church was frequently undervalued. Their talents in administration as well as in caregiving must be recognized and their partnership gained if the process of recovering the ministry and mission of the church's institutions is to succeed.

The mission outreach of the MCI in 2000 was challenged by the stark realities of homeless populations living on the streets of major cities and the rural poor barely surviving on poor agricultural production. Moving rapidly from a sluggish industrial and state-controlled economy to a market-oriented, technological, and globally based economic system has benefitted few and left most of the population behind. The local churches faithfully struggled to maintain ministries of caring and compassion that could have served as models for urban ministry in North American or European contexts.

To respond to many devastating natural disasters and promising opportunities for redevelopment, the MCI organized a relief and development component in partnership with UMCOR. The Committee on Relief looked to the agency for administering funds for community-based projects. Indian church leaders established criteria, reviewed applications, and evaluated the results of projects that made a difference in many communities served by MCI churches.

The Mission Board of the MCI supported evangelization efforts in northeast India and among indigenous tribal groups within the country. It joined GBGM in ventures beyond India by providing missionary personnel for exploring church development in Nepal and for serving the large expatriate Indian community in Fiji.

Pakistan

Methodist mission in Pakistan began in the late 1800s and was revived in 1930 with the development of a mission in the Multan region. It was part of the India mission related to the Southern Asia Central Conference until the act of partition in 1947. The independence of Pakistan gave encouragement for Islamists to create the state under Muslim religious law. Christian minority groups experienced considerable alienation and eventually hostility from official bodies. Several of the Methodist mission projects, including the successful Luci Harrison High School for Girls in Lahore, were eventually nationalized. In 1970, Protestant Christians agreed to the formation of a common church structure and founded the United Church of Pakistan. The Methodist Church brought a constituency of 60,000 persons and an active membership of 21,000 into the United Church. In recent years a new school facility was built on the grounds of the former Methodist mission compound in Lahore.

Since 1991, fundamentalist Muslim influences in government have heightened tensions within the Christian and Hindu communities. The rights of members of these minority religions were not protected and were even singled out for harsher treatment under the law. United Church Bishop Samuel Azariah assisted in the formation of a religious and human

Legend for Church Relationship to UMC	
Autonomous	A
Affiliated Autonomous	AA
Affiliated United	AU
Covenant UMC	Cov
Central Conference	CC
Concordat	Con
Cooperative Mission	CM
Ecumenical	Ecum
Independent	Ind
Mission	Msn

rights group that was instrumental in negotiating individual cases with the government. His efforts required the support of an international network of human rights groups, who stood ready to respond to his calls to enable the defense and frequently the protection of convicted individuals released to his custody.

The United Church in 2000 saw the immediate future for its mission in Pakistan in working with women, who bore the burden of discrimination by society. Finding acceptance within and becoming a vital part of Christian communities enhanced their self-esteem. The church offered special seminars and programs for women to strengthen each other and their role in family life. The church believed that a connection to the world Christian community was vital to the continuation of its witness in this conflicted context and was heartened by the support of GBGM.

Singapore and Malaysia

Witnessing to the gospel as members of a minority religious group in a religiously diverse population describes the common mission challenge faced by Methodist churches in these countries. Interacting with people of other faiths and seeking to understand them are not electives for the people called Methodist in these countries. Dialogue, not preaching, is commended to those who seek to bear a Christlike witness to their neighbors. It builds respect, shows humility, clarifies misunderstanding, adds to one's own faith enrichment, and prepares believers for effective communication of their own faith experience. Methodists in Singapore and Malaysia have grown in their faith and in their capacities for outreach and service by first seeking the unity in Christ promised by the gospel.

The Methodist churches in Singapore and Malaysia were granted autonomy in 1968. They remained in one conference until 1976, when the two countries became independent. Both churches were structured around ethnic realities, with individual conferences serving Chinese, Tamil, and English-speaking (largely British) memberships.

Both churches have been quite successful in establishing and maintaining private schools to serve both Methodist members and the larger community. The fine reputations of the schools transcended religious and cultural differences, and none were at a loss for enrollment of outstanding students. The churches also offered social services, including day care and residential services for children and elderly, medical clinics, and a hospital.

The Singapore church successfully launched its own denominational mission society (Methodist Missions Society) with a full-time executive. In 2000, the society was supporting more than one hundred missionaries at work in Asia (mostly in Nepal, Thailand, Cambodia, and Vietnam), Africa, and Europe. Singapore mission leaders invited GBGM into a partnership for a common Methodist witness in Cambodia and Vietnam.[16] The society received generous support from its members who benefitted from living and working in one of the world's fastest-growing economies.

Robert Solomon, bishop of the Methodist Church in Singapore and former faculty member at Trinity Theological College, reported in 1998 on the enthusiasm with which local churches of his conference were engaging in direct mission and evangelism efforts in the region of southeast Asia. They successfully penetrated one mission context that remained closed to regular missionaries of the church: "When I visited Lower Myanmar Methodist Church in Yangon two years ago, I met with a cell group from a Singapore church who were conducting training sessions for church members. In Chiangmai [Chiang Mai], I visited a small obscure village where a Singapore Methodist church had contributed to the building of a simple hut that serves as a chapel. Several other Singapore Methodist churches have planted daughter churches in various countries and maintain the work by supporting local pastors and workers. . . . Mission involvement moves rapidly from financial giving for mission and missionary work to more direct involvement."[17]

Trinity Theological College, an ecumenical school in which The Methodist Church was a major partner, became a center for advanced pastoral studies for students from Malaysia, Singapore, and more than forty countries. GBGM and Trinity College collaborated in establishing scholarships to enable students from partner churches around the world to pursue formal studies in theology and church leadership.

New mission initiatives of GBGM in Cambodia, Nepal, and Vietnam are discussed in chapter 9.

CHAPTER 7

Aims of Mission: A Churchwide Embrace

God, Creator, Redeemer and Life-Giver summons the
Church to mission in the world. The aims of this mission are:

    1. To witness in all the world, by word and deed, to the self-
    revelation of God in Jesus Christ and the acts of love by
    which God reconciles people to God.

    2. To evoke in all people the personal response of repentance
    and faith through which by God's grace they may find
    newness of life in righteous, loving relationships with
    God and others.

    3. To bring people together into a Christian community for
    worship and fellowship and to send them into the world
    as servants in the struggle for justice and meaning.

    4. To reveal in ministry the love of God for all who suffer.

    5. To move all people to live in awareness of the presence
    and life-giving power of God's Holy Spirit, in acknowl-
    edgment of God's rule over earthly history and in con-
    fident expectation of the ultimate consummation of God's
    purpose.[1]

THIS STATEMENT was drafted by the Board of Missions of The Methodist Church as the prologue for the paragraphs in the church's *Book of Discipline* defining its authority and mission responsibilities on behalf of the whole church. Following church union in 1968 and the restructuring of the general church in 1972, the statement was adopted as a mission statement for all of the agencies of the denomination. The statement, with slight revisions, was moved from the heading of the disciplinary paragraphs for the mission agency to the front of the administrative order section of the *Book of Discipline*. The move symbolized the intent of The United Methodist Church (UMC) that mission was not the sole domain of one agency but was becoming the general purpose of the whole church.

The embrace of the aims of mission by all of the program agencies of the general church promised new or additional resources for the traditional mission constituencies of the Board of Missions (which would become the Board of Global Ministries, then the General Board of Global Ministries). While the *Discipline* still assigned to the World Division responsibility to "administer the program of The United Methodist Church as it relates to areas outside the United States,"[2] other general agencies initiated direct contacts with church leaders in many countries in their efforts to help undergird their ministries. Since funding global mission remained a Board responsibility, the other agencies specialized in offering their services to the churches and conferences around the world. For those churches engaged in the institutional development phase of their church life, consultative services related to such endeavors as leadership training, higher education, Christian education, and publishing were highly valued. The central conferences, with direct membership representation on the boards of the general church agencies, generated the greatest demand for services from the agencies.

Africa University

The most notable foray into world mission by a general agency other than the General Board of Global Ministries (GBGM) was the development of Africa University by the General Board of Higher Education and Ministry (GBHEM). The idea evolved from discussions of higher education in Africa initiated by the Africa Task Force of the World Division of GBGM. African church leaders, anxious to become engaged in a mission initiative that would impact the entire continent, centered their energies upon the creation of a United Methodist university for Africa. The project was readily adopted by GBHEM, which packaged it for presentation and financial support from the 1980 General Conference. The General Conference approved the proposal and created a general church fund supported by direct apportionments to the conferences and churches. A former mission property in Mutare, Zimbabwe, was chosen as the site, government approval was given, and construction of buildings (with considerable volunteer labor from UMC groups in the U.S. and Europe) begun. Collaboration was sought from the mission board, but the project was administered by GBHEM and financed through the general church, generously subsidized by foundation and government grants. The popularity of the project throughout the church was the result of imaginative and strategic marketing efforts of GBHEM. It was successful in getting the connectional units of the entire church to focus on one project and to mobilize resources toward its realization. Subsequent General Conferences endorsed continued funding for the project. A board of trustees composed predominantly of African church leaders was given full responsibility for its management.

The Africa University project built confidence in GBHEM capacity to serve the educational ministries of other central conferences. Schools, universities, and seminaries in and beyond Africa begun by the missionary movement of the church found a new professional association and institutional connection in the denomination. While other general agencies did not undertake global programming in such a dramatic fashion, all of them geared up for serving the church beyond North America. The General Board of Discipleship (GBOD) structured program services and developed language materials around service requests from churches in Europe, Latin America, and Africa. GBHEM cultivated a global network of United Methodist–related college and university administrators offering consultation services to staff and trustees. This growing relationship between the churches with mission origins and the general church structures was merely the introduction to defining the denominational parameters of a global church.

Episcopal Initiatives

The leadership role of the Council of Bishops (COB) in The UMC has shifted with the evolving patterns of organization in the denomination. In 1968, the *Discipline* described the work of the council in generic terms: "Promote the evangelistic activities of the Church and . . . furnish such inspirational leadership as the need and opportunity may demand."[3] As the structures of the general church were fortified through reorganization in 1972, a special section devoted to "Superintendency" was added to the

Discipline. Superintendency was understood to be a shared task between bishops and district superintendents but was described primarily in organizational terms: "Those who superintend carry primary responsibility for ordering the life of the church. . . . to see that all matters, temporal and spiritual, are administered in a manner . . . faithful to the mandate of the church." The language in the same *Discipline* also embraced mission: "It is also their [superintendents and bishops] task to facilitate the initiation of structures and strategies for the equipping of Christian people for service in the Church and in the world in the name of Jesus Christ and to help extend the service in mission."[4]

With each new class of bishops elected to the council, the body became more inclusive in its membership. A more diverse and colorful COB began to offer evidence of qualities of teaching and leading the church into highly significant areas of program and witness.

The Bishops' Call for Peace and the Self-Development of Peoples

Acting on the initiative of the COB, the 1972 General Conference adopted a resolution titled the Bishops' Call for Peace and the Self-Development of Peoples. Its aim was to place the resources of The UMC behind the task of interpreting the root causes of poverty and injustice in the world community. Various mission initiatives in the church addressed the pressing problems of world hunger, human rights violations, and militarism from an activist or relief-oriented perspective, but the call was directed at converting the hearts and minds of church members. United Methodists in the U.S. would be exposed to a larger worldview to challenge parochial assumptions about their government's participation in global conflicts and other systemic problems producing so much human suffering. The project proposed an educational process of personalizing the issues of an increasingly interdependent world with North American church members being asked to "examine how their habits and practices within an affluent society depend on continued world deprivation."[5]

The Bishops' Call employed two staff persons, Bishop Ralph Dodge as the executive coordinator and the Reverend Michael McIntyre. Dodge was a missionary bishop fresh from the liberation struggles in former Rhodesia and in Zimbabwe following the election of the first national bishop, Abel Muzorewa. McIntyre, a clergyperson from the Central Illinois Conference, had just completed a tour with the McGovern Democratic Presidential Campaign as the national coordinator for religious leadership for McGovern. Bishop James Armstrong of the Dakotas Area was the chair of the coordinating committee. This team became engaged in a series of seminars, workshops, and consultations across the U.S. for the purpose of "opening up issues for people" on the subjects of militarism (including the arms race), nationalism and self-interest, racism, sexism, and economic exploitation. It called upon staff from mission programs in the U.S. and elsewhere to offer a fresh approach to the work of the church on the cusp of a growing global consciousness. The Bishops' Call "asks United Methodists and others to work for the day when dominance and force will be supplanted by a commitment to justice and dignity for all the world's people."[6]

The project was renewed for a second quadrennium by the 1976 General Conference. It did not suffer from any loss of enthusiasm from among academics and social activists in the church constituency. It lacked strong financial support. Most of its seminar activities were funded with the help of participants and supportive general agencies such as GBGM and the General Board of Church and Society (GBCS). Its offices were at first housed in Washington, D.C., at the United Methodist Building but were later moved to the Church Center for the United Nations in New York, where a stronger international influence was sought. Whenever possible GBGM enabled international participants with a Third World perspective to attend and/or give leadership to seminars and other events. A number of global contacts were pursued, including leadership training for women and youth in Angola, Brazil, the Caribbean, Indonesia, New Guinea, the Philippines, South Africa, Zaire, and Zambia. The staff members embraced various struggles for justice, encouraging a nonviolent movement toward independence in New Hebrides and participating in the second meeting of the Nuclear Free Pacific Conference in the South Pacific. They were involved in human rights advocacy in South Africa and the Middle East.

The aim of the educational activities of the Bishops' Call was to increase the number of church leaders who were recognizing how an alliance with movements in the Third World could become a strong force for constructive change. The leadership of the project adopted the educational methodology of "conscientization," the popular study and reflection process of Third World educators like Paulo Freire of Brazil. These educators were successful in joining a rational comprehension of issues to an existential involvement in conditions of deprivation and suffering.

Participants in this learning philosophy/process were encouraged to make personal commitments to behavioral change and to engage with like-minded persons and groups in building alternative strategies for community development. This educational process worked in a variety of contexts from urban to rural communities, workplace conditions, union organizing, and human rights movements. While it served to strengthen and add to the number of voices in annual conferences calling for the church's participation in a variety of local peace with justice efforts, there is little evidence of its success in connecting this leadership with effective global organizations and networks for social change.

The work of the project itself did not continue beyond 1980. After evaluation by the General Council on Ministries (GCOM), its programs were folded into the missional priorities and ongoing programs of the general church. Many of the issues addressed by the Bishops' Call surfaced on the agenda of the Joint Panel on International Affairs, a biannual inter-agency forum attended by representatives of GBGM, GBCS, and the General Commission on Christian Unity and Interreligious Concerns. The panel members availed themselves of expertise from academic and diplomatic circles and guided their agencies in establishing policies and drafting resolutions on sensitive international justice issues.

Ecumenical Witness

In 1982 and 1983, leadership in the church appealed to the COB to sort out the conflicted issues of denominational membership and representation on the National Council of Churches (NCC) and World Council of Churches (WCC). The precipitating issue was reporting in the popular journal *Reader's Digest* and the prime-time television program *60 Minutes* alleging misuse of church funds by these ecumenical bodies. The reports, based solely on information gleaned from critics of the ecumenical movement, alleged that councils were funding political revolutionaries and guerrilla army activities in Third World countries. In the final analysis, it was the controversial Program to Combat Racism of the WCC that provoked the interest of the public media. Grants had been made to organizations that were very much involved in the struggle to end apartheid in South Africa and to establish independence and self-rule in other southern African countries (Angola, Mozambique, Namibia, and Zimbabwe).

The agencies of The UMC that administered ecumenical funding and program relationships (GBGM and General Commission on Christian Unity and Interreligious Concerns) were bombarded with a constituency reaction to the popular media coverage. Efforts to clarify the church's position with statements issued through connectional channels were inadequate to counter the publicity the anti-ecumenical pundits had generated through the media.

The COB heeded the appeal to launch an "investigative" process and set about interviewing leaders of the councils and the appropriate agencies of the denomination. Its report affirmed the importance of the church's ecumenical witness. The bishops concluded that if the church councils were to fail because of their frailties, the denominations would have to create alternative structures to accomplish the mission programs they had chosen to do cooperatively, including a challenge to forces of international racism. The COB report questioned, however, the practices of decision making and accountability within the councils and the denominational agencies. The COB agreed to become more intentionally involved in monitoring the work of the NCC and WCC and the general church agencies that critics believed had too much autonomy. The bishops assigned to serve as directors of the general agencies and elected to the membership on policymaking bodies of the ecumenical councils began making more frequent reports to those councils. The COB also proposed giving greater scrutiny to the selection of denominational representatives to the ecumenical councils. Subsequently, the General Commission on Christian Unity and Interreligious Concerns brought all recommendations for United Methodist representation on the councils to the COB for review and final nomination.

The COB had successfully established a new standard for agency accountability as well as a new level of direct involvement in general church program. The bishops remained active in overseeing and monitoring United Methodist participation in ecumenical bodies, but by the year 2000, the intensity of the COB role in guiding interchurch program directions, funding, and cooperation had diminished. The influence of the church councils waned. Organizational complexity overwhelmed the WCC. An increasing membership base of more than 350 denominations without a corresponding financial commitment from the churches brought cutbacks in staffing and program. A similar scenario was played out in the year 2000 by the NCC, which had to call upon its largest denominational contributors—including The UMC—to make special infusions of financial aid to rescue it from burgeoning deficits. The COB, in both instances, took the lead in garnering support for these fragile but visible expressions of the unity of the church.

In Defense of Creation — The Nuclear Crisis and a Just Peace

In the 1980s, U.S. foreign policy was grounded in building a strong military, and the national economic policy offered big tax incentives for large capital investment in industry and business. There was little government attention directed to the social benefit from lifting growing segments of the population out of poverty. Gradually, leadership in the churches found its pastoral and prophetic voice. The U.S. Conference of Roman Catholic Bishops weighed into public policy debate with major position papers on the economy and peacemaking.[7] The Presbyterian Church (U.S.A.) issued "Peacemaking — the Believers' Calling" in 1980. The COB of The UMC decided to offer a teaching document that included a prophetic witness to the costliness of national and international defense policies grounded in an unrelenting dependence upon militarism and nuclear deterrents.

The Episcopal Initiatives Committee of the council, chaired by Bishop C. Dale White, developed a two-year study process for the council that would enable it to issue an informed statement to the churches. It included in-depth biblical and theological reflection, a review of historic and contemporary ethical theories guiding national policies for military engagement, a learning process regarding weapons production and capabilities of various weapons systems, a hearing process for soliciting expert opinion and a "feedback" process for receiving commentary on its early draft statement. The final statement, a hundred-page "Foundation Document" published in 1986, was accompanied by a pastoral letter to the churches and a forty-page study manual for congregations to participate in their own process of discovery and action.

The bishops found grounding for their work in the Old Testament understanding of shalom as living in harmony with all of God's creation. "The shalom of God's good creation has been broken by the falseness and violence of sinful human creatures. . . . Shalom discloses an alternative community — alternative to the idolatries, oppressions, and violence that mark the ways of many nations."[8] The bishops called for living in God's shalom, instead of living under the threat of the proliferation and use of nuclear weapons to destroy life on this planet; God's shalom, instead of

At a 1995 meeting of the World Student Christian Federation in Côte d'Ivoire, participants released a dove, symbol of their yearning for peace. Their act was a response to the news that the French government had carried out nuclear tests in the South Pacific. *(Photo courtesy of UM Archives and History)*

huge expenditures on military budgets that jeopardize funding for nutrition, health, education, housing, and other programs serving the well-being of impoverished peoples in all nations; God's shalom, instead of stockpiling and proliferating nuclear weapons among nations.

The bishops found some contemporary coherence in the ageless principles of the just war doctrine of the fourth- and fifth-century church. They could find no *reasonable hope of success* in achieving a just peace through the use of nuclear weapons. The widespread fallout effects from the use of nuclear weapons offered no form of *discrimination* between combatants and noncombatants. There could be no *norm of proportionality* in force in introducing the ultimate destructive capacity of nuclear weapons. So the message of the statement was "a clear and unconditioned 'No,' to nuclear war and to any use of nuclear weapons. . . . It is a rejection of that nuclear idolatry that presumes to usurp the sovereignty of God over all nations and peoples."[9]

The statement was released with a strategy of claiming as much public attention as possible. With the aid of public relations specialists, the message was proclaimed through the secular media. Members of the council charged themselves with interpreting the statement in each of the episcopal areas of the church. Bishops entertained dialogue in local churches. They met with officials in government, ranking officers in the military, nuclear scientists and physicists, and captains of the industrial military complex, many of whom were members of United Methodist churches or within their reach.

In their call to action, the bishops cited the *Discipline*, which placed responsibility for witnessing to the gospel of the Prince of Peace squarely upon the members of the churches:

"The people of God [the laity] are the Church made visible in the world. It is they who must convince the world of the reality of the Gospel or leave it unconvinced . . . the Church is either faithful as a witnessing and serving community, or it loses its vitality and its impact on an unbelieving world."[10]

United Methodists were being commissioned by their bishops to a mission of securing peace with justice in the world. The bishops were both commended and criticized for their leadership, but they and the church caught a vision of the magnitude of the calling to responsible Christian living in a complex contemporary world context. The bishops were unable to forecast an end to the Cold War which fueled the nuclear threat they were addressing, but the message is no less significant in the post–Cold War period, which still suffers the absence of a just peace. Conflicts among nations persist and the proliferation of nuclear power among smaller nations eludes their ultimate control and increases their threat to all human life. It is a message that must be renewed with each generation.

An Emerging Global Vision

In 1992, the COB reported to the General Conference on its preliminary discussions of organizing the denomination on a global model. This study had gained considerable momentum as the central conferences claimed a growing number of seats at each General Conference, thanks to their increasing membership at the expense of declining memberships in annual conferences in the U.S. The agenda of each General Conference continued to be centered upon the interests of the North American churches and the organizational structure housed in the U.S. Delegates from central conferences became increasingly vocal in expressing their frustration over spending days working on documents that were not trans-

lated into their languages and addressing issues that required greater familiarity with the cultural, political, and organizational domains of North
American churches. But they were equally vocal about their strong self-
identity as United Methodists and their membership rights to full participation in a global church.

The central conferences no longer wished to be considered objects of
mission of the denomination and lobbied to claim their full inheritance in
the denomination. After four more years of discussion, the bishops yielded
their leadership on the issue to the Connectional Process Team (CPT), a
body created by the 1996 General Conference to develop an entirely new
structure for the church incorporating its global connections. The CPT
proposed the creation of four regional central conferences (including
North America) that would focus on the organizational agendas and issues
of each regional context. It also proposed a quadrennial Global Conference with a base membership of five hundred, composed of one clergyperson and one layperson from each annual conference, plus additional
delegates based on size (membership) of each conference. The Global
Conference would confirm the election of bishops in the regions, legislate
on matters of church doctrine and constitution, celebrate global mission
and ministry, and address social issues of global importance. Each of the
regional bodies would be authorized to create its own program agencies.[11]

While it was generally acknowledged that the economics of the denomination would not likely undergo much change, i.e., with North
American churches financing general church programs, the CPT did not
address the financial feasibility of its proposal. For that reason, plus
the difficulty of convincing a detached North American constituency of
the importance of such a radical reorganization in the governance of the
church, the proposal was defeated by the 2000 General Conference. The
action did nothing to discourage the popularity of the concept of a global
church. In fact, it may have even encouraged the pronounced trend in The
UMC for conferences and churches to forge their own linkages with
other bodies in a global church connection for interaction and to undertake joint mission programs.

The struggles to organize the denomination around global representation did not dampen the enthusiasm of mission leaders across the global
connection for participating in events designed to celebrate their common mission. GBGM produced "global gatherings" in Louisville in 1987,
Indianapolis in 1993, and Kansas City in 1997. Four to six thousand

participants attended each of these events, thanks to conferences and churches organizing travel groups by land and air. Plenaries featured such outstanding speakers as Bishop Desmond Tutu (on South Africa's journey away from apartheid) and Jonathan Kozol (on social responsibility for children). Witnesses from the life and ministry of global mission partners challenged all participants to a higher level of commitment to mission outreach. Workshops and seminars on mission topics and program training opportunities were well attended. And the construction of a "global village" in a main convention hall dramatically depicted the importance of such issues as world hunger, threats to the environment, and the danger of land mines. Daily Bible study and worship were the highlights, especially as participants engaged in rituals and joined in singing the music of the churches from every continent.

Such an experience of global community within the context of the denominational family emphasized the gifts each country and culture brought to The UMC, something that needed to be appreciated and valued before serious conversations about organizing the church around a common mission purpose. In the recent past, the only organization capable of producing such an experience was the WCC at its general assemblies. Over the years, assembly participants found much greater satisfaction from the worship, educational forums, and fellowship opportunities of the ecumenical assemblies than from the tedious and laborious plenaries devoted to business. Few world communions produce public events of a global nature, and even the WCC was finding it increasingly difficult to manage. The UMC had the capacity and the energy to experience its global connection through international events or "gatherings." They were not intended to be at the expense of realizing a Christian unity that was ecumenical, not only denominational, in character. This larger vision of a global Christian community required considerable nurturing in difficult times.

Children and Poverty

Having established a prophetic teaching role for the council through the "In Defense of Creation" project, the bishops turned their attention to another issue with major implications for the ministry and mission of The UMC. At their fall meeting in 1996, they issued a foundation statement for an "Episcopal Initiative on Children and Poverty." The church's concern for children was a familiar theme that readily incorporated Jesus' admonition to his disciples about placing children foremost in their presence and ministries. But the statement reported on the harsh facts of the "state of the world's children." The bishops warned of the "genocide of the world's most vulnerable citizens, children in poverty." Because of "economic injustice, racial and ethnic and religious hatred, and the abuse of political power . . . children are being sacrificed" to malnutrition, diseases, military conflicts, homelessness, forced labor, crime, gun violence, sexual abuse, and general neglect." They concluded, "All children have a basic need and right to know that they are loved infinitely by God and that God seeks for them a life of joy, hope and meaning."[12]

The bishops challenged United Methodists to recover their Wesleyan heritage in which the total needs of children, and especially the impoverished, were addressed. John Wesley was noted for having "provided education, opened free health clinics, established a sewing cooperative for women in poverty, provided a lending agency, opposed slavery, visited the imprisoned, and ministered to malefactors. Methodism in the eighteenth century was a movement of the poor, by the poor and for the poor." And the bishops cited with alarm the fact that The UMC in the U.S. "is experiencing a loss of not only impoverished children but children of the middle class as well. The decline in church school enrollment and attendance among children in The UMC at a time when children are increasingly at risk physically and spiritually is a judgment upon us and a call to immediate action."

The bishops collaborated with the general church agencies of the church in producing a program resource for congregations to respond to the needs of children in the church and community. The material provided a checklist of intentional activities aimed at welcoming children into the full community of the church and including the needs of children in the scope of the church's witness. The list included: educating the congregation to the needs of children and the poor; making church facilities safe for children; reducing the risk of child abuse; helping children grow as faithful disciples; involving children in the life of the church; reaching out to children in the community; and advocating for legislation and public policies that improve children's lives and lives of poor families.

Each bishop took responsibility for elevating the profile of children and children's ministries in his or her conference. In April 1999, a report on the response of the conferences was prepared for distribution. It documented a host of creative activities and special programs stimulated by the initiative in the conferences in the U.S. There were also reflections from bishops' personal identification and continuing pastoral involvement with children's programs.

The global reach of the initiative centered upon Africa, a continent with more than its share of oppressive human conditions jeopardizing the future of its children. The council endorsed a Bishops' Appeal with the theme "Hope for the Children of Africa." In an unprecedented move, each active bishop committed herself or himself to raising new program funds for ministries with children in the African central conferences. The African bishops selected projects to benefit from these additional resources, most of which were of a capital development nature, either improvements to existing institutional ministries or the building of new facilities (schools, hostels, clinics serving children). Each funding conference in the U.S. was encouraged to develop a partnership with an enabling conference in Africa.

When the council evaluated the first six years of the Bishops' Initiative on Children and Poverty, some unusually candid observations were made.

> Our focus upon children and the poor has borne fruit. However, too often what seems to preoccupy us are our own children and children like ours. Too little attention has been paid to the economically poor, to the systemic causes of poverty, and to the theological and ecclesiological implications of God's identification and presence with the poor.
>
> We confess that our own lifestyles often reflect being in community with the affluent rather than in community with the poor. The benefits we derive from the very economic system that leaves others impoverished undercuts the credibility of our witness. We stand in need of conversion, and we yearn and commit ourselves to live, like Jesus, in more complete community with the poor.[13]

In renewing the initiative for a new quadrennium, the council became more focused on economic issues, particularly the emergence of the global economy as the cause of the growing marginalization of the poor in the world. "The global economy increasingly resembles a giant casino in which the few are enormously enriched while myriads toil without prospect of a decent chance at life's necessities." The bishops critiqued the history of U.S. Methodism as compromising the principles of Christian community in which the well-being of all is served with the values of an expanding frontier based solely upon economic gains and the spirit of individualism. They regretted the introduction of market interests into the life of the connectional church—especially that the appointment system over which they presided encouraged "pastors [to] compete for bigger salaries and larger congregations." They asked the hard question whether the church is prepared to reconstitute itself as the body of Christ in community with the poor. Their suggestions included a call for "a review" of such systemic issues as:

- How we compensate, evaluate, and appoint clergy and employ church staff;
- How and where we form new congregations;
- How we design and locate church facilities;
- How we define and practice evangelism;
- How we recruit, nurture, and deploy pastoral leaders; and
- How boards and agencies are structured and how they determine their policies.[14]

If the basis for such a review of connectional activities remained the church's mission of serving children in poverty, the Bishops' Initiative held the prospects for securing a new future for The UMC. The test became one of whether the initiative could move from being just another program emphasis to embrace this renewing power of the Spirit. The aims had to be kept in perspective, for persons of wealth do not voluntarily choose poverty. But institutions of influence and wealth, including The UMC, could refocus their work and resources upon basic values that model a human community that respects and serves the welfare of all God's people. The intentionality of the council in renewing its commitment to this initiative offered great encouragement to those in the church and the larger community who shared this vision.

Mission—Initiation and Facilitation

Managing mission outreach within a denomination with so many points of initiation has given way to the notion of "facilitating" mission. A major theme of GBGM in the reorganization and reconceptualization of its program in the late 1990s, this was not really a new discovery for the Board but rather an acknowledgment that mission has never been subject to bureaucratic direction or control. The missionary calling has always been very much centered in a personal response. Missionaries in earlier times were initiators of mission programs that were later endorsed by the denomination's mission board. They purchased properties in their own names, created institutions (schools and clinics) before churches were established, and cultivated financial support from their singularly loyal constituencies. As mission churches took root, their leaders often followed the unilateral patterns of leadership offered by their missionary tutors. United Methodist mission did not evolve with a master plan nor did it head into the twenty-first century with a comprehensive mission strategy. There were and would continue to be some duplication of efforts, some poor stewardship of resources, a mixture of motives and often undiscernible results.

Premeditated mission engagement was not the strong suit of United Methodist mission. Doing mission was preferable to thinking about it. The "Aims of Mission" statement cited at the beginning of this chapter was really an expression of faith in what God can do with everything that the people called Methodist presented through their missionary efforts. If mission was considered the prerogative of the whole church with innumerable points of entry and countervailing directions, voids would be discovered for the church to attempt to fill. For those wishing to lead this church into new mission directions, guidance was more important than stimulus. The last quarter of the twentieth century presented many such opportunities. The General Conference, the Council of Bishops, and the General Council on Ministries all took initiatives in pointing new directions for the church to be engaged in mission.

Missional Priorities

Provision for leading the whole church into a major missional program was given to GCOM. In addition to its responsibility to coordinate general agency programs, a role which the church has generally resisted because it portends a centralized authority which is reserved for General Conference, the council was also charged with recommending missional priorities to the General Conference. A "missional priority" was defined as "a response to a critical need in God's world that calls The United Methodist Church to a massive and sustained effort through primary attention and ordering or reordering of program and budget at every level of the Church." And further, "the required response is beyond the capacity of any single general agency or annual conference."[15]

The council used its power of recommendation sparingly, not for any lack of sensitivity to needs of crisis proportion but out of discretion to avoid watering down the church's response to the chosen priority. Because a missional priority had financial implications with its budgetary needs apportioned to the conferences and local churches, great care was taken to work within estimates of how much of an additional burden the churches could bear.

In order to claim the church's attention to a missional priority, broad-based church participation in implementing its program was required. Committees were structured across the lines of participating general agencies with direct accountability to the recommending body, GCOM. Some argued that this organizational overhead was too costly, and many agencies were clearly discouraged from proposing a program for missional priority status because of the multiple levels of approval and accountability. They much preferred the status of "special program," which granted General Conference recognition and special funding but remained under direct control of the sponsoring agency.

World Hunger

The pace of international development during the last quarter of the twentieth century was rapid but very uneven. While societies in the Northern Hemisphere wallowed in their technological achievements, most of the populations in the countries of the Southern Hemisphere had yet to be exposed to the accomplishments of the Industrial Revolution. As earlier noted, this historical reality prompted the Council of Bishops of The UMC to issue a "Call for Self-Development of Peoples." Its aim was to awaken the church to its responsibility to encourage and participate in the development of economic policies and intergovernmental programs that would serve the welfare of all of God's people. Many conferences were held and position papers developed to help the church membership understand the magnitude of the resource imbalance in the world community and for policymakers to hear the cry of the church for needed corrections.

The denominational mandate to assist with world development was clearly lodged with the mission board. The United Methodist Committee on Relief (UMCOR) was the agency within the Board with the greatest capacity for delivery of aid and funding programs of resource development for human survival. In the 1960s, UMCOR was fulfilling its role—in co-operation with ecumenical relief organizations—by focusing on crises

Harry Haines, the head of UMCOR, became well known throughout the denomination for his leadership in global relief and developmental work. *(Photo courtesy of UM Archives and History)*

with an ever-growing magnitude. The food emergency created by the civil war in Biafra in 1967–1970 became an all-consuming enterprise for the churches. It was but the first of many conflicts within newly independent countries of Africa that produced dislocation of the masses and a permanent presence of refugee camps across that continent.

With the 1970s came awareness that all resources that sustain human life on this planet are not renewable. The 1973 "oil crisis," prompted by the exercise of political power by the cartel of oil-producing nations, was a major wake-up call, especially to the churches of the Northern Hemisphere, that all was not well with the stewardship of the earth's scarce resources, including food. It was a time for self-examination and creative responses. The WCC sought to interpret the situation from the perspective of the poor nations:

> As a result of a combination of circumstances, many of the poor societies of the world face an even graver and more critical situation than formerly. There is a serious shortage of food in various countries and in the world as a whole. Inflation spirals; and monetary values fluctuate

alarmingly. Without some cutback in the rate of consumption of both food and energy by the rich everywhere with a view to the fairer distribution of the world's resources among the human family, the poor everywhere will face increasing misery. . . . At present oil prices, the non-oil producing countries of the Third World will have to pay as much as $10 billion in additional oil bills. The total flow of development aid and loans they receive is about $9 billion. At current rates, India will spend 80% of its export earnings for oil, Bangladesh 85%. . . . Within both rich and poor nations, it is the poorest people who are the most affected. Just as the rich nations, rich people everywhere have sufficient resources to fall back on; for the poor the problem is one of survival. The plight of the poor, more than half of the human family, is a challenge to the rich and privileged everywhere. The churches, who are committed to the service of the poor and the promotion of justice, cannot be silent in this critical period. As churches we have to examine the various factors that combine to oppress the poor of the earth everywhere.[16]

The Board of Global Ministries already had an interdivisional task force working on world hunger, defining the issues and developing a response. A 1974 report from Dr. Harry Haines, associate general secretary of UMCOR, cited the urgency and the disastrous extent of the developing world food and energy crisis:

Over the next 12 months, there may be from 10 million to 30 million incremental deaths in (less developed countries) as a result of starvation of diseases rendered by fatal malnutrition. Only a large effort by the fortunate minority of developed, well-fed nations can prevent this disaster. . . . If astronomers told us that a comet would crash into the earth one year from today, probably killing 30 million or more people and possibly spinning the whole planet out of its orbit, the whole world would mobilize its technical resources to try to deflect the comet from its path and avoid disaster. It remains to be seen whether this less tangible but equally certain threat of massive starvation and political upheaval can be dealt with in time.[17]

The Board's response was to designate the issue of hunger as "a central theme for immediate action, prayer and study" and to recommend the theme for a similar quadrennial designation by the forthcoming General Conference.[18] In anticipation of the favorable action of the conference, the interdivisional task force of the Board of Global Ministries outlined an all-encompassing program strategy. The Board aimed to accomplish strategies for both amelioration and prevention. "Combating the problem of emergency and perennial hunger has long been an essential aspect of Board program. Increasingly, churches and other bodies have become aware of the need not only to bring relief but have begun to focus on more permanent measures of development as well. There is a need to avoid a 'crisis psychology' and work for long-term development. We urge that in order to address the chronic situation of hunger, new and creative efforts be made which link economic development with consciousness raising of people, leading to self-reliance and their participation in decision-making."[19]

Proposals in the plan included direct assistance to affected nations and groups. This assistance took the form of funds for and cooperation with other ecumenical and development-oriented organizations. It included programs of training and deployment of personnel in development programs. It also provided for funds for projects to encourage small farming and appropriate technologies. The role of women in rural development was recognized globally. Finally, the plan provided for work with community development programs emphasizing holistic development (health, education, population growth, nutrition, agriculture, and evangelism). Within the U.S., the plan encouraged advocacy of accountability of agribusinesses, changes in governmental policies and programs related to food production, and support for publicly funded food assistance programs for the poor. Within the church, there was a call for education of the constituency on the issues of world hunger and even a call for a "disciplined fellowship of at least 300,000 United Methodists to give themselves a new and simpler life style based on the need to eradicate world hunger."

When the 1976 General Conference approved World Hunger as a missional priority for the 1977–1980 quadrennium, most of the elements of the Board's program were endorsed. The legislation identified four areas of responsibility:

(1) Services and resources to help alleviate hunger, and the basic causes of hunger in the U.S. and abroad (assigned to GBGM);

(2) Lifestyles for acting out Christian discipleship (assigned to GBOD);

(3) Public policy and legislation involving hunger and poverty (assigned to GBCS); and

(4) Training opportunities with United Methodist educational institutions (assigned to GBHEM).

A goal for funding for the missional priority was established at $5 million annually. Two million dollars was to be included in the general church Missional Priority Fund apportioned to the conferences and churches, and $3 million was to be raised through Advance Special offerings. Fifty-eight percent of the funding was to be used to fund the services and resources area of work assigned to GBGM. The program was to be administered by a Coordinating Committee on Hunger with representation from each of the administering general program agencies.

C. Dean Freudenberger, professor at the School of Theology in Claremont, California, and a former agricultural missionary, assisted GBGM with training and development of church leaders to advance the goals of the program. He opined, "Church leaders have had little orientation, let alone systematic training, to fathom the mystery of rural community and agricultural development for food production." With the aid of government and foundation funding, he helped other church leaders design a 1976 Vatican conference on agricultural development in tropical and monsoon conditions. Accompanying him to Rome were key mission leaders from churches in Tonga, Kenya, the Philippines, and India. He was gratified to hear these participants interviewed by Vatican Radio and committing themselves to strategic involvement in their respective countries. The Reverend David M. Geconcillio and his wife Marcina, Filipino Crusade Scholars, "told of correspondence with their church in the Philippines requesting a rural appointment in spite of the hardships which it will bring." Mr. and Mrs. John Nyesi of Kenya "spoke in very moving terms about how they would begin the integration of their new knowledge into the life and ministry of the United Theological College and its rural outreach throughout the life and work of the National Council of Churches in Kenya."[20]

Hunger remained a missional priority program of The UMC for one quadrennium. Similar programs emerged in other denominations, which reinforced the urgency of the message and the solicitation of a generous response. The participating agencies collaborated with a host of organizations working on the issues of world hunger. An entire infrastructure of

U.S. regional and community organizations that had developed in the 1960s in response to President Lyndon Johnson's declared War on Poverty quickly shifted its focus to hunger-related issues and was at the disposal of the churches. The church membership became acquainted and began to support significant allies in the struggle to eliminate hunger. Bread for the World, an independent, interdenominationally supported advocacy group located in Washington, D.C., became a vital resource in the analysis of public policy issues and in the mobilization of a constituency response to proposed legislation. Local chapters recruited church members into action groups working with state and municipal governments on programs of social welfare, health, and nutrition.

By action of the 1980 General Conference, the missional priority on world hunger became a special program in 1981 and was assigned to GBGM for direct administration. The program thrust remained the same, and interagency cooperation was maintained. The substantial change was in funding, since the program no longer benefitted from a general church apportionment. Generous support continued through designated gifts to the Advance. A discussion of the management of this program within GBGM can be found in chapter 5.

Strengthening and Developing Racial / Ethnic Churches

The mission focus of the church upon injustices that provoked so much social conflict and turmoil in the late 1960s shifted in the following decade to highlight inequalities within its internal or institutional life. In 1976, Dr. Grant Shockley, then president of the Interdenominational Theological Seminary in Atlanta, was engaged in a study on the "Crisis in the Ethnic Minority Churches" for presentation to General Conference later that year. He presented some of his findings to the Board of Global Ministries meeting in March of that year. His data was drawn from the black church experience but could be readily applied to Native American, Hispanic, and Asian churches as well. He cited a declining black church membership in spite of population increases. Less than 50 percent of the black population belonged to churches. He noted that most black United Methodist members attended predominantly black membership churches, with little change since the dissolution of the Central Jurisdiction. He questioned the resolve of the denomination to create an inclusive church and challenged the false assumption that minorities would continue to remain in a denomination in which they do not share equally in its life and authority.

Finally, he reminded the directors of the mission agency that most of the black and minority churches were situated on the cutting edge of mission opportunities in both inner city neighborhoods and rural areas.[21] With that challenge, the directors were prepared to support the call at the forthcoming General Conference for a missional priority on strengthening and developing racial and ethnic churches.

The approach to the 1976 General Conference depicted the condition of racial/ethnic minorities within the denomination as in a state of crisis. Delegates recognized that even the small number of racial/ethnic members in the denomination were an institutional asset the church could not afford to lose, and the General Conference voted to establish a missional priority on Strengthening and Developing the Ethnic Minority Local Church. A goal of $5 million was approved, with $2.5 million earmarked as a new general church fund for apportionment to the conferences and churches and $2.5 million to be raised through voluntary "second mile gifts" through the Advance. Each of the four major program boards were given a share in the administration of the funds for programs in three major categories: church development, leadership development, and community outreach.

Constituencies directly benefitting from the new missional priority were African-American, Asian-American, Hispanic, and Native American United Methodists, distributed unevenly among a small number of annual conferences. By embracing the distinct racial/ethnic groups within the priority, the church signaled its recognition that cultural affirmation of these individual groups was the defining principle for mission development. The hopes for their integration into predominantly white churches would not be realized. Conferences with few, if any, racial/ethnic congregations either opted out or speculated whether they were included in this churchwide missional priority. The challenge became clearer as patterns of migration became more diffuse and opportunities for new church development among racial/ethnic populations were staring them in the face. Conferences with established racial/ethnic populations and churches were challenged to think about growth and to begin comprehensive planning for programs of development and outreach.

Each of the racial ethnic/groups had a special agenda of needs and issues to address; all relied upon their nationally organized caucuses to keep them before the administrators of the missional priority funds. Among the African-American churches, those with ties to the former

Central Jurisdiction were still trying to appropriate the gains (and losses) of their incorporation into the denomination in 1968. An aging supply of black pastors was not being replaced at the rate of termination by retirement or death. Many black churches in the rural South required major repairs or building renovations. The expanding African-American populations in urban areas, especially in the North, were underserved by black United Methodist churches. New church development and strategies for ministries in transitional communities (from white to black) were needed.

Hispanics in the U.S. were moving far beyond the reach of the historic ethnic-language missions of the denomination located along the Río Grande and in Puerto Rico. The major metropolitan areas of the northern states were greatly augmented by Hispanic population growth. The Spanish language was the common cultural characteristic among the various national groups, and it was not sacrificed in the process of their acculturation within new communities. Neighborhood churches began opening their doors to fellowship groups of Hispanic Christians wishing to use their facilities for worship and service. Conferences required Spanish-speaking pastors, a commodity that was in short supply. Latin American Methodist churches provided a small pool of talent from which to draw, but national origin of the congregations to be supplied usually dictated the recruitment of acceptable pastors.

Asian Americans comprised the most diverse nationally organized racial/ethnic constituency in the church. The historic mission among Japanese-American immigrants of earlier generations had dissolved into the conferences. A few congregations of Nisei (second-generation) Japanese-American families remained and offered encouragement to newly arriving immigrant groups with Methodist origins or seeking out relationships to The UMC. Most prominent were the Korean Methodists, who came with considerable evangelistic zeal. Pastors educated in Methodist schools in Korea were included in the immigrating population and found their way to local United Methodist churches and other meeting places to gather congregations of immigrant families. Getting their Korean Methodist clergy credentials recognized by United Methodist conferences was the first hurdle to gaining the support of the United Methodist connection. Another was a requirement that their congregations become financially self-supporting before they could be received into full conference membership. Similar problems were encountered by immigrant Philippine United Methodists and Methodists from India,

Indochina, and the Pacific Islands, who were among those that the growing North American economy attracted to the U.S.

The Native American mission within Methodism historically focused on the reservation populations of the Southwestern U.S. Accepting the comity agreements among the churches enforced by the Bureau of Indian Affairs, The Methodist Church created the Oklahoma Indian Missionary Conference (OIMC).[22] Few ministries were established by conferences for Native Americans who took up residence off their reservations. The new missional priority had to keep both populations in focus when developing program and funding strategies. It was not easy, since loyalties to the historic work were strong, and the base of leadership for work with nonreservation populations was very small. This distinction among the Native American constituency became aggravated and an independent caucus was soon organized to represent nonreservation Native American constituents — the Native American International Caucus (NAIC). For both groups, leadership development and program funding were crucial to the enhancement of Christian witness among Native people by United Methodists. Poverty conditions prevailed in both reservations and among the diaspora tribal communities. The paucity of seminary-trained clergy available for service in Native American churches required a long-term strategy.

With the administration of the missional priority programs decentralized among four general agencies and implemented in seventy-three annual conferences, collecting quantitative data to evaluate the overall impact of the priority had been a challenge. In 1988, the missional priority coordinating committee reported to General Conference on some of the results of four quadrennia of funding totaling more than $57 million:

116 new ethnic congregations formed,

85 ethnic congregation buildings constructed,

56 parsonages for ten congregations built,

289 ethnic minority elders ordained, and

21 ethnic minority diaconal ministers consecrated.[23]

Statistically, the most significant contribution of the missional priority on Strengthening and Developing the Ethnic Minority Local Church (later renamed a missional priority on Racial Ethnic Local Churches) may have been helping the church to maintain its distinction as the most racially diverse mainline Protestant denomination in the U.S. The UMC is often recognized by its ecumenical partners for its diversity, and leaders from the ranks of its racial/ethnic membership were frequently drafted for denominational and ecumenical program offices. Bishop Melvin G. Talbert recalled that the program was in part created in response to "vacancies left by minorities moving into positions at the conference and general church levels. . . . There was a lack of leadership — we could not supply adequate leadership to the existing black churches. So far from talking about expanding our ministries, we couldn't take care of those we had. . . . I think it's been a tremendous success if we've simply stopped the tide of decline."[24]

Helping the church understand and affirm the value of inclusiveness is another acknowledged achievement of the missional priority. According to Yolanda Rivas, an Hispanic pastor elected to the position of associate general secretary of the General Commission on Religion and Race, the missional priority required the majority church to enter into a process of reexamination or, theologically speaking, "repentance." The result was that "the ethnic church is not any longer an alien group in the visible body of the church, but is part of the same family, not second or third cousins, but equals." At every level of denominational life, stifling attitudes of condescension and dependence were challenged and ethnic minorities were able "to assess their own problems and needs, and to take the needed steps required to change conditions and determine where they wanted to be."[25]

Early into the experience of the quadrennial missional priority, Dr. John Graham, a black pastor, district superintendent, and mission board executive, cautioned leaders about the limited effectiveness of short-term programs in addressing the systemic needs of black United Methodists: "Crash programs, or occasional quadrennial emphases, will not solve the problem. It must be addressed by every general board, every institution, every bishop and district superintendent within the church. Short-term programs at best will serve only as a bandage and raise inflated hopes among Black people in the church."[26]

Graham's warnings applied to all ethnic minority groups in the church that together advocated for the "incorporation" of the missional priority as a regular (or continuing) program emphasis of the denomination. This concept was adopted by the 1988 General Conference and embraced by succeeding conferences, which earmarked a quadrennial amount of $5.5

million in general church funds to underwrite racial/ethnic programs through the participating general agencies.[27]

While the missional priority program emphasis may not have stimulated much membership growth among these expanding population groups, the denomination grew in appreciation of the cultural values and learned to accept the leadership gifts of its broad-based membership. More racial/ethnic persons were elected to serve in leadership positions. In 1984, the largest class of racial/ethnic bishops was elected. While many of the obvious statistics of development can be cited, including the number of church buildings built or remodeled and the rate of growth in leaders recruited and trained for ministry, the program resources needed to sustain the future of culturally distinct groups in the church should also be recognized. During the life of the missional priority, hymnal supplements were published: *Songs of Zion*, African American; *Celebremos*, Hispanic; and *Voices and Hymns from the Four Winds*, Native American. In addition, the denomination published the *Korean-English Bilingual Hymnal*.[28] Church school curricula and program publications were produced for the primary language groups.

The symbolic significance of the missional priority outweighed the substance of the program. While The UMC declared itself in favor of inclusiveness as a denomination, it was not aggressively stating that it was "open for business" in communities of color. The priority was focused more on the internal agenda of the local church than on the public image of a denomination in a competitive church membership marketplace. The needs of those already in the fold were fortified, without asking what the church must do to offer an attractive witness and ministry in unfamiliar communities.

For instance, investing in alternative (church-based) educational opportunities for Hispanic children was never considered, even though their failure and dropout rate from public schools was higher than other minority groups. Church schools are part and parcel of the Latin American culture and would provide a more intimate and supportive environment for immigrant children than large classes in the poorly financed neighborhood schools they were forced to attend. Such a strategy implemented nationally would have made a significant welcoming statement from a Protestant denomination to the fastest-growing minority population in the U.S. and with historical roots in Catholic cultures.

Similarly, encouraging strong black churches in poor urban neigh-borhoods to develop business enterprises in order to stimulate local economies and provide jobs for church and community members was not a "church development" strategy. Many independent nondenominational churches successfully undertook such ventures and saw their memberships grow and thrive as a result. Recruiting proven pastoral leadership from beyond the Methodist streams of church experience was considered "off base." Black storefront churches in many of the nation's cities were train-ing grounds for pastors but were not cultivated for United Methodist membership under the missional priority.

The missional priority did not pursue property ownership as a strategy for racial/ethnic church growth and expansion. Though The UMC was a connectional organization wherein local properties were held in trust for the denomination, most local churches were inclined to act on property matters with rights of immediate ownership. Efforts at trying to solve the problems of sharing building space by two or more United Methodist congregations or fellowship groups often engendered more hard feelings than acceptance. A denominational investment fund that would preempt properties in changing communities for future church development was not considered. Leaders were content to see millions of United Methodist dollars wasted on rental contracts or in borrowing from secular financial institutions.

Racial/Ethnic Plans for Ministry

As the missional priority for Strengthening and Developing Racial Ethnic Local Churches was "mainstreamed" into the life of the church, mission strategies for each of the individual racial/ethnic constituent groups began to emerge. These efforts were developed by the leadership of the respective racial/ethnic caucuses, who sought the attention of the General Conference and then proposed major program initiatives with general church funding.

Two plans were adopted by the 1992 General Conference: a Compre-hensive Plan for Hispanic Ministry, and a Comprehensive Plan for Native American Ministries. Both were to be administered by leadership groups selected from within their racial/ethnic membership. The initiatives were assigned to GBGM for general supervision.

The Hispanic plan laid out an aggressive program for church and lead-ership development for annual conferences to "buy in." Recognizing existing strongholds for their work in major metro areas of the regions of the church, Hispanic church leaders — especially laity — were trained in church development methodologies for starting new chapels. (Chapels are informal gathering places for small groups of immigrant inquirers and believers, many of whom are disaffected by the traditional authority of the Roman Catholic tradition in Latin American cultures reflected in the rites and symbols of austere parish churches of their adopted North American urban neighborhoods.) Attention was also given to conferences and local churches with no Hispanic ministries but with signs of growing Hispanic populations to be served. Hispanic missionary personnel were recruited and trained by GBGM to work with the conferences and churches in strategic planning and program development. Teams of Hispanic church leaders were recruited to develop program resources and conduct training events. A strong solidarity of purpose and resolve for full and comprehensive implementation was cultivated and an impact felt across the connection. In the 1997–2000 quadrennium, the program peaked with nineteen deployed missionary personnel, program development initiated with forty-one conferences, twenty-nine congregations chartered, 176 missions established, 318 faith communities gathered, and Sunday schools extended in 201 locations.[29]

The Native American plan continued to address the leadership shortage and used available funding to sponsor constituency events. Some were programmatic, such as congregational development and evangelism and camping, while others were more developmental, such as research into how to stimulate economic development within Native communities and cultivating Native American spirituality. The Center for Native American Ministry housed at Claremont School of Theology provided a base for a coordinator. Unfortunately, the plan did not cultivate a closer working relationship between the OIMC and the NAIC. Both claimed resources from the missional initiative but failed to work or strategize together about the future of the United Methodist witness among Native Americans.

The 1992 General Conference approved research proposals that led to the formation of two more program initiatives. The Asian American Language Ministries study identified the scarce resources available to the small but growing number of Indochinese, South Asian, and Pacific Islander congregations or fellowships developing within the conferences in the U.S.[30] An effort was made by GBGM, working with other general agencies, to network the leaders of these fledgling groups and to become their advocates within the general church and the conferences. General church funding, on a rather limited basis, was also made available as incentive grants for the developing congregations.

The second proposal focused on Strengthening the Black Church for the Twenty-First Century. It surveyed the status of black churches and developed a strategy of creating teaching centers at those churches that evidenced a record of institutional growth and/or program development of a specialized nature that deserved replication. The 1996 General Conference adopted both of these proposals and assigned them to general agencies for supervision (Asian American Language Ministries to GBGM, and Strengthening the Black Church to GCOM).

While these initiatives provided a specific focus and direction for the ministry and mission development of the individual racial/ethnic groups within the denomination, it is questionable whether their learnings benefitted the whole connection. Though ownership was gained through the participation and leadership of members of the racial/ethnic caucuses in the denomination, their administration tended to be rather independent, even under the supervision of assigned general program agencies. Each of the initiatives had to approach the same institutions and agencies of the denomination with individual messages and appeals. The guiding hope was that there might be some cumulative effect, but by the year 2000 the denomination was without a comprehensive strategy for defining and developing its mission to an increasingly diverse and pluralistic population. A greater concern, however, was the adequacy of resources committed to this effort. If the whole denomination was to benefit from these initiatives extended on its behalf, it had to be sure that both funding and accountability were well established.

Special Programs

The *Discipline* anticipated the creation of special programs which responded to "a distinct opportunity or need in God's world that is evidenced by research or other supporting data."[31] A "special program" endured quadrennium by quadrennium with the recommendation of GCOM and the blessing of the General Conference. It was assigned to a general program agency for administration and had to find its funding within the resources of the general church approved quadrennially by the General Conference.

Africa Church Growth and Development

Upon recommendation of GCOM, the General Conference of 1980 gave Africa Church Growth and Development the status of a "special program." It authorized GBGM, the originating agency, to administer and promote the program.

The aim of the program was to bring to the attention of the whole church the unusual opportunities for undergirding the growth of Christianity and the development of United Methodist churches on the continent. Missiologists were predicting that the rate of growth of Christianity in Africa would result in the continent having a larger Christian population than all of North America. The United Methodist conferences in Africa were experiencing rapid growth, more than doubling their total membership between 1980 and 1990, from a reported membership of 430,000 to 1,100,000.

The program was designed to respond to the profound vision and the initiative for spiritual renewal from within the African churches. John W. Z. Kurewa articulated the theological and missional significance of the claims of African leadership upon the new directions of mission on the continent. Kurewa was a United Methodist clergyman from Zimbabwe who served as an administrative assistant to a bishop and a staff member of the WCC. He became the first president of Africa University. Kurewa wrote in 1979: "God called his Church in Africa around Christ for a purpose, and that mission is to be carried out by the African Church. . . . A Church which has no consciousness of mission of its own may be living on convictions of other people or on faith of past generations. . . . The renewal of the United Methodist Church [in Africa] which started in 1980 was God's activity to liberate . . . the Church from being mission-station bound and from missionary control to a church that would adapt itself to the indigenous life-style of the African people. The Church had to be African — praying, singing and proclaiming the Gospel in the African ways and thought-forms."[32]

Kurewa and other African United Methodist leaders insisted that Africans have the same opportunity for understanding and mobilizing their resources for mission as did their missionary-minded North American United Methodist ancestors earlier in the century. In spite of the manner in which missionaries worked, which he described as "crude" and only in "collaboration with their own kind," their "obedience" created a strong

As this art from the Democratic Republic of the Congo demonstrates, Africa is the source of many valuable and positive contributions to humanity, even though the media in the West typically reports on Africa only when the continent suffers famine, civil conflict, or other disasters there. *(Photo by Robert J. Harman)*

"mission consciousness" for cultivation.[33] While establishing a financial goal of $7 million to be raised through the Advance in the first quadrennium, the program design honored the concept of self-determination and introduced mutuality into the process of decision making by creating a committee structure with a majority of representatives from African United Methodist churches. Twenty-seven members came from the African annual conferences and provisional conferences, three from conferences in Europe, and fourteen from conferences in the U.S. African United Methodists were peers in decision making with their European and North American church colleagues.

The Africa Church Growth and Development Committee met annually to administer funding decisions related to three areas of work: (1) evangelism and community development; (2) leadership development; and (3) church construction. But a uniqueness of the program was in the form of administration it established. The committee took a holistic view of the church development needs and challenges of United Methodist churches on the continent. It set priorities in order to increase the impact of its grants. In 1986, the committee voted to concentrate on funding the construction of a new church in Maputo, the capital city of Mozambique.

United Methodist mission in Mozambique had been confined, by colonial authorities, to rural areas. With the movement of population to the capital city during the difficult struggles after independence, a strong church presence was needed. A beautiful new edifice for the Chomuncula UMC was dedicated on Easter Sunday 1989 and was especially well suited to serve a growing congregation and a large community of internally displaced persons because of a postrevolutionary conflict. The service was attended by representatives of conferences across the continent, expressing the solidarity of the United Methodists in Africa who were willing to subordinate their own conference projects to the funding of the completion of the priority project in Mozambique.

Another distinctive feature in the program design was the commitment of the African churches to participate in the fund raising as well as the administration of grants. Of the $7 million to be raised in the first quadrennium of the program, the African churches subscribed to a goal of $1 million. There was considerable enthusiasm in African churches to participate fully in this program. Within the first two years of the program, it was reported that the African churches gave $147,126. That represented a rate of per capita giving for Angolan United Methodists of 99 cents and $1.50 for Mozambique United Methodists.[34] The European churches were also generous in their funding of the program.

The promotion and the administration of the program was placed in the hands of an executive director, Dr. Nathan Goto of Zimbabwe. Goto, a former school administrator and lay leader in the Zimbabwe Annual Conference, worked tirelessly in his itineration of projects of the African churches and in telling their stories to conferences and churches in the U.S. He praised the program for its capacity to unite the conferences in Africa in a significant effort of development: Africa Church Growth and Development, he said, "is unique in that it brings to the conference table our African United Methodist people and those from Europe and the United States in order to discuss projects crucial to the future of the Church in Africa. . . . This is the first time we Africans have been directly involved in determining which of our priorities will be served. We do it, not on an individual basis to church bodies in Mozambique, Zimbabwe, Angola, Zaire, Nigeria, Liberia and Sierra Leone, where The United Methodist Church is present, but with a view to the good of the continent as a whole."[35]

The marks of Africa Church Growth and Development were found not only in church structures and organizational achievements but in valuing the gifts of persons. The United Methodist churches in Africa were growing because of outstanding leadership. Young people selected by their churches to benefit from scholarship assistance through this special program were prominent in the leadership roles of their churches, communities, and the ecumenical movement in Africa. Leadership development was the assurance of the future influence of the churches in Africa. In the Africa Church Growth and Development arena the early conversations about the need for a denominational university in Africa were held. Ironically, as the Africa University project ascended in prominence, Africa Church Growth and Development descended. Funding diminished and the costly style of administration with a large committee had to be reconsidered. By 2000, income through the Advance for each of the program categories had trailed to almost insignificant levels and the executive committee of the fund was left to preside over limited resources and opportunities for funding. Africa Church Growth and Development had not captured the key to effective promotion of mission in the last quarter of the twentieth century, namely, direct participation by constituents. Nevertheless, it successfully introduced the notion of a cooperative strategy and vision for the United Methodist witness on the entire continent.

Communities of Shalom

The General Conference of 1992, meeting in its capacity as the highest policymaking body of the denomination, demonstrated its ability to respond to a "kairos moment." The conference met in Louisville, Kentucky, shortly after devastating riots consumed the neighborhoods of south Los Angeles. The incident that sparked the uprising was the abuse of a black motorist, Rodney King, by white policemen, an incident that was caught on videotape and then televised nationally. Reactions to this obvious injustice became a prolonged rebellion in the minority neighborhoods overwhelmed by similar problems with police and community relations and also severe economic conditions. The violence and destruction occupied national attention for weeks.

The General Conference members in Louisville received a briefing on the situation from the bishop and superintendent of the Los Angeles Area. They concluded that the General Conference could not proceed with business as usual until it had made a response. Long hours were spent on reflection, meditation, and deliberation. Joseph Sprague, a clergy

Richard Abrams, a church and community worker who was a part of Communities of Shalom, helped Kimberly King, left, and Jeremy Mosely at the Bethlehem Centers of Nashville in 1999. *(Photo courtesy of UM Archives and History)*

member of the West Ohio Annual Conference, gave passionate and articulate leadership to the discussion of developing a program response of establishing community foundations based upon biblical and theological principles of peace with justice. He called upon the body to introduce to Los Angeles and to communities across the nation a response based upon the biblical concept of shalom. He envisioned churches and people of all faiths working together to rebuild their neighborhoods and create viable communities. A working group was delegated to bring a proposal to the body. Sprague's idea was refined and then defined in a formal proposal which the General Conference then adopted as a special program for immediate implementation. A national committee was named and the program assigned to GBGM for supervision and funding.

Los Angeles was designated a "Shalom Zone," and leaders from across the connectional church descended on the affected neighborhoods with the hopes of modeling community-based programs that could be replicated in other places with similar critical needs. Church and community leaders were encouraged to look first within their own community for available leadership and resources before turning to outside groups. Religious leaders, not only United Methodists, were encouraged to work together and to provide a highly visible profile for religious values to guide the response. Attention was given to the fears and uncertainties of ethnic groups that had become part of the hostilities and would prevent them from joining hands in a rebuilding effort. Offering a united front and working with a plan that valued self-directed development for the good of the whole community, requests for funding were presented to governmental agencies and private groups or foundations.

The denominational intervention in Los Angeles became a demonstration project for the whole church. Soon personnel were recruited from across the church for training and mobilization of similar efforts in their communities. Staff provided by GBGM worked directly with the general committee that established policy and direction for the program. The program did not promise funding but offered training methodologies that included techniques for leveraging local community resources as a stimulus for external sources to recognize and respond. The number of such training events multiplied and the leaders from each were included in a continuing network of mutual support.

In 1996, the Shalom Committee reported on its activities to the General Conference, using the theme, "Shalom is on the Move." The General Conference endorsed the program for continuation. The general committee began wrestling with how it could institutionalize its work, including the establishment of a foundation to support its work. It also began testing the feasibility of its community development strategies for deployment in Third World contexts. Churches in Africa issued invitations for the Communities of Shalom to work with them.

Special Program on Substance Abuse and Related Violence (SPSARV)

The growing chemical dependency among significant segments of the U.S. population reached crisis proportions in the last quarter of the twentieth century. Drug dealers and their constituencies became a dominant part of local economies and a deterrent to the social welfare of hard-pressed inner city communities. Students were admitting to "experimental" use of drugs, and addiction rates among youth were rising. Recreational use of drugs became popular among more affluent and success-oriented personnel in the corporate business world. Acts of violence and crime traditionally correlative to drug abuse were on the rise nationally.

Leadership in The UMC—a denomination with an historic role in temperance work—became increasingly restless about the situation. Discussion was initiated by the COB, which eventuated in a missional initiative with both pastoral and prophetic consequences. In 1990, Bishop Felton May of the Harrisburg Area offered himself for a special assignment by his colleagues. A little-exercised disciplinary provision for the COB to assign one of its members "to some specific churchwide responsibility deemed of sufficient importance to the welfare of the total Church" was employed to appoint May to a year-long, highly visible ministry of combatting drug abuse.[36] His assignment included taking up residence in Washington, D.C., in order to mobilize pastors and congregations in effective ministries in city neighborhoods that had become notorious for drug trafficking.

With funding provided through Advance Special promotion, guidance from the leadership of the Baltimore-Washington Annual Conference, and staff assistance from GBGM, various program strategies were developed. Claiming drug addiction as a spiritual matter, local D.C. churches sponsored Soul Saving Stations. Tents, reminiscent of revival services, were erected in neighborhoods. Preaching and gospel music attracted gatherings of people from the neighborhoods on warm summer evenings. Counseling and social services were offered to all who requested help. Direct action programs were planned against purveyors of drugs. Leaders did not overlook the complicity of landlords and tenants who allowed their properties to be used by drug dealers. City officials were invited to the neighborhoods and stirred to action by improving law enforcement as well as improving programs of prevention.

A model for churches becoming proactive in reclaiming their urban neighborhoods from the pestilence of drug addiction and violence began to emerge. But the bishop's activities were not limited to one city or to the urban context. With the help of GBCS, training seminars were designed for congregations to undertake supportive and healing ministries for their membership and constituencies to implement. May was tireless in his travels across the connection, helping congregations establish patterns of communication about the problem of drugs and then offering suggestions for program development. When his "special assignment" ended, he had established a significant momentum within the church for a special program on drug abuse.

The 1992 General Conference approved the creation of SPSARV. GBGM and GBCS shared in direct supervision, but all general agencies cooperated in developing program guidelines and resources. Staff members of SPSARV worked with annual conference leaders in identifying

and resourcing model development programs at five sites. They participated in numerous workshops and training events that developed strong
leadership teams in the conferences. In addition, the staff members cultivated ties with other service providers to reach critical constituencies,
e.g., college campuses, with their program. And they collaborated on a
legislative agenda with GBCS to address problematic sentencing laws and
counter-productive treatment modalities.

Once established as a general church program, the popularity of the
substance abuse program grew among central conferences. Training programs were developed in cooperation with the leadership of the central conferences in Europe, and the leadership base of the SPSARV was
greatly enriched and expanded. The Northern Europe Central Conference included the new mission conference in Russia, which welcomed the
program resources to enable it to serve better in communities that were
devastated by the effects of alcoholism. Early in the new millennium, a
global conference was held in Zimbabwe to bring leaders from Europe
and Africa together for the first time to resource one another in establishing ministries of outreach and service.

Holy Boldness—National Plan for Urban Ministry

The ministry of Methodism in the major cities of North America
traces its beginnings to the settlement of immigrant communities in the
late nineteenth and early twentieth centuries. They are, to a great extent,
conditioned by the same social and political dynamics today. Where European and Scandinavian congregations once gathered, congregations
composed of people from Latin America, Africa, Asia, and the Pacific met
in the late twentieth century. Pastors and parishioners who waited at the
Eastern shore docks to receive their loved ones from passenger vessels
lined the baggage claim areas at international airports to assist family
members in making their entry into U.S. society. Immigrant congregations often provided new arrivals with their first foothold in a strange and
fast-paced way of life driven largely by unfamiliar forces of economic accumulation and consumption. They clung desperately to language and
cultural values protected by ethnic-centered fellowship groups that helped
them absorb the risks of entering places of work, classrooms, markets, and
public or social service agencies.

The missional priority on the Racial Ethnic Local Church helped focus the church's attention to this reality but not to the extent realized by

earlier generations. At the turn of the century, not only local churches, but also church-based social institutions — hospitals, homes, and community centers — were established to serve these new communities without reliable public services. It was clear that the denomination had an intentional strategy and a commitment to cultivate and conserve its valued constituencies. Evidence of a similar development-oriented strategy for the late-twentieth century church was not readily found.

Contemporary strategies for urban ministry were too often crisis oriented and therefore distracted from actively cultivating opportunities for growth and development. The mid-twentieth century decline in labor-intensive agricultural economies in the Southern states forced African Americans to move to Northern cities for employment. This movement found neighborhood institutions — and especially the churches — ill prepared. Congregations reverted to the same discriminatory behaviors as local businesses and their political leaders who inspired panic-selling of homes and relocation to new neighborhoods, often the suburbs. Church buildings were sold and even abandoned to enable congregations to rebuild in newly segregated neighborhoods. Conferences were focused on new church development in "high potential" communities that excluded those where newly arriving African-American populations sought out church relationships. Most efforts at garnering support for highly pressured urban churches found little interest among a growing church constituency that had intentionally left the city behind.

The deprivation in the urban neighborhoods that fueled rebellion in several cities during the 1960s provoked a variety of responses from The UMC. (Several urban programs are described in chapter 1.) The denomination was losing ground in major population areas and needed a strategy for recovery and rebuilding. The National Division of the Board of Missions sought out the advice and counsel of key leadership from the annual conferences. Known as the "Linkage Group," these leaders were convened in the role of a denominational urban brain trust. They found counterparts in other denominations, relations that soon expanded their ideological reach and range of strategy development and influence. One of their conclusions was that neither denominational agencies nor conciliar ecumenism was structured to implement a strategic response that included urgent decision making and a direct funding capacity. They formed a coalition among Protestant denominational national mission agencies known as the Joint Action and Strategy Committee (JSAC). Mission heads at the JSAC table collaborated on funding programs and projects for which they did not have time to develop popular support within denominational or conciliar church bodies. Primary among them were community-organizing efforts, including Saul Alinsky's controversial Industrial Area Foundation that specialized in conflict-oriented tactics to create momentum for changes in public policy. For several years denominational funding through JSAC enabled surviving urban churches in many cities to participate in efforts at stabilizing their communities. Grants encouraged new forms of denominational cooperation at local levels to address community issues like public education, housing, employment, health, and safety.

JSAC had a limited future in that it suffered from a generationally based membership. The participants were the last of a vanishing breed of "white male" urban church leaders in their denominations. By the late 1970s, women and persons of color gradually came into the denominational agency ranks and replaced them. The structures they had built for interdenominational strategies for urban ministries did not survive the transition. New denominational priorities preempted cooperative mission strategies. In The UMC, the pendulum had clearly swung to racial and ethnic church development missional priority and emerging special programs.

The most consistent strategy development for United Methodist urban work came through a network of United Methodist urban ministers and program personnel. It was nurtured by the Urban Ministries Office of the National Division of GBGM and its director, the late Reverend Kinmoth Jefferson. Organized into jurisdictional subunits, the urban network provided the Board with a liaison relationship with a variety of creative local programs for which only limited funding was made available. Participants placed a high value on the networking relationship with like-minded church leaders. They organized occasional training events and encouraged advocacy for urban issues like "redlining," mortgage banking's practice of excluding neighborhoods with persons of color from access to credit sources. They also worked on criminal justice reforms, plant closings and relocations, and more sensitive church strategies for ministries in racially transitional communities.

From a new generation of leaders in this network in the early 1990s came a forward-looking proposal to develop a national plan for urban ministry for The UMC. With assistance from GBGM, these leaders sponsored a national convocation on urban ministries in Birmingham, Alabama, in 1995, the first such gathering in almost two decades. Workshops were held on a variety of topics, and platform speakers urged the 3,000 participants to generate a new interest within the whole church for undertaking vital ministries in cities of the U.S. A rising national economy was producing new investment in urban economies and neighborhoods. While some populations were profiting, others languished in conditions of poverty. The churches needed to offer leadership. Bishop May addressed the body, admonishing participants to act with the "boldness" of the early Apostles, whose mission was recognized both in the synagogues and by secular authorities.

The 1996 General Conference received a proposal for a national plan for urban ministry endorsed by GBGM but produced by a revitalized national urban network or association. It was entitled "Holy Boldness — A National Plan for Urban Ministry." The document stated: "The objective is not to create new national structures or priorities, but work within present structures and existing resources to leverage new opportunities for urban ministry."[37] The plan mandated all of the general agency staff with responsibility for urban concerns to collaborate in addressing the program needs in local urban settings. The strategy consisted of the sponsorship of training events or "academies" across the connectional church that would produce a corps of leaders to reach neighborhood churches with a teaching and planning process to activate new and "bold" beginnings in urban ministries. Members of the network produced a training curriculum. It included an introduction to a comprehensive list of subjects: contextual urban theology, urban evangelism, leadership development, community economic development, eradication of racism, strengthening multicultural collaboration, and health and healing. The trainers were recruited from within and beyond the network. The program was not dependent upon raising new funds, only a committed cadre of leaders to carry the plan to the conferences. General Conference approved, and the enthusiasm for the work was soon contagious.

In 1997, a second major conference with the Holy Boldness theme was held in San Francisco with an even larger attendance than the first. Participants were energized by a growing momentum within the denomination to take into account once again the faithful witness of The UMC in urban centers. It was a national plan, so a strategy for reaffirming it by the 2000 General Conference was developed at the event. The plan was approved at General Conference. The grassroots leadership and energy that emerged within the conferences continued to expand. Much of the movement's success was credited to its genuine acknowledgment of and response to the growing pluralism experienced in churches located in the growing metropolitan centers.

Restorative Justice and Mercy Ministries

The 1996 General Conference acted favorably on a petition from participants in church- and conference-based programs for criminal justice and prison reform. The petition called for the general church to command the resources of its general agencies for heightening the church's witness (nationally and internationally) to systems of criminal justice. Law enforcement and judicial systems at state and local levels were overwhelmed by a rising volume of offenders and were failing to serve either the victims or the perpetrators of crime.

Behind the language of the petition was a changing philosophy of treatment for participants in criminal justice proceedings. The emphasis had been upon retributive justice, i.e., seeking punishment and then rehabilitation of offenders. In contrast, the concept of restorative justice was promoted with a new objective of treatment programs aimed at correcting behaviors: Punishment for criminal behavior would not result in a change of conduct without a commitment to restoring—to whatever extent possible—what was taken from the victim and the community in the criminal act. Seeking punishment of the offender as a primary means of providing a sense of satisfaction for the victim would not afford a new sense of well being. Neither would it provide much personal protection without securing some measure of reconciliation with the offender. The judicial system was not sufficiently patient to accomplish these aims. In the words of the 1996 General Conference petition: "We understand that justice-making is restorative rather than retributive, seeks to create wholeness rather than isolate blame, cares for both victim and offender, and seeks the ultimate restoration of right relationships among God, persons, and people until we see peace restored to the community."[38]

The special program on Restorative Justice and Mercy Ministries brought together leadership from the general program agencies to determine how each could use its resources to influence church and public opinion on such a sensitive matter. The UMC was already noted for its stand against the death penalty, but in the context of state legislatures passing stronger and more repressive crime bills to handle a rising number of drug-related offenses, there was not a ready audience. A coordinator was hired. Church constituencies with any affinity to the issue, from prison chaplains to social ethicists, were consulted. A range of services and programs were planned, including:

- the development of Victim Offender Reconciliation Programs and neighborhood conflict resolution programs based on restorative justice ministries models;
- the training of mediators to respond to community conflicts;
- a restorative justice curriculum addressing violence and criminal justice issues for introduction at seminaries; and
- constituency education programs on the restorative justice philosophy.

GBGM devoted staff and director time to discerning its response. Connections were made with annual conferences within the U.S. jurisdictions and the central conferences that were active in prison ministries, and the results were encouraging. The new mission in Senegal reported on a vital ministry in a women's prison. Congregations in Czechoslovakia, emerging from years of Communist government restrictions on their ministries, reached out to prisons and jails with ministries of visitation. The two North Carolina conferences recruited local church graduates of the *Disciple* Bible Study program to conduct study groups in their state prison system. The Oklahoma Conference developed a new church to serve families of incarcerated persons and parolees. The Board established a model program for transporting family members from Philadelphia and New York City for visitation in federal prisons in central Pennsylvania. Counseling and job training programs were also made available to participants. A national mission initiative was considered to encourage local churches to offer assistance to ministries and emerging congregations behind prison walls. The aim was to extend not only the sense of community and service of their local churches but also the hand of church membership to inmates. Once becoming familiar with this context of the criminal justice system, it was believed that congregations would become strong advocates and participants in movements for change.

It was readily recognized that establishing patterns of restorative justice was a long-term proposition. It deserved continued emphasis and strategy development. Meanwhile, without an intentional and proactive ministry within the judicial and prison systems by mainline Protestant denominations, other religious groups were active. There was a cry from within prisons for a ministry to the whole person that The UMC sought to fulfill. If the church were content to leave this ministry in the hands of the small number of chaplains it recruited, the full potential of its ministry would never be realized. The mandate of the special program would have to be expanded and more creative minds set to work in realizing the possibilities.

Cooperative Mission—Ecumenical Engagement

Dr. Masao Takenaka, a distinguished ecumenist and theology professor from Doshisha University in Japan, addressed the 1973 annual meeting of the Board of Global Ministries. Reporting on the program of the WCC Urban and Rural Mission in the Asia region, he discussed the plight of the urban workers whose annual income averaged a meager $180. With the rapid increase in the standard of living in the industrialized nations of the world, he questioned whether it was possible for the comfortable to "grasp the human agony of the other peoples of the world." Then he recalled the disturbing impact of recent struggles for justice in the U.S., namely civil rights, the Vietnam War, and even Watergate, as well as the longing among many for an "intermission." But for others, there was the realization that "it was just the beginning of a long struggle toward the liberation of Asia."[39]

"Struggle and solidarity" was the common ecumenical theme marking the decades of the 1970s and 1980s. The WCC, which had encouraged the formation of representative ecumenical structures in each region of the world, was uniquely positioned to hear the voices of leaders of liberation movements. The favorite text for exegesis and explication at interchurch gatherings was the prophetic words of Jesus' call to ministry: "'The Spirit of the Lord is upon me, because he has anointed me to bring good news to the poor. He has sent me to proclaim release to the captives and recovery of sight to the blind, to let the oppressed go free, and to proclaim the year of the Lord's favor'" (Luke 4:18–20). Delegates to various ecumenical gatherings often heard compelling witnesses from those engaged in liberation movements: the struggle to end apartheid in South Africa, to throw off the vestiges of colonialism among the newly independent nations of Africa, to end the autocratic rule of governments in Latin America, and to protect human rights in the industrialization of Asia.

There was no "intermission" for the churches that by membership in the WCC declared their resolve to relate to the struggles for human rights in which their global partners were engaged. The reflections and analyses on underlying justice issues produced strong self-criticism of the churches' complicity with the economic and social systems that oppressed the majority of the world's population. Statements and actions of the WCC generally embraced the perspective of Liberation Theology or showed sensitivity to the emergence of other local theologies with a so-called preference for the poor. Council programs that supported the justifiable ends of liberation struggles, such as the Program to Combat Racism, invited much scrutiny and criticism. Considerable stamina was required for leaders of the churches to stay in dialogue with their ecumenical partners embroiled in revolutionary movements and a constituency of local church members who wanted to remain at a comfortable distance from the conflicts of the world.[40]

The Board of Missions was clearly on record in support of the WCC. As early as 1971, Bishop James K. Mathews, chair of the Board Committee on Policy and Program, introduced a strong endorsement at the annual meeting:

> The Board of Missions of The United Methodist Church reaffirms its support of the World Council of Churches as the principal ecumenical instrumentality of our day. . . . Recently the World Council of Churches has been under fire for attempts to fight racism and to create fellowship among churches of widely differing backgrounds. Specifically the council has been the target of numerous attacks concerning its funding of projects which fight racism on all continents. The purpose and program of the grants have been improperly described in an effort to discredit the council and its work. The vital work of building bridges between churches living in many different societies, including those under Marxist governments, has been portrayed as naive submission to spread communist influence. To remain silent while such charges are given widespread circulation would be to turn from our duty not only to the ecumenical witness but to our Church and its members who live under many governmental systems. . . . We believe that faith and justice go together and that the World Council of Churches seeks to be obedient to the Gospel as it proclaims Christ in the context of a broken world

hungering for righteousness and justice. Christians should not be frightened from the task of witnessing to Christ because of false and misleading accusations.[41]

The foundations for such an unwavering commitment to the ecumenical movement within the Board were unquestionably laid by the Women's Division. In his opening address as the president of the Board of Missions, Bishop Lloyd Wicke lauded the women's leadership:
"I would pay tribute to the women of The United Methodist Church who in so large a degree have laid their institutional life upon the altar of intra-church unity so that the united body would be served more adequately. I salute the ladies, and trust their deed may increasingly 'infect' the whole body."[42]

The Women's Division's mission within ecumenical organizations as well as the denomination was a catalyst for reform. Within the WCC, women participants from The UMC were committed to developing program resources for women and children and a stronger leadership role in the organization for women. A major effort organized by the council to address the concerns of women adequately was the Ecumenical Decade: Churches in Solidarity with Women. The program paralleled the United Nations Decade for Women: Equality, Development and Peace. A delegation of women directors from GBGM to the 1985 World Conference to Review and Appraise the Achievements of the UN Decade held in Nairobi, Kenya, returned with an enthusiastic report.[43] The directors joined with other women delegates of the World Council attending the event in urging the adoption of the UN's "Forward Looking Strategies," aimed at improving the status of women in all aspects of society.

The Women's Division took leadership within GBGM to follow up on the implementation of the Ecumenical Decade. The delegates to the Nairobi conference called upon the WCC to work with greater intentionality at programs for women's development by strengthening the role of its "women's desk." The World Division and the Women's Division collaborated in the financial sponsorship of the staffing of this position. The Health and Welfare Program Department fashioned a series of initiatives that pressed forward its program concentration on women's health issues. Rehearsing the principle that health is not a medical issue, the department committed itself to leadership development programs and advocacy of public policies which would produce "a better life for women and children in poverty, better access to permanent housing, health and human services, retirement and long term care."[44]

While the ecumenical stance of the Women's Division was anchored in resolutions of the General Conference affirming the goal of ecclesiastical unity, the division directors broadened the base to incorporate those for and with whom the aims of mission were to be accomplished:

"We believe in the oneness of God's children, God's children everywhere: Christian and non-Christian, poor and affluent, minority and majority groups, youth and adults, national and international. We believe ecumenical concern means concern for the whole world: the religious, the secular, the academic, the political, the social, the economic."[45]

The Women's Division's first commitment identified those organizations whose "goals permeate the life of society with the Christian imperative." Major church councils benefitted from their direct support and participation along with the Church Women United and the World Federation of Methodist Women. Grants to regional ecumenical bodies (e.g., East Asia Christian Conference or the Commission on Religion in Appalachia) were made with a designation for specific programs with women and children.

The women's "ecumenical stance" also committed them to cooperation with other "organized groups which share our concern for meeting the needs of all [persons]." In addition to church-based organizations, the Women's Division cooperated with secular groups with whom it shared a common purpose, e.g., the National Welfare Rights Organization. This strategy of coalition building with secular groups mitigated against the proliferation of church-sponsored groups to address each and every mission objective in the larger society. Working through coalitions, however, often presented complications. Relinquishing responsibility for articulating public statements to a coalition spokesperson sacrificed leadership recognition and sometimes quality control. Church representatives on coalitions were frequently required to provide complementary interpretation designed to address the needs of their respective constituencies, especially when coalitions gained a special public notoriety. The division's work on the controversial issues such as the protection of women's reproductive rights and the passage of the equal rights amendment to the U.S. Constitution required deft defenses of its position and choice of allies in the struggles.

Participation in conciliar forums and assemblies that defined directions or challenged policy positions was time-consuming and arduous work. Speaking to and for the churches was not taken lightly. Contrary to the opinion of critics of the ecumenical movement, much research, analysis, and care was given to the crafting of language and the due process of gaining approval of delegated bodies. The process broke down, however, with the meager efforts of member churches to educate their constituencies to the role of the councils and issues they addressed. Again, the Women's Division led The UMC in its commitment to mission education. Its sponsorship of the annual Schools of Christian Mission engaged their own members of United Methodist Women and other leaders in conferences and churches in mission studies. When ecumenical partners chose to abandon cooperative efforts in selecting themes and publishing materials in 1996, the Women's Division led the Board into sole sponsorship of the venture within The UMC.

Ecumenical cooperation did not stop with rhetorical leadership on justice issues. Programs were sponsored and/or networked by ecumenical organizations to achieve the greatest possible reach for Christian witness worldwide. These programs included education and leadership development, mission and evangelism, health, student movements, women's issues, urban-rural ministries, community development, and emergency relief. The extent to which member churches agreed to provide financial support through the councils for these activities was perhaps the litmus test for their commitment to the ecumenical movement. The popular ecumenical program theme of the 1960s, "Mission on Six Continents," signaled the encouraging rise of Christian witness from within the churches of the Third World and end of the dominant missionary influence from the churches of North America and Europe. Regional councils or conferences of churches were established to enhance the cooperation of the growing churches of the Southern Hemisphere. Denominational mission boards were challenged to think and act cooperatively. "Cooperative" meant broad-based funding for all churches of the region administered through the councils rather than bilateral actions, like transfer of funds between churches of the same denomination only. The program budgets of GBGM administered by the World Division earmarked some funds for administration through church councils, but direct funding for the United Methodist central conferences and autonomous Methodist churches in the regions remained the predominant method.[46] Other denominational boards followed the same pattern favoring traditional fund transfers.

In the decade of the 1980s, the WCC made one more effort to tip the organization's balance of economic power in the same direction as its membership growth, that is, to the churches of the South. A study and dialogue among leaders on the theme, "Ecumenical Sharing of Resources," concluded that a just stewardship of God's resources would require a radical readjustment in order to empower adequately ecumenical partners from the Third World. The project proposed a common principle that in God's economy there was no such thing as an "absolute donor" or "absolute recipient." The common good of the Christian community required the relinquishing of individual control of gifts in favor of a genuine sharing of the resources each member committed to the ecumenical store. It also embraced the concept of adequate participation of representatives from the Third World in the decision-making bodies of ecumenical members. When the published report from the Escorial Consultation in Spain on this matter was shared with the member churches, the response was subdued. The World Council had begun to experience difficult financial straits because of falling world currency rates and internal organizational problems. The timing was poor for discussions on erasing "donor" from the ecumenical lexicon, and the whole project was too soon forgotten.

With the geopolitical changes occurring in the last decade of the twentieth century, the victory over apartheid in South Africa and the collapse of Communism in the Soviet Union and its satellite states, the theme of ecumenical dialogue and action shifted from "struggle and solidarity" to "revisioning." In 1993 another distinguished ecumenical visitor addressed GBGM with an invitation "to discern the signs of the time, to discern what is the will of God." Dr. Konrad Raiser, a German Lutheran theologian, elected to the post of general secretary of the WCC in 1992, shared his vision of the kind of ecumenical movement that would be needed at the end of the millennium. He cited the changing mission context in which confrontation between external enemy forces (i.e., Cold War hostilities) is replaced with the legitimate claims of "increased liberty and well being for all [amidst] contradictions of increasing marginalization, poverty, structural unemployment, and a young generation that does not seem to have any hope for its own future." He described a new moment for ecumenism:

> The ecumenical movement . . . has to find a new language for the ecumenical vision which inspired people in the first half of the century at the time when the awareness of our one world was slowly beginning to

emerge. Today the appeal to think globally seems to reach people less and less as they are preoccupied with their very local concerns and seek security and insurance in the face of growing uncertainties in the world around. Maybe for too long we have engaged in an ecumenical approach from above, relying on the functioning of administrative structures, disregarding the needs of people in local communities. What we need is a language and a methodology which reflect the fact that the ecumenical movement is much less of an institutional structure but a network of living communities, of communities where the local perspectives can retain their integrity.[47]

Raiser did not shrink from a critique of the waning commitment of the churches to the movement, decrying "the spirit of competition in the value system of our society that seems to erode the links which have grown in decades of ecumenical work [prompting] the re-emerging of denominational identities." He tried to make the case for churches working together. "All are in need of support only in the sense of sustaining mutuality in their hope and receiving spiritual encouragement through the witness of others." And then he called for the fiftieth anniversary of the council in 1998 to be declared a jubilee year, "a year of mutual forgiveness of renouncing the ownership claims of our church, of our traditions, of transcending our competitive struggles, to enter into the liberty of freely sharing with one another the gifts of the spirit."

The new millennium began with fewer voices and a much-reduced rhetoric espousing the ecumenical vision. The ecumenical institutions were weakening and financial woes of the major councils dominated the ecumenical agenda.[48] The good faith of member churches in the capacity of church councils to deliver on cooperative program strategies continued on the decline. A resurgence in denominationalism might not be so much the result of a rising competitive spirit but a need to step back and reassess what type of mission witness can and should be accomplished through structures of ecumenism. In North America, for instance, the culmination of the important work on the Ecumenical Decade: Churches in Solidarity with Women was remembered more for its ill-fated 1997 Minneapolis conference on the feminist theme of biblical and theological "Re-imagining God" than for the kinds of transformation it stimulated in women's life and work in churches and communities around the world. The exclusive focus given by the planners of this conference to the controversial theological issue of developing a more inclusive language for people of faith to talk about God overlooked the more globally sensitive and action-oriented objectives of the decade program, including advocacy for women's rights and justice issues, especially the ratification of the UN Convention on the Elimination of All Forms of Discrimination Against Women. Reporting on the event was effectively preempted by the press coverage of the conservative or religious right that characterized the event as a radical feminist threat to basic biblical teachings and traditional church values. This treatment was followed by well-orchestrated publicity campaigns to discredit sponsoring groups, including the Women's Division of GBGM. If the grand goal of "revisioning" the role of ecumenism was not successfully achieved, a modest effort at reinventing ecumenism was becoming an urgent task. Needed was a conciliar structure that was truly a "common witness of its member churches, not something over, above, or against them," as the 1971 statement of the Board of Missions declared.

CHAPTER 8

A Survey of Europe

*T*HE UNITED METHODIST CHURCH (UMC) in European countries has been seen generally as an evangelical Protestant alternative to the state church. Of course, no generalization can describe every national context, but European United Methodists have distinctively chosen their church affiliation rather than accept a nominal membership in a state-recognized church. The community of United Methodists on the continent up to 2000 was small but vital. The three central conferences[1] were represented in the European Council on Ministries, which sought to provide general oversight of the ministry and witness of the denomination in the region. The British Methodist Church chose an observer relationship to the council, but in the 1990s the council was restructured to accommodate full membership for the parent church of all Methodism from the British Isles, the Methodist Church in Great Britain.

Throughout the Cold War period, European United Methodism was forced to accommodate to political realities. The 1970 General Conference received a request from the annual conference in the German Democratic Republic to be recognized as a central conference "because of the developments of state law and church necessities." The General Conference granted the request, acknowledging that "national identity," in this case recognizing that the political distinction between East and West Germany was a legitimate or necessary consideration in forming judicatory boundaries.[2] It further granted the new conference the right to elect its own bishop. The bishops serving the Central and Southern Central Conference were severely restricted in their supervision of organized conferences in Eastern Europe. In some cases, such as Bulgaria and Czechoslovakia, where United Methodist churches continued to exist, the governmental ministries of religious affairs took over their direct supervision.

Episcopal visitations were restricted, and the bishops' role of presiding over official meetings was denied. A similar pattern prevailed in northern Europe, where the superintendent in Estonia functioned in the role of bishop, and Soviet authorities closely guarded his activities.

State control of the churches in Eastern Europe required considerable sacrifice the on part of United Methodist pastors and congregations. Where United Methodist churches were given official permission to continue their ministry, they were to have no foreign contacts or receive any financial support from abroad. The state took charge of church finances, paying pastoral salaries at a rate far below other professionals and making occasional grants for building repairs. Pastoral ministry was restricted to caring for the existing membership, and no calls were to be made on non-members without a special invitation. Ministers and priests who failed to comply were subjected to arrest and imprisonment. Nevertheless, church leaders found a sharper purpose for their mission in a Marxist context. Vilem Schneeberger, superintendent of the United Methodist Church in Czechoslovakia, wrote about the Christian witness in an atheistic political system: "The Christians believe they have to show a real sense of human existence—to answer a question that atheists are unable to answer satisfactorily. It is not only a question for Christians. But, are we truly able to live a life that can be a model for our unbelieving neighbors? Do we really have the bread of life for them? Are we real witnesses of the love of God that changes our lives and our relations to our fellowman? We Christians have a great task of reconciliation. This is not only a question of our inner life. The reconciliation of God means a change in human relations. The Christians in a radical secularized and unbelieving society have to show this reconciliation in their lives."[3]

Given the state of political isolation for many of their churches and their minority status among the established churches of the region, United Methodists in Europe valued the connectional relationship to a larger denominational identity and church structure. Even though the association with churches in the West complicated or compromised their standing with Eastern European governments, church leaders proudly claimed their organic relationship to The UMC. Fiercely independent in their respective central conference structures and ministries, the European delegates to General Conferences and representatives on general church agencies always commanded recognition as full participants in all proceedings of the church. European United Methodists were among the strongest advocates of the formulation of a global denominational structure for The UMC.

Mission Program Relationships

After the Second World War rebuilding program in Europe was completed, the continent was not a strong venue for United Methodist mission. The philosophy of political coexistence also shaped East and West church relationships. Representatives from theological academies and mission leaders from both sides participated in various forms of an ongoing Christian-Marxist dialogue. There were few harbingers of the rapid decline and collapse of Communist control that began with the destruction of the Berlin Wall in 1990. The changes exposed much vulnerability.

Political instability in Yugoslavia quickly deteriorated into conflicts fueled by the exploitation of ethnic and religious differences. The world community was poised to intervene in the Balkans, and church relief agencies and other nongovernmental organizations (NGOs) were invited to help. In 1993, the United Methodist Committee on Relief (UMCOR) began rebuilding destroyed housing in Bosnia with funding from international development grants. UMCOR-Bosnia became the largest field office of the unit's NGO program, a channel for a voluntary agency to receive sizable development grants from government sources. Following the North Atlantic Treaty Organization military campaign in 1998, a project office was opened in Kosovo working on shelter reconstruction and agricultural and community development programs. A Europe headquarters office for UMCOR-NGO was opened in Vienna in 1999 to meet requirements for funding from the European Union. The Vienna office also coordinated the participation of European UMC leaders in the program.

The changes occurring in the post–Cold War period also presented new and urgent opportunities for church development. As the countries in the former Eastern Europe gained their independence, the churches experienced new freedoms. When the state economies crumbled, the financial resources of the connectional relationships in Western Europe and the U.S. were in great demand. Pastoral salaries and benefits once paid by socialist governments were forgotten. Church buildings needed repairs and new church facilities were required. Confiscated church properties had to be recovered through uncertain governmental processes.

Map of Europe with cities and countries labeled, including church relationship codes:

- NORWAY (CC) — Oslo★
- SWEDEN (CC) — Stockholm
- FINLAND (CC) — Helsinki
- ESTONIA (CC) — Tallinn★
- RUSSIA (CC)
- Pärnu
- LATVIA (CC) — Riga★
- Liepaja
- LITHUANIA (CC) — Kaunas, Vilnius
- BELARUS
- DENMARK (CC) — Copenhagen★
- Belfast
- Dublin★
- IRELAND (A)
- GREAT BRITAIN (Con) — London★
- BELGIUM (AU) — Brussels★
- POLAND (CC) — Warsaw★
- UKRAINE (CC)
- Konstancin
- GERMANY (CC) — Berlin★, Frankfurt
- Paris★
- Reutlingen
- Pilsen, Prague, Jihlava
- CZECH REP. (CC)
- SLOVAKIA (CC)
- MOLDOVO (CC)
- Basel, Zurich
- Vienna★
- SWITZERLAND (CC) — Kusnacht, Geneva
- AUSTRIA (CC) — Graz
- Budapest★
- HUNGARY (CC)
- ROMANIA
- SLOVENIA
- Novi Sad region, Syd
- FRANCE (CC)
- ITALY (A)
- CROATIA
- Belgrade★
- Black Sea
- BOSNIA — Sarajevo
- YUGOSLAVIA (CC)
- Lovech, Varna
- Sofia★
- BULGARIA (CC)
- MACEDONIA (CC)
- Rome★
- PORTUGAL (A) — Lisbon★
- Madrid★
- SPAIN (Ind)
- Atlantic Ocean
- English Channel
- Strait of Gibraltar

Legend for Church Relationship to UMC	
Autonomous	A
Affiliated Autonomous	AA
Affiliated United	AU
Covenant UMC	Cov
Central Conference	CC
Concordat	Con
Cooperative Mission	CM
Ecumenical	Ecum
Independent	Ind
Mission	Msn

The European Council on Ministries began a serious review of program directions for an enlarged European constituency. The strategy for responding was left to each of the central conferences to initiate. A special fund for assisting United Methodists in neighboring conferences was established by the Zurich Episcopal Area in the Central and Southern Europe Central Conference. The new Germany Conference assumed a large financial burden for the reuniting of the two central conferences in Germany. The Northern Europe Central Conference stimulated the formation of "support groups" within the conferences for the recovery of the UMC witness and ministry in the Baltic States. But the European conferences also enlisted the General Board of Global Ministries (GBGM), the World Methodist Council, and many local churches and conferences into supportive relationships. The GBGM Millennium Fund approved major grants for church properties and pastoral support that in many cases were matched by contributions from churches. The Connecting Congregations program of World Evangelism in the World Methodist Council recruited supporting churches that helped pay salary support for congregations in the Czech Republic, Slovakia (Slovak Republic), Estonia, Latvia, and other European countries.

The strategy for recovery did not feature the receiving of traditional mission personnel. Though a few commissioned missionaries were recruited by the GBGM for service in Russia, Bulgaria, Latvia, and Lithuania, there was a strong desire to maintain a respectable level of self-sufficiency when it came to personnel. New recruits for pastoral leadership were found within their churches or invited to transfer from other denominations, presenting a major challenge in the areas of orientation and training. The 2000 General Conference set aside new funds for developing seminaries and other schools in the region to serve the growing demand for formal education for clergy and lay leadership.

In the 1990s, Europe became a dynamic mission context for The UMC. European church leaders exercised strong leadership skills required to maintain local direction and momentum for the emergence of a new United Methodist witness in many places. The rush of goodwill and generosity from beyond the continent was creatively channelled to serve the development of congregations within the United Methodist churches in each country. Hani Hanschinn, coordinator of Methodist Women's Work for the Central and Southern Europe Central Conference, gave counsel and guidance to the women of the Eastern European churches who were expressing a strong desire to take advantage of their newfound religious freedom and begin mission programs. In 1992 she heard them describe their situation as follows: "We now have many opportunities for witness and mission, and we see many needs around us, but we are not trained to do all this special work." Four years later, at a follow-up consultation, the same women reported having successfully established structures for women's organizations on national levels, conducted training for leaders, and experienced strong membership growth among younger women in their local units. And further, "The diaconal work of Methodist women . . . involved soup kitchens in Bulgaria, summer camps for children from industrial areas in Poland, prison ministry in Hungary and Slovakia, visiting of a children's home in Macedonia, and help with the distribution of humanitarian aid in Yugoslavia."[4]

Some of the conferences in Western Europe addressed various social challenges facing the continent. Multiculturalism was on the rise and with it the increase of hate groups that sparked reactions of xenophobia and racism against the increasing presence of persons of color from Asia, Africa, and the Caribbean. Many foreign students and workers who migrated to large urban areas were gathered into Christian congregations along national and ethnic lines. Among them were persons of Methodist traditions who turned to the United Methodist conferences for recognition. Korean Methodist churches sent missionaries to begin churches among their diaspora in Europe. Churches in Africa did the same. There was a need for strategies for serving these populations through shared facilities and limited financial support as well as strategies of incorporation emerging racial/ethnic churches into the connectional life and mission of The UMC in Europe.

World Mission

European United Methodists have had a strong heart for world mission. Missionaries from European churches were recruited and mission projects supported through the predecessor bodies of GBGM. Bishop Franz W. Schäfer of the Zurich Episcopal Area and other leaders concluded that greater support would be generated from their churches if the European conferences established their own mission boards. In addition, the non-state churches in Europe were often entitled to a rebate for that portion of their members' income tax earmarked for support of the budget of the state church—provided that it be used for charitable international development work. Considerable sums of money were made available for the service projects of the churches in Africa, Asia, and Latin America.

In 1971, the Council of the United Methodist Central Conferences in Europe created the European Commission on Mission (ECOM) to coordinate mission activities beyond the continent. There was an intentional distribution of world mission program relationships among the participating conferences. For example, Norway accepted Angola, Liberia, Zimbabwe, and India; Sweden accepted Mozambique, Zimbabwe, Liberia, Sierra Leone, and India; Denmark accepted Zaire/Congo (Southern); Switzerland/France accepted Zaire/Congo and North Africa (Algeria and Tunisia); Germany accepted Sierra Leone, Nigeria, Burundi, Brazil, and India. Representatives of the mission boards of the Methodist churches in Great Britain and Ireland as well as GBGM participated in the annual meetings of ECOM, where reports were shared along with valuable guidance and counsel. Each conference board (or mission agency) managed its own administration of mission funds, program evaluation, personnel recruitment, training, and supervision. The relationship of each board to the host church leaders and funded projects in their mission relationships was direct or bilateral, partially necessitated by accountability for the use of public funds. The mission partners welcomed the additional source of funding and attention.[5] European United Methodists took great pride in having a direct stake in the global mission of the denomination. GBGM welcomed the partnership but failed to develop joint strategies and patterns of program administration with the European boards. In the case of North Africa, the Zurich Area bishop and the Switzerland and France board directly administered the fragile UMC relationships and most mission personnel matters in Algeria and Tunisia amidst frequent interfaith and political hostilities.

Northern Europe

The following narratives provide summary updates as of 2000 on the mission and ministry of the UMCs through the central conferences in Europe, save for the Baltic States and European Russia, treated in the next chapter.

United Methodism in northern Europe originated in the harbor of New York City in the middle of the nineteenth century. The mission society of the Methodist Episcopal Church purchased an old ship and renamed it *Bethel* to start a ministry among Scandinavian immigrants and sailors. The converts were quick to start congregations in the New York vicinity but also to return to their homelands and introduce a Wesleyan interpretation of the gospel under the restrictions of state-approved churches.

Norway

The UMC here comprised fifty-two congregations with a membership of nearly 6,000. The church maintained a strong social ministry through the administration of two hospitals, two nursing schools, several retirement homes and a senior center, three kindergartens, and two homes for delinquent children. The Norway church recruited mission personnel for the world mission program of The UMC in numbers that far exceeded its proportionate share. The church maintained a special relationship to United Methodist mission in Angola, having sent mission personnel and substantial financial support without interruption during the country's political isolation from the West during its turbulent liberation struggle and civil war. The church sought to minister to new immigrant populations in its own urban centers. A Pakistani pastor was appointed to a growing immigrant congregation in Oslo.

Denmark

Twenty-nine congregations served about 2,500 United Methodists. The church sought to balance its ministry between outreach and a strong emphasis upon the teachings of the Christian faith and the witness of the church. Special attention has been given to ministries with youth and young adults who are influenced by strong secular values. The conference has also adopted a mission to the homeless in the city of Copenhagen. Its world mission connection was to the Zaire/Congo, where at least one of its members served as a missionary. It also provided support for The UMC in Estonia and for re-establishing United Methodist churches in Latvia and Lithuania.

Sweden

There were sixty-nine United Methodist congregations with approximately 4,000 members. The United Methodist Theological Seminary serving northern Europe conferences was located in Göteborg. The Sweden conference operated a hospital in Stockholm and several homes for the elderly. Most of the churches provided programs for children and youth. In addition to its world mission connections in Africa and Asia, Sweden United Methodists have been active in providing support for the re-emerging churches in the Baltic States.

Finland

Here the United Methodist mission embraced both Swedish-speaking and Finnish-speaking populations in two provisional conferences. Because of Finland's historical association with Russia, members of The UMC maintained ties to ethnic groups along their Russian border. With changing political conditions following the fall of Communism, new ministries have been initiated. Both conferences have been active in new church development, starting new congregations in several locations.

Germany

In 1992, after the political reunification of Germany, the two central conferences serving East and West Germany merged under one bishop, Dr. Walter F. Klaiber. The new Germany Central Conference included

A cornerstone was laid for the United Methodist Church of Reconciliation in East Berlin in the early 1980s, proving that even during Communist rule Methodists continued to have hope. *(Photo courtesy of UM Archives and History)*

650 local churches with 42,000 members and a constituency of nearly 70,000. Its social mission has been largely defined by the historic work of the deaconess movement that established and operated sixteen hospitals, twenty homes for seniors, and about twenty recreational centers. More recent ministries of social involvement have focused upon treatment for alcohol and drug abuse, sharing resources and leadership expertise with the general church Special Program on Substance Abuse and Related Violence (SPSARV). Several local churches in urban areas have been affected by the arrival of immigrant populations from Africa and Asia. The conference Board of Mission has fostered a relationship with Methodist churches in Africa and Korea for shared support of missionary pastors developing ministries among a growing number of their expatriates. In world mission, the Germany Conference provided more than DM 2 million annually for programs in Africa, Latin America, and India and maintained as many as fifteen mission personnel on assignment to partner Methodist churches.

Central and Southern Europe

The churches in these countries originated in various ways, including initiation by immigrants returning from the U.S. Besides the obvious effects of the Second World War and the ensuing Cold War, their ministries have been shaped by the conflict in the Balkans in the 1990s and continuing emigration from Africa into Europe.

Austria

With the culmination of the Second World War, Austria became a haven for refugees from various countries, especially Eastern Europe. The churches in Austria were instrumental in providing Christian hospitality and aid with the help of international assistance. Austrian United Methodists maintained their expertise in delivering aid as they worked ecumenically in providing assistance to unsettled populations throughout the region. The provisional annual conference comprised nine congregations and six pastors serving a membership of about 600 and a constituency of 1,300. Though small in relationship to other churches, The UMC in Austria enjoyed the same governmental recognition given to Roman Catholic, Lutheran, and Reformed churches. The capital city of Vienna, host to many international organizations, attracted large numbers of residents from other countries, increasingly from Africa. With financial assistance from GBGM, the conference has employed international persons in mission from the Democratic Republic of the Congo and Yugoslavia to offer pastoral ministries, create congregations, and develop outreach ministries to expatriates living in Vienna. Centrally located in Europe, the conference became a frequent host to regional and global meetings and consultations for United Methodists and ecumenical groups.

Bulgaria

Communist rule in Bulgaria was noted for its brutality. Methodism in the country was singled out for persecution because of its denominational affiliations with the West. The mission school for girls in Lovech was closed and the property taken by the government. All but two of sixteen local congregations were officially disbanded, and many of the pastors were jailed on false charges of treason or espionage. United Methodists in Bulgaria lost all connection with the larger church until 1989. Bishop Heinrich Bolleter was able to meet with surviving members in two congregations and began to lay the groundwork for the revival of their Christian witness and ministry. In 1993, the annual conference was able to meet for the first time since 1947. By 1995 there were ten congregations and several small Bible study groups meeting. The congregation in Varna was compensated for the confiscation of its former church property with a new site in the city center. With assistance from the Millennium Fund, church partners in Europe and supporting congregations in the U.S., a new building was constructed that would serve its growing membership of about 400. Local churches became engaged in ministries of social outreach to refugees and prisoners. As a minority church presence in a predominantly Orthodox religious context, there were occasional conflicts or misunderstandings to reconcile, but Methodism was finding its place and its mission in a newly democratic Bulgaria.

Czech Republic and Slovakia

The UMC in the former Czechoslovakia grew out of the mission work of the Methodist Episcopal Church, South in the 1920s. When the Communist regime took power in 1948, the church was restrained from continuing any contacts outside the country. By the 1980s, church leaders were, however, permitted travel to meetings abroad. In 1993 the country was divided into two distinct nations, the Czech Republic and Slovakia. The annual conference accommodated the split by creating two districts: The Czech District with fifteen circuits and the Slovak District with four circuits. The new political context provided the church with new opportunities for ministry. The church established a halfway house for newly released prisoners in Pilsen and a shelter for homeless in Jihlava. Recovery of church properties and building new structures has been a major challenge. The Millennium Fund of GBGM provided help with a new church start for a congregation in the Lochotin neighborhood in Pilsen. The congregation began in the pastor's apartment and continued in rented schoolrooms. The city conveyed the use (long-term lease) of property in a neighborhood where no other Protestant churches were located. A chapel to seat seventy persons and with several meeting rooms for church activities was planned and built. Meanwhile, the parent church in Pilsen undertook a $400,000 renovation project of its facility with the help of partner churches in Europe.

France

The Evangelical United Brethren Church was the main root of United Methodist mission history in France. The eleven circuits related to the Switzerland-France Annual Conference. They served about 1,500 members. Deaconesses established several institutions of the church, including a clinic in Strasbourg and three homes for the elderly. Some local churches have played host to immigrant congregations of largely Asian origins. One congregation serving Kampucheans contributed leadership and support for the joint missionary effort of the Switzerland-France Conference, GBGM, and the Singapore and Korean Methodist churches in Cambodia.

Hungary

The Hungary Provisional Annual Conference comprised ten circuits with thirty congregations serving about 2,000 members. The United Methodist witness has survived two world wars and the Communist occupation. Since 1989, Hungary has no longer been the pawn of foreign powers and the church became at last free to minister to the needs of Hungarians. This ministry included Hungarians living in the neighboring Carpathian Ukraine, where two local United Methodist congregations in Kamenica and Ushhorod were thriving after enduring more than forty years of separation from connectional relationships to The UMC. Local congregations in Hungary were engaged in social outreach by starting ministries in prisons and treatment programs with abusers of alcohol and drugs. Opportunities for Christian education in the schools were also being pursued. Most congregations met in homes or in inadequate church buildings. The Millennium Fund assisted the construction of a new church and conference headquarters in Budapest. The striking new facility included a state-of-the-art meeting center for church conferences.

Poland

One of the strongest of the European missions established by the Methodist Episcopal Church, South, The UMC in Poland comprised forty congregations serving a constituency of about 6,000. When the Communist government took power in 1945, all churches experienced forms of repression, but a lighter hand may have been applied to United Methodists. The missionaries departed in 1949, and the local leadership nurtured the congregations. The church has always been active in education. Its English-language school in Warsaw was and continues to be considered a prestigious institution. Similar schools have been started in several other cities. Income from the schools helped underwrite the ministry and programs of the churches. Pastoral supply and supervision remained a challenge for the church, but new students enrolled in the seminary at Konstancin. A major project for the church was the rebuilding of the conference center at Klarysew, near Warsaw. The property was owned by the Poland Annual Conference and conveniently located in the Warsaw metropolitan area. The conference wished to develop it for conferences and meetings for both church and other groups. The government has identified more than twenty additional properties once owned by the church. Their recovery by the church would greatly extend the ministry of United Methodism in Poland, but resources for their maintenance and supplying leadership for additional congregations present obstacles to their immediate acquisition.

Switzerland

The UMC in Switzerland comprised eighty-four circuits and ninety-five active pastors. It was one of the most active conferences in world mission, with twenty missionary personnel assigned to posts in Algeria, Argentina, the Democratic Republic of the Congo, Zimbabwe, and the

Carpathian Ukraine. The conference also supported the new mission initiative in Cambodia. Swiss congregations have been most generous in their support of new United Methodist ministries emerging in the former Eastern European conferences. Institutional ministries in Switzerland include a hospital and AIDS clinic in Zurich operated by deaconesses, and two other hospitals in Basel and Küsnacht. The conference has also taken initiatives in developing congregations among Kampuchean residents in their own cities and in advocating for asylum seekers in general.

Yugoslavia/Macedonia

United Methodist mission in the former Yugoslavia was originated by German Methodist missionaries, who sought out their own kin in southern Europe. Germans were no longer welcome in the region following the Second World War, so the mission of congregations refocused upon the Slovakian- and Hungarian-speaking populations in the northern province and Serbo-Croatian-speaking populations in the Novi Sad region. In 1991, Macedonia declared independence from Yugoslavia, but one annual

In a forboding portrayal of future conflicts to come, a Roman Catholic church and a Muslim mosque stand facing each other near Gornji Vakuf, Bosnia, in 1995. Even while the fighting was still going during the Bosnia war, the United Methodist Committee on Relief (UMCOR) had established a presence to provide shelter, clothing, and other help to refugees and war victims. *(Photo by Mike DuBose for UM Communications)*

conference remained with two districts. There were fourteen congregations in the Vojvodina region of Yugoslavia and ten congregations in Macedonia. The presiding bishop and the superintendent in Austria supervised the work. Candidates for ministry were invited to pursue studies in the seminary at Graz, Austria. Civil wars have plagued both regions, but the churches—with assistance from United Methodists in Austria, Switzerland, and Germany—were constant in their witness and in efforts at providing relief. The Millennium Fund provided funds to complete the rebuilding of The UMC in Syd. Church members began rebuilding the structure until their own resources were exhausted. Partners in Europe also helped. In 1999, a United Methodist lay pastor, Boris Trajkovski, was elected president of Macedonia. His government was embroiled in mediating historic differences between ethnic Albanians and Macedonians that were exacerbated by the Kosovo conflict. He died in a plane crash in 2003.

Autonomous Methodist Churches

The UMC enjoyed fraternal relationships with autonomous Methodist churches in several European countries. Opportunities for frequent consultation and cooperation were mutually initiated. All European Methodist bodies with roots in either The UMC or the Methodist Church in Great Britain now participate in regular meetings of the European Council on Ministries, a formal channel for communication and joint action. Autonomous churches with beginnings in the Methodist Church in Great Britain included The Methodist Church of Ireland and the Evangelical Methodist Church of Portugal. Autonomous churches with beginnings in U.S. Methodism included: The Evangelical Church of Spain, the Methodist Evangelical Church of Italy, and the United Protestant Church in Belgium. These churches functioned within small Protestant communities in predominantly Catholic or secular settings. Each developed patterns of cooperation with other Protestant bodies in order to maintain a witness with diminishing memberships and resources.[6]

CHAPTER 9

Initiatives for a New Mission Age

*The church is being swept by the Spirit into a new
mission age. We may not yet know where or how
the Spirit will lead, but we look forward with faith
and hope to a new pentecostal moment in mission.*[1]

"GOD WILL BRING back what [inhumanity] tears apart." These were
the words of Bodo Schwabe, executive secretary of the German
United Methodist Mission Board as he handed rocks from the remains of
the Berlin Wall to Bishop Woodrow Hearn, president of the General
Board of Global Ministries (GBGM). It was April 1990, and the occasion
of the first meeting of the Board following the historic culmination of the
Communist experiment in Russia and throughout Eastern Europe. Few in
that gathering could begin to contemplate the new beginnings in mission
that moment in history would present. For the mission agency of the
church, the decade of the 1990s became its most active period in the century and offered the most far-reaching consequences for Christian mission for The United Methodist Church (UMC). Events in Europe caught
the public's attention, but the response of the church was not limited to
one continent. The following narratives recap the major global mission
initiatives begun and developed by GBGM and capture the dynamic of
the Spirit's leading of the church into a new mission age.

Russia Initiative

The Russia Initiative began with a visit to Moscow in January 1991 by
GBGM General Secretary Randolph Nugent and Hearn. The visit was
arranged by Suzanne Stafford, a United Methodist laywoman from North

Arctic Ocean

Kara Sea

Barents Sea

RUSSIA (CC)

St. Petersburg

★ Moscow

Yekaterinburg •

Kaliningrad

• Samara

BELARUS
(Msn, CC)

Semipalatinsk
region

Chernobyl • ★ Kiev

• Ushhorod

UKRAINE
(CC)

KAZAKHSTAN (CC)

MOLDOVO
(CC)

GEORGIA
REPUBLIC

Sevastapol

Black Sea

Caspian
Sea

TAJIKISTAN

Legend for Church Relationship to UMC	
Autonomous	A
Affiliated Autonomous	AA
Affiliated United	AU
Covenant UMC	Cov
Central Conference	CC
Concordat	Con
Cooperative Mission	CM
Ecumenical	Ecum
Independent	Ind
Mission	Msn

Carolina who was exploring business opportunities in the post-*glasnost* period in Russia. The principal contacts made by Nugent and Hearn were with the Department of External Affairs in the Moscow Patriarchate of the Russian Orthodox Church and officers of the Soviet Peace Federation. Father Ioann Ekonomtsev, one of the newest and most forward-looking members of the church hierarchy, warmly received the visitors from The UMC. He was anxious for cooperation with mission partners in the development of a new Department of Catechism and Christian Education that he was asked to head. He was not averse to cooperation with secular as well as church organizations and revived the church's relationship with the Soviet Peace Federation, an agency of the Soviet government that promoted humanitarian work at home and abroad. He invited representatives of that organization to join him in the consultations with his visitors from the GBGM.

In a practice familiar to Russians, the conversations were summarized in a formal "agreement" among the parties to establish a Joint Commission on Humanitarian Assistance. The Russian participants promised assistance to GBGM in shipping (waiver of duty) and acquiring visas and accommodations for United Methodist personnel. They also offered an infrastructure for distributing humanitarian aid to programs related to the church and the Peace Fund in Russia. The agreement also referred to dialogue "in matters of theology and spiritual development," which Nugent and Hearn interpreted as cooperation from the Russian Orthodox Church in future church development work of the UMC. The agreement would "make possible the presence of The UMC within the Soviet Union in cooperative alliance with the Russian Orthodox Church." In their report to GBGM, they concluded, "While at work cooperatively with the Russian Orthodox Church, we would also be able to pursue denominational, UMC-based programming."[2] In further dialogue with leaders of the Russian Orthodox Church, there was greater receptivity to United Methodist assistance with the rebuilding of church properties that were returned to the church during the post-Communist period than enabling the startup of a United Methodist ministry in Russia.

In their recommendations to GBGM, Nugent and Hearn laid out an ambitious agenda including: (1) the establishment of a Joint Commission on Humanitarian Assistance between the GBGM and the Soviet Peace Fund to channel United Methodist humanitarian assistance; (2) the placement of missionary personnel in Moscow to oversee "the development of church and humanitarian aid"; (3) exploration of the development of ministries in the region with the Northern Europe Central Conference; (4) establishment of communication with the Russian Orthodox Church External Affairs Department "to provide help to The United Methodist Church through the GBGM in the establishment of United Methodist churches"; (5) development of plans for the acquisition of property for church buildings; (6) assistance to Russian Orthodox clergy and laity to pursue training in United Methodist seminaries; and (7) review of alternative methods of church development suitable for Russia, i.e., to respond to high-profile initiatives (independent of GBGM) from local churches in the U.S. to plant churches in Russia.

Efforts were immediately undertaken to establish the proposed joint commission. Participants from GBGM (and then other general agencies of The UMC) and European central conferences met with representatives of the Soviet Peace Fund and Father Ioann to implement the agreements. The logistics of establishing a "commission" quickly eluded the participants, but channels of direct and productive communication were well established thanks to the continuing efforts of consultant Stafford. The most aggressive activities focused on assistance with medical health and food programs in the Moscow region. With the help of the Soviet Peace Fund, the Health and Welfare Program Department of GBGM made contact with administrators of state-run hospitals in Moscow and outlying cities. They brokered partnerships with hospitals associated with The United Methodist Association of Health and Welfare Ministries. The prototype for such partnerships was developed between the Scientific Research Institute of Childhood Hematology in Moscow and the Memphis Methodist Health Systems. Administrators of both institutions met in Moscow and in Memphis and developed programs for personnel training, short-term exchanges of medical personnel, increase in the supply of drugs available to the institute, and the shipment of needed equipment and medical supplies. Soon other partnerships developed, resulting in the transfer of considerable resources and expertise.

The Board believed that the health initiative and other work related to this new initiative would be greatly assisted by placing a missionary in the Moscow region. Christiana Hena, a Liberian trained as a medical doctor in Krasnadar, Georgia, Soviet Union, was in Oklahoma completing studies for a graduate degree in public health. She was befriended by local United Methodists and made known to them her desire to return to Russia as a missionary. In addition to her calling to missionary service, Hena's medical background, previous experience in Russia, and Russian language skill commended her to GBGM for missionary candidacy. There was only one drawback. Hena had been part of a Christian student movement in Russia that became unpopular with the government for establishing "underground churches." Because of these activities, her student visa was invalidated and she had to depart from the Soviet Union. While she finished training for United Methodist missionary service, GBGM worked with immigration lawyers to clear up her record and to define her work in acceptable terms to officials in the new Russian government. Hena was commissioned in the spring of 1991 and was sent to Moscow to take up ministry as a United Methodist missionary. She served initially as a liaison for the partners in the health program, maintaining connections between Russian health institutions and health professionals in Memphis, as well as other programs in the U.S. In Moscow, she also volunteered her professional services to a hard-pressed state orphanage. She renewed her association with Christian students who were instrumental in helping her form a congregation of Russian believers. The Church of Love and Salvation chose not to affiliate with the emerging UMC in Russia. Hena served as the medical consultant to the churches of the conference and also established a network of rural community-based clinics in the Ukraine.

With the economic uncertainties that followed the demise of the Communist system and predictions of severe food shortages in the winter of 1991–1992, humanitarian organizations developed emergency programs for food distribution. The World Council of Churches (WCC) organized a massive church aid response through its network of relief agencies. The United Methodist Committee on Relief (UMCOR), another unit of GBGM, was asked to serve as the lead agency for the distribution of food in the Moscow region. The Department of Charities of the Russian Orthodox Church was the principal church partner for the project, but the Russian partners serving on the joint commission offered the logistical support of the Soviet Peace Fund. Dr. Bruce Weaver, UMCOR head, decided to mobilize the participation of local United Methodist churches in the U.S. in the response. Directions for supplying food for packaging and shipping were sent to the conferences and churches. Opportunities were offered to enclose letters of greeting inside the food boxes. Regional collection points were set up and international shipping channels cleared with church and government agencies. In all, 50,000 food boxes were sent in this manner.[3] With only incidental problems in the ports of St. Petersburg or in the warehouses in Moscow, the boxes of food were distributed to local organizations serving the elderly or children. Slowly but surely responses to the enclosed notes of greeting were received, connecting United Methodists with recipient families in Russia.

A generous response to financial appeals from UMCOR made it possible to purchase additional food for shipping and distribution. U.S. Government agencies were anxious to help nongovernmental organizations respond to the crisis in Russia, and UMCOR received matching grants to help defray shipping costs. The success of the program was met by doubts and questions from many traditional allies and critics alike. Ecumenical organizations like the National Council of the Churches of Christ in the U.S.A. (NCC) balked at the notion of cooperating with the Soviet Peace Fund. Under the Communist regime, that organization was closely tied to the state, and, unlike charitable organizations in the West, participation in its program was hardly voluntary. Worker "contributions" were mandatory, and there was little public accountability for its work. But it was the only organizational structure in existence that was strategically placed to make things happen. The Peace Fund, and its successor organization, remained a steadfast partner of the Russia Initiative program throughout the decade. Vladimir Shaporenko, executive of the fund's Moscow office, became a consultant to the program and later a staff member of GBGM.

Considerable intrigue and much skepticism marked the initiation of UMC development in the post-Soviet period. This period's earliest initiation of missionary activity leading to the formation of Methodist or United Methodist ministries in Russia or other former states of the Soviet Union can be traced to the Korean Methodist Church and to an association of Korean Methodist pastors with Korean-American pastors of The UMC. An estimated 500,000 Koreans resided in the Soviet Union, the remnant of a migration from North Korea to the Soviet Union during the Korean War. As soon as the political situation opened up, the Kwan Lim Methodist Church (a large institutional church) in Seoul deputized a Russian-Korean layman, Michael Kang, to initiate work in Moscow. He was instructed to locate property for a church center, and he sought assistance from the Department of External Affairs of the Russian Orthodox Church. The Orthodox Church had no ministry for the Koreans and had no objection to a foreign-based Protestant ministry with a non-Russian

Bishop Rüdiger Minor, far right, met with United Methodist missionaries in Moscow in the 1990s. Left to right are Christiana Hena, the Reverend and Mrs. Young Chuel Cho, and Robert J. Harman, then a deputy general secretary for GBGM. *(Photo by Robert J. Harman)*

ethnic group. There was a change of attitude when more aggressive evangelists from other churches in Korea began public revivals that drew much attention and sometimes criticized Orthodox practices. Assistance from the Moscow Patriarchate was provided in locating a building site to begin the Korean Methodist ministry. Upon completion of the center, the Reverend Yoon Chol was assigned by the Kwan Lim Methodist Church to provide pastoral oversight.

The Korean Methodist Mission Association to the Soviet Union, a group of missionary-minded pastors of Korean and Korean-American congregations, began recruiting pastors from Korea and the U.S. to start churches in the former Soviet Union. The Reverend Young Chuel Cho, a deacon in the New York Annual Conference, answered the call to begin a ministry in Moscow. He sought only the blessing of some of the Korean elders in the conference and, with the financial support of the association, prepared to take his family to Moscow. The cabinet of the conference quickly arranged for a special appointment and requested guidance and assistance with supervision from GBGM. Cho speedily and effectively gathered a congregation of Korean ethnic Russians and expatriate Korean business people in Moscow. Services of worship were conducted in Korean and translated into Russian. The church was chartered by the government as a "soviet" or society with the name United Methodist prominent in the Russian title. Reverend and Mrs. Cho were received into the missionary community of GBGM. Pastor Cho organized Korean culture and language classes for the second- and third-generation Russian Koreans who had little opportunity to appreciate their national/cultural heritage in a xenophobic Russian context. He also found comradeship among other missionary pastors from independent churches in Korea and joined them in forming a "seminary" to train some of their converts in theological and ministerial disciplines.

Meanwhile, the Reverend Dwight Ramsey, an elder from the Louisiana Annual Conference, was introduced to the former Soviet Union through a travel seminar group in 1990. He scheduled a return visit and arranged to conduct public gatherings and services of worship at the university in the city of Sverdlosk (Yekaterinburg) in the Ural mountain region of Russia. His meetings were well attended by curious students and others interested in religious dialogue or just conversation with this personality from the West. One inquirer, Lydia Istomina, was a former Intourist (government travel bureau) guide who volunteered to serve as a translator for Ramsey. Istomina, a young mother and teacher, became a convert to his preaching. She was anxious to lead others into the Christian faith and to form a United Methodist church in Yekaterinburg. Under Ramsey's tutelage (through frequent visits and fax communications) she organized the First United Methodist Church of Yekaterinburg and soon had a following of up to five hundred. Istomina also provided contacts for Ramsey to extend his evangelistic ministry in other cities, especially Sevastapol in the Ukraine and Moscow. Ramsey's church, the Broadmoor UMC in Shreveport, Louisiana, became enthusiastic supporters of this Russian mission and provided generous financial support for its development. The church also enlisted the support of the annual conference. Bishop William B. Oden led a delegation to Yekaterinburg in September 1991, where he and Bishop Hans Växby of the Northern Europe Central Conference recognized Istomina as a local pastor and assisted her in baptizing and receiving the first members into The UMC.[4]

The Council of Bishops received reports from Bishops Hearn and Oden and General Secretary Nugent on the growing potential for United Methodist work in Russia and determined that a coordinator should be named. The bishops turned to one of their number, Rüdiger Minor of the Dresden Area in East Germany. Minor had studied Russian in East German schools and was generally familiar with the region. Moreover, he was a leader of European Methodists who had expressed their concerns to GBGM that United Methodist initiatives from the U.S. were too unilateral and would "build a bridge to Russia over the heads of the European United Methodist connection."[5]

Minor accepted the role of coordinator and set out on an arduous journey to the places and people in the former Soviet Union where evidences of United Methodism were emerging. In addition to the work in the Moscow region, he visited a United Methodist church in Samara, a city on the Volga River. The founding pastor of the growing congregation was Vladislov Spekterov, a young man who accepted Christ while visiting in Estonia and attending an evangelistic youth meeting at the Tallinn UMC. Arriving by automobile at the outskirts of Samara, Minor spotted a sign with a United Methodist cross and flame directing him — not to the church, but to the food pantry sponsored by the church. This experience was an early indicator of the holistic nature of the ministry Minor would find among the emerging United Methodist churches in Russia. In Yekaterinburg, First UMC also established a feeding program, a preschool, and a prison ministry. The last produced a second local United Methodist congregation within the walls of the prison and introduced an extended ministry to family members who came to Yekaterinburg for prisoner visitation days. While this holistic ministry had its own distinctive origins within the young congregations in Russia, it was further encouraged by financial grants from UMCOR enabling all churches to engage in food pantry or feeding station programs.

Minor also visited the Carpathian region of the Ukraine, the only place other than Estonia where there was a continuing ministry of The UMC in the former Soviet Union. In the town of Kamenica he met an aging United Methodist pastor, the Reverend Ivan Vuksta, who successfully resisted attempts by authorities to limit the "free church" presence in local communities to one church, in this case a Baptist congregation. When the Methodist church was taken over by the state government, he gathered family members each Sunday in his home for Methodist worship. He journeyed to Estonia annually to take courses for pastoral ministry and was ordained deacon in 1968 and elder in 1982. In 1984 he was successful in registering the Kamenica United Methodist congregation with the government. In 1991 he reopened the United Methodist ministry in neighboring Uzhhorod. The churches remained in association with the Hungarian United Methodist Church, whose members provided spiritual and material support until incorporated into the recently formed Ukraine United Methodist Church, which was officially registered in February 2003 under the name: "The Spiritual Administration of the United Methodist Church in the Ukraine."[6]

Minor additionally checked out contacts in Latvia that were seeking the recovery of Methodist church properties and beginning United Methodist ministries. He visited with church leaders in Poland who were encouraging Bible distribution to churches in communities along the borders of Ukraine and Belarus.

Mission leaders in several annual conferences and pastors or members of a significant number of United Methodist congregations in the U.S. developed a strong interest in evangelistic and church development activity in the former Soviet Union. Some were in contact with GBGM, and others ventured into Russia through other channels. The United Methodist banner was unfurled in various locations without the benefit of communication or joint strategy development. General Secretary Nugent and Deputy General Secretary Robert Harman approached Weaver about becoming the director of a Russia Initiative program of GBGM. Weaver was completing service as interim head of UMCOR and was acquainted with the Russian context from his leadership of the food program for Russia. In order to scope out the possibilities of a program, Harman and Weaver called a consultation for May 1992 in Nashville, inviting any and all United Methodist groups or individuals with an interest in mission in Russia to participate. More than fifty persons attended the consultation, representing such groups as the Korean Association, the Mission Society for United Methodists, the Broadmoor UMC in Shreveport, Louisiana, Christians Associated for Religion in Eastern Europe, the Soviet Peace Fund, GBGM, and other general agencies. Minor was the keynote speaker, and the GBGM leadership helped the representatives begin informal conversations about their activities and future plans.

Minor's reports to GBGM and the Council of Bishops kept both bodies well-informed about church activities. Minor's initial contacts with the Russian Orthodox Church revealed a discomfort with the growth of foreign evangelistic groups beginning work in Russia without the blessing of its church hierarchy. Ekonomtsev, the Russian Orthodox signatory to the agreements with The UMC, had departed from the church's influential Department of External Affairs. Though he remained a partner to GBGM, the open door to official cooperation he provided had closed. The UMC was included in public indictments of proselytizing missionary activity. The need for a stronger coordinating function for the United Methodist presence in Russia was becoming evident. In March 1992, GBGM endorsed a recommendation to establish and provide administrative support for a mission in Russia. The Council of Bishops received and supported the recommendation but favored the assignment of a full-time resident bishop.[7] The council offered a proposal to the 1992 General Conference to establish a new episcopal area to serve Russia. It would be situated in Moscow and administer the emerging mission in Russia with a relationship to both the Northern Europe Central Conference and GBGM. With the merger of the Dresden Area into a newly united Germany Conference, only one bishop was needed in Germany. Minor was the obvious candidate for the position but required election by the Northern Europe Central Conference.

The favorable action of the 1992 General Conference and the anticipated election of Minor by the Northern Europe Central Conference gave United Methodism an official standing in Russia. It was celebrated in an installation event planned for Moscow in August 1992. United Methodists from across Russia, Europe, and the U.S. gathered in the rented auditorium that was home to First Korean UMC in Moscow. Organizational tensions were present in abundance. Some of the Russian United Methodists did not feel fully franchised in the episcopal election process and were voicing historic animosities toward a German influence in Russian Methodism. Regional interests were expressed by participants from the Urals in their reaction to the selection of Moscow for the new episcopal area office. Some new Russian United Methodists were appalled to learn that ecumenical protocol had been followed and an official invitation had been sent to the Russian Orthodox Church. The External Affairs Office of the Russian Orthodox Church did not respond to the invitation of Minor, but Ekonomtsev was present to bring the greetings of the Patriarch Alexy II and speak to the assembly.

The celebratory event surrounding Bishop Minor's election and appointment to Russia provided an occasion for recent converts and other participants to connect with the historical beginnings of the Methodist work in Russia. The mission of Methodism in the late 1800s and early 1900s from Europe and the U.S. had successfully established congregations in the St. Petersburg area and in the Far East. The Reverend George Simons, a missionary and member of the New York Annual Conference of the Methodist Episcopal Church, supervised the mission. He successfully recruited and trained a handful of indigenous pastors, published a hymnal, and circulated a regular conference newspaper. Those in the Methodist mission befriended members of a branch of the Orthodox Church (The Living Church) and channelled financial assistance from the mission board in New York to help with the training of priests. Methodism in Russia lost ground during the Bolshevik revolution, but provided substantial humanitarian assistance from Europe and the U.S., thanks to the courageous administrative efforts of Deaconess Anna Eklund of Finland, who remained in Russia long after Superintendent Simons and others were forced to take refuge in Lithuania. The extent to which the Russian United Methodists gathering in 1992 understood their descent from these origins was questionable, as was the measure of their commitment to the future formation of a United Methodist connectional conference. But the foundations were laid, and little more could be expected of the state of United Methodist mission in Russia at that moment, unless it was from the provocation of ecumenical partners, especially the Russian Orthodox Church.

The establishment of a United Methodist church in Russia, and especially the assignment of a bishop of the church to take up residence and supervisory responsibilities in the country, became a major obstacle in the degenerating relations between The UMC and the Russian Orthodox Church. United Methodist representatives attending meetings of the WCC were singled out for harsh criticism by Russian Orthodox participants. Bishop Melvin G. Talbert, secretary of the Council of Bishops, and Dr. Bruce W. Robbins, general secretary of the General Commission on Christian Unity and Interreligious Concerns, met the Russian Orthodox delegation during the WCC Central Committee meeting in Geneva in August 1992. They arranged for representatives of the two churches to have a consultation, held in Moscow in January 1993.

The dialogue opened with an audience with His Holiness Alexy II, Patriarch of Moscow and All Russia. The patriarch reminded the United Methodist delegation that the Russian Orthodox Church was emerging from a period of seventy years of hardship and repression. The church was assuming a strong leadership role in the rebuilding of the country following the failed Communist experiment. It welcomed cooperation and assistance in the form of humanitarian aid but regretted the missionary opportunists who were coming to Russia in great numbers to engage in proselytism. He saw a regrettable pattern of exploitation in the progression of United Methodist work, which began with humanitarian aid and resulted in the creation of a mission and the establishment of an episcopal office. He concluded: "We question now whether we can accept aid. Can the Russian Orthodox Church maintain ecumenical relations with the Methodists?"[8]

The most vocal Orthodox critic of United Methodist congregational development in Russia was Metropolitan Kyrill (a single titular name given by the church for the office of metropolitan), head of the Department of External Affairs in the Moscow Patriarchate. He claimed Russia's Orthodox history to be undefiled by the influence of Communism and 80 percent of the Russian population to be baptized Orthodox. Without any acknowledgment of inactivity or nominal memberships in Russian Orthodoxy, he concluded that the presence of United Methodist work in this Orthodox context could not be anything other than proselytism. He questioned the sincerity of the United Methodist ecumenical commitment.

The United Methodist delegation cited the brief history of the Methodist movement in Russia at the beginning of the century and its strong desire to see its continuation in a post-Communist renewal of ministry in the following terms: The historical preeminence of the Russian Orthodox Church was acknowledged and certainly never to be challenged by a UMC in Russia, whose ministry would be complementary and not competitive. The great suffering and persecution of the church under Communism would always be honored as an act of faithful witness for which United Methodists and other ecumenical partners were highly motivated to respond. The UMC was already officially cooperating with the Department of Charity and the Department of Christian Education and Catechism, and hundreds of United Methodist volunteers were working in local Russian communities side by side with Orthodox members in the rebuilding of Orthodox churches and institutions.

In spite of these efforts at rapprochement through dialogue, Orthodox criticism of United Methodism in Russia continued. A second dialogue took place in 1994 with little change in posture. The acrimony in the relationship reached a high when the Russian Orthodox Church gave its endorsement to the drafting of a new and more restrictive law on religious freedom. The law prevented the official recognition by the government of any religious group that had not been in continuous ministry in Russia throughout the seventy-year Soviet period. While that provision in the final bill precluded the newly reconstituted Russian UMC from being counted among the official religious groups, it opened the door to a registration process for which The UMC could claim its historical beginnings in Russia as a denomination. It eventually allowed The UMC to register as a central denominational body, sparing member churches the onerous process of filing registrations individually. It also assured the legal presence of The UMC in Russia.

The Russia Initiative program of GBGM successfully promoted a concept of partnership for initiating and supporting church development in Russia. The program was directed by consultant Weaver from his home and office in Dallas and offered a variety of opportunities for participation. Because it has become a model for other new mission initiatives of GBGM, its components are worthy of a full description.

Supporting Congregations

This program was a way of raising salary support for Russian United Methodist congregations from local congregations, districts, and annual conferences in the U.S. The Russia United Methodist Annual Conference approved a basic salary plan for all its pastors.[9] The Supporting Congregations program solicited pledges to cover the salary support package of the ninety-five pastors under appointment in 2001. The support was raised in the name of a specific partner church but directed to the conference for the basic salary plan for all pastors. All funds were sent through the GBGM Advance program.

The Partnership Program

This program was aimed at recruiting local churches and other connectional bodies to initiate work in cities, towns, and villages in Russia. New locations were chosen where there was no UMC presence. It involved selecting a place to work with the help of the Russia Peace Foundation (formerly Soviet Peace Fund). Shaporenko, a GBGM staff specialist and former director of the Soviet Peace Fund in Moscow, was in charge of the site selection and the management of communications between the local church and the host group in the receiving community, usually a service agency (orphanage, hospital, or other institution). United Methodist churches in the partnership program agreed to cultivate a relationship in the host community and to develop it over a three-year period. This was done largely through visits (often exchange visits) funded entirely by the local church. Anywhere from thirty-five to fifty such visits were conducted by the program each year. Agreements were reached about the nature of a partnership between the two groups. The visitors from the partner United Methodist church were invited and hosted for an initial visit. A special emphasis was placed upon introducing the host group to The UMC and to the nature and work of the local congregation in its home community in the U.S. Before the end of the initial visit, a service of worship or some form of faith-sharing took place. The church visitors also brought some forms of material assistance for the work of the host agency (medicines, recreational equipment for children, etc.). They also presented a small grant from UMCOR for humanitarian work of the host group or other community project. The grants created enormous goodwill and opened the way to a continuing project relationship. Follow-up visits were planned, and a partnership "agreement" of some kind was signed.

Partner Church Development

The Partnership Program accounted for much of the expansion of United Methodist work in Russia and the Commonwealth of Independent States. GBGM missionaries in Russia followed up the local contacts made in communities by the partner churches. They traveled to the local communities of every host group and introduced the possibility of forming Bible study groups. Many of these local groups organized as house churches. Local leaders were identified and nurtured. As the leaders matured and the groups grew, they were presented to the annual conference for chartering and membership and the leaders were given opportunities for training.

Mission Volunteers in Russia

Projects were developed for work teams interested in a short-term, work-related exposure in Russia. Sponsoring groups raised funds for travel and for any material needed at the work site. A few groups were recruited from campus ministries in the U.S. and sent to Russian universities. Shenandoah University, a United Methodist–related college in Virginia, developed a significant exchange program with a state university which sponsored annual opportunities for faculty and student exchanges. The Russia United Methodist Conference and churches had yet to develop an adequate infrastructure to benefit directly from this program.

The Russian Leadership Program

This program was the creation of Dr. James Billington, the Librarian of Congress. A Russophile and strong advocate in the nation's capital for progressive policies toward Russia in the post–Cold War political context, Billington espoused bringing young or aspiring political leaders from Russia to visit local communities in the U.S. to see how democratic institutions were operated and supported by the citizenry. He was convinced that this would be the only way to address the cynicism that was developing within the body politic in Russia. Billington was invited to address the Russia Initiative consultation in Dallas in February 1999. He took encouragement from participants in the United Methodist Russia Initiative to seek funding for such a program from the Congress. When the funding was approved, he came back to the Russia Initiative to help in hosting more than 1,500 visitors in the summers of 1999 and 2000. The Russia Initiative program gained about 600 new participants and a strong and influential advocate in Washington, D.C.

Russia Initiative Annual Consultations

Since the first consultation in Nashville in 1992, annual consultations have been sponsored by GBGM, with the number of participants increasing each year. The learning from that first consultation was that there would be little likelihood of drawing a master plan for the involvement of the diverse elements of United Methodism working in Russia. But the benefits from encouraging communication with each other were obvious. Participants in the annual consultations were individuals, churches, and groups engaged in one or more of the programs described. Attendance grew to nearly three hundred, with expenses covered by registration fees. Only the travel expenses for leaders from Russia, missionary personnel, or special guests were covered by GBGM.

Russia United Methodist Theological Seminary, Moscow

The viability of a United Methodist ministry in Russia, or elsewhere, hinges on the effectiveness of indigenous leadership. This principle was readily grasped by the insightful and visionary ministry of the Korean Methodists and Korean-American United Methodists who started missionary work in Russia and the Commonwealth of Independent States in the early 1990s. They worked with other Korean mission groups in Moscow to establish an independent (nondenominational) school for pastoral candidates. Visiting professors from seminaries in Korea helped with the teaching. It soon fell on hard times and was rescued by Rev. Cho, whose Moscow congregation was strong enough to continue its support temporarily. Bishop Minor, once a dean and director of a United Methodist seminary in East Germany, gravitated to the work of the seminary and sought increased resources to develop it into an institution that would distinctly serve the leadership development needs of the emerging United Methodist churches in Russia.

GBGM enlisted Dr. Donald Messer (then president at Iliff School of Theology) to organize a Seminary Advisory Committee, comprising representatives of other United Methodist theological schools.[10] After consultation with a small group of educators in Russia, their first effort was to strengthen the organizational and academic life of the fledgling Russian seminary. Dr. Clarence Snelling, a retired professor of church administration from Iliff, was recruited to serve as an administrator and general instructor in Moscow. He was succeeded by Tobias Dietze, a German United Methodist pastor with Russian-language skills, who was recruited by Minor to be the dean, a position supported by the GBGM International Person in Mission program.

The Academic Subcommittee of the advisory committee continued to recruit retired and active professors to supplement the small faculty in Russia by serving as visiting scholars (for periods of six weeks). At least one professor from the participating seminaries was scheduled to teach a course in Moscow each semester. Dr. Robin W. Lovin, dean of Perkins School of Theology at Southern Methodist University, took a turn at lecturing at the fledgling Moscow seminary. Upon returning he penned these reflections upon the experience:

> Methodism has always thought of itself as a movement that became a church by historical accident. In the U.S., the movement is mostly a memory and the denomination is a very big reality. But I've learned what it must have been like to be a movement by being in Russia. I am convinced that the evening I spent talking to thirty lay leaders who come twice a week from all over Moscow for training at the seminary is as close as I will ever get to what it was like to be in one of John Wesley's conferences with his lay preachers. I don't expect that the history that will come out of that classroom in Moscow will flow through just the same channels that Methodism followed in Western Europe and North

America. But I think I see the Holy Spirit at work in Russian Methodism, and I want to stay with it until we see what God has in mind.[11]

The seminary program moved rapidly toward developing a fully indigenous leadership. Some graduates were encouraged to pursue postgraduate studies and become members of a resident faculty. The Reverend
Andre Kim completed a master's degree program at a Korean seminary
and headed the distant learning program. Sergei V. Nikolaev, a student
at Perkins School of Theology, and others were scheduled to return to
teaching posts upon completion of their postgraduate studies abroad.

The advisory committee took up other issues, e.g., curriculum. An an-
thology of contemporary writings in biblical criticism was assembled by
Dr. David Petersen, Old Testament professor at Iliff, and translated by
Elena Stepanova, chair of the Board of Ordained Ministry of the Russia
Annual Conference and former dean and professor of philosophy at Yekaterinburg University. Stepanova also provided an extensive introduction
to the work written especially for Russian students. Dr. S T Kimbrough,
associate general secretary for Mission Evangelism of GBGM, made substantial contributions by identifying and locating in archives in Russia and
the U.S. various Wesley theological works published in Russian during the
time of the initial Methodist mission presence in the early twentieth century. Seminary professors suggested contemporary pieces for translation
and publication by the United Methodist Publishing House.

The United Methodist Theological Seminary in Moscow graduated its
first class in 1997. It maintained a residential student enrollment of about
twenty students, with more than forty students in the distant learning
program. The members of each graduating class received appointments to
the expanding number of churches of the Russia Annual Conference. The
GBGM provided annual grants to underwrite the budget of the seminary
and the expenses of the advisory committee. The Women's Division provided scholarship grants for women students who composed a large proportion of each class as well as the itinerant ministry of the conference.
The General Board of Higher Education and Ministry (GBHEM), an
active member of the Advisory Committee, underwrote the expenses of
sending exchange professors to Moscow. GBHEM gave overall guidance
to the development of leadership training programs for the Russia Annual
Conference. The Reverend Robert Kohler, GBHEM staff member, was
instrumental in creating an independent study program for local pastors

in outlying regions, a project that became part of the seminary's distance learning program.

The seminary was located in an inadequate, small, and expensive rental property. With a large grant from the GBGM Millennium Fund, a substantial grant from GBHEM, and other matching gifts, an abandoned school facility in Moscow was purchased as a site for the seminary. A fundraising goal of $2 million was established to underwrite the redevelopment of the building into classrooms, a student residence, and an office for the bishop and conference headquarters. The advisory committee oversaw the fund-raising campaign.

Church Building Projects

At the end of the first decade of the renewal of United Methodist ministry in Russia, property acquisition and church construction were on the ascendency. Local churches were meeting in shared public facilities or renting from landlords with rather capricious attitudes toward their presence and the amount of their rent. The first new church building project in Yekaterinburg dramatized the challenge and level of difficulty in undertaking a construction project in Russia. The project started from one of the first partnerships (Yekaterinburg/Broadmoor UMC and the Louisiana Annual Conference). Full funding for the project was not available from local sources in the U.S. or Russia so GBGM became a major financial backer. The Yekaterinburg pastor, Istomina, left Russia for residence and a ministry in the U.S. While the new pastor and her building committee wished to manage the project, the factor of sponsorship from the U.S. remained to be exploited by all of the participants. The major donors in Louisiana wanted assurances of the security of their investment in the project and offered one of their talented church members, James Gillespie, as a project supervisor. Contractual negotiations and disputes were a dominant factor throughout the project. Enforcement was lacking. City bureaucrats worked their self-interest agendas. Contractors walked off the job. The project took five years to complete. Meanwhile, the congregation that would ultimately occupy the structure was smaller than the one that planned it. Congregational morale was tested as it assumed responsibility for maintaining the building. The partnership concept of the Russia Initiative was tested on its ability to rise above familiar patterns of mission and financial dependency.

Other church building projects have proceeded surprisingly well, but until the economy in Russia yields a greater potential for self-supporting congregations, a bold agenda for church construction was waiting to unfold gradually.

Women's Association

In 1994, in fulfillment of a Centennial Fund program goal to enter into dialogue with constituencies worldwide, the Women's Division of GBGM sponsored a major consultation with Russian women. Participants were invited from the newly established United Methodist churches and from other religious (Orthodox/ecumenical) and secular and commercial organizations (some planning business careers in the new Russian economy). The outcome was the establishment of a network, the Russian Women's Association, of largely professional women working in social service organizations dedicated to strengthening the role of women and children in the Russian society. Annette Funk, Women's Division staff in Financial Development, was assigned to oversee the follow-up work of the conference and association. Periodic grants were made to the organization or to social agencies headed by women who were related to this organizing effort. While the support and nurture of this women's network was the major commitment of the Women's Division, the division also cultivated a community among women leadership in the Russia UMC. The church had a proportionately high number of women among the clergy and lay leadership. Encouraging their leadership efforts offered great potential for influencing the direction of the church. The organizing of a women's unit in the life of a conference within a central conference was not the role of the Women's Division. In Russia, women United Methodists looked to the European Methodist Women's Federation to take this on, with financial assistance from the division if requested.

Ecumenical Relationships

The UMC was one the few major (U.S.-based) Protestant denominations to organize a denominational presence in contemporary Russia. Lutheran bodies were accepted largely because of their history in ministry to German-speaking populations in Russia. The Presbyterians assisted Reform church partners. Episcopalians worked directly with the Orthodox Church. The UMC also worked ecumenically on European church strategies through the Europe office of the NCC and indirectly through the European Council of Churches. As previously reported, the Russian

Lydia Istomina, an Intourist translator, became a United Methodist through the influence of the Reverend Dwight Ramsey in 1990. She organized a congregation in Yakterinburg that soon had five hundred members. *(Photo courtesy of UM Archives and History)*

Orthodox Church made known its discontent with the United Methodist presence in Russia, accusing The UMC of violating its ecumenical commitment to support the ministries of the Orthodox Church, of proselytism, and using humanitarian aid to win over Orthodox believers. These were serious charges that the Russian Orthodox Church broadcast widely. Father Leonid Kishkovsky, ecumenical officer of the Orthodox Church in America, served as an advisor to GBGM and was a frequent interpreter of the UMC presence in Russia to the leadership of the Russian Orthodox Church.

The early contacts of The UMC with the Russian Orthodox Church were with rather progressive members of the church hierarchy (Ekonomtsev and Archbishop Sergei of Charities). Their perspectives on cooperation were not shared by the prevailing center(s) of power in the Moscow Patriarchate, especially by Kyrill. UMC assistance to the Russian Orthodox Church was through these two leaders for the programs of their departments. The Department of Charities was a principal partner in the food distribution program(s) of UMCOR in the early stages of the country's post-Communist economic crisis. The Department of Christian Education and Catechism received consultative assistance from GBGM and the General Board of Discipleship in the development and publication of church school curricula. Orthodox University, the first church-sponsored higher education project in Russia and a project of the director of the department, received financial and material assistance from GBGM. Ecumenical cooperation within Russia was limited to work with and through other international agencies like the WCC or the Bible Society in Russia. Cooperative efforts among representative denominational leadership in Russia were permanently eroded by the Russian Orthodox Church advocacy for the restrictions of the religious freedom legislation.

International Congregation in Moscow

The UMC and other member churches of the NCC supported a congregation for expatriates in Moscow. In the Soviet days, the church served U.S. citizens (and some Europeans) who occupied the limited number of government or cultural posts in Moscow. It was known as the "embassy church." Later it took on a more international character, serving expatriates from more than thirty nations, many of whom were student refugees from African countries that were caught up in military conflicts or political turmoil. Africans in Russia have suffered from severe acts of racial violence, and the congregation became a leading advocate for the protection of human and civil rights by the government. The congregation reached many poor Muscovites, especially pensioners in need of food, clothing, and other forms of assistance. Pastoral appointments were made by the sponsoring denominations on a three-year rotating cycle.

Publications and Communications

United Methodist efforts in developing resources for this mission initiative were insufficient. Church publications in the Russian language were very limited. While one of the early missionaries, Kim Lae Sun, worked on a Christian education curriculum, priority attention was directed at providing curriculum resources for the seminary. A group of partners in the Russia Initiative put together a publishing enterprise but had to be selective about what they printed. Kimbrough teamed up with the Reverend Ludmylla Gorbosova, a professionally trained musician and Moscow United Methodist pastor, in the publishing of a United Methodist hymnal in Russian. It had 250 hymns of the church, including several Russian hymns that appeared in the first Russian Methodist Hymnal published in the early 1900s, and some contemporary and original contributions of Rev. Gorbosova. The Women's Division participated in the funding of this project. Minor appointed a church commission to work on matters of content, publication, and introduction to the churches.

At an early stage in the development of the United Methodist mission in Russia, media communications was thought to be an important strategy for creating religious dialogue and promoting the ministries of the churches. The Mission Resources unit of GBGM worked with the United Methodist Commission on Communication and church partners in Russia to sponsor a religious radio program, *Religious Digest*, on a major network. Produced in Moscow with program content from the Russian Orthodox Church and other cooperative church agencies, the program had potential for reaching a national audience. The good news was that it was done in cooperation with other denominations — including the Orthodox. The bad news was that it was terribly expensive to reach the expansive Russian media audience and lacked a firm funding base. The alternative, less-expensive locally based church media efforts, were much more difficult to develop and had yet to be organized.

Rural and Small Towns

One of the program needs presented to GBGM by Ekonomtsev was the development of rural areas, especially small towns and cities which benefitted neither from the Moscow-based services of the former Communist government nor from today's global attractions. This need was discussed with the Rural Chaplains program of the GBGM Town and Country Ministries network. The chaplains promptly organized a representative group to travel to rural areas in Russia and Tajikistan to develop some proposals. They envisioned work among farm cooperatives in these contexts, even assisting with machinery and marketing techniques. Their attention has been concentrated upon a conflicted area in Tajikistan where conditions prevented their return. Communications continued and provided the basis for future development. The Rural Chaplains provided scholarship assistance for a student, Parvina Ndjabulla, from Tajikistan to obtain a U.S. college education. She was employed by GBGM on the seminar staff at the Church Center for the United Nations.

Missionaries

A relatively small number of GBGM missionaries were assigned for work in Russia. The emphasis of their work lay in developing local leaders. Few expatriate missionaries had to fill major leadership roles, e.g., local pastors or conference administrators. The missionary portfolio with highest program visibility was that assigned to following up on partner church visits, mentioned in the previous section on church development. As trained leadership emerged in the church, the Russia UMC was ready to meet this and other internal missionary requirements. It was already sending missionaries to Kazakhstan and the Russian province of Kaliningrad to engage in church and community development. Because Russia provided a high level of educational achievement, recruitment of Russians for skilled positions or professions such as medicine or social work was relatively easy.

Some Methodist missionary activity in Russia originated from other sources than GBGM or within the Russian United Methodist conference. The Korean Russian constituencies in the church continued to relate well to personnel of their Korean ethnic background and welcomed such personnel from the U.S. or Korea. Also, the Mission Society for United Methodists (MSUM) assigned personnel to Russia and the Commonwealth of Independent States. There was no consultation with GBGM about this activity, but the MSUM initiated communication with Minor regarding the need for MSUM personnel to have an organizational "cover" in Russia that met the requirements of the religious freedom law. The unsettled issues of the MSUM relationship to the formal structures of the denomination precluded any formal agreement.

Continuing Consultation Task Force

Coordination of GBGM initiatives in Russia required the creation of a task force which included representation from Southern Europe and Northern Europe central conferences and representatives from the emerging Russia UMC. From 1992 to 1996, it met annually to review the developing work and to make recommendations. The first meeting of the group laid down a good theological rationale for initiating United Methodist work in Russia. Any hope that the committee would be able to "rein in" independent mission activities of United Methodists as well as the agencies of the church was soon given up. In 1997, after the mission had gained its

standing as a provisional annual conference, it was agreed that a full committee was no longer needed but that a consultation process between the
Russia UMC and the GBGM should continue. A new committee was
proposed, the Continuing Consultation Committee, made up of equal
representation from the Russia UMC and GBGM. The group met annually, shifting sites between Russia and the U.S. The meeting agendas
included briefings on program development, budget, and other general
matters. It was also an arena to address some of the tensions, expectations,
and disappointments created by the many-faceted approaches of partner
churches from the U.S. to those in Russia. The Russian leaders on the
committee began to use this arena as a sounding board for policy development in their annual conference and to offer assessments of program and
policy directions of GBGM and other agencies of the church.[12]

Kazakhstan: Nuclear Radiation and Health

GBGM began its work in Kazakhstan in 1993 as an extension of the
health component of the Russia Initiative. Cathie Lyons, associate general
secretary for the Health and Welfare Ministries Program Department,
traveled to Kazakhstan with the aim of identifying new hospital partnerships for United Methodist–related hospitals.[13]

Kazakhstan achieved its long-awaited independence from Russia in
1991. Since then there had been only limited contact between Kazakhstani
health professionals and their peers in the West. Lyons was encouraged
to visit the remote Semipalatinsk region that Joseph Stalin had closed for
the Soviet Union's atomic and nuclear weapons proving ground. Out-
siders were forbidden to travel there during the period of Soviet control.
The story of its oppression was just beginning to be told. From 1949 to
1991 more than 550 atomic, nuclear, and thermonuclear weapons were
tested at the site. The people of the region were never informed of the
health risks to the population from the tests being undertaken.

The Minister of Health of Kazakhstan described the Semipalatinsk region as "our place of weeping and our place of sorrow."[14] Health professionals and scientists in the region recognized that the health and developmental problems that would overwhelm future generations would likely
overshadow past and current sufferings of the people. Lyons successfully
brokered partner relationships between four hospitals in Semipalatinsk
with four major hospitals in the Houston area, including the Methodist

Hospital in Houston. Administrators and physicians from the participating institutions developed a three-year plan of cooperation. Humanitarian relief was also provided, with UMCOR shipping medicines, general hospital supplies, food, and learning aids for children in orphanages and special schools. These efforts received local media coverage in Kazakhstan, where there was increasing curiosity about The UMC.

In September 1993, Dr. Boris Ivanovich Gusev invited a GBGM team to visit him at the Kazakh Scientific Research Institute of Radiation Medicine and Ecology. He became director of the institute during the Soviet period and was privy to information collected by the institute on the effects of radiation exposure on the general population during the years of nuclear tests. Citing his familiarity with the Christian teaching that "the truth shall set you free," he asked his visitors from GBGM for help. Would they help him meet U.S. scientists who were interested in radiation research and would work with him to help tell the truth about human health and ecological effects of forty years of nuclear weapons testing in

This young girl was affected by nuclear tests whose radiation polluted the Semipalatinsk region of Kazakhstan during the Soviet Union period. The Health and Welfare Ministries unit of GBGM sent representatives to Kazakhstan in the 1990s to provide relief and to develop a series of dialogues with scientists there and in the U.S. about the effects of nuclear radiation. *(Photo by Cathie Lyons, courtesy of UM Archives and History)*

the region? It was estimated that 62 percent of the current population were born to parents exposed to radiation, among whom were excessively high rates of mental retardation, physical deformities, and cancer.

The Health and Welfare Department organized two dialogues, one in New York and the other in Semipalatinsk. A U.S. team of radiation professionals was carefully recruited with the growing awareness of the sensitivity of the issues to be addressed in a dialogue that would attract interest in the larger scientific and public policy communities. Hearn, Houston Area bishop and president of GBGM at the outset of this initiative, chaired the dialogue sessions. Participants expressed great interest in Gusev's data, perhaps the most complete longitudinal study of a radiation-exposed population. There was immediate concern for the care and treatment of future generations in Semipalatinsk who would suffer the effects of their parents' long-term exposure to ionizing radiation. There was also a desire to see Gusev's research and analysis expanded through further consultation with international experts on radiation research and ecology.

In 1995, after legal reviews in the U.S. and Kazakhstan, GBGM entertained a proposal from the department to establish a United States/Kazakhstan International Foundation on Radiation, Ecology, and Health. The foundation would seek funding from other foundations to enable further cooperative research efforts with the Semipalatinsk radiation scientists and to establish a clinical treatment and research center in Semipalatinsk. The foundation with a small membership of five persons from each country had offices in the GBGM New York headquarters. Among its goals was the increase of rehabilitation capacity—in particular a new clinical center, publication of selected scientific reports on the health problems in Semipalatinsk, and sponsorship of training seminars for health care workers.[15]

In 1999, the Board received a proposal from the U.S./Kazakhstan Foundation for the building of a primary medical care center in Semipalatinsk. The center would be located in the city of Kurchatov and serve the general population so dramatically contaminated by the effects of nuclear testing radiology. It would also be a training site for medical personnel and medical students from the former Semipalatinsk nuclear testing polygon and the surrounding region. Three million dollars in unrealized capital gains were restricted for this purpose. The government Ministry of Health constructed the center under the supervision of the foundation. A distinction in this partnership was the high level of cooperation between the government whose officials were primarily of the Muslim religious tradition and The UMC.[16]

The health initiative in Kazakhstan also stimulated other mission efforts. A relationship developed with the local Russian Orthodox Church, which asked for assistance in developing a church school and help with Bible distribution. The Russia Annual Conference of The UMC assigned a missionary pastor in 1999 who developed a youth and counseling ministry and assessed the prospects for congregational development.

When the first GBGM team visited Kazakhstan, local leaders recalled how other visitors from the West came but never returned. On one occasion a Kazakhstani host invited a United Methodist delegation to tell her more about their church searching for some explanation for why it is that United Methodists keep returning to Semipalatinsk. Her inquiry underscored the aptness of the United Methodist public relations theme that describes the nature of the church's witness: "It is not *who* goes to your church, but *where* your church goes."

Renewal of The UMC in the Baltic States

The early witness of Methodism in Russia and the Baltic states at the beginning of the twentieth century lost ground to two world wars and the rise of Communism in the Soviet Union. In 1918, the Bolshevik revolution forced the closing of foreign embassies and the relocation of the headquarters of Methodist mission in Russia and the Baltic states from St. Petersburg (Petrograd) to Riga, Latvia. A seminary and superintendent's office serving the region was maintained. The mission work among the German-speaking population in Latvia was initiated by both the *Evangelische Kirche* (former Evangelical United Brethren Church) and the Methodist Church in Germany. The Methodist Church in Germany supported a similar ministry in Lithuania. Efforts in both countries were dependent upon missionary pastors from Germany who were forced to return home or emigrate to the U.S. following the outbreak of the Second World War. At the end of the war, the countries of Lithuania, Latvia, and Estonia became the spoils of Russia's participation in the Allied campaign in Europe. Each country had distinct cultures and languages, making the transition most difficult. It ultimately took the bombing of Tallinn by the Russian air force to convince Estonia to fold itself into the Soviet Union.

In the Soviet period, Methodist churches had no official standing in

Latvia and Lithuania. Their pastors had emigrated, and the church buildings were confiscated. Members were offered the ministry of the Lutheran or the Baptist churches, which were among the few Protestant churches recognized by governmental authorities. Methodism managed to survive in Estonia, the only province in the Soviet Union where officials allowed Methodists to worship, but Methodists were not free from persecution. Superintendent Andre Kum and many of the Estonian Methodist leaders were arrested, deported, and imprisoned in Siberian camps. The Estonian church was permitted to entertain occasional visitors from the world Methodist family and was allowed to receive its bishop from the Northern Europe Central Conference, but for all practical purposes the church was cut off from connectionalism. Superintendent Olaf Parnamets provided stalwart leadership for the small communities of Methodists in his care.

With the post–Cold War breakup of the Soviet Union, the Baltic countries regained their independence. There was immediately a stirring of new religious activity in each country. Latvian Americans and Lithuanian Americans began returning to the homelands to make contact with family members and friends. Among them were United Methodists who had past associations with Methodist ministries in Latvia and Lithuania. There was a growing advocacy for GBGM to assist with the redevelopment of the churches.

Latvia

The Board held title to three church properties in Latvia, two in Riga (including the prestigious old seminary and office building) and one in Leipaja. When Bishop Minor visited Riga in his role as coordinator of emerging mission in the former Soviet Union, he found the former First Methodist Church building occupied by an athletic association. A boxing ring had been erected in the sanctuary. But he also met a small group of persons interested in re-establishing a (United) Methodist Church in Latvia. No Methodist clergy had survived the period of official absence of Methodism, but a handful of Lutherans volunteered themselves to lead and rebuild Methodist congregations.

Research into church and public records indicated that the properties of the Methodist Church were registered in the name of the Board of Missions (Global Ministries) in New York. A Riga law firm was contacted to assist with the recovery of the properties from state ownership, which the Board agreed to finance. In 1995, the properties were among the first in the country to be returned by the government to a church organization. Of course, they were in varying states of disrepair, but they represented a major program asset and public statement for a new United Methodist witness in Latvia.

In 1996 the Latvia District of The UMC was constituted and formally related to the Northern Europe Central Conference. Bishop Hans Växby presided over the first district conference at which Arijs Viksna (a Lutheran pastor with a convincing Wesleyan theology, serving a United Methodist Church in Leipaja) was named superintendent and delegate to the forthcoming Northern Europe Central Conference. The mission district consisted of two churches in Riga and one in Leipaja with reports of several "fellowship groups" in formation. Of course, financing the emerging ministries in a slowly developing economy was a major concern. The restoration and maintenance of church buildings was a preoccupation. Växby brokered relationships with GBGM, the World Evangelism Connecting Congregations program of the World Methodist Council, and leaders of the Northern Europe Central Conference to generate basic support for the efforts of the congregations.

Plans for United Methodist church development (or redevelopment) in Latvia were in the custody of the small group of pastors and their recruits to whom Växby provided necessary oversight and pastoral encouragement. Each of the newly established congregations benefitted from partnerships cultivated by United Methodist churches in northern Europe and the U.S., but the culturally distinct and insular context of Latvia necessitated local initiative and follow-through. Not until the year 2000, when it became obvious that the leadership in the churches required a stronger connectional relationship and training, were missionaries introduced. The churches began gradually serving the needs of new communities and age groups with distinctive ministries.

Lithuania

A small aging group of former Methodists who saw their churches close and pastors leave Lithuania in 1941–1942 became anxious to find United Methodists among the religious groups entering their country to begin new ministries. Vally Nance, a Lithuanian-American United Methodist lay member from Birmingham, Alabama, spent eight months in the country in 1994–1995. She was the child of a refugee family who fled Lithuania for Europe and then the U.S. Baptized as a Methodist in Lithuania, she was raised in The UMC. The family members whom she visited in Lithuania asked if she knew when the Methodists would return. She presented that query to Kimbrough, who was familiar with the history of Methodism in Europe and Lithuania and urged the Board to make a commitment.

Kimbrough made several visits to Lithuania, one with Dr. James White, Europe secretary of the World Division and retired Pastor Arthur Leifert of the Germany Conference. Leifert began his ministry in Lithuania and was anxious to be of assistance in locating surviving church members and identifying church-owned properties. Contacts were also made with Bishop Jonas Kalvanus of the Lithuanian Lutheran Church who welcomed the possibility of a return of Methodism to his country.

On August 30, 1995, Växby presided over a service of renewal and celebration of Holy Communion that was held in a Lutheran Church in Kaunas, the old capital of Lithuania that was the seat of Methodism in the country. Twenty-two members (former and new) of the Kaunas congregation signed the membership roll and became the nucleus of United Methodism in the city and country. The reorganization of the Kaunas church enabled The UMC to register and to begin the process of property recovery.

The newly established UMC in Lithuania set ambitious goals, including the reconstituting of local churches in every community where they had earlier existed. By the end of the decade, considerable progress had been made. Not only were sites with historical significance for Methodism identified for development, but programs of social service and outreach to communities of need were planned and implemented. A ministry to incarcerated youthful offenders has become a model for treatment reform. A preventive health program utilizing the congregations as the base for ministry introduced the holistic nature of United Methodist ministry to many in Lithuania.

GBGM provided resources for this ministry with a team of staff members. They effectively utilized missionary personnel in directing the mission. The Reverend Bill and Grace Warnock were invited to transfer from Moscow to Kaunas to provide administrative, program, and pastoral support. The Reverends David and Kristin Markay from Ohio joined them in a missionary assignment to develop the mission. Bill Warnock was appointed by Växby as the superintendent and represented the interests of the church in all proceedings with the government in re-registering the church and reclaiming properties. He served as superintendent and pastor at the parent church in Kaunas that was thoroughly renovated and restored to its original state. The Warnocks retired in 1999. After assisting Warnock with the redeveloping of the Kaunas congregation, the Markays took on the assignment of starting a new UMC in the capital of Vilnius, a new site for Methodist witness and ministry. David succeeded Warnock as superintendent. The encouragement and enlistment of local personnel to assume pastoral leadership became a priority for the mission.

Estonia

The demise of Soviet control presented a small but energetic United Methodist Church in Estonia with a new opportunity to extend its witness and service to the population. The church lived in the shadow of the state, since Soviet authorities gave close scrutiny to all church activities. The church in Tallinn had lost its church building in the Russian bombardment of the city in 1944. Its two Sunday services, one in Estonian and one in Russian, were conducted in the Adventist church building. Church headquarters was located in a small building in the old historic section of the city. Methodism in Estonia also included small congregations occupying very modest facilities in several smaller cities and towns and a band of "Sunday schools" or unofficial house churches.

A strategy for developing its ministry in the new context of political and religious freedom unfolded with the cooperation and encouragement of the Reverend Eddie Fox of the World Evangelism program of the World Methodist Council. The immediate focus was upon developing leadership. A seminary was developed in the small headquarters building of the church in Tallinn. World Evangelism provided missionary and financial support for the venture, and Asbury Theological Seminary, Wilmore, Kentucky, helped with curriculum development and contributed visiting professors. Student recruits came from across the small nation, and classes were offered in both Estonian and Russian languages.

Superintendent Parnamets received a surprise visit from the Reverend Sundo Kim, pastor of the large and prestigious Kwan Lim Methodist Church in Seoul, Korea. The two leaders became acquainted while serving in the leadership ranks of the World Methodist Council. Kim's church was pursuing a rather aggressive program of world mission and evangelization that featured Western Europe, Russia, Asia, and Africa. After experiencing the vitality of the Estonian United Methodists, Kim offered his help along with a challenge. He wanted to help Parnamets with the construction of a new church building for the Tallinn congregations that would also house the growing student body of the fledgling seminary. He offered a contribution of $1 million, with the understanding that a similar amount would be raised from world Methodism.

Parnamets accepted the challenge, began dialogue with the government about a possible site, and commissioned local architects to design a structure. GBGM assisted in providing records to document previous property ownership that would entitle Tallinn United Methodists to a replacement site that was at least of equivalent value. A large land parcel was offered in a semi-industrial area of the city, offering striking vistas of the harbor. The local architects were enamored with the site and the opportunity presented to design the first newly constructed building in the city in the post-Soviet period. Their final design featuring a nautical exterior exploited the physical amenities of the harbor site. The space would easily accommodate the existing congregations and the seminary as well as a variety of church programs and community services. The initial cost estimates for construction required more than a simple matching of the Korean church million-dollar grant. Parnamets was up to the challenge. The new church would become both a symbol of the strength of his peoples' faith throughout the difficulties of the past and the fulfillment of a vision for a strong Methodist witness in the future.

The new building project was promoted as the Baltic Mission Center. Construction was begun with the funds available from Korea and good faith in the generosity of Methodism worldwide. Special fund-raising projects were begun by World Evangelism and by GBGM. When the Korean funds were spent and before fund-raising efforts began to produce new monies, GBGM advanced loan funds to keep the construction on course. The Board later made two sizable grants from its Millennium Fund, which were matched by the fund-raising efforts of World Evangelism and churches and leaders in several conferences working as a network of "The Friends of Estonia." Several mission volunteer trips were organized by "The Friends" to generate more interest in the project and to provide "free labor" on the project. The seminary moved into its classrooms before the facility was fully completed. After nearly five years of construction, the finished building was consecrated in the fall of 2000.

The renewal of Methodism in Estonia not only made its mark on the skyline of Tallinn but in the heart of the community of Parnu. There the

Reverend Ulas Tankler, a young Estonian pastor who benefitted from receiving his theological training at the United Methodist seminary in Reutlingen, Germany, took up his ministry with a small church membership but a vision for serving the larger community. After successfully recruiting a new generation of church leaders, Ulas began conversations with city authorities regarding population groups with special needs. An agreement was reached that allowed the church to build a new facility on a large tract of land in a neighborhood without any existing church, in return for creating a treatment program for dependent and neglected youth. Eager for just such an opportunity, Tankler had a multipurpose building designed. It featured worship space for the congregation that would also accommodate musical concerts. It had educational space that doubled as program space for a city-sponsored youth treatment center. And it provided dormitory space and dining services for young people requiring residential care. The name given to the project was Agape Center.

Tankler's agreement with the city of Parnu provided for limited government funding for program and required that most of the construction costs be raised through church sources. Northern European United Methodist conferences provided generous support through their Estonian Support Group. GBGM provided sustaining grants and made it possible for Tankler to itinerate among United Methodist churches in the U.S., where he was well received. He worked tirelessly at presenting the needs and opportunities, and churches responded with funds and volunteer assistance with projects at the church. When the building was near completion in 1997, the church proudly hosted the quadrennial meeting of the Northern Europe Central Conference.

With the stirring of a revitalized Methodist witness and ministry in the region, Estonian church leadership prepared to undergird its connectional neighbors in the area of training. The Baltic Mission Center trained Russian-speaking church leaders, some of whom intended to serve in the Russian Annual Conference, in spite of historical and cultural differences. A pastor from Riga enrolled in studies at the center to receive his first formal training as a United Methodist minister called to serve in Latvia. At the close of the century, United Methodists in the three countries comprising the three districts of the UMC in the Baltic states remained organizationally distinct. They have yet to create opportunities for community and sharing of their respective visions for ministry. They, along with Russian United Methodists, have been warmly received into the Northern

Europe Central Conference, but their combined presence there outnumbered the membership of the more established conferences in the region. Benefitting from the spiritual gifts of these new conferences would require further cultivation and a strategy for integration by this regional connectional body.

Latin America: New Church Relationships and Initiative

In a review of its mission relationships in Latin America, GBGM questioned whether the partnership with the Council of Evangelical Methodist Churches in Latin America (CIEMAL) was sufficiently committed to initiating new relationships in the region. The cooperation between the Board and CIEMAL seemed to favor support for internal church programs through cooperative relationships with mission agencies in North America and Europe.

In the decades of the 1980s and 1990s, mission journals devoted increasing attention to the growth of evangelical (i.e., Christian but not Roman Catholic) groups and churches in the region. Because much of this activity was being sponsored by a wave of independent missionary and evangelistic groups from North America, the trend was quickly dismissed by most Protestant churches as Pentecostal and uncooperative.

Among Methodists in Latin America, the Brazil church demonstrated a strong will to begin work in newly designated missionary areas in the country and to send missionaries to care for a growing diaspora in the U.S. The Costa Rica church made evangelism its priority by establishing a training school for pastors and evangelists. The only new church relationship nurtured in the region was with the Primitive Methodist Church in Guatemala, which expressed a desire to leave its very conservative missionary sponsorship and affiliate with a Methodist body in the region. CIEMAL opened its doors to this strongly indigenous church, which then entered a covenant relationship to The UMC at the 1992 General Conference.

GBGM began hearing new reports of independently developing congregations and church entities with Methodist identities in several countries where there were no established Methodist churches. Some were initiated through direct contact with United Methodist congregations in the States that were directly engaged in sending volunteer work teams to the region. Others were the result of local charismatic leaders organizing churches that they believed reflected Methodist doctrinal or organizational principles. The issue was discussed with CIEMAL. An agreement was reached to fund a ministry of "accompaniment" in order to make contact with and assess the strength of such groups in Venezuela, Colombia, El Salvador, and Nicaragua. Bishop Emeritus Isaías Gutiérrez of Chile was assigned the task of visiting the groups.

In Venezuela two groups were vying for recognition as "Methodists," and discussions focused on the organizational implications of choosing the Methodist heritage in the Latin American context. In Colombia, the MSUM introduced Methodism to local communities and leaders. Follow-up discussions with CIEMAL were punctuated with much doubt and uncertainty over the prospects of relating to other Methodist bodies in the region.

In El Salvador, Juan F. Mayorga, an ambitious young pastor, enrolled in the Spanish-language local pastor's course at Garrett-Evangelical Theological Seminary in Evanston, Illinois. He was determined to introduce a Methodist church to his country. He welcomed the initiative from CIEMAL and proceeded with the development of a constitution and organizational structures and encouraged the recruitment and training of leadership for an autonomous Methodist church in El Salvador.

In Nicaragua, where GBGM had worked ecumenically on economic and social development programs, Bishop Gutiérrez and the Board were surprised to find two congregations in Managua with the identifiable United Methodist cross and flame designating their places of worship. They were the fruits of a local church ministry from the Florida Annual Conference with a strong desire to make a connection to the denomination in the region. GBGM missionaries in Nicaragua were committed to the ecumenical community development agenda, but CIEMAL nominated a pastor to serve in the GBGM International Person in Mission program as a church developer in Nicaragua.

At the Rio de Janeiro site of the World Methodist Conference in August 1996, GBGM staff met with the leaders of CIEMAL to discuss their understandings of any existing accords on mission initiatives in Latin America. The staff shared with the CIEMAL leaders the growing commitment within GBGM to concentrate on mission evangelism and its program goal to "Witness to the Gospel for Initial Decision to Follow Jesus Christ." The implementation of this goal should reflect an expanding Methodist presence in Latin America. How would the two bodies cooperate? An agreement was reached: "Either CIEMAL or GBGM could make initial contact to establish a new project and in each case the group initiating the work would inform the other in order to establish a process of discernment and accompaniment for the new group.

"Both groups would inform each other of the methodology to follow, including aspects of economic support.

"Both CIEMAL and GBGM will help the new project discern progress toward becoming a church and work with people associated with the new initiative on the mission to be developed."[17]

In the fall of 1996, the GBGM began a formal exploration of initiating a church development program in Honduras. Methodism was already present in the country but limited to the historic communities of English-speaking settlers. The several Methodist churches composed a district of the Methodist Church of the Caribbean in the Americas (MCCA), also a CIEMAL partner along with the GBGM. MCCA was beginning new ministries among the Spanish-speaking and also among the indigenous Garifuna-speaking and expressed an interest in the GBGM initiative.

The Reverend Armando Rodríguez, a retired minister and former bishop of the Methodist Church in Cuba, and his wife Alida volunteered for missionary service with GBGM and were given a short-term assignment to explore the feasibility of a United Methodist mission in Honduras. Under their enthusiastic leadership, preaching points and community ministries were established in the Tegucigalpa regions of Marzo, Colonia Satélite, Colonia Fuerzas Unidas, Colonia Loma Linda Norte, Uscaran Prison, Donli, and Yoro. By 1998, the MCCA district in Honduras was active in channelling GBGM funds for the work of the mission and using its registration to assist in the acquisition of properties. Volunteer teams and short-term missionary personnel were recruited from the Puerto Rico Autonomous Methodist Church, the Cuba Methodist Church, and The UMC, especially Hispanic congregations.

At the end of their three-year term, the Rodríguezes were replaced by full-time missionaries selected from the local context. In the fall of 1998, Hurricane Mitch presented an immediate challenge to the continuation of this initiative. Mitch was the most devastating storm to hit the region in years, leaving thousands without homes, food, medical care, employment, schools and churches. The small but growing United Methodist churches and fellowships reached out to their neighbors and provided temporary housing and other relief measures within the limits of their own resources.

UMCOR recognized the capacity of the church to assist with redevelopment efforts and began channelling funds and material resources to the church for construction of houses, distribution of clothing and medicines, reopening of schools, and counseling.

By 2000, the United Methodist mission initiative in Honduras was still in its preliminary stages and far from being recognized as an established church presence. But it was making a distinctive mark. Visitors reported a great enthusiasm among the people for a Methodist ministry strongly grounded in firm spiritual foundations and expressed in a commitment to social development of its members and larger community. The young church was discovering the value of working with other Christian churches and groups in extending their witness of word and service. This cooperative reach was recognized as a significant departure from the work of many of the evangelical missions initiated in the country, which were very dogmatic and discouraged forms of cooperative engagement in ministries.

Cambodia/Vietnam/Nepal

Autonomous Methodist churches have a heart for mission. The products of missionary outreach from the West, they are secure in their own ministries and reach out to other countries with the good news of the gospel of Christ. In Asia, the Korean Methodist Church has been the most active in creating local church missionary societies that are reportedly sending hundreds of missionaries to more than fifty countries. Methodist Churches in Singapore, Malaysia, and Taiwan have followed suit with a particular focus on neighboring countries as opportunities permit.

Cambodia

In 1995, GBGM was invited to a consultation with the Singapore Methodist Church on the prospects of its new missionary outreach to Cambodia, Vietnam, and Nepal. The changing political situation in these countries resulted in openings for exploration of Christian missionary presence which authoritarian governments had always strongly resisted. Relief and development, i.e., humanitarian work by ecumenical agencies like Church World Service, was welcomed but strictly limited and monitored by the governments. Singaporean Methodists invited the Board into a partnership in this venture that would introduce Methodism into countries where it had no recognition. The invitation echoed similar overtures

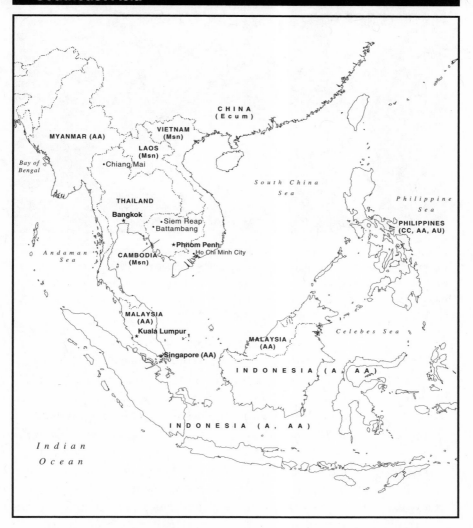

CHINA
(Ecum)

MYANMAR (AA)

VIETNAM
(Msn)

LAOS
(Msn)

•Chiang Mai

Bay of
Bengal

South China
Sea

Philippine
Sea

THAILAND

Bangkok ★

PHILIPPINES
(CC, AA, AU)

•Siem Reap
•Battambang

Andaman
Sea

★Phnom Penh
•Ho Chi Minh City

CAMBODIA
(Msn)

MALAYSIA
(AA)

Kuala Lumpur ★

Celebes Sea

MALAYSIA
(AA)

•Singapore (AA)

INDONESIA (A, AA)

INDONESIA (A, AA)

Indian
Ocean

Legend for Church Relationship to UMC	
Autonomous	A
Affiliated Autonomous	AA
Affiliated United	AU
Covenant UMC	Cov
Central Conference	CC
Concordat	Con
Cooperative Mission	CM
Ecumenical	Ecum
Independent	Ind
Mission	Msn

Cambodia lost most of its educators to the atrocities of the Khmer Rouge government in the late 1970s. These remains from the "killing fields" are a reminder of the estimated 250,000 deaths. The Singapore Methodist Church has used its experience with a quality parochial school system to develop education in Cambodia. *(Photo by Robert J. Harman)*

to the Board from Cambodian- and Vietnamese-American UMC members who had begun Christian ministries in their homelands with the aid of family members still living there. The Board was informed of the existence of several United Methodist churches in Cambodia and fellowship groups in Vietnam benefitting from United Methodist support from the U.S.

The Board was anxious to learn more about these developments. Board representatives accompanied Cambodian- and Vietnamese-American United Methodists on mission journeys to their homelands. A joint staff visit was also planned by the Singapore Methodist Missionary Society to unveil plans for mission in these countries. These visits in Cambodia introduced the Board to Methodist missionary personnel from Korea, Malaysia, Singapore, and the Switzerland-France Conference of The UMC. There was clear evidence that Methodism had been introduced to this Buddhist context, but the question remaining to be answered was whether a cooperative approach to representing Methodism could be developed.

The Singapore Methodist mission strategy for Cambodia was focused upon education. Methodist churches in Singapore operated a first-rate parochial school system. Such expertise was needed in Cambodia, a country that had lost most of its educators to the atrocities of the Khmer Rouge government in the late 1970s. A generous Singaporean Methodist donor made a grant available to the church for the purpose of purchasing a hotel complex in Phnom Penh and redeveloping it into a school and service center. The Cambodian authorities granted a registration for this activity.

A mission society of the Korean Methodist Church sent the Reverend Jin Sup Song to Cambodia with a "priority of proclaiming the Word, guiding people to the saving knowledge of Jesus Christ, and establishing faith communities across the country."[18] He found the Cambodians especially receptive to his preaching of the gospel and soon established many local churches and recruited a number of his converts for ministry. He established a Bible training school in his missionary residence and brought the local leaders to Phnom Penh each week for classes under his instruction. With financial support from Korean Methodists, he soon purchased a site and built a school to house his teaching activities. He summarized the aims of his ministry: "Prepare pastors who have a passion to start and build up churches, and give continuous formation to persons responsible for church work."[19]

The mission board of The UMC in Switzerland and France commissioned one of its members of Cambodian descent to a ministry of church development in his homeland. He was successful in gathering congregations in several rural settings and wanted the connectional embrace of Methodism to include them.

GBGM decided upon a strategy of letting Cambodian-American United Methodists lead the way into Cambodia with the understanding that their efforts would be coordinated with other Methodist bodies already present in the country. Two couples were recruited into missionary service and sent to Phnom Penh. One couple, Joseph and Marilyn Chan, were charged with church development responsibilities. They immediately linked up with their Methodist colleagues from other countries and worked cooperatively to achieve a unified witness for Methodism in Cambodia. In their first three-year term they were responsible for starting more than forty congregations. The second couple was inclined more to self-direction and was therefore ineffective in bringing community development efforts into a corporate Methodist mission activity.

Three autonomous branches of Methodism coming from five countries

(Singapore, Korea, Switzerland, France, and the U.S.) were developing a model of cooperative mission development and administration in Cambodia. While the work of each mission agency had independent registrations for its local churches, agencies, and institutions, all worked under one common administrative registry with the government, known as the Cambodian Christian Methodist Association. A representative governance structure was established with participation from the mission agencies of the sponsoring autonomous Methodist churches, but a majority of the membership comprised local Cambodian leadership. The association was in agreement that the church in Cambodia would advance through creating vital worshiping, learning, and serving communities of people called Methodist. To that end they cooperated in the development of Sunday school and Christian nurture materials and a joint hymnbook and worship resources. They also recognized the importance of social witness to the Wesleyan tradition and were engaged in programs of economic development and health services. The purchase of property and program investments by the Women's Division provided the young church with a program center in Phnom Penh for training activities, administrative offices, and a place of worship.

A visitor to the joint mission initiative in Cambodia found the Methodist Association concept to be "a wonderful, and refreshing model" but cautioned:

> To cooperate with the other Methodists for the best interests of the reign of God, and of the people of Cambodia could be a formidable task. Since it is a journey on an uncharted road, it would require deep understanding and trust among all the mission agencies. . . . Since Christian mission should point to the kingdom rather than focusing on the representation of any particular church, the decision and commitment to work together may need to continue to be renewed. Conflicts often take place, when groups work with different cultural values, assumptions, and beliefs. Thus, all involved are called to seek to learn and understand hidden internal cultural values of each other. It would be important to continue to keep the power dynamics among the three Methodists egalitarian and mutual.[20]

The small Methodist missionary presence in Cambodia remained committed to developing indigenous leaders. More than one hundred congregations were related to the Methodist Association, each under local pastoral leadership. Each week representatives from the regions were invited to Phnom Penh to participate in leadership development opportunities and to maintain the bond of unity that all acknowledged was needed to be effective in their ministry. Building the connectional structures and the institutions needed for a continuing witness and church presence required further commitment and cooperation on the part of the initiating bodies. The foundations for such further development were being laid with care. Only as leadership and program directions emerged from within the Cambodian church would the international Methodist partners be given a clearer vision on issues of further organization and relationships.

Vietnam

A United Methodist presence in Vietnam was the primary vision of Vietnamese-American United Methodists, who like their Cambodian-American sisters and brothers wanted to share their adoptive faith experience with family and friends in the homeland. The government in Vietnam was opening to the West, and with the resumption of diplomatic ties with the U.S. in 1998, the leading activity was on the economic front.

Church life continued to exist under strict government control, with the Roman Catholic tradition still dominant in the small Christian community. The Vietnam government had only recently recognized one Protestant Christian denomination: the Evangelical Church of Vietnam (EVC), the indigenous form of the missionary work of the Christian Missionary Alliance. There seemed to be no inclination on the part of the government to entertain the presence of other denominations.

The encouragement of tourism interests in Vietnam permitted frequent home visits by expatriate Vietnamese, including United Methodists from the U.S. They made contact with individuals and groups cultivating Christian ministries. In 1998, GBGM enabled Bishop Roy I. Sano to accompany GBGM and GBHEM staff to assess the prospects for a relationship to these Vietnamese pastors and their church development efforts. They had conversations with several pastors who wanted to know more about The UMC. One had been under house arrest because he refused to give up his ministry at the government's direction in 1975. While formalizing a relationship to The UMC was the pastors' expressed desire, government restrictions precluded the organization of a United Methodist church identity at that time.

The Indochinese National Federation of Asian American United

Bishop Roy I. Sano, former president of the World Division, traveled to Vietnam in 1998 for GBGM to assess the prospects for a relationship to Vietnamese pastors and their church development efforts. *(Photo courtesy of UM Archives and History)*

Methodists has continued its accompaniment of the pastors in Vietnam. In the summer of 2000, it reported contacts with nine pastors who oversee as many house churches. It also reported a large number of pastors and lay leaders who expressed an interest in pursuing formal educational opportunities and training as pastors and church workers. Caucus members succeeded in raising funds among their U.S. congregations and from the Korean Methodist Church for the construction of a new church building in Cu Chi. The first floor of the building housed a sewing enterprise and the second floor the congregation. A clinic has been established in Ho Chi Minh City and received financial support and occasional visits from mission volunteers to assist with their ministry.

The Vietnamese National Caucus requested missionary status for one of its members by GBGM. Since The UMC was not recognized in Vietnam, the placement of an expatriate national back in his/her homeland as a missionary required third-party assistance. Caucus members believed the placement would assist in meeting many of their mission objectives. They wished to provide support for Vietnamese pastors and develop training for house church leaders. They recognized the need for print resources for personal faith development and for a network of Christian women engaged in outreach to other women. A social service center was envisioned for Ho Chi Minh City.

Nepal

Because of strict government and religious sanctions, the mission of Protestant Christianity to Nepal was limited to aid and development through a cooperative agency, the United Mission in Nepal (UMN). Mission boards from Europe and the U.S. recruited professionally trained mission personnel to engage in health and educational programs. These efforts represented the most progressive forms of social development in the country and benefitted from intergovernmental and foundation grants and donations.

While the kingdom remained steeped in its ancient monarchical and religious (Hindu and Buddhist) traditions, and in spite of laws prohibiting religious conversion, a small Christian presence was developing. Indigenous churches were being cultivated in response to—but without any official connection with—the mission activities of the United Mission in Nepal. Missionaries from neighboring countries, especially India, began to penetrate local communities. Most came from independent mission organizations without any connection to historic Protestant traditions. In 1998, the Methodist Church in Singapore commissioned a missionary couple, the Reverend Erik and Shanti Tan, to begin work in church development activities. GBGM responded by sending the Reverend Naveen and Esther Rao from the Methodist Church in India. They were sent under the International Persons in Mission program of the Board to explore opportunities for developing a program of pastoral education and leadership development. They were to collaborate with the Reverend and Mrs. Devi Bhujel, who were completing graduate studies at Trinity Methodist College/Seminary in Singapore. They were the first known Nepalese to receive graduate degrees in Christian studies. Both had participated in the indigenous church movement in Nepal and were prepared to help guide the Methodist entry into the country. GBGM agreed to commission them as missionaries of The UMC.

Leaders of the UMN protested this direct missionary initiative in church development by one of its member bodies. As the only officially recognized Christian organization in the country, the UMN was not prepared to represent the independent activity of the Methodists. Moreover, the UMN did not want any conflict with the government over missionary protocol to jeopardize the many outstanding social programs it administered on behalf of the government. The government had not seen the apparent threat, perhaps because it was distracted by more serious revolutionary political and military activity in its provinces or was lacking in the enforcement capacity to keep in check the proliferation of missionary activity. The hesitation gave the Methodist partners an opportunity to evaluate and undergird their cooperative efforts in extending the witness of the church in this place. Small Methodist fellowships or churches have been formed in relatively secure areas of Biratnagar, Kathmandu Valley, and Kathmandu City. Rev. Bhujel recruited a faculty of indigenous church leaders and opened a theological college in Kathmandu in 2002. The institution offered much-needed training and support but also an introduction to a larger world church community for indigenous leaders to make better decisions regarding the appropriation of missionary activity from the West, including Methodism.

Africa: Initiatives, Reconstruction, and Development

New mission initiatives in Africa in the closing decades of the twentieth century were stimulated by distinctive mission activities. First and foremost was the evangelistic zeal of the African United Methodist churches that impelled their witness to Christ far beyond juridical limits or national boundaries; second was the goodwill response of the global UMC that sought to bring comfort and support to the many lives suffering from devastating crises (political and natural) that engulfed the continent. Finally was the intentional resolve of GBGM to fulfill its first program goal "to give witness to the gospel for initial decisions to follow Christ." This survey begins with an examination of the Board's program innovations.

Senegal Mission Initiative

In developing its program objectives for the early 1980s, GBGM found itself engaged in a protracted dialogue on evangelization and church development in the global context. The Research and Development Committee challenged the World Division to develop a model for initiating a new United Methodist ministry in an African country in which there was no registered UMC. Senegal, a predominantly Muslim country in which UMCOR had made significant contributions to a successful program of community-based agricultural development, was chosen as the location. Though the endorsement of the initiative was given in 1991, a strategy for beginning work as a registered Protestant denomination in this predominantly Muslim country took months, then years of dialogue and discussion with government officials, friendly nongovernmental organizations, and the small existing indigenous and missionary churches.[21]

A team leadership was decided upon for initiating a United Methodist presence in Senegal. The team would be GBGM missionary personnel with experience in church development, youth work, women's ministries, and primary health care. At least one member of the team would be recruited from French-speaking African United Methodists. The first members of the team, the Reverend Harold (Bill) and Roberta Smith, entered Dakar in 1995. They handled legal and property matters and prepared the way for other assigned personnel. Contact was made with a remnant of a mission started by Methodist missionaries from Korea, but this initial effort did not successfully yield a means of cooperative mission development. A fresh approach to developing a ministry in an urban context was proposed, relying heavily upon social services for women (including women prisoners) and youth and an economic development program for young adults.

The Reverend Nkemba and Mbwizu Ndjungu from Southern Congo in the Democratic Republic of the Congo (DRC) joined the team in 1997. Rev. Ndjungu brought with him strong gifts and skills for leading a ministry of "direct proclamation" or evangelism. This approach required great sensitivity in the Muslim context, in which converts to Christianity were generally forced to leave their family. The team's commitment to the church development goals of the mission had to be re-evaluated and resulted in a change of assignment for some team members. The remaining missionaries, the Reverend Al and Mavis Streyfeller, the Ndjungus, and Sebastian and Karen Ujereh recovenanted around the assignment, summarized by Pastor Ndjungu as divinely led: "The Holy Spirit is working in Senegal to gather the church."[22]

Converts to Christianity were led to a deeper appreciation of the common religious heritage of the two great faiths. After declaring their intention to become Christians, all converts were given six months to contemplate their decisions. The Senegal UMC consisted of four hundred believers in nine small congregations served by a local lay preacher in each charge. Three of the lay pastors were engaged in theological studies leading to ordination. The church maintained a strong program of outreach through literacy, women's shelter, prison ministry, job skill development, microcredit, and children's nutrition.

East Africa

The 1984 General Conference received leaders of the Evangelical Episcopal Church of Burundi and paved the way for this church to become part of the Africa Central Conference of The UMC in August of that year. A church founded by missionaries of the World Gospel Mission, who only reluctantly yielded leadership to nationals, it yearned for a relationship to a larger church family. Bishop J. Alfred Ndoricimpa devoted his leadership to orienting his members to Methodist doctrine and polity. He cultivated relationships with bishops and conference leaders in the connectional UMC family to help him with the building of a strong church, but their efforts were often dictated by the social and political conflicts that were a daily part of life in Burundi and the larger region.

In 1993, jubilation followed the first free elections in Burundi, making Melchoir Ndadaye the first head of state from the country's suppressed Hutu tribe. Ndadaye was assassinated within months of his inauguration, producing the civil unrest and armed conflict between the rival Hutu and Tutsi tribes that consumed the country. Ndoricimpa, along with other Hutu religious and political leaders, sought refuge in Nairobi, Kenya. He continued to supervise the work in Burundi and gathered other Burundi United Methodists in temporary residence in Nairobi. In 1994, the civil war in Rwanda spiraled out of control, resulting in the genocide of more than 100,000 citizens, generating further dislocation of the general populations of both Burundi and Rwanda.

Refugee encampments in eastern Zaire (now DRC) took on proportions of major cities. While governments were slow to respond to the crisis, causing such massive death and destruction, nongovernmental organizations were called to the scene. UMCOR set up offices in Nairobi as a secure base from which to administer aid programs for refugees from Burundi and Rwanda living in the large UN camps near the cities of Uvira and Bukavu in Zaire.

The Council of Bishops sent representatives to the region and summoned a response from the entire church for all of Africa. Bishop Felton May reported that the refugee count on the continent exceeded six million. Three out of four countries in Africa produced or received refugees requiring the poorest on the continent to share their own minimal resources with newcomers. The Bishops' Appeal and Campaign for Africa would assist United Methodist churches and ecumenical agencies in Africa with the awesome task of relief, rehabilitation, and repatriation of refugees and displaced persons on the continent.[23]

GBGM responded to the appeal by mobilizing teams of volunteers to work in the camps where UMCOR had staked out a presence. The first line of recruits were doctors and nurses who were later joined by childcare workers for the great number of orphans populating the camps. The teams were recruited, trained, and sent in regular intervals to assist with the projects established by The UMC and NGOs serving in the region. Conferences from the U.S. and Europe sent personnel who were joined by volunteers from the African central conferences.

There were some concerns about whether this short-term volunteer commitment was a cost-effective method of delivering aid, but the Board was responding to an undeniable personal need to identify with the magnitude of human suffering in the region. Health professionals in the first group to visit the region told the Board that they went to Africa to "deliver the greatest honor that human beings could be a part of—the honor of service." They commended the Board for creating a positive vision of the African continent, "because only a positive vision and faith can make a difference."[24]

The region became the focus of coordinated efforts by the Board staff in planning for a longer-term response to the crisis. UMCOR played the lead role in managing direct assistance to refugee populations from its Nairobi office. It maximized the contributions of United Methodist churches by applying for governmental and intergovernmental (e.g., the UN and European Community) grants for aid and development projects. The Women's Division provided grants for the Office of Women and Children's Ministry in the World Division to organize efforts to reduce the vulnerability of women and children to the violence in the camps. Mission Personnel administered the movement of United Methodist volunteers into the area.

The National Division, with its history of administering institutions for childcare, was charged with developing an orphanage in cooperation with the Central Zaire (now DRC) Conference. The site chosen was Goma, the principal city in the eastern region where a developing UMC was serving the new permanent population of immigrants. Mission partnerships were developed with such congregations as the Ben Hill UMC in Atlanta to fund the construction of the orphanage and church facility.

One of the unanticipated byproducts of the enhanced United Methodist presence in this troubled region was its significant prospect for a continuing ministry. The UMCOR banner and the added presence of teams of United Methodist volunteers in the camps gave the denomination a high profile. United Methodist representatives were sought out by refugees who wanted to know more about the church. Some were leaders of church groups meeting in the camps and desiring a connection. One such group of Rwandans contacted Ndoricimpa in Nairobi seeking recognition by The UMC. The bishop offered immediate pastoral oversight, and when the group returned to Rwanda, a United Methodist Church was officially registered with the government. The Rwanda church under the superintendency of the Reverend Kaberuka Jupa was recognized as a district of the newly formed East Africa Annual Conference in 1996. With an estimated membership of more than 20,000, the Rwanda District actively engaged in providing community services in the true Wesleyan tradition. Its schools have been recognized by the Rwanda government and benefitted from modest state financial assistance.

With Ndoricimpa's presence in Nairobi, the scope of his ministry was gradually expanded from Burundi (and Rwanda) to include United Methodist church development in Uganda, Kenya, and Sudan. Methodism was introduced to Uganda by the mission outreach of the Kenya Methodist Church (KMC). The Reverend Solomon Muwanga, a Ugandan and a missionary pastor of the Kenya Methodist Church, received his theological training in the U.S. There he made friends with many UMC leaders who expressed interest in supporting his ministry in Uganda. When he returned, Muwanga used those connections for financial support quite independent of the KMC. He organized and registered a United Methodist Church in Uganda as a commercial organization under his own leadership. A visit in 1990 by a delegation from the Africa Central Conference College of Bishops reviewed his ministry and approved its standing in the central conference. The visiting bishops recognized Muwanga's credentials and function as a superintendent. They participated in the ordination of several of the pastors Muwanga had recruited.

Muwanga's charismatic style of leadership won many new members, and the church was extended into three geographical districts, Busia (Kenya), Jinja, and Arua. When the Uganda work was assigned by the

Africa Central Conference to the supervision of Bishop Ndoricimpa there was immediate tension. While historic ethnic conflicts were cited as the problem, Muwanga's lack of accountability for decisions he made regarding property acquisition and donor program funds severely tested the connectional system. Pastors began complaining of capricious use of the superintendent's authority. GBGM missionaries were not supported, were undermined, and then were dismissed by their superintendent. When the East Africa Annual Conference was formed in 1996, Muwanga made it clear that he wanted Uganda United Methodists to be independent. The more he offered resistance to incorporation into the regional conference of United Methodist churches, the greater was the resistance to his leadership from within Uganda. In 1998, his ministerial orders were revoked by the East Africa Conference and a new superintendent named for the Uganda District. The Uganda District under Superintendent Daniel Wandabula was organized into three subdistricts comprising 15,000 adherents.

The United Methodist mission in Uganda established liaison relationships to evangelists and pastors working in neighboring Sudan. Hostilities in the Sudan have a history of exploiting religious traditions and values. The East Africa Conference is reaching out to those claiming a United Methodist relationship but as of 2005 had not made a decision on their petition to incorporate their pastors and church members, now estimated at 3,500, into the conference.

After Ndoricimpa relocated in Kenya, the KMC struggled to maintain and extend its hospitality in the face of confusing, if not conflicting, judicatory relationships. The KMC continued its work in Uganda even after the defection of its chosen leader to United Methodist influence. The ministry of the Uganda United Methodists in Busia, in Kenya, has resulted in converts to Methodism in Kenya where the KMC had not chosen to work. The UMC, on the other hand, agreed to accept a proposal from an independent fellowship of Christians to become United Methodists in a newly formed UMC in Kenya. The official presence of a United Methodist connectional body or district in Kenya remained very tenuous. Efforts were made to draw the work in Busia together with independent contacts with The UMC from at least one other indigenous church group. The combined United Methodist membership in the Kenya district was estimated at 4,500. The United Methodist presence was small in comparison to the established KMC but still troubling to the KMC.

The KMC entered into a covenant relationship with The UMC and en-joyed strong financial support from many mission-minded churches and several conferences.

The mission initiative in East Africa evolved largely from overwhelm-ing political events, not from a strategy or action plan. The tragic suffer-ing of humanity in Burundi and Rwanda had an impact on the entire re-gion and continued with the factional fighting in the DRC, supported by neighbors more interested in repositioning their political influence on the continent than in establishing stability in the region. In the midst of so much human need came recognition of a spiritual hunger that the churches needed to fill. In the words of Ndoricimpa, the East African con-text is primed for a holistic evangelism:

- In a community where internal or external wars are ways of control-ling the power . . . people want to see an evangelist as an agent of rec-onciliation; they want to hear of a God who cares, a God who is Prince of Peace.

- In a community dominated by politics of division, exclusion, etc., people want to see an evangelist as the best politician. . . . They want to hear of a God who controls the universe and all that are in it in-cluding politics.

- In a community where a group of people have maintained a tradition that does not promote the well being of everybody . . . people expect an evangelist to be an instrument of social change.[25]

Witnessing in God's World: Academies for Evangelization

If this was a *kairos* moment for witnessing to the gospel in places like East Africa, the challenge to the church was one of developing a comprehensive strategy for leadership development. The effectiveness of communicating the gospel is always increased when indigenous personnel are in charge of the effort. The young churches that emerged from refugee camps in Africa or were re-established in post-Communist Russia or Eastern Eu-rope had leaders, but they did not always have exposure to the training op-portunities that would make them effective leaders.

The Evangelization and Church Growth Program Area of GBGM celebrated the growth of partner Methodist churches and United Meth-odist conferences by inviting practitioner evangelists from twenty-seven countries to a Global Consultation in Atlanta, Georgia, in June 1999. Participants were eager to share with one another their successes and challenges in their work. Given only a three- to five-year frame for reporting on their work, the following were among the results shared:

- A single Liberian Crusade produced sixty-three new churches with a membership of 8,741 and 200 persons making decisions for Christ.

- In Zimbabwe the church is growing in leaps and bounds. Everywhere you go in large cities you find congregations worshiping in open air services and sanctuaries are always overcrowded. Forty-two new circuits have been established in the last four years and a total number of 18,057 converts were won to Christ.

- In Sierra Leone, a rebel war is a primitive, cruel, barbaric and contemptible war. Nevertheless, fourteen new churches were established.

- In Nigeria, 169 new churches and 10,250 persons responded to the call to Christian discipleship.

- In East Africa, the work extended from Burundi to four other nations with the development of 241 new churches and 30,365 persons responding to the call to Christian discipleship.

- Six new churches were started in Malaysia. A minister was sent to thirty logging camps to conduct weekly worship services with 400 attendees. The church in Indonesia expanded to six new areas.

- Germany has developed twenty-three new church planting projects, and Brazil increased by seventy new churches.

- Only three churches survived in the Communist era in Bulgaria. Now there are twenty-eight churches.

- Chinese churches in metropolitan areas of the U.S. increased from two to five churches, while a congregation in New England experienced an increase in worship attendance from less than 50 to 180 persons weekly.[26]

In addressing hindrances to their work, participants in the consultation cited the increasing influence of other faith traditions, the rise of new religious movements, extreme fundamentalism among religious groups inciting conflicts, religious persecution in some areas, government restrictions on church development, civil unrest, and wars. In contemplating the future challenges and new directions for their work, they cited the following: the need for greater flexibility to embrace new ideas, greater sensitivity to needs of multicultural and multiple language groups, greater openness to issues of economic justice to address the growing distance between rich and poor, and training of church leadership for mission and evangelism.

As a response to this outpouring of the fruits of the Spirit at work in their churches, participants made a commitment to develop a continuing network of church leaders working in areas of mission and evangelism. The network members would share resources and develop training opportunities for others to benefit from the experience and expertise extant in the churches. The commitment to training was formalized in a proposal for Board sponsorship of Academies of Evangelization and Church Growth on each continent. Subregional training events were scheduled for Africa and conducted in 2001, featuring such subjects as biblical foundations for evangelization, evangelization in the Wesleyan tradition, gospel and culture, and gospel in the African context. The leaders were chosen from the African church contexts. The agenda provided a forum for discussion of sensitive issues at the very center of African life such as HIV/AIDS, polygamy, secret societies, syncretism, gender issues, corruption, and war and peace. The events also included opportunities for leaders from the conferences to develop comprehensive plans and strategies for deepening the training and enhancing the leadership skills of local pastors and church leaders.

Other academies were scheduled for Europe, Latin America, Asia, and North America. A strong cadre of leaders from the conferences and churches was emerging to contribute articulate perspectives to a global reflection on the leading of God's people to witness to the gospel and experience the growth of their churches.

Investments for Mission

Along with the geopolitical changes occurring in the post–Cold War period, a strong wave of economic growth prevailed in industrialized countries. The bullish stock market rise in the decade of the 1990s put GBGM into the enviable position of being able to declare a strong program dividend from its stock holdings. In April 1997, the Board set aside $30 million from realized gains in its investment portfolio to benefit various mission programs. More than $20 million was designated for underwriting the cost of current and future pensions and health benefits for missionary personnel. This action had the effect of removing this item from the annual appropriations budgets of the Board, thus freeing up apportionment and other income sources for other program opportunities.

Millennium Fund

An amount of $9 million was placed into a "Millennium Fund" account designated for meeting "infrastructure needs" of developing and redeveloping churches in Europe, Africa, and the inner cities of the U.S. The announcement of this fund was to be a highly visible response to the hard-to-promote "fixed costs" of a growing mission engagement in key places. In particular, it would focus on helping churches with new opportunities for mission to recover from cataclysmic events—government property confiscation, devastating wars or civil disasters, and the effects of inflated or deteriorating local economies. The Board realized that the needs were greater than the funding available, so the Millennium Fund was presented as a challenge fund for the conferences and churches to match with their contributions of money, volunteer time, and material supplies.

The initial interest and follow-up requests for funding overwhelmed the Board. The Millennium Fund Committee decided on a strategy designed to help complete major projects, rather than administering smaller amounts to a greater number of projects. The availability of a partnership to assist with the completion of the funding required for each project was a key decision criteria.

Millennium Fund projects in Europe consisted of helping to establish a church development revolving loan fund for the Russia Annual Conference, the purchase of a site for the Russia United Methodist Church Seminary, the construction of the Baltic Mission Center in Tallinn, the acquisition and site preparation for churches in the East German Conference, the pastors equitable salary and benefits program for the Central and Southern Europe Central Conference, and new church construction in Bulgaria, Poland, Hungary, and the Czech Republic and Slovakia.

In Africa, the Millennium Fund grants restored church properties damaged by war and funded new church development among new constituencies. The trauma of war in various locations on the continent brought new opportunities for ministry. In East Africa new work was begun with refugee populations in Uganda and in Rwanda and with dislocated Burundians in Kenya and Tanzania. In West Africa, ministries were initiated in Côte d'Ivoire, among Liberians in exile, and in Guinea with a diaspora from Sierra Leone. In the DRC, the evangelical fervor of the churches was not dampened by the incursion of neighboring armies and internal rebel groups seeking to gain control of the post-Mobutu political vacuum. In South Africa, new United Methodist churches were forming among guest workers from Mozambique and the newly evangelized groups by missionary pastors from Zimbabwe.

In the U.S., Millennium Fund grants reinforced new urban strategies for United Methodist ministries in Los Angeles, Chicago, East St. Louis, Miami, Columbus, Pittsburgh, New York, and Baltimore. Care was given to ensure that investments complemented strong program commitments such as the extensive Communities of Shalom ministries in Baltimore, a new black church development program in the Western North Carolina Conference, and parish and community revitalization in Chicago. In October 1999, the Board honored mission leaders with Millennium Fund awards for their mission vision and inspiration among United Methodists.[27]

The Millennium Fund was not the only evidence of a new program thrust to benefit from the stock market largess. In 1998, the Board received recommendations from the Finance and Mission Development committees to realize capital gains amounting to an additional $25 million. There was no hesitation in identifying program areas that would benefit from this further blessing from Board investments in a burgeoning U.S. economy. Thus the Board approved a variety of new program initiatives.

Partnership Fund

A $5 million fund was established for churches and projects in Latin America and Asia (particularly the Philippines Central Conference), regions not addressed by the Millennium Fund. The key element of the fund was the deepening of the concept of resource-sharing across the traditional economic divide between donor and recipient. Faith resources that sustain so many partner churches and programs through oppressive conditions of poverty and exploitation were to be celebrated and valued as gifts to be exchanged, just as stewardship of wealth was to be given and received through grants in aid. The mechanisms for this kind of sharing were to be developed in collaboration with the mission partners, a process that would precede any distribution of funds.

Innovative Mission Volunteers

An amount of $2.5 million was designated for developing the Board's program area of Mission Volunteers. In the restructure of 1996, this program area was designed but not fully funded to realize the growing expectations of mission constituents. The new funding would permit the Board to resource the conferences outside the U.S. to create a capacity to improve their readiness to receive volunteers and also to participate fully in the sending of volunteers. This reciprocal aspect of volunteering was widely recognized as an unmet goal of United Methodist volunteer programs. The new program would also take a more proactive role in cultivating projects and placing volunteers, especially in countries engaged in rebuilding after catastrophic events. This rebuilding effort would involve temporary assignment of field personnel to administer support for assigned volunteers. Finally, the new program would categorize placement opportunities for special skill/professional groups and individuals. It would seek to accommodate groups of medical, educational, administrative, or financial personnel in strategic placements but also serve individuals with similar skills as opportunities arose.

Web Page Development

Various constituencies, e.g., professionals and clients seeking information via the AIDS Information Network, readily recognized the Board's intentional application of new communications technology for mission development. As the internet became a household concept in communications, considerable thought had to be given to a comprehensive strategy for employing it for mission purposes. A $5 million grant was made to increase the Board's ability to use this technology for communicating the good news. On a given day the Board's web page was receiving 20,000 to 30,000 "hits" or contacts from computer users. Proposals were developed for updating and servicing the Board's web page and for new online publications to be posted on the Board's site. The Board had to hire the technical staff members needed to support such a program, but their talent also served a larger church constituency with their internet ministries. The Board offered internet access services to conferences and local churches wishing to develop their own web pages. This popular service of the Board linked thousands of congregations to the medium by using Board access as a host. It resulted in a geometric increase in the frequency and quality of constituency communications as more and more Board program resources and financial information were posted on the web.

Missioners of Hope and Bishop Handy Young Adult Missioners

The changing patterns of missionary service from lifetime to short-term engagement required the Board to be proactive in its recruitment programs. It was estimated that the majority of its missionaries would retire or leave service within ten years. Youth had to become the focus of missionary recruitment. Two new programs would offer guidance. The Missioners of Hope focused upon missionary recruitment and service in Africa. It paralleled the Council of Bishops appeal, Hope for the Children of Africa, discussed previously, but looked to Africa, not the U.S., for a response from the churches. A goal of one hundred African youth was set, and the conferences readily responded with their brightest and best for training and commissioning by the Board as missionaries to children's projects in the African central conferences. This program marked the Board's most significant effort in globalizing its missionary force.[28] It was celebrated in Africa as a new day in mission when the gifts and graces of young Africans would be recognized and shared in missionary service across conference boundaries.

The Handy program was aimed at challenging young adults from the churches in the U.S. to work along side the Missioners of Hope in Africa and elsewhere. As African churches identified programs and projects to benefit from the Missioners of Hope program, the Board was presented with a quantum increase in new personnel placement opportunities. Its recruitment base would be global, i.e., it would draw upon central conference sources for applications as well as conferences in the U.S. The promotion of the program and the initial screening of applicants would take place through specially trained conference mission personnel committees, a model the Board wanted to apply to all missionary recruitment.

An amount of $5 million was designated for the two programs. Both required introduction of new administrative, training, and supervisory procedures.

Central Conference Pensions

The capacity of individual central conferences to provide pension and other benefit coverage for increasing numbers of clergy and other church workers varied greatly. The block grants from the former World Division were used to set aside only meager amounts of assistance to retired workers in the Africa and Philippine central conferences. Occasionally special grants were made with the intent of increasing reserve funds available to fund pensions with interest earnings. Both the growing demand and the failing economies of most countries rendered the programs very inadequate. An amount of $2.5 million was set aside to work on the development of a comprehensive pension and benefit program for the affected central conferences. This need was further acknowledged by the 2000 General Conference, which mandated the General Board of Pensions and Health Benefits to develop a global pension program with the assistance of GBGM and the General Board of Publication, which administered a pension grant-making program from its annual profits from sales.

Agricultural Development

A common strategy employed by missionaries was food production for the communities they served. Missionaries specializing in agricultural development acquired acreage, planted crops, managed livestock, and taught their skills to the converts to help them and their families become self-sustaining. Much of this historic development activity has been lost to changing program priorities, discouraging local politics, and frustrating national economic conditions. By the 1990s few mission agricultural programs survived to help churches face the onslaught of poverty in many parts of the developing world. The Board wished to reverse the trend. It approved a $2.5 million proposal for a program of sustainable agricultural and rural development. Recognizing that some agricultural missions failed because they were too dependent upon external resources and technical methods of production, the new proposal emphasized local capacity building, increase of sustainable methods of production, active networking and training of leaders (especially women), and developing local church-based (UMC) initiatives for community agricultural development. The program would set long-term, not immediate, goals since its success would require leadership training and development, region by region, community by community. Many of the partner church leaders who suffered the missionary legacy of idle farmlands were anxious to be part of the Board's new initiative. The principle activity of a Board staff team would be to encourage networking to share expertise and provide training opportunities for local leaders. The program was not a traditional grant-making form of mission. Approved and implemented in 1998, it lived a short life when expectations failed to be shaped around the long-term transformational nature of the program.

Reflections

The significance of the new mission initiatives that were funded by the stock market largess is not the quality of the programs but the quantity of resources. To have mission dollars in the tens of millions available for new program ventures was precedent setting. The motivation for taking the realized gains for investment in new mission programs emerged from the conservative forces prevailing in the church's General Council on Finance and Administration. Each quadrennium the council recommended the amount of general church program funds (World Service) to be apportioned to the conferences and churches. Members sought an explanation for the accumulating balances in all general agency reserve funds but especially GBGM. They believed that the council should not recommend apportioning new general church funds to the churches while agencies were holding sufficient funds in reserve accounts or in unrealized capital gains.

GBGM had never been entirely successful in interpreting the complexity of its financial holdings to the general public. For instance, large amounts of reserve funds were donor restricted for specific projects and others designated for such capital-intensive items as administering missionary health insurance and pensions, property maintenance, and self-insurance. Moreover, changing audit and accounting procedures requiring the annual reporting of the book value of capital gains brought more attention to the total assets managed by the Board.

Having had more experience in preparing budgets with shrinking income sources, the staff welcomed the opportunity to think creatively about allocating these new resources to programs. Proposals came quickly to the Board Cabinet table, where, with the exception of vesting missionary benefits, new program directions were given more favorable consideration than bolstering existing programs. The *modus operandi* was responding to a changing world context that was presenting new mission opportunities in places where the Board was previously unable to be engaged. Because the motivation was to spend down reserves, most of the program proposals involved administering grants to others and did not adequately consider developing the Board's long-term sustaining capacity for these and other vital programs. Negative reactions were anticipated to expenditures for Board infrastructure, such as communications, including web page development. So the transforming effect of investing new resources in mission was to help others achieve it. Historically, project funding without solid development strategies in place generally produces greater dependency. With shrinking or no financial reserves left on hand for future management, history will determine the effectiveness of the Board's strategy for investing in new global mission relationships by spending its way out of accumulated wealth.

HIV/AIDS Interagency Task Force

AIDS (Acquired Immune Deficiency Syndrome) was recognized by the World Health Organization as a health crisis of pandemic proportions. In 1985 it estimated that more than 10 million people worldwide had been infected by the Human Immunodeficiency Virus (HIV) believed to cause AIDS, and that as many as 100 million people could become infected by the virus over the next five years. Traces of the disease had been identified in 127 countries in the Americas, Europe, Africa, Asia, and Oceania. In the U.S. alone, more than 57,000 cases had occurred, more than half of whom had died.

In November 1987, three general agencies of The UMC collaborated in the sponsorship of a National Consultation on AIDS Ministries. Sixty-two of the seventy-three annual conferences sent representatives to the event in Millbrae, California. Participants heard reports from health specialists, persons diagnosed with AIDS, caregivers, pastors, theologians, psychologists, researchers, educators, and therapists. They shared plans for ministries unfolding in their annual conferences but mostly took encouragement from one another on how to begin a substantial witness by their churches.[29]

In 1988, GBGM sent a resolution to General Conference on "AIDS and the Healing Ministry of the Church."[30] The contents of the resolution reflected pioneering research and development on a complex and disturbing global health issue by the Health and Welfare Ministries Program Department. Recognizing the appalling dimensions of the growing AIDS pandemic, the Board believed the church would rise to the challenge of an "unparalleled opportunity for witness to the Gospel and service to human need among persons, many of whom would otherwise be alone and alienated from themselves, other people and from God." In a parallel petition the Board asked the General Conference to establish an Interagency Task Force on AIDS to guide the response of the denomination.

An outline for the work of the task force was contained in the 1988

Viewing the many panels on the AIDS quilt displayed at the Mall in Washington, D.C., were United Methodists from Toledo, Ohio: the Reverend Scott Campbell, Marilyn DuFour (kneeling), and standing, Becky Tucker and Jessica Miller. *(Photo by Jay Mallin for UM News Service)*

resolution. The first act was a call to confession by the church not only for its "tardy and inadequate" response to the crisis, but for its rush to judgment that the disease is "God's punishment." This attitude toward a disease that was in large part transmitted by homosexual activity and abusive substance injections would have to be the focus of considerable education and advocacy efforts within the church. Achieving the goal of the resolution that "churches should be places of openness and caring for persons with AIDS and their loved ones" was complicated by subsequent General Conference actions condemning homosexual activity as "incompatible with Christian teaching." And the aim of enabling the church's ministry to this population was further complicated or confused by another General Conference action that restricted the use of general church funds for any program advocating homosexuality.

GBGM was assigned responsibility for coordinating the Interagency

Task Force on AIDS. The task force monitored the work of the agencies and educated members on latest developments in treatment modalities. It conducted a survey of conferences to determine the extent to which the connectional church was offering ministries and services to the affected population. More than 2,000 respondents to the survey were added to a growing HIV/AIDS Ministries Network, which received program resources prepared by the participating general agencies. Under the creative leadership of Cathie Lyons, associate general secretary for the Health and Welfare Ministries Program Department, a newsletter and occasional papers were published for distribution utilizing emerging computer information technologies to communicate with this growing leadership group. When the internet became operative, the department made large amounts of data available to an even larger public surfing the net. Professionals in the field and government officials recognized their web site as one of the primary sources of technical and legal information. A growing number of pastors and church leaders found resources for their difficult and challenging ministries among persons living with AIDS and their family members.

The global reach of the church was used to extend educational opportunities for church leaders. The Health and Welfare Ministries Program Department and the World Division sponsored consultations in Zaire, Bolivia, India, and Zimbabwe in cooperation with church leaders in those and surrounding countries. In some country contexts, church leaders discussed sensitive issues which social customs and local religious beliefs had protected for too long. They worked on action plans for their conferences and churches to become engaged in significant ministries. In Africa the serious effects of the pandemic had been mounting with little or no public health infrastructure able to ameliorate them. Church memberships were diminished by rising death rates and communities overwhelmed by orphaned children. The consultations provided them with some assurance that they were not alone in facing these challenges. A global network of church leaders covenanted to combine efforts at education, advocacy, services, and spiritual support was emerging.

The interagency task force membership was intentionally inclusive of HIV positive persons and those living with AIDS. The Reverend Paul Dirdak, chair of the task force, commented on its mission to heightening the sensitivity of the task force to its limitations. While "the disease is absolutely not a homosexual disease . . . the vast majority of people who are dying horribly are gay men. Task force members realized that churches have yet to comprehend fully just how the churches' attitudes have left gay men, their loved ones and families, either able or unable to weather the assault of AIDS. Task Force members realized that the credibility of the church is at stake whenever and wherever the church remains aloof or fretful."[31] That is where the mission of the church on this frontier remained.

UMCOR-NGO Funding

The United Methodist Committee on Relief (UMCOR) became a household name among United Methodists. UMCOR was known for extending the church's ministries of compassion and relief worldwide. It was a "brand name" that gave "quality assurance" to local churches that their contributions to aid others in communities struck by natural disaster or civil unrest would be well invested and would not be charged the cost of administrative overhead.

A highly regarded ecumenical connection of church-related relief and development programs provided UMCOR with the delivery channels for the funding of direct services for forty years. Then came a heightening of the level of competition for the charitable dollar. When disasters received increased media coverage with such innovations as twenty-four hour television news, the appeals for funding by religious and secular relief organizations also flourished. A proliferation of organizations of goodwill requesting financial support often beat church organizations to their donors' pocketbooks.

Also, governments and intergovernmental organizations were finding it increasingly difficult to administer direct relief and redevelopment programs in many of the locations where their foreign policy interests required them to be involved. The negative reaction to the U.S. Government's abortive peacekeeping and humanitarian role in Somalia during 1992 and 1993 provided a case study for reducing a high-level profile in unstable countries. The practice of contracting for the aid and development services of nongovernmental organizations (NGOs) became the popular alternative for most Western governments.

In this climate, UMCOR and other church relief organizations found the need to make adjustments. In times of disaster and distress, advertising was strategic. Before they heard it in church, United Methodists needed to know UMCOR to be a recipient of gifts along with other prominent church organizations such as Catholic Relief Services and Lutheran World Relief, independent religious groups like World Vision, or secular groups like CARE (Cooperative for American Relief Everywhere). UMCOR became an independent member of InterAction, a Washington-based network of relief organizations that represented its members in national media promotions during crises. This connection put the UMCOR name before public and church donors in advertisements in the secular press.

The InterAction membership also introduced UMCOR to opportunities for NGO funding. Contracts for development-related work in key crisis locations were offered by the U.S. State Department, UN agencies, the European Community, and other national or regional bodies. The first venture for UMCOR was a multimillion-dollar U.S. Government contract for building housing in Bosnia and Herzegovina. Instead of transferring funds from church donors to another operational group (usually church-related) on the ground, UMCOR became responsible for managing government funds and directly administering the reconstruction effort through the hiring and supervision of personnel.

While being an agent for government funds required UMCOR to be nonsectarian in its project management, persons related to the program (employees, contractors, local governments, other agencies, and recipients) came to know the organization as a church-based group. Expectations and perceptions of UMCOR's presence offered opportunities for a growing witness. According to Kenneth Lutgen, deputy general secretary for UMCOR, 1992–1997, a Bosnian couple of mixed religious origin (Muslim and Orthodox Christian) brought their child to one of the UMCOR workers inquiring about baptism. They wanted the child reared as a "Methodist" because of the good work they saw UMCOR doing in their country. "Youth houses" were created in some of the UMCOR properties and funded by the Women's Division, providing programs that reached young people distraught by deteriorating conditions in their country.

UMCOR's positive experience in Bosnia won the organization recognition and additional NGO contracts. Economic development and housing projects in East Africa addressed the plight of refugee families in the camps in Zaire (DRC) and prepared for their return in the villages of Rwanda. UMCOR administered monetization programs in Eastern Europe and Central Asia where U.S. commodities were sold for local currency and new local business ventures established with the proceeds. It moved into Kosovo with a contract for rebuilding neighborhoods after the 1998 NATO strategic bombing campaign aimed at removing the Serbian armies of Yugoslavia President Slobadan Milosêvić.

UMCOR was becoming involved in creative enterprises beyond any previous experience. Opening an office in Washington became an administrative necessity. A new corps of personnel familiar with global project management had to be recruited. Field offices were opened in a variety of locations, including Turkey, Tajikistan, Rwanda, Liberia, Kosovo, Haiti, Republic of Georgia, Azerbaijan, and Armenia, and a coordinating office in Vienna.

This growing new dimension of the organization's work also produced some tensions and uncertainties. There were many questions. UMCOR was becoming dependent upon government funding, perhaps too much so? Were government program directions rather than the mission of the church driving UMCOR? Would it have an effect upon church contributions? Was government project funding sufficient to cover the additional costs of the UMCOR operation as an NGO, or did church funds have to be used to subsidize government-sponsored programs? Were the new program personnel sufficiently familiar with the mission objectives of The UMC? How much involvement was expected of United Methodist leaders in countries where NGO-funded projects were located?

A special task force of Board members was appointed to wrestle with such questions and express Board policy regarding NGO project relationships. In their recommendations to the Board, they affirmed a mission relationship between the church and governmental units. Citing Wesley's ministry to the poor as being uncompromised by "political implications," and remembering the broad mission mandate of the 1996 *Discipline*, they declared: "Whenever United Methodism has had a clear sense of mission, God has used our Church to save persons, heal relationships, transform social structures, and spread scriptural holiness, thereby changing the world."[32]

The report then provided policy guidelines that limited the Board's involvement in NGO programs to those that "complement [GBGM's] basic program mandates and strategic directions." UMCOR would be discouraged from soliciting donor (governmental program) funds "simply because they are available, or . . . solely for the purpose of implementing government programs." United Methodist leaders in affected episcopal areas were to be informed of the NGO activities of UMCOR. Procedures were put in place for approving project grants, financial accountability, and development of personnel.

This movement of UMCOR had significant program implications. It shifted the focus of the organization's commitment to development strategies from "micro project funding" to a major program emphasis. More attention was given to contractual relationships with large governmental funding agencies than to encouraging small projects, usually under sponsorship of church-related organizations. In 1996, many of the small church projects, which had always received guaranteed funding from UMCOR, were notified that they would only receive what funds the churches contributed directly to the Advance. The funds that UMCOR used to subsidize these projects had to be directed toward paying the administrative costs of the NGO program.

When it came to boasting of accomplishments, UMCOR could, however, produce new balance sheets with matching funds from governments that doubled or tripled the upfront church funding.

Open to question was whether the funded programs could match the virtues of the smaller church-based programs, such as encouraging community control, local leadership development, appropriate technology, environmental responsiveness, and cost-effectiveness. Also unknown was the true impact of this program emphasis and related funding decisions upon ecumenical cooperation where UMCOR had been a leader. The NGO activity also influenced other denomination-based and ecumenical relief and development activities. Without a doubt, the contractual government projects certainly gave UMCOR a higher profile and a greater sense of independence among other church-related agencies with which it has historically shared a similar mission.

Land Mines

More than 100 million antipersonnel land mines were a dangerous residue of military conflicts in more than sixty countries of the world. These devices were planted to discourage invading armies but remained active long after hostilities ceased. They killed 10,000 and maimed another 12,000 persons every year. Many organizations, including the UN and the Nobel Peace Prize Campaign to Ban Landmines, were actively at work in gaining signatories to a comprehensive treaty banning the production, sale, stockpiling, and deployment of land mines.

Among the countries most affected were Cambodia, Vietnam, Angola,

Mozambique, Bosnia, Afghanistan, El Salvador, and Nicaragua. In all these countries, The UMC has been engaged in relief and development activities, and in all but Afghanistan, United Methodist churches were organized or in formation. In response, the Health and Relief Program Area of the Board developed a model program of direct assistance to victims of land mines in Angola. Brokering a relationship with a program partner in India, a method of making inexpensive prostheses was transported to Angola along with an Indian practitioner experienced in installing the devices. Angolan United Methodists were trained in the production and fitting of the inexpensive but high-quality prostheses. Planning began for further distribution of this cost-effective medical technology to other settings.

In October 1997 GBGM voted overwhelmingly to support the comprehensive treaty banning land mines. General Secretary Nugent was convinced that the Board's mission responsibility demanded more: "When weapons of war take the insidious and hidden form of land mines, becoming stealthy stalkers and potential killers of children, so that children are afraid to play in the fields or to help in the harvesting of food, then it is not enough nor is it sufficient to simply condemn the planting of the mines. It is essential to also actively participate in land mine removal. . . . Beyond land mine removal, we must also be engaged in helping to replant and till the soil, sowing the newly safe fields with seeds of grain and foods for life."[33]

The Board established a task force to outline a strategy for Board participation in efforts of land mine removal. A group of prominent experts on the subject were invited to serve in an advisory capacity to UMCOR. A good number were United Methodist in background and welcomed strong church leadership into a highly technical field of work. Their recommendations to the Board focused upon initiating efforts in Mozambique where the local United Methodist church could offer leadership and logistical support. A further recommendation focused upon the introduction of state of the art technologies for removing land mines by machine, rather than the painstaking and life-threatening removal by hand. At the annual meeting in 1999, the Board enthusiastically endorsed the recommendations, and staff was charged with seeking financial partners (governmental or nongovernmental) for making the kind of investment such a program required.[34]

Ministries with Women in Crisis

Dedicated to a mission of empowerment to oppressed persons, the National Division of GBGM turned its attention to women in crisis. In the follow-up to a 1978 national consultation on the issue, the division readily identified constituencies of women in crisis—battered, imprisoned, addicted, exploited, and abused—with whom the church was only peripherally involved. The challenge of moving the church forward into ministry to the lives of women and their families who were overwhelmed by circumstances and problems beyond their control was well suited to a division that had networks of mission leaders, projects, and institutions that had ready access to the affected population groups. Under the leadership of division staff Peggy Halsey, a new program was launched. A formidable number of local and regional groups engaged in direct and enabling ministries with women in crisis situations was identified. From those a network of model programs was cultivated and resourced by the division. They provided the division and each other with valuable experience and information about services, funding, and policies that enabled or hindered their work.

Halsey expected some uneasiness with the church agency addressing such sensitive and controversial issues as family violence, rape, prostitution, pornography, teen pregnancy, abortion, drug and alcohol abuse, incarceration, incest, and child abuse. So long as the constituency served remained outside the church the reaction would be manageable. But Halsey and the division also had their sights fixed on a ministry to women "sitting in our pews, singing in our choirs, teaching in our Sunday schools, or preaching in our pulpits." For many women, there was no immunity from abuse and life-threatening experiences from which they cannot escape. To document her hunches, Halsey conducted a churchwide survey of United Methodist Women that revealed that:

- One in every twenty-four had been raped.
- One in six had been abused by their husbands (for one-fourth of those, the abusive treatment involved physical battering).
- One-third of the employed women reported having experienced sexual harassment on their jobs.
- One in eight had been widowed; one in nine divorced.[35]

Moreover, the respondents reported a general reluctance to seek help from their churches for dealing with their problems. In some cases, a pastor or church member may have been a party to their crisis situation and the procedure for recourse within church structures was unclear. Few expected to find help from the ministry of their churches.

With the documentation in hand, the division prepared a resolution for the 1980 General Conference that called for "supportive, non-judgmental ministry to women in situations of stress and transition" and cited the reconciling and empowering love of God as a fundamental ingredient for such a ministry. The General Conference resolution gave a strong endorsement for the Office for Ministries with Women in Crisis to help the church:

- advocate community services which respond to specific needs, such as those of battered women, displaced homemakers, rape victims, women in prison, unemployed women, and victims of substance abuse;
- provide awareness training for clergy to sensitize them to the needs of women in crisis;
- provide educational and training opportunities for clergy and laity to deal with issues of physical violence, sexual and economic exploitation, loss, and dependency; and
- support public policies and programs that provide needed research and social services to women in crisis.

Through the efforts of the office, many congregations became equipped and found opportunities for developing ministries with women experiencing crises. They supported local programs such as shelters for battered women and their children, ministries to women in prison, peer support groups for women in transition, and community-organizing efforts of poor and underemployed women. They explored the root causes of abuse and crisis and developed programs of advocacy and prevention. The office served as a valuable resource to the United Methodist Bishops' Initiative on Children in Poverty and the general church Special Program on Substance Abuse and Related Violence.

New Challenges for U.S. Mission Institutions

A rich legacy of the women's missionary enterprise from The Methodist Church was a network of one hundred national mission institutions located in communities across the U.S., including Puerto Rico and the Virgin Islands. The largest component was a collection of seventy community centers in thirty-five states, serving primarily low-income families of all races and cultural backgrounds. There were nine residential treatment centers providing therapeutic services to emotionally troubled children and youth. There were six colleges and two universities, all founded as Methodist mission schools and which still provided academic opportunities or alternatives for deserving populations at affordable costs. There were six residences offering temporary safe shelter for women in transition from confinement in prisons, hospitals, or mental health institutions or women exiting disruptive and abusive family relationships.

Each institution was locally autonomous, with its own policymaking board and economic base, but all received services and/or financial support from the Joint Committee on Institutional Ministries of Women's Division and GBGM. The Women's Division held title to a large number of properties occupied by these agencies and contributed generously to their maintenance and improvement. Units of United Methodist Women promoted the funding of the agencies located within their conference boundaries and raised support for both apportioned funding and special program grants administered by the Women's Division.

While most of the agencies had a long history of effective service, their traditional modes of providing direct services were interpreted as somewhat outmoded during the social upheavals facing many communities in the 1960s and 1970s. Their programs were sometimes characterized by mission agency staff persons as "Band-Aids" and irrelevant to effectuating changes in public policies that promised longer-term solutions to changing neighborhoods.[36] The agencies soon faced competition for mission board funding by new ventures in community organizing, economic development, and public policy advocacy. With great frequency, these historic, church-based agencies turned to government-sponsored programs and secular foundation funding to continue to serve their communities and balance their budgets. New dollars were welcome, but these funding sources also required greater client participation at policymaking levels. Community representation on their boards began to displace church representatives, resulting in a gradual drift away from church influence, locally and nationally.

The agenda for administering the national mission agencies in the decades of the 1970s and 1980s was occupied by revisiting the definition of "church-relatedness." Funding from church sources was no longer the

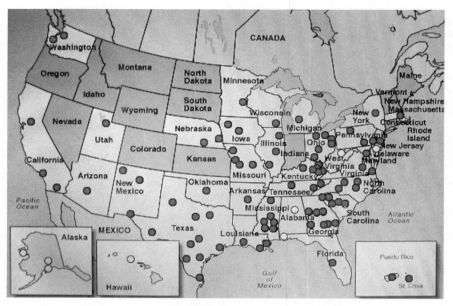

UMW institutions in U.S. (*GBGM map*)

primary criteria. Programs funded from government and other sources for most agencies far outweighed the financial support (past or future) garnered from the churches or the mission board. Funding sources also shaped the quality of programming offered by the agencies. While the agencies continued to serve the historic constituencies of women and children identified by deaconesses who founded them, government funding introduced restrictions on religious practices that previously accompanied their programs. Staffing decisions were handled locally and often produced executive leaders who had little or no association with the church. Moreover, the heads of the agencies were disproportionately male professionals who reluctantly adjusted to an organizational history and culture that was shaped and administered by church women in mission service. Property ownership by the Women's Division became one determining variable for a relationship, but the division was sometimes treated as the "absentee landlord" who received all of the tenants' complaints along with little accountability for the actual stewardship of their properties.

New strategies for administration of the national mission institutions were soon developed and implemented. The Women's Division hired a property administrator who surveyed and documented the condition of all agency properties. The agency occupying each property owned by the division was required to enter into a lease agreement binding it to policies of utilization and management that observed the rights of ownership and the responsibilities of the lessee. In March 1976, the Women's Division issued a new policy statement on "Ministries to Women and Ministries to Children," discussed later in this work. It refocused attention on the role of women in policymaking and administration: "Women should participate in every aspect of an institution providing services to women and children, not only as recipients of services but in designing programs, carrying them out, and serving on governing boards and in executive leadership."[37]

New staff and Board member training events were designed and conducted with the help of Women's Division directors and the staff of the National Division assigned to the Institutional Ministries unit.

The renewed attention to issues of agency affiliation closed the distance between the mission board and the agencies, but cultivating a sense of engagement in a corporate mission with the other national mission institutions became the ultimate challenge. In the decade of the 1990s, the Joint Committee on Institutional Ministries proposed the concept of the "Caring Connection." It asked for the commitment of each of the national mission institutions related to GBGM to enter into a process of caring for one another. It acknowledged the financial limitations that prevented the Board from assuming the levels of support the agencies' programs deserved but promised a strong presence and partnership with and among all agencies. Agencies would agree to share resources with each other upon request or referral from the Board. An agency with an expertise in financial development would offer consultation or leadership development to another agency in need of such. An agency with program expertise in an area of organizational development desired by another agency would offer its assistance. The stories of the mission of these institutions would be highlighted and developed for publication in church periodicals and professional service bulletins. Agency executives would cultivate opportunities for consultation and support. National mission institutions would overcome their isolation and find a "relatedness" together that would strengthen them to serve new constituencies and develop greater resources.

The "Caring Connection" enabled national mission agencies to work together on issues of public policy advocacy. It attempted to speak with a strong, united voice on subjects of welfare reform, faith-based initiatives, living wage, and health benefits for workers. Testimonies from agency administrators about the economic hardships of their clients were shared with advocacy coalitions that presented them to congressional hearings. These administrators also shaped resolutions by the Women's Division and GBGM that called for support from the larger church constituency.

The distinction of being counted among the national mission institutions related to GBGM afforded the benefit of national church sponsorship and networking among related agencies. It has also been a differentiating factor among similar church-related agencies established within the annual conferences. Many national mission agencies were excluded from conference financial support because of their funding relationship to United Methodist Women locally and to GBGM. The origins of a significant number of these institutions date back to the era of racial segregation when church initiatives in mission and ministry in the African-American communities were taken by the Women's Division because opportunities for service were ignored by the annual conferences. The conferences that have come to terms with their complicity with racism have taken intentional steps toward inclusiveness in their support of the national mission institutions within their conference boundaries. Sadly, the institutional barriers of racism still limit partnership and service in too many places within the church connection.

A Changing Mission in Rural America: The Farm Crisis

Rural America, always considered the bedrock of the nation's cultural and social welfare, was hit hard by an encroaching global economy. Mechanized agriculture, benefitting from improved technologies, became the focus of large agribusinesses. These multinational firms with an eye toward gaining a major share of the larger world market succeeded in driving down prices small farmers received for their products. With insufficient income to meet rising expenses, farmers in the heartland, especially the small number of black farmers in the South, were forced out of farming and off their family-owned lands at alarming rates. In 1987, the American Bankers Association midyear report indicated that 2,100 farmers were leaving farming each week.[38] According to the Federation of Southern

Cooperatives/Emergency Land Fund, 9,000 acres of black-owned rural land were being lost each week. The more fortunate were able to gain some return on their investment while leaving behind cherished properties and their lifelong work. Others faced financial losses through bankruptcy with little confidence in rebuilding their lives.

With more than half of all United Methodist churches in the U.S. located in rural communities, this crisis could not be avoided by the denomination. Reports from annual conferences indicated severe challenges to a pastoral leadership poorly prepared for ministry with an economic disaster in the making. In communities with histories of ecumenical cooperation, joint strategies for ministries of sharing and caring were effective. The Office of Town and Country Ministries of the National Division provided financial assistance to regional training centers specializing in rural ministries to develop leadership resources for dealing with the crisis. Seminars, workshops, and strategy sessions were sponsored through the network of town and country ministry leaders in conferences and the national Rural Ministries Fellowship.

In a 1985 Resolution on the Rural Farm Crisis in the U.S.A, GBGM expressed pastoral concern for the families so severely affected by the crisis, noting the rising incidence of child and spouse abuse and suicide. It expressed alarm over the rate at which black farmers were losing their land and vocations, with more than 50 percent of the total national black-owned acreage lost within a ten-year period. The Board endorsed several emergency actions to help stanch the crisis. It committed Board resources to assist annual conferences in conducting workshops for pastors serving in crisis communities. It committed Board leadership to organize and participate in hearings on agricultural and rural life concerns along with other general agencies and annual conferences. It called upon Board and church-related agencies to move investments in rural banks committed to reinvestment in communities facing economic depression.[39]

The Women's Division offered its leadership by mounting a Small Family Farm Project. The first phase was educational. Two national workshops were planned for bringing farmers into dialogue with conference officers of United Methodist Women. That was followed by the development of program resources to be used by local units and then a series of events in the conference for planning action strategies and organizing task forces to work at district and local church levels of the organization. Women leaders were evident in the churches by their grasp of the issues from the local farm economies to agribusiness policies and global economic systems that seemed to be driving government and industry actions.[40]

A creative leadership group, adopting the name "Prairiefire," developed a community-organizing response to the rural crisis. With encouragement from mission boards of most major denominations, Prairiefire developed a linkage between church and community leaders in affected regions who were searching for systemic causes in political and economic policies and developing legislative solutions. The organization gained public attention to the rural crisis through well-written and strategically placed editorials and articles in regional and national publications and by sponsoring community events and demonstrations in support of hurting farm families and declining small town businesses. But the response of most politicians lacked the kind of concrete assistance given to the bailout of a major company, such as Chrysler, and left most farmers fending for themselves. The politicians seemed content with the notion that the rural U.S. was at the end of the passing of an era and that the emerging global economy held the answers.

In 1988, General Conference adopted the "Rural Crisis" as a special program for the 1989–1992 quadrennium. In search of program strategies for churches to strengthen ministries to small and declining rural communities, the National Division turned to the Center for Town and Rural Ministries in Columbus, Ohio, and the Upper Sand Mountain Cooperative Parish in north Alabama. These training centers were cooperating with the United Methodist Rural Fellowship in the development of a new leadership cadre of "Rural Chaplains." The chaplains were recruited from among ordained ministers of their conferences who were called to work on issues of crisis intervention in struggling rural communities and churches. They would be certified chaplains of the denomination, a process administered by the GBHEM. The Town and Country Ministries Office endorsed the program and helped it develop into a national association.

In a 1998 newsletter of the Rural Chaplains Association, the leadership identified its purpose with the mission statement of the Program Unit on Rural Life Issues of the Kentucky Council of Churches: "We are witnessing profound and disturbing changes in rural America. Land ownership is being restructured, agricultural production is becoming more heavily industrialized . . . and the earth is being subjected to harmful farming, mining and development practices. Such changes adversely affect rural people, their way of life and their land. The toll attributable to the crisis includes increased suicide, family violence and individual breakdown. This level of human suffering is incompatible with our commitment to social and economic justice."[41]

The Rural Chaplains could become a force for United Methodist mission in rural communities by understanding and interpreting the changing context and introducing programs with long-term consequences. Rural America was still the heartland of the nation but was not immune from the negative impact of certain changing social and economic values. A team of leaders committed to ministry with an evangelical spirit and grounded in the values of inclusiveness and justice could offer a promise of renewal and transformation for the rural churches and communities. But they need not look for creative new programs.

The national mission model for Cooperative Parish Development adequately fitted the contemporary context. It called for local small-membership churches to find a common ministry and develop a cooperative structure to realize their mission together. It valued the principles of shared ministry for the building of strong communities of faith, ecumenical or interdenominational cooperation, disciplined planning and program administration, compassion for the poor and powerless, and a commitment to correcting injustices. In the National Comprehensive Plan for Town and Country Ministry adopted by the General Conference of 2000, cooperative ministry was commended as a key organizing strategy for mission: "Practitioners involved in the cooperative approach believe that cooperative ministry is the most helpful and promising way of going about ministry within the United Methodist connection. Cooperative ministry is more a style of ministry than a particular structure or organizing technique. It is a form of ministry that helps focus on both the health and the strength of the local congregation and on witness and outreach across a larger geographical area. Some successful examples are denominational while others are thoroughly ecumenical."[42]

Cooperative ministry required adopting a philosophy of mission, not just implementing a packaged program. It had to be intentionally chosen and cultivated by conference leadership. The report to the 2000 General Conference identified only 729 cooperative ministries within the United

Methodist connection. Had more conferences and churches availed themselves of this form of ministry and committed their personnel and financial resources to its full implementation, United Methodist churches and their ecumenical cohorts would have been in a stronger position of leadership in the rural crisis and better prepared to lead into the coming new day for rural America.

CHAPTER 10

A Survey of the Middle East
and North Africa

*T*HE ORIGINS OF Christianity in the region date back to the apostolic mission of James in Jerusalem, Peter and Paul in Antioch and Rome, Thomas in Babylonia, Mark in Alexandria, and Barnabas in Cyprus. The early missionary strides of the Eastern churches extended the witness of the faith beyond the region, only to be overcome by the Islamic conquest in the seventh century. Orthodox Christianity was forced into retreat and settled for a minority status in a region that was strained by religious antagonisms. Christian missionary strategies have historically respected the role of Orthodox leaders in preserving the faith in the face of Muslim dominance. Roman Catholic missionaries learned after the Crusades to accommodate their Latin rituals and structures to the recognized rites of the Eastern Church. Protestant missionaries entering the region in the nineteenth century worked within the Eastern churches rather than establish separate churches.

Political and religious conflicts characterized the Middle East during the last half of the twentieth century. Governments in the region have become more restrictive of church-based mission initiatives from the outside. The Middle East Council of Churches (MECC) was established in 1974 and served as a bridge to the universal Christian community. The MECC specialized in developing strategies for cooperative ministries with Orthodox, Anglican, and Protestant churches in the region. It was the principal agency through which UMCOR funds and administers relief and development throughout the Middle East.

Israel

Working with the council and church entities, the General Board of Global Ministries (GBGM) created a United Methodist "liaison office" in Jerusalem and created a nontraditional missionary posting with the blessing of church leaders there. The liaison office would not directly engage in promulgating the gospel but work to strengthen the Christian witness of the historic churches. The office would assist the Board in identifying social and human development programs deserving financial support. It would also specialize in interpreting the churches' point of view on conflicts in Israel to the North American church constituency, which was subject to one-sided editorial perspectives in support of the U.S. pro-Israel foreign policy and vocal religious opinion makers in the conservative political right in the United States.

The Reverend Romeo del Rosario, a United Methodist pastor and scholar from the Philippines, became the first missionary to staff the liaison office in Jerusalem. He related to the church officials in Jerusalem who were mobilizing leaders of the strong but diminishing Christian community there to make known their prayers and dreams for their people and the unrepresented uprooted Palestinian masses who were destined to spend their lifetimes in refugee camps. Using the occasions of frequent visits from United Methodists and other groups making Holy Land pilgrimages, del Rosario introduced them to the social and political realities of the Palestinian population that some educational tour groups overlooked. He and his successors in the liaison office became confidants of United Methodist bishops and other church leaders who would take the Palestinian cause back to the United States Government in the form of letter-writing campaigns and visits with their representatives.

In 1990, GBGM honored the request of an ecumenical partner, the Bethlehem Bible College, to send a missionary couple to strengthen the faculty and help with the administration of the school. Alex Awad, a Palestinian American, and his spouse Brenda were available for the assignment. Alex's father had been instrumental in the development of this Baptist elementary and secondary school. Upon completion of missionary candidacy and training, it came time to send the couple and their small family to Bethlehem. Alex, the holder of a U.S. passport, was denied a visa and work permit by the Israeli government. Many attempts at intervening by the Board, prominent church leaders, and political representatives failed to

Palestinians threw back gas canisters fired at them by Israelis during the Intifada of the 1990s. *(Photo by Cover, used with permission of The Image Works)*

convince the Israeli government of the wisdom of permitting an expatriate Palestinian to re-enter the country as a missionary among his people. Previous visa infractions were cited as the reason, but his family associations with Palestinian liberation efforts were more likely the cause. Leaders at the Bethlehem school and GBGM remained patient and hopeful. Influential members of the academic community in Jerusalem were persuaded to take up the issue. After nearly three years, the Israelis relented and the Awads were on their way.

Other missionary connections to the Middle East have been short-term or special assignments. The young adult Mission Intern program recruited personnel for assignment to the schools, hospitals, and other projects in Israel that were by and large supported from abroad. Relationships with other institutions and agencies such as the Young Men's and Young Women's Christian associations also provided continuity of Christian presence in the country. All work remained ecumenical with the exception of a mission school endorsed by United Methodist mission volunteers from North Carolina, who enthusiastically adopted it and blessed it with the denominational imprimatur without repercussion.

The struggle for a just resolution to the conflict between Israelis and Arabs over their common right and aspirations for their ancient lands has occupied the attention of policymakers. UN Resolution #799, adopted in 1967, called for the withdrawal of Israel from all occupied territory it claimed after the "Six Days War." Israel ignored the will of the international community and began establishing settlements on appropriated Arab lands. Palestinians were generally excluded from major negotiations on the future of the region. Their claims to the formation of a recognized state went unheeded until 1995 when Palestine Liberation Organization Chairman Yassir Arafat and Israel Prime Minister Yitzakh Rabin agreed on a peace process. It provided self-rule under the Palestinian Authority and paved the way for a graduated return of land to it. Reactions to this progressive process toward a peaceful settlement provoked rebellion and resistance among extremists of both Israeli and Arab descent. Violent responses emerged from both parties. Among Palestinians they ranged from a rock throwing "Intifada" among the poor and the powerless to strategic acts against the general Israeli population by terrorist groups. Progressively conservative Israeli governments responded with strategic military strikes against civilian targets and invasions of the Palestinian territory to destroy homes, shops, and villages of supposed terrorist families.

As the violence escalated, United Methodists joined with other Christians and representatives of most major religions in a variety of measures to protect human rights and the establishment of a lasting peace between Arabs and Israelis. Every General Conference of The United Methodist Church (UMC) since 1980 has addressed the issue. The policy objectives of the 1980 position and following statements of the denomination were shaped by a high-level, interdenominational study team of church leaders headed by Dr. Tracey Jones and sponsored by the National Council of the Churches of Christ in the U.S.A (NCC). The principal issues did not change, while the urgency of their resolution increased. The right of self-determination of both Israelis and Palestinians received general acclamation. But the call for recognition of the claims of Palestinians to a sovereign state within historic Palestine divided world political bodies and created interreligious tensions. The failure to reach an accord on this issue only provoked other conflicts throughout the region. On the occasion of the invasion of Kuwait in 1990 by the army of neighboring Iraq, sides were drawn between Arab states as well as Arab and non-Arab nations. But it was the military presence of the U.S. and "coalition" forces recruited largely from other Western nations that was readily exploited by radical Islamists who successfully fanned anti-Jewish and Christian sentiment in the region. The challenge of engaging in significant interreligious dialogue in the region and among world faith communities seemed to have a greater urgency than pursuing an exact articulation of political formulae for peace.[1]

Algeria

With the conclusion of the long and difficult struggle for independence in Algeria in which Islam had been the major unifying force, the future of a Christian witness in the country changed markedly. French nationals left the country by the hundreds of thousands. Algerians in exile returned. The Christian community waned from 10 percent to less than 1 percent of the population, The new government proceeded to nationalize many of the institutions that were served by Christian missionary personnel. Protestants, a scattered minority fraction in an Islamic context, discovered the importance of cooperation. In 1972, The United Methodist Church in Algeria united with the Mennonite and Reformed Churches to create the Protestant Church of Algeria. While each denomination maintained a liaison with its church judicatories abroad, all shared a common life of worship and service in Algeria. Services were conducted in the French language, but participation became more international with a growing number of expatriates from many nations.

Hugh Johnson, United Methodist missionary pastor and superintendent for Algeria, reported a growing fellowship between Protestants and Roman Catholics. The Christian festivals of Christmas and Easter were celebrated together, Bible study groups were united, pulpit exchanges were encouraged, and Christian education and catechism classes were joint enterprises. In smaller cities such as Thenia and Tizi-Ouzou, pastoral care became an ecumenical project. In other locations Protestants used Catholic facilities and vice versa. Sisters from the Catholic White Sisters missionary order taught in a former Methodist mission school in L'Arbaa Naït Irathen. A Methodist missionary family assigned to Oran took up temporary housing in a Catholic-owned apartment.

Maintaining the Christian presence in this North African country where Christianity once thrived became the focus of the mission of the small Protestant and Catholic communities in Algeria. The rise of

Muslim fundamentalism produced considerable uncertainty and periods of unrest in the political and social life of the country. The United Methodist presence remained in Algeria largely because of the constant oversight of the Zurich Episcopal Area and the support of partner conferences in Central and Southern Europe. Hugh and Fritzie Johnson devoted their entire missionary lives to leading and accompanying Algerians through times of crisis and efforts at rebuilding. Hugh Johnson took the long-term perspective in understanding the problems of the past and the potential for the future of Christian witness: "Largely due to internal dissension, Christianity spent itself out, indeed was already in its death throes before the arrival of the Muslims from the East in the eighth century. No one wishes to see that happen a second time. For this reason, the emphasis in Algeria is much more on the unity of diverse components than it is upon uniformity. Differences are considered less as points of division than as source of mutual enrichment." [2]

Mission strategies for establishing a witness in places where Christians are a distinct minority can be informed by the Algerian mission.

CHAPTER 11

A New World Vision

*Because the church envisions the coming of a new
heaven and a new earth, its mission proclaims the
authority and reign of God which transcends the lesser
claims of the powers and principalities of this world.*[1]

$\mathcal{T}$HE MISSION OF THE CHURCH is guided by the eschatological vision of a new heaven and new earth (Revelation 21). Establishing a just world order with the full realization of an abundant life for all of God's children becomes a missionary preoccupation wherever suffering prevails. A missionary doctor who treats recurring diseases among villagers soon tires of attending to the symptoms and begins to search for the cause. Dispensing medicines will temporarily heal the sick, but only clean water, nutritious food, and sanitary disposal will sustain a healthy village. The mission vision elevates from service to embrace development. But one healthy village will not survive in a nation of sick villages. Other villages must catch the vision, so the mission vision is lifted from a local focus to the national horizon. The goodwill and direct action of a few in a single context can create an effective model, but its successful replication requires mobilizing others to create additional resources and to establish a policy of universal enforcement.

The above scenario is the natural cycle of the missionary journey from a personal intervention to create change to generating a strong public advocacy in order to sustain change. The journey will almost certainly be accompanied by notoriety and conflict as the vision of the larger social good challenges the controlling interests of a few who benefit from the status quo. Such polarities stimulate debate about means versus ends or the virtues of personal versus social or corporate engagement in fulfilling

God's mission. The United Methodist Church (UMC) seems to have endless energies for such spiritual polemics. The truth is that both are prerequisites for the kind of transformation visualized in a new heaven and a new earth. There is no mission without a deep personal calling to help or convert individuals, and there is no completion of that mission without sharing its fruits with all of God's people.

The mission of The UMC in the second half of the twentieth century was strongly influenced by a growing sense of urgency about world problems. Troubling social indicators including high illiteracy rates, shortage of schools and teachers, high infant mortality, alarming population increases, food deficiencies, and economic gaps were found to exist not only in the developing nations but also in the United States. Reporting on the rising expectations of oppressed peoples filled the nightly news, and the eloquent voices of their leaders calling for a moral revolution resonated strongly within The UMC. The struggles within and the responses by the denomination are recited in an earlier section of this volume, but the range of issues on which the church found its prophetic voice during this period is addressed here. The concerns identified in this reporting may take on the appearance of a public policy agenda, but the origins of each issue are grounded in the church's mission commitment to enhancing human dignity through improving the quality of life. The story may be as much about what the church has learned in becoming an advocate for human development as about what it has achieved.

Social Welfare and Health Policies

In 1908, the Methodist Episcopal Church (the Northern denomination of Methodism in the U.S.) became the first in the Methodist family and one of the earliest denominations in the U.S. to articulate a formal social creed. In the last quarter of the twentieth century, The UMC frequently employed the credo's prophetic force in addressing the causes of social injustices and transforming its ministries of compassion for the disadvantaged by embracing a larger vision of fully inclusive communities serving the general welfare of all citizens.

Health for All/Comprehensive Community-Based Primary Health

The history of Methodist mission, both national and international, reveals a strong preference for institutionalizing the various forms of compassionate ministries the church founded. Church clinics, hospitals, and homes for children and the aging (and schools in international mission settings) were initiated in villages and communities where none previously existed. Institutions were designed to formalize the delivery and assure the continuity of vital social welfare services. But the maintenance of voluntary-based institutions became costly, and donor interest was often difficult to sustain in these institutions. Their services sometimes became redundant or obsolete as government programs became available, but seldom were the needs of the poor adequately addressed.

In 1969, the National Division of the Board of Missions considered a policy for its social welfare and health programs. In the North American context, it celebrated the creative role of the church in initiating social ministries and knowing when to release them to the local communities to continue. It acknowledged the legitimate role of governmental agencies in providing many of the social services that mission projects and institutions of the churches provided but questioned the will of the state to accomplish the job. The expanding economy would provide the resources, but the churches would need to become advocates by "doing what is necessary to get the state to start what needs to be started in the places where social welfare and health services are either nonexistent or inadequate." Two approaches were suggested: (1) Model development, i.e., start temporary programs to demonstrate to the state the locations, the types, and the modes of delivery of needed services. And (2) work in concert with the state in developing needed programs. In either case, the church's mission would be to "convert the state to undertake its responsibilities."[2]

The Women's Division of the Board was not supportive of a policy that would result in the outright release of their historic social welfare institutions to community-based groups or to state authorities. Furthermore, the agencies the division founded were drawn closer to the Board by adopting policies requiring greater accountability to the division for use of funds, maintenance of properties, and administration. But the division lent its support to the growing momentum for a comprehensive national health care policy. In a statement referred to units for study in 1971, the division declared the privatized health care system in the U.S. to be in a state of crisis. The statement decried Third World conditions prevailing in an affluent country: shortage and unequal distribution of medical professionals, an infant mortality rate higher than eleven other countries, a male life expectancy lower than eighteen other countries, chronic illnesses among people in poverty, and alarming disparities between the races in various health problems. The women outlined proposed principles for the restructuring of the health care system, especially the right to equal access to the best (and comprehensive) services by all citizens, national standards and policy formation for health care services and professions, consumer participation in policymaking, and public financing through taxation.[3]

The fate of a national health care policy in the U.S. remained a much-debated issue. Church-based advocacy continued to be focused on an improved quality of service with equal access guaranteed through federal financing, but the context was enlarged to incorporate a global perspective. In 1977 the member states of the World Health Organization, including the U.S., adopted a policy of Health for All by the Year 2000. It set this threshold for the world community to attain a level of health enabling all peoples to live socially and economically productive lives. The Health and Welfare Division of the General Board of Global Ministries (GBGM) embraced this program theme, and the Board brought a resolution to the 1980 General Conference that committed the denomination to a whole new approach to understanding and solving health issues in the global context.

Without completely abandoning curative medicine and its dependence upon chemical and surgical treatments, technical equipment, medical professionals, and institutionalized care, preventive health care was given a new prominence: "It is recognized that more than anything else people's health is affected by the circumstances of their lives including living and environmental conditions, education and employment opportunities, resources and life style, political and socio-economic realities, spiritual nurture and supportive relationships."[4]

The means of ministry commended to the churches in the resolution adopted by the 1984 General Conference was advocacy: "To focus clearly on those factors which impede individuals and communities in their search for health and wholeness; and to point to what must be done if people are to be freed from those powers and practices which stand in the way of health development, physically, mentally, socially and spiritually." Community and individual health was no longer understood to be solely a medical problem. Factors thwarting healthy living included "unequal distribution of political, economic and social opportunities, goods and services." Primary health was the focus, and the delivery system would not be exclusively hospitals or a clinic but also the social policy development processes of governments at all levels.

The principles of the Health for All program were readily applied to various mission contexts and constituencies. Health for All was especially compatible with the program commitment of the Women's Division to ministries with women and children. At a 1978 seminar on Women in Development, a range of concerns surfaced, including occupational safety, sterilization, abuse, rape and battering, human sexuality, and biomedical ethics. A new program focus was emerging on increasing awareness of women about personal medical health decisions and the impact of marketing and prescribing of pharmaceutical products by their physicians

The Health and Welfare Ministries Program Department sponsored a symposium on the subject of Women's Health that received coverage in the November 13, 1983, edition of the *New York Times*. The specific nature of the impact of economic, political, and social factors on women's health was traced to several communities of women, including refugee women, adolescent women, older women, women in jail, and Third World women. The attention given to issues of maternal health and child welfare drew the attention of the Pan-American Health Organization of UNICEF, which asked the department to provide it with literature on the subject. The work of the Department on Women's Health also received recognition at the 1985 UN Conference on the Decade for Women held in Nairobi in 1985.[5]

The community-based Health for All program philosophy required some new learnings on the part of Western health practitioners who understood healing in physical and organic terms. Cultures of the Southern Hemisphere were more likely to attribute powers of healing to spiritual well being. Missionary doctors generally dismissed spiritual healers as a heathen vestige. Holistic health acknowledged a role for counselors and spiritual practitioners who were equipped to deal with a patient's emotional problems also affecting one's physical health. A resolution prepared by units of the GBGM for the 1980 General Conference commended alternative programs that included: "educational efforts and programs which help people understand the spiritual, emotional, mental, and physical components of health in their personal lives and circumstances; [and] development of holistic health centers within the context of the Church's ministry."[6]

The Health and Welfare Program Department began a consultative process in 1990 on the program theme of Health for All with partner church and conference leadership in Latin America, Asia, and Africa. The consultations examined the biblical foundations for ministries of healing, analyzed social and political issues that not only restrain the development of healthy communities but aggravate social violence and military conflicts, and identified strategies for engaging churches in preventive and holistic health programs. A pastoral letter issued by the participants in the Latin America Consultation held in La Paz, Bolivia, in 1990, called upon the churches to counter "social and political policies and practices that bring suffering and early death to millions of people." Signers urged their churches and others: "To reclaim the prophetic ministry of Jesus by exposing and challenging cruel systems of exploitation, destruction, oppression and death; by exercising our political ministry to advocate for policies which assure that the people live in dignity and safety, health and wholeness; for standing in solidarity with people's movements which struggle for justice, peace, and the integrity of creation."[7]

Encouraged by the responses of regional church leaders, the department committed major resources to the training of partner church practitioners in comprehensive community-based primary health care. In 1993, the department entered into a working relationship with the Comprehensive Rural Health Project in Jamkhed, India. The work of the project in helping a community of the poorest of the poor take charge of their own health received the acclaim of international health organizations. The department was so convinced of the value of extending its mission from providing health services to developing healthy communities that it redirected budget resources that previously underwrote the professional services of a missionary physician to utilizing the Jamkhed project for leadership training seminars in community development. ·

Drs. Mabel and Rajnikant Arole, graduates of Christian Medical College and Hospital in Vellore, India, started the Comprehensive Rural Health Project. The Aroles dedicated their professional lives not only to curing diseases but demonstrating the viability of a community-based primary health program. They emphasized education and development of villagers in preventive strategies for healthy living through production of their own food supply, drilling wells for clean drinking water, creating sanitary systems of waste disposal, and utilizing natural/cultural healing techniques. Yammunabai Kulkarni, a health worker in the village of Ghodegon encompassed by the project, offered testimony to the effectiveness

Mabel Arole, center, founded a community-based primary health program along with her husband, Rajnikant, in Jamkhed, India. The holistic program became the model for comprehensive health care developed in many other countries by GBGM. (*GBGM photo*)

of the program among the poor inhabitants: "Ghodegon was a different village before I became a village health worker. Most of the adults suffered from guinea worm infection. We still have scars on our ankles, knees and backs from this infestation. Now it is no longer a problem. We were superstitious. We thought that most diseases were the curse of the goddess. In the past there were epidemics of cholera. We used to sacrifice goats and chickens to appease the goddess. The cholera did not disappear. Now, since I became a village health worker, the cholera is no more. Every year, 10 to 15 children used to die in the village. Now hardly a baby dies."[8]

The model community at Jamkhed became the training site for teams of personnel recruited by partner churches and conferences and at the direction of regional missionary coordinators employed by GBGM. The basic components of primary health care taught at Jamkhed seemed to have a ready application for most mission contexts in the Southern Hemisphere. They were also seen as an economical alternative to the rural and urban clinics located among marginalized poor communities in industrialized contexts of the Northern Hemisphere. Given the enduring popularity of the high-cost, high-technology model of institutionally based curative care, the alternative community-based programs were not an easy sell. Medical professionals did not readily accept the cadre leaders trained for developing alternative health practices and methodologies. Some church leaders were also disappointed in the declining emphasis upon building medical institutions which proudly carried the Methodist name and gave a stronger identity to their ministries in countries where their churches existed in relative obscurity. But the local churches that developed community-based programs with the help of the newly trained leaders found a new opportunities and excitement for their ministry.[9]

Aging

Through study and research, the Health and Welfare Division of the Board of Missions counseled the Board on the growing impact of an aging population upon the church and the society. In 1975, the division recommended that the Board oppose mandatory retirement policies for UMC personnel. This matter was referred to the Board Personnel Committee for a review of its own policies that required retirement at age sixty-five and was inconsistent with the general church policy that set retirement age at sixty-eight. The division also asked the Board to petition the 1976 General Conference for a change in the general church employment policies which it considered nondiscriminatory for persons under age sixty-eight but discriminatory for those older. In addition to "race, color or sex," the division wanted "age" inserted in the Disciplinary statement of nondiscrimination in hiring, paying, and promoting church personnel.[10]

To develop further the capacity of the church to address issues of its graying membership, the Health and Welfare Division offered an incentive grant to a United Methodist seminary that would emphasize gerontology in its training of pastors. A grant of $700,000 was awarded to St. Paul School of Theology in Kansas City, Missouri, to set up a chair on gerontology and establish a center of health and welfare ministries on its campus. The source of funds was the sale of a farm in Illinois, which the late Ms. Oubri Poppele had left to the division.[11] The grant was to be used for research on the problems of aging and the status of the church's ministries with the elderly. St. Paul seminary would share the results of its research with other academic institutions focusing on preparing persons for careers in fields of aging.

In 1979, a policy statement on aging was prepared by the Health and Welfare Division for submission to General Conference. It documented the growth in the aging population in the U.S. and cited the economic burdens, health problems, psychological needs, and yet strong potentials for living productive lives. It called upon The UMC to "engage in sustained advocacy for the elimination of age discrimination in personal attitudes and institutional structures." In the private sector, the resolution urged religious institutions to establish the "context for care" provided for older persons and to infuse their values into neighborhood and community life. It affirmed the role of government as the "guarantor of last resort that no persons are left outside the system of services" without absolving the "institutional church or individual Christians from responsibility for persons in need." Society was expected to "define a minimum standard of basic and necessary support" for its aging population, assuring that required services "be provided at a cost within the financial means of the elderly with appropriate public subsidy when necessary." It committed The UMC to "call upon society to respond to the basic human right of the elderly, the right to die with dignity and to have personal wishes respected concerning the number and type of life sustaining measures that should be used to prolong life."[12]

The resolution on aging adopted by the 1980 General Conference set forth a number of prescriptions for affirming and including the aging in the ministries of the church. Churches were called upon to "recognize that older persons represent a creative resource bank available to the church, and involve them in service to the community as persons of insight and wisdom. This could include not only ministry to one another, but also to the larger mission of the church for redemption of the world, including reaching the unchurched." The General Conference authorized an Interagency Task Force on Aging to develop specific program and policy recommendations for embracing the church's mission by and to the aging. The task force worked for a full quadrennium reworking the 1980 policy statement and proposing many new program directions for the general church. At the 1984 General Conference, the task force succeeded in including age as a category for the selection of general church agency directors, thus providing a corps of peers in each agency to monitor implementation of the resolution and the task force recommendations.

Advocacy within the Board of Global Ministries escalated the issue of aging on the mission agenda. The Board established a staff portfolio on aging and lodged it in the Health and Welfare Ministries Division. The staff worked with other organizations in advocating federal nondiscriminatory legislation. It promoted Board membership in a "Generations United Coalition," a group of voluntary and church organizations working creatively to address the tendency in political arenas to pit the young against the old rather than promote the justifiable needs of both within society. Since the policy statement adopted in 1980 was aimed entirely at the U.S. context, the division began work on a statement on international aging. This important work was joined by the World Division, which urged

GBGM to become one of the NGO signatories of the UN Resolution on "Older Persons and Human Rights." This resolution called attention to the absence of any reference to the aging in the Universal Declaration on Human Rights and other UN covenants. It sought the inclusion of both age and gender factors in the preparation of all instruments that deal with issues of "employment, housing, economic security, food security, criminal acts and physical abuse, the family, media and indigenous peoples." It pledged the UN to work with other governmental organizations and NGOs to "work toward finding solutions for the long term care of the elderly, especially those who are disabled, single and live alone."[13]

In 1999, GBGM endorsed the UN International Year of Older Persons. A course on aging was included in the summer Schools of Christian Mission that year. It informed participants about preparing for the experience of aging and how to protect the rights of the elderly in societies that honor their seniors with sentiment but not always through practice.

Children's Health: Infant Formula

With increasing frequency, reports on children's health linked infant malnutrition in the Third World to the promotion of artificial milk formula feeding practices. The product was marketed in many countries as an alternative feeding method for women who could not, or chose not to, breast-feed their infants. It was also sold as a supplement for older babies experiencing a nutrition deficiency. The lack of clean water standards and the unavailability of satisfactory sanitizing techniques required for the preparation of milk formula caused the spread of bacteria, disease, and, ultimately, death to babies.

The Third World Action Group organized a global campaign to mobilize world opinion against promoting the use of artificial milk for infant feeding in poor nations. It focused on the activities of the Nestlé Company, the world's largest and most visible company distributing the product worldwide. Nestlé was accused of unethical and immoral behavior with respect to selling infant formula in developing countries. The company used general advertising and distributed free samples to attract interest and generate sales. The labeling seldom used local languages and failed to include warnings about misuse.

In 1974, the Interfaith Center on Corporate Responsibility (ICCR), representing the Women's Division and other church groups, began filing shareholder resolutions with U.S. formula companies asking about their practices. In 1977, the Infant Formula Action Coalition composed of international health organizations, church bodies, and NGOs, launched a boycott against the Nestlé Company. Several annual conferences of The UMC immediately supported the boycott. At the 1978 annual meeting of GBGM, the Women's Division initiated a resolution supporting the boycott and the Board followed suit: "That in view of growing concern over promotional campaigns in Third World areas stimulating the use of infant formulas and bottle feeding of babies, and in view of the refusal of the Nestlé Corporation to cease promotional activities, the Board of Global Ministries join in support of the boycott of Nestlé products."[14]

The decision to engage in economic sanctions was not taken lightly nor was an early resolution of the matter likely. The Board worked closely with the General Board of Church and Society (GBCS), which had taken the same action, and both agencies gave leadership to the broad-based Infant Formula Action Coalition. Even though as many as thirty-four annual conferences endorsed the boycott of Nestlé, sentiment was growing against the involvement of general agencies of the denomination in economic embargoes. Some saw the hand of the Nestlé Company maliciously stirring up dissent among influential members of the boycotting churches. The 1980 General Conference responded to the controversy by creating a "third force strategy" in the establishment of a task force accountable to the General Council on Ministries to oversee the church's involvement in the Nestlé boycott.

By 1982, pressure from the boycotting groups and criticisms by international organizations produced some results. The Nestlé Company issued a revised set of instructions to its field staff, explaining how to implement the World Health Organization (WHO) and UNICEF international code of marketing. The International Nestlé Boycott Committee, including GBCS and GBGM, welcomed the progress and then outlined their provisions for "ending the boycott." A commitment to universal and strict implementation and enforcement of the WHO/UNICEF codes, regular meetings between Nestlé executives and the International Nestlé Boycott Committee to assure compliance, and a mutually agreeable process for monitoring results were the coalition's "conditions."

At the same time the United Methodist Task Force began its independent appraisal of the protracted dispute and was preparing to ask the General Council on Ministries to request the boycotting GBGM, GBCS, and the thirty-four annual conferences to "re-examine their position and

Theressa Hoover served as head of the Women's Division in the tumultuous years when the division was actively engaged in debates over abortion, women's rights, the rights of children, and apartheid in South Africa. *(Photo courtesy of UM Archives and History)*

consider concluding their participation." Dr. Richard Tholin, social ethics professor at Garrett-Evangelical Theological Seminary in Illinois and the articulate and persistent chair of the GBGM Nestlé Boycott Task Force, urged the Board to "continue to honor the grass roots commitment of the participating conferences . . . and to maintain our ecumenical relationships, particularly with Roman Catholic bodies . . . in order to continue the boycott and get complete approval of the Code." As much time and energy would be spent on maintaining unity among United Methodists in the struggle as in negotiations with Nestlé.

By the time GBCS and the GBGM met in the spring of 1984, sufficient progress was made on the issues of compliance for the International Nestlé Boycott Committee to recommend a six-month suspension of the boycott. A confrontation on the Nestlé boycott issue at the 1984 General Conference was successfully sidestepped. The General Conference urged the entire infant formula industry "to respect the universal applicability of the WHO Code by adopting its provisions in all countries except where prohibited from doing so by law." On October 4, 1984, the International

Nestlé Boycott Committee recommended an end to the international boycott of Nestlé and announced a new phase of activity in its efforts to improve infant and young child health.

The Nestlé boycott demonstrated the effectiveness of coalitional efforts in developing or shaping social and economic policy. The International Nestlé Boycott Committee was a formidable international coalition, producing a strong tide of influence and power. For United Methodists, there was a byproduct from the protracted corporate action against Nestlé. The 1984 General Conference enacted a strict limitation or prohibition upon agencies and connectional bodies in instituting churchwide boycotts. An amendment to appropriate paragraphs of the *Discipline* served as a warning label: "The General Conference is the only body that can initiate, empower, or join a boycott in the name of The United Methodist Church."[15]

Advocacy for Children

"Until children have strong advocates in the general population, we will champion their cause. Our call is for the whole of church and society to share the urgency of this concern." This was the mission "manifesto" issued by the Women's Division in its 1993 policy statement on Ministries with Women and Ministries with Children and Youth. It echoed a 1976 policy statement on Ministries to Women and Children in which advocacy was linked to providing new services for children to reflect the changing role and expectations of children. For more than a century United Methodist Women (UMW) and predecessor groups of women organized for mission had been strong advocates for the rights and needs of children. In October 1972, the Women's Division adopted a report from its Task Force on Child Advocacy, committing the division to:

- Develop, establish and test models of child advocacy, demonstrating the functioning of the churchwomen's organizations as advocates for children and using the church structure and operations as resources.

- Encourage local United Methodist Women units to develop models of child advocacy in keeping with community needs.

- Encourage local units of United Methodist Women to investigate the need for infant care, day care, after-school care, and mental health programs for children in their communities.

  - Participate in developing a system to monitor community services to eliminate dehumanization.
  - Take steps in consultation with the National Division and Health and Welfare Division to support church-related children's services already in existence.

The need for adequate childcare was being addressed in legislative arenas in the 1970s. Women's Division resolutions supported public funding for quality childcare, with the assurance of sensitivity to cultural and other local issues that require flexibility in the types of services offered as well as their administration.

During the International Year of the Child in 1979, the Women's Division commended for study by local units the nine goals of the year recommended by the Specialized Seminar on International Affairs: Focus — Human Rights. The division also sponsored two regional (U.S.) Child Advocates' Conferences, attended by conference and district UMW representatives who were active in child advocacy or were service providers or directors/board members of agencies related to the National (and Women's) Division. The agenda for conferences focused on the needs of children for which public support should be generated by church leadership in advocacy circles.

Between 1988 and 1993, nearly 10,000 local units of UMW participated in the division's Campaign for Children program. The local units made commitments to make a difference in the lives of children through worship, educational community service, and legislative action. The program was so successful that a phase II was adopted for 1994–1999 with the subtheme: "Making the World Safe for Children and Youth in the 21st Century." In keeping with this theme, the division became an active member of the Child Labor Coalition, participating in a national network of organizations working to protect working minors and end child labor exploitation. The division actively supported several campaigns:

The Rugmark Campaign aimed at raising awareness and changing business practices in the rug-making industries in India.

The Foul Ball Campaign sought to end child labor in the production of soccer balls in Pakistan. The Soccer Industry Council of America responded with a draft code of conduct that became part of a labor agreement between the International Labor Organization (ILO), UNICEF, and the Pakistan Chamber of Commerce.

The anti-sweatshop campaign was directed at employment practices of the Disney Corporation in countries where it manufactured products.

Global March Against Child Labor was an international campaign to promote the rights of children worldwide to receive an education and to be free from work that exploited or hindered their development.

A major goal in advocating the protection of children was aimed at gaining U.S. Government adoption of the UN Convention on the Rights of the Child. The convention was a universally agreed set of nonnegotiable standards and obligations of governments. It was carefully drafted over a ten-year period. It spelled out the basic human rights of children everywhere:

- The right to survival;
- The right to develop to the fullest;
- The right to protection from harmful influences, abuse, and exploitation; and
- The right to participate fully in family, cultural, and social life.

Every country but two, the U.S. and Somalia, ratified the convention. A sticking point was the military's objection to a provision that prohibited the enlistment of persons under the age of eighteen into military service. The convention was adopted as international law by the General Assembly of November 1989, and efforts to obtain U.S. Government ratification persisted. The National Division approved a resolution in support of the convention in 1989 and the Women's Division promoted letter-writing campaigns to legislators. The Women's Division continued to work on the issue of military conscription of children. The division sent a resolution to the 2000 General Conference on Banning the Use of the Child Soldier.[16]

The general boards of Global Ministries, Church and Society, and Discipleship of The UMC endorsed participation in Stand for Children: A National Day of Commitment, coordinated by the Children's Defense Fund on June 1, 1996, at the Lincoln Memorial in Washington, D.C. The Women's Division became a sponsoring agency of the event and worked with the National Division in organizing UMW and the national mission constituencies to attend the event. A resolution drafted by the Women's Division for the 1996 General Conference reflected the long-standing partnership of the division by endorsing much of the legislative agenda of the Children's Defense Fund. Many General Conference delegates perceived the leadership of the Children's Defense Fund to be "too liberal," but few organizations have accomplished so much in focusing Washington's attention on the needs of children.

Welfare Reform

The UMC mission board has a strong history of engagement in welfare reform. In the 1960s and 1970s, the Women's Division maintained a liaison with the National Welfare Rights Organization, which organized participants into forms of direct action to effect needed changes in welfare policies and practices. Church families were asked to try living on a welfare family's income for one week. A study book authored by Edward Carothers, *Christians and Cruelty Systems*, helped church members understand the oppressive nature of poverty and the injustices of the economic and political systems which kept people poor.

Public welfare systems remained a potent political issue, and for most activists a national disgrace. The passage of the landmark Welfare Reform legislation by the U.S. Congress in 1996 and signed into law by President William Clinton represented a major setback for advocates of a stronger social policy for children. The political goal of the legislation was to stimulate a reduction in the welfare rolls by requiring state governments to develop work programs for participants in welfare programs. Employment opportunities were developed but without the promised financial incentives that would lead to self-sufficiency. Moreover, there were seldom adequate provisions for the care of children when heads of welfare households entered the workforce.

GBGM created a Welfare Reform Crossfunctional Team that solicited information from national mission agencies and other constituencies about the effects of the new law in their communities. Economic and social hardships upon individuals and the correlative impact on services provided by private (and church-based) social agencies were documented and shared with lawmakers at local, state, and federal levels. These efforts certainly heightened the quality of the national dialogue on issues of poverty and human dignity, but the practical outcome was limited to influencing administrative implementation of the legislation in various locales.

Civil Rights and Human Rights

By 1969, The UMC was engaged in the structural appropriation of the changes wrought by the civil rights movement in the U.S. The 1968 abolition of the black Central Jurisdiction and integration of churches in The UMC was on the way to becoming reality. The churches were supporting the Fund for Reconciliation, the denomination's response to the need for healing and redevelopment in communities deeply affected by the rebellion of persons of color against systems of prejudice and discrimination. But the challenge to the churches was not over. The Black Economic Development Conference/Forum issued its "Black Manifesto."

The conference/forum was organized by the Interreligious Foundation on Community Organization (IFCO), which brought together the leadership of major community groups and national civil rights organizations into partnership with religious (Jewish and Christian) bodies to work on programs of community empowerment and development. A "manifesto" issued by the forum addressed the churches as "socio-economic institutions with great wealth and power" and demanded the payment of reparations for the unpaid labor that black enslavement contributed to the economic strength of the U.S.

The manifesto was given a dramatic presentation at a Sunday service in Riverside Church in New York. It was delivered by James Forman, a former leader in the Student Nonviolent Coordinating Committee, who had an equally dramatic strategy for enforcing it. He and his supporters staged a sit-in at the Interchurch Center, which became the fortified symbol of the movement's "enemy." The action provoked a legal restraining order from the building's tenants, the National Council of Churches (NCC) and major denominations. Tensions were rising and little was being done to mediate the conflict. Peggy Billings, assistant general secretary for the Women's Division Section on Christian Social Relations, reported on her contacts with Tracey Jones, general secretary of the Board of Missions, who encouraged the formation of a Crisis Intervention Team to prevent the intervention of law enforcement in the sensitive matter. The team provided liaison communication with influential civil rights leaders and denominational officials and invited John Adams of GBCS, whose conflict-resolution proficiency had been well demonstrated in other public arenas.

The standoff lasted several weeks. The rhetoric of the confrontation was heightened and along with it the efforts to seek a peaceful resolution. Consultants were hired to negotiate between the NCC and Forman. The Crisis Intervention Team briefed the consultants on programs and strategies that the churches could offer as options in the negotiations and thus strengthen their response to the urban crisis that provoked the conference/forum actions. Finally, the churches agreed to drop their re-straining order, and the Forman forces agreed to end their occupation of the building. Reparations, the expressed purpose of the confrontation, were a stumblingblock for the churches and remained so whenever the is-sue was raised. Escalating the demands of the black community to sub-stantial financial considerations required the churches to be sensitive to what their holdings reflected in a society in which there was an ever-widening gap between rich and poor. Those making black financial de-mands also insisted upon a review of church program priorities that would effectively demonstrate how the white leadership establishment in the churches was wont to control denominational assets.[17]

The confrontation between the churches and the forces of the civil rights movement escalated the dialogue on the need for reform within the churches. It provoked the formation of caucuses within the denomina-tions to pursue issues of racial justice and equitable distribution of re-sources as well as equal opportunities for leadership and service in the churches. This impact has been addressed in the early part of this book. The manifesto event also opened the door to issues of financial empower-ment in the minority communities. The special session of General Con-ference in 1970 reaffirmed the initial endorsement of Project Equality given by the 1968 uniting conference. Project Equality was the creation of national religious bodies providing a regional reference service of ven-dors of supplies and services that subscribed to its high standards for affirmative action policies and submitted to its annual performance re-views. All units of the church were pledged to use the services of Project Equality and purchase supplies and contract for the services from ap-proved companies.[18]

Church investments in minority-owned banks was another empower-ment issue that gained prominence in policymaking arenas of the church. In 1968, the Women's Division approved a study of its accounts on de-posit with banks to determine how to leverage its influence around issues of equal employment opportunities. It led the other units of the Board to make similar studies and selected investments in minority banks that met federal banking standards.[19]

Protecting the gains of the civil rights movement required diligence on the part of advocates for racial justice. Through its program networks and participation in national coalitions, GBGM was poised to give its support to key legislative issues. In 1981, the Board supported the renewal of the critical Voting Rights Act of 1965 that secured the civil rights of minority groups. The act had been responsible for increasing the number of minorities registered to vote and helped increase the number of black and Hispanic elected officials. The new legislation went further in providing voter assistance in languages other than English and made it easier to process voter discrimination complaints by requiring proof of a procedure's discriminatory effect rather than intentional discrimination.[20]

The National and Women's divisions of GBGM provided financial support for local community organizations working on open housing. These groups organized a national coalition to support enforcement of fair real estate lending and marketing practices through federal legislation. In 1981, the Board petitioned members of Congress to strengthen the Fair Housing Act to outlaw such practices as: "steering" minority persons to seek housing only in minority neighborhoods; "redlining," or refusing to finance or insure homes because of the racial composition of the neighborhood or setting higher rates to finance or insure those homes; and requiring different security deposits, down payments, or interest rates depending on the race of the buyer or renter.[21]

In the area of employment, the doctrine of separation of church and state left religious institutions outside of the enforcement of equal opportunity legislation. Church agencies and organizations were obliged to create their own policies and practices. The UMC created a General Commission on Religion and Race with corresponding units in every annual conference to promote and monitor affirmative action practices within the church. The commission provided guidelines for general agencies to develop individual affirmative action plans. Then, through formal review processes and periodic visits to agencies, the commission sought to fulfill its task and to be a court of appeal for complainants. GBGM sought to play a similar role for the mission agencies and institutions under the administration of its program divisions. Plans submitted covered categories of racial/ethnic minority persons and women in both staff employment and board memberships.[22]

In spite of protections offered by federal civil rights legislation, black citizens faced issues of discrimination. The Federation of Southern Cooperatives brought national attention to the perils of black farmers in mostly rural Southern states. As the market value of farmland increased with regional patterns of urbanization, black farmers were confronted with escalating property taxes and operating expenses. Forced sales of family-owned farms increased at an alarming rate. Blacks remaining on their farms experienced hardships in production and reported a high incidence of discrimination in the distribution of federal aid. The redress of their grievances involved time-consuming administrative and legal appeals that often brought too little relief too late. Because the viability of rural black churches and communities depended upon members with strong livelihoods, GBGM responded to grant requests for legal representation and advocacy. Most were administered through ecumenical channels.

The Tchula Episode

While progress on hard-fought civil rights causes moved slowly on the economic front, advances in political representation were even harder to achieve and maintain. A case study from rural Mississippi was presented for the churches' consideration in 1981. In the small biracial town of Tchula, Eddie James Carthan, age twenty-seven, was elected mayor in 1977, the first black to be elected since reconstruction. Dissenting aldermen immediately challenged Carthan's leadership. They employed several obstructive tactics, even installing their own police officers, accountable to them rather than the mayor. When Carthan and his supporters tried to "take back" the department with the use of force, he was charged with assault on a duty officer. Carthan (along with six others known collectively as the "Tchula Seven") was convicted on the charge and sentenced to three years in prison. Subsequently, other charges were brought against the embattled mayor, including fraud and complicity in the murder of an alderman. Without stronger legal representation, Carthan faced the certainty of long-term imprisonment.

To the Carthan supporters and other observers, the Tchula case was not only a political injustice in removing an elected official from office but was a racially motivated abuse of the justice system. They saw the local white power structure influencing the courts to send a message to other blacks to abandon any aspirations for political office. An appeal was made to the Racial Justice Working Group of the NCC, which reviewed the situation and asked for financial contributions from member denominations for Carthan's legal defense and a full redress of grievances. The National Division had already provided grants of $3,000 and $8,000 to the United League of Holmes Country, a local black community-organizing project related to the division's United Methodist Voluntary Services program. The league had taken up the cause of Carthan by helping with his legal defense and also by mobilizing public interest in the case and providing material support for the Carthan family.

United Methodists in Mississippi were soon drawn into the conflict and controversy over the issues of Carthan's case, but some especially objected to the financial involvement of GBGM in his defense. Similar to the logic employed by Southerners in the heat of the civil rights challenges, staunch United Methodists in white congregations expressed their opinion that the Tchula matter was a local issue and did not merit intervention from the "outside." In writing to René Bideaux, the associate general secretary of the National Division, about the matter, a local pastor summarized the attitude of his church members: "The situation in Tchula was not, and has never been, a race issue. It was a matter of criminal investigation and judicial process. But it seems as though the UMC under the unwise concern of the Board of Global Ministries has made it a race issue."[23]

With additional voices of local church members rising in opposition and proposing the withholding of contributions to World Service, the North Mississippi Annual Conference expressed its objections to the Board's involvement in this case. It was careful, however, to make its case on procedural grounds. The *Discipline* required a consultation process with annual conference leaders before financial grants are made by any general church agency to programs within conference boundaries. The North Mississippi Conference officials claimed that National Division staff members did not provide notice or consultation regarding its decision to make a grant to the United League of Holmes County for the Carthan defense. While the division cited a staff member's visit in December 1981 to the conference offices during which an opinion on the matter was solicited, it finally acknowledged that this form of consultation was "inadequate." The General Council of Ministries was asked to review the matter and ruled that the consultation requirement had not been fulfilled. As the controversy swelled, the procedural impasse was offered as the rationale for the suspension of three National Division staff members with direct program responsibilities for the funding decision.

The actions of the National Division provoked activists to ask whether the cause of racial justice in this case was being sacrificed to bureaucratic technicalities. The opposition forces within the church had successfully established the grounds by which the issue would be joined — church protocol, not race. At the annual meeting in October 1982, both the National Division and the full Board responded by adopting a "Resolution on Justice Ministries and the Crisis in Civil Rights." It reaffirmed the Board's "commitment to equal justice for all in society" and its "work with groups and communities across the country," responding to "victims of injustice or possible violations of civil rights with contributions to funds for legal defense."[24] In March 1983, the National Division, after consultation with the North Mississippi Conference, approved the request of the NCC for a $10,000 grant to its Racial Justice Working Group for the Carthan Legal Defense Fund.

In the minds of some civil rights veterans, the Carthan episode prompted a question of strategy. Was this the right issue to choose for a high-profile involvement of the churches in racial justice matters. Did the Carthan case (i.e., securing an adequate legal defense of one small-town mayor) offer sufficient potential for changing the national trend of eroding political gains of civil rights legislation? The case certainly illustrated how far the mission of the church had drifted from its high resolve after church union in 1968 to work on issues of reconciliation. It was the Fund for Reconciliation that created a channel of support for the program of United Methodist Voluntary Services whose purpose was to bridge the distance between the churches and the powerless—especially racial and ethnic minorities—in rural and urban communities. The United League of Holmes County fit the profile of the marginalized groups to whom United Methodists were urged to "listen and minister." Choosing to debate the process rather than having an honest encounter over the abiding influence of racial prejudice had the effect of turning a deaf ear to the victims. The public controversy over the funding reduced the opportunity for ministry to a mere gesture of support.

Ironically, the focus on reconciliation in the Carthan matter was largely internal to church structures. The National Division and the North Mississippi Conference entered into intensive dialogue regarding mission in the rural and largely black Holmes County. They agreed to new initiatives in parish ministry and community outreach to a predominantly black population, initiatives that might not have occurred without the eruption of the Carthan matter. GBGM provided funding. In October 1983, the National Division informed the church that Carthan had been released from a federal prison and that he had been exonerated by acquittal and withdrawal of charges for the major charges against him and freed for time served for a minor offense. The division concluded this episode with these comments: "Support from GBGM played an important part in the long struggle to free and vindicate Mayor Carthan and the Tchula Seven, and to preserve Black political rights. We ask all members of the Board to receive this report of progress with joy."[25]

Racism and Organized Hate/Violence

Racial attitudes in the North American culture are shaped and influenced by the activities of extremist groups that utilize or exploit a Christian identity. The notorious functioning of the Ku Klux Klan (KKK) gained headlines from time to time, but other hate groups made their presence felt through acts and threats of violence. In 1978, the Division on Ecumenical and Interreligious Concerns brought to the attention of the Board of Global Ministries a resurgence of the KKK and its tactics in singling out persons of color, Roman Catholics, and Jews for condemnation. In 1980, Dr. C. T. Vivian, acting director of the Southern Christian Leadership Conference, spoke to the Board about the activities of the Klan in all regions of the nation. He called upon Christians to create a national environment in which the KKK could not survive.[26]

In 1981, Board Ombudsman Harry Gibson presented the Reverend Michael and Ella Curry, whose United Methodist church in West Virginia had become an object of KKK threats. Their lives had been threatened if they refused to permit the Klan to hold a fully robed preaching and recruitment rally in the church building. After hearing their witness to the faith in the face of continued harassment, the Board commended them for their faithfulness. Gibson proposed a program response to "counteract the current mood of terrorism, violence and militarism." He invited the Board to consider "the creation, recruitment and deployment of a new cadre of missionary personnel to speak to this nation and carry the message of peace, justice and equality which is basic to our missional and Biblical faith [and] give authenticity to our witness on all six continents."[27]

In creating a new missionary category entitled Peace with Justice Educators, the Board took into consideration the quality of a United Methodist witness in churches and communities of the U.S. that would address the roots of racial hatred, exploitation, and other injustices that produce social conflict. Working in cooperation with GBCS, World Division missionaries were recruited to spend up to one term on assignment to annual conferences willing to support their itineration. The missionaries taught classes, conducted seminars, and were frequent speakers in public meetings and assemblies where issues of interracial and international relations were being addressed.

Acts of terror and hatred were again addressed by GBGM following the 1995 bombing of the Murrah Federal Office Building in Oklahoma City. A Board-sponsored National Consultation in St. Louis in July 1995 on the subject of "Ministry in the Midst of Hate and Violence" brought together mission leaders from the annual conferences to reflect on the tragedy of the rising influence and escalating violence of extremists in local communities. The consultation also developed plans for the conferences and churches to respond. The United Methodist Rural Fellowship offered the services of its rural chaplains program, which had been created and its membership trained and deployed to respond to crisis conditions in many rural communities caused by the decline of the agricultural economy. It was joined by specialists in conflict resolution and persons with expertise in the behaviors of hate groups in leading consultations and seminars with conference and local church leaders. A resource entitled "When Hate Groups Come to Town" served as a manual for preparing local church members to give leadership to conflict resolution in their communities.

A rash of black church burnings across Southern states finally received national attention in the late 1990s. Civil rights leaders were convinced of conspiratorial activities of hate groups. Church leaders demanded governmental intervention. Federal investigations seemed to give some credence to their conclusion, but institutional racism was evident in trivial efforts at improving local law enforcement or other programs aimed at prevention. The NCC issued an appeal for financial support for the rebuilding of the churches, which were either uninsured or underinsured. GBGM cooperated with the NCC but also developed its own campaign, which included the recruitment of volunteer work teams to assist with the rebuilding efforts of the members of the burned churches.

Charter for Racial Justice

The Woman's Division, Methodist Board of Missions, pioneered in engaging the church on issues of racial justice. It adopted a "Charter for Racial Justice" in 1952, long before civil rights became a national fascination. The charter aimed to challenge the practice of legal segregation and to assure that the programs and institutions of the Woman's Division were open to all without any form of discrimination. In 1962, the charter was revised to address structural inclusiveness within the division as well as a new emphasis on international human rights. In 1978, the charter was again revised to focus on institutional racism, with foci both internationally and in the U.S.

In summary, the charter was a policy statement of the Woman's and later Women's Division and a commitment of UMW organizations "to struggle for the rights and the self determination of every person and group of persons." Directors and staff of the division insisted that the policy was more than a statement and was a process of working on issues of institutional racism that deny full recognition and participation to persons of color in the organized church and in the institutions supported by the church. Consequently, the charter was used in training sessions for leaders and members at every level of the UMW organizational structure. A study/action guide was developed that probed the meaning of racism, helped with the identification of racist behaviors, encouraged the use of a survey to develop a proactive agenda for confronting racism in local church and community contexts, and offered a guide for action. Frequent inventories were made, which produced reports on how the commitment to antiracist conduct was being fulfilled.

In 1980, the Women's Division successfully presented the charter to the General Conference for adoption as a policy and commitment to achieving racial justice within the church and the world community to which it was in mission.[28]

Human Rights

Ever since the adoption of the Universal Declaration of Human Rights in 1948, religious bodies have been active in the discourse occurring in various world forums on issues ranging from the rights of children, women, and refugees to the preservation of the environment. The contributions of the Christian community have strongly influenced the course of the secular debate and the language of official documents on these subjects. The active involvement of the churches in the human rights arena has also served to recognize and strengthen an international commitment to defending the freedom of religion as a basic human right.

In August 1967, at the height of the civil unrest in North American cities, the Woman's Division convened a National Seminar for selected leaders of Methodist women on the theme, "Human Rights in World Perspective." Participants heard speakers who linked the explosion of angry, anguished urban black populations to the rising expectations of the worldwide human rights revolution. There were calls for radical changes in the U.S. power structures and social order for which persons of color had been waiting for two hundred years. A voice from Africa urged the importance of basic forms of economic and social development needed to sustain and protect human rights in newly independent nations. Mrs. Pumla Kisosonkole, a former member of the Uganda parliament and the Uganda delegation to the UN, and a member of the executive board of the All Africa Conference of Churches, said: "Economic and social revolution should go side by side in emerging nations. Economic progress depends on social individuals who enjoy their personal freedom. Too often, the insistence on human rights in new nations is still left at the level of the United Nations. Human rights should be included in the school curricula of developing nations. Government social workers must be involved in vigorous campaigns in favor of freedom of the individual if the rest of independence is to be meaningful."[29]

The UMC gave careful definition to human rights in the 1980 *Book of Resolutions*. It also embraced the need to incorporate human rights into its communal life and witness:

> We affirm that all persons and groups are of equal worth in the sight of God. We, therefore, work toward societies in which each person's or group's worth is recognized, maintained, and strengthened. We deplore all political and economic ideologies that lead to repression or totalitarianism, that pit persons against each other, that deny hope, that seek to enhance privilege and power of the few at the expense of the well-being of the many. We condemn violations of human rights in all political and economic structures. The Church, while proclaiming the gospel message of a God of love and justice, must be wary lest it compromise its own witness and unwittingly become an uncritical ally of repressive power and privilege in society around it.

The urgency and importance of the church's witness to the protection and fulfillment of human rights was rehearsed in a 1981 open letter from GBGM to The UMC. A new administration was in place in Washington giving signals of a shift away from the recognition of fundamental human rights in developing and implementing government programs and policies in both foreign and domestic affairs. A new secretary of state boldly declared in his first press conference that "International terrorism will take the place of human rights in our concern, because it is the ultimate abuse of human rights." The Board responded: "No one argues with opposition to terrorism. But to substitute anti-international terrorism for our concerns for human rights obscures the struggles of those seeking basic rights, even food and shelter, by overcoming structures of oppression.

And the label, 'terrorism,' is particularly open to selective application, used only to those we condemn."[30]

A diminution of the importance of human rights was reflected in congressional testimony by the new leadership in the State Department that it would not hold the observance of human rights standards by other countries as a condition for U.S. transaction of official relationships with them. And the department declared its intent to enlist missionaries as agents of the Central Intelligence Agency (CIA). A Board-sponsored amendment to the *Discipline* was aimed at precluding missionaries from becoming government agents: "The World Division shall prohibit the use of its personnel as paid or unpaid informer to any official or unofficial intelligence agency of any government."[31] And the Board appealed to United Methodists to embrace actively human rights for others, as they expected their government to protect the rights they demanded for themselves. "When the U.S. supports highly repressive governments that consistently violate the rights we demand for ourselves, then it is our integrity that is at stake — the integrity of our nation and our integrity as Christians within that nation. For these actions, it is we who will have to answer to God. And, the Bible makes clear that we as all nations are judged by our seal for righteousness and justice, not our military strength, by what happens to the poor, the widow and sojourner, not by our material success."[32]

The Board, along with other church groups, was becoming increasingly alarmed over reports of increased U.S. military involvement in Central America, where the death toll of innocents slaughtered by government armies and private militia had reached the tens of thousands. The martyrdom of a church leader like Archbishop Romero and the murders of Maryknoll missionary nuns in El Salvador aroused Christians of both Roman Catholic and Protestant evangelical persuasions to appeal for solidarity from the world church community. The increasing tide of refugees into the U.S. from El Salvador, Guatemala, and Nicaragua found sympathy and hospitality from churches in the Southwestern U.S. whose members became increasingly politicized around U.S. foreign policy in the region.[33] Church members were mobilized to participate in visits to Central America to strengthen the church presence in the face of repressive acts by military forces against their own populations.

Having taken a strong stand against apartheid in South Africa and backing it up by exerting the shareholder leverage of Board investment portfolios, many in the mission community expressed great dismay upon

At a Quito, Ecuador, conference in 1988, church leaders discussed human rights in Latin America. Left to right are Bishop Jesse DeWitt, former president of GBGM; Bishop Secundio Morales of Panamá; and Bishop Frederico Pagura of Argentina. *(Photo courtesy of UM Archives and History)*

learning that the Reagan administration would be entering into a policy of "constructive engagement" with the South African regime. Under Cold War protocol and tensions, access to the strategic mineral deposits in the region which the U.S. Government consumed for its own armament production prompted the encouragement of South African military ventures in Angola and Mozambique. The destabilization of these countries produced homeless families and refugees in record numbers. The churches were overburdened with their care. Their suffering and oppression could no longer be kept secret from a compassionate world church community that began to echo their cries for justice. The Interfaith Center on Corporate Responsibility was effective in leading the North American churches in a corporate investment strategy aimed at heightening the economic pressure on the South African government. GBGM was a major participant in the strategy which moved from shareholder resolutions and dialogue with corporations doing business in South Africa to selective divestment from companies in key industries that showed no response.[34] While detractors complained that such a strategy would hurt the poorest citizens more than the wealthy establishment, it was credited with the final collapse of the white-only South African government and the building of a free democratic republic.

In Asia, the U.S. Government continued to look to South Korea to secure its influence in the region with a massive military presence. At the same time, the human rights abuses of Korean governments were historically overlooked, even though faithfully reported by congressional investigators. A coalition of church groups and NGOs was formed to monitor events in South Korea and Washington in order to inform the advocacy efforts of supportive constituencies in the U.S.[35] The efforts of human rights advocates within South Korea and with support from abroad assisted in the emergence of democratic election processes leading to the election of President Kim Dae Jung in 1996. Kim, a dissident and opposition political leader who suffered imprisonment and persecution under the repressive post–Korean War governments of the South, had been befriended by many church and human rights groups. He accelerated the process of dialogue with leadership of the recalcitrant Communist regime in the North. The gradual opening of the North provided family visits and reunions (North and South) and stimulated the prospects for re-engagement of mission relationships in the North where Christian mission had a strong base. At the 1991 Assembly of the World Council of Churches in Canberra, Australia, representatives of the church councils from the South and North met for the first time.

In the North American context, the churches devoted considerable energy to addressing the subject of women's rights. In the period under review (1968–2000), two issues commanded the attention of women organized for mission in The UMC. The first was to establish the legal rights of women through the adoption of an amendment to the U.S. constitution. The national movement for adopting the language and then ratifying an Equal Rights Amendment educated the church and the political constituency on how limited were the legal protections for women in areas of financial security, health care, education, and employment. The campaign prompted a national groundswell of litigation and advocacy that opened up a host of new opportunities for women in U.S. society, ranging from participation in school sports to representation in state, local, and federal governments, from employment in the private sector to participation in the military.

Defending a woman's right of choice when it came to abortion was a more protracted struggle. The polarizing effect this issue had within U.S.

society, including The UMC and other churches, should not be under-estimated. In the interest of unity, the NCC left discussion and debate of the issue to its member communions. The Women's Division engaged the issue by becoming a founding member of the Religious Coalition for Abortion Rights (RCAR). It was a strong interfaith network of organizations, including national Jewish groups, which was instrumental in keeping the prochoice position prominent in the public debate. The division found allies in the ranks of General Conference delegates and successfully introduced a similar position in social policy statements adopted by General Conference. The issue was thoroughly debated at each General Conference, where the growing influence of prolife supporters narrowed the church's endorsement of legal abortions to limited situations under proper medical procedures. The 2000 General Conference added a ban on partial-birth abortion.

In 1977, the Women's Division decided to focus the church's abortion debate on the implications for women in poverty. The division voted to file a friend of the court brief in a legal contest known as *McRae* v. *Califano*. Cora McRae, a New York citizen and welfare recipient, was denied Medicare coverage for an abortion. Ellen Kirby, a division staff member, and Theressa Hoover, associate general secretary, testified on behalf of McRae, arguing the denial of her religious rights. The division argued: "If a woman's religious faith included a provision for supporting her conscientious decision to have an abortion, then a governmental policy that imposed restrictions on her ability to exercise her decision would be a limitation to her religious faith."[36] Although the division's argument was upheld in a 1979 decision by a Federal District Court in New York, it was overturned on government appeal to the U.S. Supreme Court, where the religious arguments were ruled out of order.

The advocacy of human rights by the churches, including The UMC, depended upon strong ecumenical cooperation provided by the NCC and the WCC. It was not without controversy over the issues chosen to address or not to address. At the 1983 Assembly of the WCC in Vancouver, critics from within and outside the council membership questioned its silence on the matter of human rights abuse by the Soviet Union in its military incursion into Afghanistan. Council leadership demurred on the grounds that a strong statement could have jeopardized the effectiveness of the continuing witness of the Russian Orthodox Church at home. Prior to the collapse of the Communism in Eastern Europe, Protestant leaders in the region voiced their dissatisfaction with ecumenical leadership over its failure to speak out in a timely and forceful manner on repressive actions of their governments. Nevertheless, member communions worked assiduously to maintain a balance between their global outlook and the parochial concerns of member bodies. Their representatives participated in frequent roundtables designed to bring together viewpoints directly from regions where crises existed and those from a more objective distance. They sought expert analysis and prepared texts of statements to be endorsed by the policymaking bodies of church councils and member communions. More importantly, they sought to develop a strategy for a cooperative response by the churches to the problems their statements addressed. Churches that tried to be responsible about their witness in a global context could not be faithful to their task without participating in such a process of listening, dialogue, critique, and support that the ecumenical fellowship afforded.

Economic Justice

With a firm belief that all aspects of life, including economic systems, fall under the judgment of God, the mission of the church sought to examine the economic order using the teachings of the gospel.

Global Economic Crisis

With the general prosperity and affluence the U.S. enjoys, the cycles of the economic life have always enriched the wealthy minority and marginalized a growing number of the poor. The mission of the church has historically been focused on those left behind. As the economy globalized, an increasing number of U.S. workers in both urban industrial and rural agricultural communities felt disenfranchised. In the mid 1970s, large corporations needing to improve the "bottom line" of their profit-and-loss statements had opted for multinational operations. To compete successfully in a global market, they relocated to cheaper labor markets in Third World countries, abandoning local communities and workers who had been loyal to them for many years. Agribusinesses built upon the efficiency principle of volume production soon depleted the previously competitive advantage of family farms. Mortgage foreclosures and bankruptcies ruled the day in farm communities.

As their local economies declined, churches faced a growing demand for pastoral care and endured a declining income needed to assure the continuation of their ministries. Many churches started collecting donations of food for distribution to members and neighbors. Therapy and grief counselors were mobilized and trained for deployment to affected communities by denominational judicatories.[37] Community organizers and activists tried to stimulate interest and support from elected officials. It was becoming evermore evident that legislation would not be written to reverse the forces of the global economy. Local communities would have to cope.

National denominational staff met and worked cooperatively to develop proposals on economic alternatives for the survival of local churches and communities. The prevailing notion was that making investment funds available to firms promising to stay local, employ locally, and reinvest locally should encourage a new community-based economy. In 1983, the National Division brought a proposal to the Board creating a "United Methodist Community Economic Development Fund." The aim of the proposal was: "To support existing and new community-based economic development ventures (credit unions, cooperatives, community development corporations, entrepreneurial small businesses) that provide job opportunities and the recycling of money with local communities. In these endeavors, churches can take responsibility for providing leadership and credibility."[38]

Several program-funding channels were proposed for providing the financial resources to establish the fund. The fund featured a revolving loan program that would enable it to be self-generating once a sufficient capital reserve was created. The administration of the fund would benefit from the division's participation in ecumenical and interfaith organizations that had been created to establish priorities. The fund was launched without much fanfare and only limited financial support. Rather than getting engaged in direct funding, the Board chose to invest its funds in other lending or grant-making intermediaries with similar objectives. The program benefit was multiplied by continuing to support a cooperative venture by ecumenical and interfaith groups seeking to attain the same economic justice goals.

The World Division reported the global dimensions of the economic crisis to the Board. In 1986, Deputy General Secretary Peggy Billings reported to directors on consultations with partner church leaders in several countries where economic conditions were causing personal hardships and compromising basic programs of their churches. Devaluation of currency in Bolivia reduced the value of monthly pastoral stipends from $50 to $10. In Brazil, annual conferences struggled to meet pastoral subsidies and solved the problem by encouraging early retirements. Inflation in Zaire forced the government to withhold financial assistance to schools, hospitals, and other social programs. Churches tried to stand in the breach but lacked financial resources to meet the challenge.[39] The Board responded with the creation of a special fund for Partner Churches in Crisis. Board units agreed to set aside considerable funding to administer grants on an emergency basis, and the directors approved an appeal to supporting churches to provide Advance giving designated for a crisis response.

The Partner Churches in Crisis appeal led the Board into a thorough examination of the cause, effect, and remedies for the deterioration of the economies and the stifling of the ministries of their mission partners. The churches recognized that their economic crises might result in their unwanted return to dependence upon financial assistance from the Board and other external sources. The Board did not want to sacrifice the painful and deliberate growth in its mission partnerships. In 1988, an Economic Crisis Task Force was created and charged with study, sharing of information, assessing impacts, and recommending action plans and strategies for the Board to implement. The work was to be accomplished over two years and was extended in order to complete a thorough exploration of issues in partnership with mission colleagues in both the U.S. and other countries.

The study process documented the problems in the emerging global economy. The shift in employment in the U.S. from production-oriented jobs to predominantly service providers resulted in more but lower-paying jobs. Consequently, U. S. workers were working more hours, on the average, while earning and saving less. Meanwhile, taxes were reduced for high-income families but increased for the middle-class working families in order to underwrite federal budget priorities that were focused on military expenditures. There were fewer federally funded programs aimed at helping poor families achieve financial and/or social security.

Countries in the Third World experienced similar problems and to a greater degree. Capital investments by private industries of the global economy provided only small local returns through low wages and small tax obligations. Therefore, local resources were exploited and the profits returned to investors in the industrial world economy. Repayment of massive national debts preempted public funds available for education, health, and other social benefits. Additional borrowing only accelerated the consequences of indebtedness and left many countries strapped for resources to strengthen local economies.

The task force found economic conditions in poor countries and communities especially vulnerable to illicit underground transactions. It completed an analysis of the codependency of unstable governments and drug cartels in Third World countries and their linkage to growing market demand and drug dealers in affluent countries in a published report, *Intricate Web: Drugs and the Economic Crisis*. The publication found a ready market beyond the Board, with 4,000 copies sold within weeks of its release.

While the frequent reports of the task force were informative and enlightening, implementation of its recommendations for engaging the larger church in both study and advocacy to correct injustices in global financial institutions and policies was never monitored. The Partner Churches in Crisis appeal had a fairly generous financial return and helped the Board respond to many requests for maintaining the infrastructure and ministries of the churches. Meanwhile, mission administrators expressed their dismay in preparing minimal annual budget appropriations for churches from which the prize of economic independence had been literally stolen by self-serving national interests and global economies.

Fair Labor Practices

The Social Principles of The UMC supported the right of workers to seek organized representation in issues related to the management of the workplace. This principle was, of course, easier to articulate than implement in a church shaped by the values of a rising and somewhat comfortable middle-class constituency. The leaders of national mission, however, were not discouraged from taking the side of labor in controversial conflicts with industry.

In 1973 and 1974, the National Division and the Health and Welfare Ministries Division struggled with each other over how to enter constructively a collective bargaining dispute in the Methodist Hospital of Kentucky at Pikesville. After months of contact with the area bishop, other annual conference leaders, the hospital administration, and striking as well as nonstriking workers, the Board found the leadership of the hospital to be resisting the right of workers to collective bargaining. The Board asked for the resignation of all members of the board of directors who were not in sympathy with the Social Principles of The UMC. In 1978,

the Women's Division joined in a national boycott of products made by
the J. P. Stevens Company in North Carolina in support of textile workers
who were seeking union recognition and improvement of working conditions. Both of these forays into fair labor practices earned rebuke and
condemnation, the most forceful from local church constituencies whose
sensibilities were seemingly offended by the actions of denominational
bodies.

Migrant farm workers in North America frequently received the ministry of local churches as they moved from community to community
harvesting crops. When these low-income workers organized to demand
better salaries and protection of their rights under state laws, they turned
to and received support from the councils of churches. The ecumenical
National Farm Worker Ministry (NFWM) was formed to assist in the
organizing of farm workers into collective bargaining units. The ministry
served as an effective liaison between churches, growers, government
bodies, and the leaders of the farm workers.

In 1972, at the request of César Chávez of the United Farm Workers of
America (UFW) and with the endorsement of the NFWM, the National
Division approved a boycott of nonunion lettuce.[40] Similar actions were
taken in support of the boycott by several annual conferences. At its annual meeting in 1973, Board members expressed further solidarity with
the farm workers by voting to restrain individually from eating table lettuce served by the banquet service of the Shelburne Hotel in Atlantic City
unless it carried the UFW label. They also instructed Board management
to make the lettuce boycott an issue in all future negotiations for Board
meeting sites.[41] In 1976, the National Division endorsed the union's
"Farm Worker Week," again expressing its "support for farm workers in
their struggles for justice through words and action."[42]

In 1985, the National Division endorsed the UFW boycott of California table grapes.[43] The boycott would expire when 60 percent of the table
grapes from California were harvested under contracts with the UFW.
This action embroiled the division in a debate with members of the California Pacific Annual Conference who had been successful in getting
a resolution of support for the growers through their conference. The
NFWM found the growers receiving considerable financial backing
for their defense from the agribusiness industry. The ministry also alleged industry collusion with the California state government against the
UFW. There were legislative attempts to diminish the authority of the

Agricultural Labor Relations Board and charges of rigging the board's process for reviewing UFW complaints in favor of the growers. The National Division's position in support of the right of farm labor to organize and in defense of the boycott of nonunion produce remained firm throughout the dialogue with the conference.

Also in 1985, the National Division, supported by the Women's Division, recommended and the Board approved participation in a boycott of the Campbell Soup Company. The Farm Labor Organizing Committee (FLOC) was organizing farm workers in Ohio and Michigan for collective bargaining rights with growers of cucumbers and tomatoes in Ohio and Michigan. Negotiations conducted by John Dunlop, former U.S. Secretary of Labor, failed to bring growers and workers into agreement on the conduct of representational elections. The Campbell Company, to whom the products were sold, refused to exert its leverage with the growers. United Methodists in the annual conferences participated in on-site investigations of the issues and their bishops (Edsell Ammons and Judith Craig) chaired special committees to review their findings and advise constituents on developments. Local church members were not only caught up in conflicting local loyalties, but regretted the prospects of a boycott which included withdrawing from the Campbell's label collection campaign which provided generous contributions to charitable organizations. Among the organizations promoting the label redemption program was the United Methodist Red Bird Mission in nearby Kentucky, a mission agency related to the National Division. Local United Methodist Women felt caught in a bind. Visits by Women's Division staff briefed women's unit leaders on the issues, especially the poor working conditions and living conditions of workers' families. With the support of the churches, including endorsement by the NCC, the boycott was relatively brief and effective in encouraging all of the growers to permit and recognize the results of union representation elections.

Organized labor in the U.S. experienced a decline in membership and popular support in the 1980s. The Reagan administration succeeded in standing down the air traffic controllers' union in a job action. All the striking workers were replaced, and the union never fully recovered. The industrial unions were ineffective in protecting the jobs in traditional U.S. industries from relocation to cheaper labor markets abroad. Unions tried to adapt to the changing economy by organizing workers in the expanding service sector of the economy but lagged in their support for immigrant or minority workers who were filling the unwanted, underpaid, and unskilled jobs remaining in the U.S. labor market. In this situation, support from the churches was critical for the organizing efforts of the largely racial minority members of the workforce. Embracing the philosophy of nonviolence employed so successfully by the civil rights movement strengthened the appeal of the farm labor organizers. Other organizers using similar strategies, e.g., those of the Southern Association of Woodcutters and women office workers, requested and received church support, but the churches lacked a long-term strategy for supporting the unorganized ranks of labor. An expanding economy helped both industry and labor absorb small victories and defeats, while new issues of worker exploitation received little notice. The reduction in full-time jobs with paid benefits and the reluctance of the Congress to raise the minimum wage to an adequate level have eroded the economic security of many middle-class families, the very heart of the church and union constituencies.

Corporate Responsibility

In 1971, the World Division of the Board of Missions commissioned its investment committee to develop a proposal for "coordinating social consciousness considerations with investment and proxy voting matters." The committee recommended that in addition to traditional United Methodist policies objecting to gambling, alcoholic beverages, tobacco, and the reduction of armaments, issues such as "reduction of pollution, betterment in fair employment and equitable conditions of work in the United States, and the reduction (or preferably elimination) of apartheid in South Africa should be taken into account as far as practicable in the making (and retention) of investments in corporate securities and in the voting of corporate proxies."[44] The change in strategy was summarized as moving away from expressing a "distaste for the particular corporation's products . . . [to] the manner in which the particular corporation conducts its business."

The recommended tactic for exercising a new level of corporate responsibility was not disposing of securities but applying "economic leverage through the most effective use of proxies." A proxy committee would review all company or shareholder resolutions on the ballots for corporation meetings that addressed an issue of "social consciousness." A process was established for taking a position on each such resolution and selecting representatives to the respective corporate meetings.

This process was the modest beginning for one division of the Board of

Missions that evolved into a major program of advocacy for the denomination. The most effective engagement in addressing social injustices through strategies of corporate responsibility was the churches' campaign to end apartheid in South Africa, details of which were described previously in this history.

The major divisions of the Board of Global Ministries became founding members of the ICCR. This body orchestrated an ecumenical witness for the churches wishing to exercise a more faithful stewardship of their holdings in corporate ownership. Collectively, the members of the ICCR identified issues and developed strategies for employing their economic leverage on companies to effect corporate and social change.

Florence Little, a treasurer of the Women's Division and then the World Division, was assigned to oversee the Board's early corporate responsibility activities. According to Little, the Board engaged corporate management on issues of economic justice, "Because we believe that God created, sustains and redeems His [*sic*] people; because we believe that we, as followers of Jesus Christ, have a responsibility to live the whole of our lives in love and concern for justice and humanity for all peoples; and because we believe the Church Universal is God's representative in society."[45]

In the trying process of dialogue with companies doing business in South Africa, Little always looked for the silver lining. While many church-sponsored stockholder resolutions went down to defeat at shareholder meetings because of the opposition of corporate management, she took credit for prompting these corporations to begin "thinking about their operations in Southern Africa and to decide whether to oppose the resolution." Some corporations began to comply with voluntary disclosure of information requested about their management policies and employment practices. Listing the names of each company, Little would recite for the Board members the responses received to each of their requests/demands. She commended those that reported even small achievements and did not overlook calling public attention to those with disappointing results.

By 1972, General Conference bought into the corporate responsibility strategy by mandating the Council on Finance and Administration to develop guidelines for investments by all general church funds. The proposed guidelines focused on international involvement, military contracts, the environment, consumerism, and employment practices. The

Social Principles of the church provided the historical and theological basis for their work. Enforcing the guidelines was not an easy route. The General Board of Pensions, with the largest investment portfolio, maintained the "prudent person" principle for investing, which focused primarily on increasing the returns. Gradually it submitted to public pressure from participants and structured portfolios for individual investment that featured firms with strong records on ethical business practices and social consciousness. And the Board of Pensions became an influential participant in the shareholder strategies of the ICCR.

In a 1978 report to GBGM on the first ten years of corporate responsibility activity, Little identified a range of issues for public witness and advocacy: children's welfare through responsible marketing and utilization of infant formula; human rights/social justice and equal employment opportunities; labor practices and policies within companies; apartheid in South Africa — asking for the withdrawal of U.S. companies from South Africa until the system was changed; honoring sanctions against Rhodesia/Zimbabwe; bank loans to South Africa; and redlining in the U.S.[46]

Immigration Reform and Protection of Immigrant Rights

The United Methodist Committee on Relief (UMCOR) has a long and distinguished history of involvement in refugee resettlement programs. Dating back to its founding in 1940 in response to massive displacement brought about by the Second World War, UMCOR has invited congregations to host families and individuals seeking to re-establish their lives in U.S. communities under their sponsorship. In the years since, regional conflicts, repressive governments, and deteriorating economies have produced a permanent global refugee population estimated between sixteen and twenty million people.

UMCOR has assisted refugees in surviving in temporary quarters and enabling them to return to their homelands as soon as conditions permit. Some refugees, fearing persecution by repressive governments or hostile communities, sought asylum in a friendly country. In the U.S., a complicated and expensive legal process has been designed to discourage asylum applications. And because the process was particularly vulnerable to political exploitation, advocacy for asylum seekers has become a primary occupation of the Refugee Concerns office of UMCOR. Lilia V. Fernandez, executive secretary of the UMCOR office and a Cuban expatriate, was the principal resource for this highly specialized mission of The UMC during this period.[47]

At the conclusion of the Vietnam War, the U.S. Government urged compassion and leniency on the part of southeast Asian governments affected by the arrival of boatloads of refugees fearing their safety under the new government. By 1980, flotillas of Cubans and Haitians escaping repressive governments began arriving in south Florida. Guatemalans and Salvadorans seeking safe haven in the U.S. from military juntas and private armies began crossing over the porous Río Grande border.

To get control of the situation, the U.S. Congress passed the Refugee Act of 1980, establishing quota ceilings for the reception of refugees from various countries or regions. Geopolitical and racial interests were clearly reflected in establishing the quotas. For instance, Africa, with the largest number of the world's refugees, received the smallest percentage (2.14 percent) of the 140,000 approved for admission to the U.S. for refugee status in 1982. Countries in Asia, on the other hand, were given a higher 7.43 percent of the total number admitted.

Aggressive law enforcement compounded the hardships. The Reagan administration, followed by its successors, instituted a policy of interdicting makeshift vessels carrying Cubans and Haitians hopeful of making it to harbor in the U.S. and returning them to their homelands. Many became victims of storms and seas at high tide. In 1994, at the height of a massive deportation by the Cuban government that included convicted criminals and social outcasts, U.S. immigration authorities placed a large number of the new arrivals in detention centers. Because there was no limitation on the term of immigrant detentions and most were held without access to legal representation, the centers functioned as prisons for long-term incarcerations. Strict border enforcement policies were implemented in the Southwest to halt the exodus of Salvadoran and Guatemalan refugees. Many were undaunted only to try again but assumed even greater risks and paying a higher price to the "coyotes" who would illegally escort them over the border.

Different treatment awaited "illegals" who were apprehended in the U.S. after successfully entering the country. The anti-Communist foreign policy interests of the U.S. Government were reflected in the larger number of Cubans admitted through the asylum process as political refugees. Those fleeing the right-wing Haitian dictatorships, either the Duvalier regime or the leadership that deposed the first popularly elected President Jean Bertrande Aristide, were generally declared "economic refugees" and sent home to face certain recriminations. Charges of racism were frequently leveled against the actions of the Immigration and Naturalization Service (INS) of the government.

Advocates of fair and equitable administration of justice sought relief from the INS repatriation practices through legal restraining orders. In January 1992, a Supreme Court ruling lifted the temporary ban on repatriation, and the government was free to begin deporting the more than 10,000 Haitians who were detained at the Guantánamo naval base. The Women's Division endorsed a resolution from the Church World Service and Witness unit of the NCC taking exception to the ruling. They called for the U.S. to suspend "forced repatriation of Haitian boat people" and urged "fair, consistent, generous and expeditious consideration of all requests by Haitians for asylum."[48]

Of the 40,000 Haitian refugees indicted in twelve months, fewer than 10,000 were permitted to pursue asylum in the U.S.[49] Those "screened in" to the U.S. were accepted on the condition that they would apply for political asylum. While refugees from other countries were granted entry to the U.S. with full refugee status, adjustable to permanent residency after twelve months, the Haitians' status required a detailed administrative and legal procedure. Sponsors, such as Church World Service and UMCOR, had to assure the Department of Justice that asylum applications would be filed and find representation for the applicants.

All immigrants to the U.S., whether undocumented or legal, faced new restrictions in the 1996 Illegal Immigration Reform and Immigrant Responsibility Act. The "hard line" legislation made deportations easier by redefining felonies as one of the grounds. It made it more difficult for undocumented immigrants to seek adjustment in their status without a lengthy period of removal from the country to complete a reapplication process. It made family reunions more difficult by raising the income level of sponsoring family member to 125 percent of the federal poverty level (i.e., over $20,000 for a family of four). It introduced new health requirements for immigrant visas, including mandatory vaccinations with medicines unavailable in certain countries. It made the process for declaring asylum more demanding by initiating interrogation within forty-eight hours of detention by a single immigration officer who was the sole arbiter of the appeal. Moreover, the law prohibited the federal courts from holding the INS accountable in discretionary matters related to deportation. And the act addressed the political "hot button" issue for immigration reform by increasing the number of patrolling officers along the border with México by a thousand.

The effect of the new legislation was felt immediately in an enforcement crackdown on immigrant communities. There were increased arrests and utter confusion. Immigration services and local attorneys were overwhelmed by requests for assistance. UMCOR hastened to initiate a new program called Justice for Our Neighbors. UMCOR provided training and technical assistance in immigration counseling to local churches in affected communities. Members of churches accompanied immigrants to INS offices. In cases where English was a second language, they helped with letter writing and found interpreters to present their cases in English. The church members provided immigrants a needed buffer from the harsh realities of U.S. political life, but they were also educated and have chosen to become advocates for justice in the administration and revision of repressive laws. They embraced the spirit if not the letter of the teachings of the United Methodist Council of Bishops, who in 1988 issued an official statement of concern to United Methodists in the U.S.:

> We invite all those whose hearts are as ours to join hands with us in declaring our uncompromising intention to welcome the sojourners in our midst and to walk with them toward our mutual fulfillment as human beings. We pledge ourselves to know them, their circumstances and needs; to love them, to embrace them and their struggle; to bid them warm welcome to our communities, religious and civil, for as long as is necessary, or as they should decide to remain. . . . Fully to love the sojourners, acting justly on their behalf, challenges the ultimate commitments and fundamental values of the sociopolitical and economic systems of which we are all a part. The church cannot easily extricate itself from those unjust systems and wash its hands of the problems. The United Methodist Church can act justly within the systems by challenging them through the management of its considerable resources, and through advocacy of foreign and domestic policies that value human welfare above a narrow concept of national security.[50]

While monitoring federal legislation and contracting with the government for managing refugee resettlement projects on a national basis was accomplished through such ecumenical and denominational entities as Church World Service and UMCOR, local churches were the agents of the church's mission and ministry to uprooted and displaced persons. This partnership between a general agency and local churches was yet another illustration of utilizing the connectional structure of the denomination to accomplish its mission. Seldom have so many in the church been asked to enter upon a ministry of direct compassion and completed the journey with a mastery of a complex system that both protected and frustrated the exercise of individual freedoms under law.

Environmental Justice

"Insofar as the Church is committed to men and women becoming more fully human, it cannot justifiably remain indifferent to [human] acts which ravage nature and upset delicate ecological balances." With these words the Board of Missions challenged the 1972 General Conference to consider seriously its mission to the preservation of the earth's resources. The rising development and use of technology to command natural resources for production and human consumption was threatening the welfare of creation. United Methodists were called upon to express a growing concern for the worsening of air and water quality, depletion of animal species, diminishing wilderness, deteriorating cities, and increasing din of noise pollution, all of which diminish the quality of human life. Suggestions for achieving a responsible "environmental stewardship" focused upon behavioral changes, from reduction of individual consumption patterns to educational advocacy in church and society, including opposing the U.S. "military's imperious claim upon our nation's resources and their willingness to risk massive environmental contamination."[51]

A resolution on "Agricultural and Rural Life Issues," adopted by the 1972 General Conference also focused on environmental issues. The General Conference action read in part:

"The United Methodist Church calls upon its millions of members across America and upon all Americans working both individually and through the structures and institutions of society—both public and private—to dedicate themselves to curbing excessive and unnecessary use and abuse of the resources of the earth, appropriately conservative uses of land, water, forests and wild life, and to a life style which expresses a spirit and a practice of responsible stewardship of spaceship earth."[52]

These statements provided a policy foundation for further engagement by the church in addressing sensitive ecological issues. At the height of the energy crisis in 1973, participants in national mission projects and programs in Appalachia urged the Board to give a stronger voice to their concerns regarding the impact of strip mining in their region. In the search for new domestic energy sources and the development of new technologies for mining for coal, vast areas of once-scenic natural resources were being decimated for limited returns. Without sufficient federal regulations, stripped lands were being left barren and mountainous areas denuded, causing erosion and flooding of local communities. The Board joined the issue by calling for federal regulation of strip mining and the restoration of all stripped land to its premined condition. In conclusion, the Board returned to a familiar theme of individual responsibility for conservation: "We call upon the American people to embark on a serious search for a life style which more adequately 'expresses a spirit and practice of responsible stewardship of spaceship earth' by checking the awesome momentum of our economy toward ever-increasing dissipation of finite energy resources."[53]

In 1975, the Women's Division entered upon a decade-long environmental international treaty development process through the UN Conference on the Law of the Sea. In 1976, the division petitioned General Conference to join the process of drafting a treaty to protect the ocean resources that comprise more than two-thirds of the earth's surface. Through the UN, the world community was expressing its growing concerns for oceanic pollution causing the extermination of aquatic life and for the insufficiency of regulations to address the advancing technology for the mining of energy and mineral resources under the oceans. The Women's Division utilized its mission education channels to inform its constituency and the membership of the church of the progress of the project. Barbara Weaver, the division's principal staff person assigned to the project, traveled to UN-sponsored meetings and conferences on the treaty facilitating the participation of NGOs and especially representatives of poor countries who were left out of the process. In 1981, a concluding conference was held to reach final agreement among participating nations and to develop a process for ratification. The landmark treaty was submitted for ratification through the constitutional provisions of member nations. The treaty was eagerly adopted after sixty nations ratified its provisions. The Women's Division was present at the final signing ceremony in Jamaica in 1982 and received special recognition from the UN for its pioneering role on behalf of United Methodism.[54]

Environmental issues were also addressed through the corporate re-

Some 63,000 gallons of oil were spilled by the tanker *Prestige* off the coast of Galicia, Spain, in 2002, causing $2 billion in damage. *(Photo by Imapress, used with permission of The Image Works)*

sponsibility agenda of GBGM. In 1989, the Board adopted the Valdez Principles, addressing the protection of nature from industrial accidents. The principles, named after the oil tanker that ran aground with devastating effects on Prudhoe Bay in Alaska, committed industries to a higher standard of safety precautions and greater responsibility for damages. The Ceres Principles addressed agricultural firms that relied upon chemical fertilizers and other high-tech production methods that depleted soil fertility and water contamination. In partnership with ICCR, the Board offered shareholder resolutions at annual corporate meetings supporting these statements on environmental protection.

The 1983 Vancouver Assembly of the WCC called upon the member churches to "engage . . . in a conciliar process of mutual commitment [covenant] to justice, peace and integrity of creation." For years the ecumenical movement addressed the sufferings resulting from poverty, lack of peace, and the misuse of the environment. Now the policymaking process of the council came to a new recognition. The Christian concern for creation was seen as having both social and ecological dimensions providing a common ground for addressing these critical issues. At the World Convocation on the theme, "Justice, Peace and the Integrity of Creation," in Seoul, Korea, in March 1990, participants made declarations that harmonized familiar elements of their claims for peace with justice and the self-renewing, sustainable character of natural ecosystems. "Today all life in the world, both present and future generations, are endangered because humanity has failed to love the living earth and the rich and powerful in particular have plundered it as if it were created for selfish purposes. . . . We resist the claim that anything in creation is merely a resource for human exploitation. . . . We commit ourselves to be members of both the living community of creation in which we are but one species, and members of the Covenant community of Christ; full co-workers with God, with moral responsibility . . . to conserve and work for the integrity of creation."[55]

The linkage of social justice and ecological justice brought a theological and ethical coherence to the missional thrusts of the council and its member churches. The trinitarian theme of "Justice, Peace and Integrity of Creation" was quickly accepted parlance in addressing the compelling issues of the closing decade of the twentieth century. It embraced concerns for a just economic order and the liberation from global debt. It accompanied calls for a true security for all nations and people living with the continuing misery of warfare. It signaled the concern for a universal protection of the earth's atmosphere and resources for the nurturing and sustaining of all life. And it emphasized the inclusive nature of community through the eradication of racism, sexism, and all forms of discrimination on both national and international levels.

In June 1992, the Women's Division and the World Division sent delegates to the UN-sponsored Earth Summit in Rio de Janeiro, Brazil. They participated in the Global Forum especially designed for NGOs to influence the proceedings of the conference. They joined with the NCC in addressing the U.S. delegation to consider that "over-development and consumption have led to a disproportionate level of resource use and destruction of our natural environment and human communities by the industrialized nations." They also joined with other representatives of the world's major religious bodies in a creative two-day interfaith prayer service. At the Rio event, an indigenous peoples' conference was also conducted, at which a declaration was issued: "We, the indigenous peoples, maintain . . . our inalienable rights to our lands and territories, to all our resources — above and below — and to our waters. We assert our ongoing responsibility to pass these on to the future generations."[56] The "product" of the official Earth Summit fell short of the high expectations of most environmentalists, but the final Earth Pledge set forth twenty-seven principles outlining the rights and responsibilities of states. It embraced such priorities as: eradicating poverty and reducing disparities in worldwide standards of living; ensuring the success of programs of sustainable development though including full participation of women; and making the polluter bear the cost of pollution.[57]

The summit also established international forest principles, which called for a universal commitment to sustainable forest management. The World Division greeted this decision with enthusiasm. The division was an owner of substantial acreage of forestlands in northern California. In partnership with the Collins Pine Company, founded by the donor family, the forests have been successfully managed under sustainable yield policies. The income was used to assist with the underwriting of missionary pensions. The Collins Company has been widely recognized for its contribution to environmentally sound forestry techniques. Following the Rio summit, the division became an active member (along with the Collins Company) of the international Forest Stewardship Council that had taken up the charge of implementing the Rio forestry principles.

The Women's Division established an Office of Environmental Justice and focused upon a number of practical matters for implementation throughout the membership of UMW. The division assemblies of 1994 and 1998 were governed by a policy limiting the quantity of paper and other expendable items. Recycle bins were placed in convenient locations at the assemblies and at Board meetings for recyclable paper, bottles, and aluminum cans. In 1997, the division committed itself to use chlorine-free paper for all its copying and publishing needs and to use chlorine-free products wherever possible in its offices and program facilities. Eight principles guided the division and all UMW units toward environmentally responsible activity: practice garbage prevention; recycle and buy recycled goods; maintain a zero tolerance for toxicities; avoid plastics; conserve energy; produce and consume locally grown food; use natural, safe materials; and promote the total well being of people when making purchases and planning decisions. In 1999, the division funded the development of a pilot Green Teams project, which would identify, train, and support selected UMW members to engage in intensive multiyear environmental justice advocacy efforts.[58]

Militarism

The Social Principles of The United Methodist Church reject violence and warfare as a means to resolving national and international conflicts and oppose increased military spending on increasingly sophisticated weapons of war at the expense of social priorities. Acting on that foundational premise, military adventures of all governments are brought under the scrutiny of the church. The military prowess of the U.S. Government comes under strongest judgment for its direct military engagements but also for its dominant influence in so many regional conflicts that too often threaten the security and well being of many countries where the church has cultivated strong mission or ecumenical relationships.

Vietnam Again

The stance of the mission agency of The UMC regarding U.S. participation in the Vietnam War was influenced by the Women's Division unequivocal opposition and its early call for "an immediate end of the war and an immediate end to our participation."[59] The Board's engagement of this issue was part of its commitment to the program theme of reconciliation established by the uniting General Conference of 1968, as described in the first chapter of this book.

The advocacy strategies that contributed to the development of a national consensus regarding the termination of U.S. military involvement in Vietnam were renewed in Board statements and actions in postwar reconstruction. The Indochina Task Force of the Board called upon the U.S. Government to take aggressive steps toward building "new relationships with Indochinese people and assist in the healing of the wounds of war throughout the battle-scarred peninsula." In order to facilitate the work of redevelopment agencies like UMCOR that the U.S. Government would be looking to for assistance, the Board demanded the government:

- Remove the Democratic Republic of Vietnam (DRVN) and the Provisional Revolutionary Government (PRG) from the listing of countries included in the Enemy Act.
- Explore immediately the formal recognition of the DRVN and PRG.
- Support presence of observer missions at the UN for the DRVN and PRG.
- Withdraw U.S.–imposed restrictions on use of its UN and UNICEF funds in DRVN- and PRG-controlled areas.
- Support congressional proposal for humanitarian aid.
- Support pending legislation concerned with amnesty.
- Permit no further U.S. military intervention in Vietnam.
- Lift travel restrictions to the U.S. of religious, cultural, and scientific groups.[60]

The children left as orphans of the Vietnam War were vulnerable to aggressive activities of adoption agencies seeking to fulfill requests for placement of international children. UMCOR became active in the resettlement of Amerasian children, the offspring of U.S. soldiers and Vietnamese or Cambodian nationals. A review of the circumstances in which many of the children were removed from Vietnam during the turbulent period of the conclusion of the war revealed violations of international treaties protecting the rights of children. Some of the adopted children were taken without consent of parents or guardians. The Board agreed to "assist in the litigation on behalf of Vietnamese children in the United States who wish to return to their extended families in Vietnam and Cambodia." The Board further urged the U.S. Congress not to seal the identities of Indochinese children brought to the U.S. until authorities in Vietnam completed their investigations and all appeals were heard.

The Board supported the resettlement of Indochinese refugees in the U.S. and the facilitating roles of UMCOR and Church World Service in providing services to an estimated 45,000 individuals. The action was qualified by cultural sensitivities stating: "Every effort be made to resettle those refugees who so desire, in countries which more nearly resemble climatic and cultural conditions of the countries from which they came, before resettlement in the United States is decided on." The Health and Welfare Division of the Board filed an *amicus* brief on behalf of the Vietnamese children brought to the U.S.

The Board also endorsed a cooperative approach to redevelopment efforts in Vietnam. The Fund for Reconstruction and Reconciliation in Indochina managed by the WCC would be the channel through which mission resources of The UMC would be directed. Dr. Aaron Tolen of Cameroon, vice chair for the fund, told the Board that the fund, administered by a diverse body of church representatives from the region, would "not do things for the Indochinese but to support what they choose to do for themselves." And further, "As the fund is for reconstruction and reconciliation none of the factions concerned are excluded. The ability to bring all factions together in discussion has been a witness for reconciliation."

The Board took a strong stand on the need for general amnesty. "We believe that in order to obtain genuine reconciliation within our country, a broad and general amnesty is required, without qualifications or conditions, for all who are in legal or other jeopardy because of the war in Southeast Asia. This we affirm and to this we pledge our support." Through a Working Group on Vietnam Generation Ministries of the NCC, national mission representatives worked diligently on pressing for reconciliation with a host of Vietnam era constituencies. They included thousands of war resisters and military deserters and also an estimated half-million Vietnam veterans with less-than-honorable discharges. Addressing problems of discrimination (minorities were a disproportionate percentage of veterans), unemployment, imprisonment, drug addiction and mental illness occupied their attention. President Gerald Ford's "clemency" or "re-entry" program progressed slowly and was unsatisfactory for many war resisters to accept. Without a full amnesty, all persons in legal jeopardy would require a time-consuming and expensive case-by-case process of support and advocacy.

The tactics of warfare employed in Vietnam also came under the scrutiny of the churches. The NCC investigated the use of chemical agents, in particular a substance known as Agent Orange. A wide range of serious physical and psychological ailments were attributed to the chemical, which was released in order to destroy natural ground cover so the U.S. military could better observe enemy movements and targets from the air. When evidence of chronic symptoms of illness of U.S. veterans and allies deployed in Vietnam was presented to agencies of the U.S. Government, there were immediate denials of responsibility. At the same time, manufacturers were asking the government to liberalize environmental protection legislation to accommodate future production of the chemical weapon. With NCC coordination, the churches adopted resolutions and mounted support for a "complete and permanent ban on the use of toxic herbicides and related chemicals." They called for "both government and independent studies to determine the symptoms of, and possible treatment for, the effects of these chemicals . . . on persons exposed to them."[61] In addition to pressing the government for a fair hearing of the facts, GBGM also entered into dialogue with producers of Agent Orange, especially the Dow Chemical Company. At the Dow headquarters in Midland, Michigan, local United Methodists were briefed on the position of the Board and entered into a heated and controversial discussion of issues. While the witness in the public and corporate sectors continued, churches were encouraged to work with local veterans' groups and to provide pastoral care and counsel to families of those affected.

Military Spending and Military Interventions

Federal budgets for the U.S. Government in the early 1980s placed an emphasis upon the Reagan administration's platform of strengthening the military. New expenditures were proposed for the development of highly sophisticated missile systems and the upgrading of other basic military hardware. These new expenditures, aimed at subsidizing an overfed defense industry, were to be offset by reductions in human services, such as Medicaid, food stamps, unemployment compensation, Aid to Families of Dependent Children, and the Comprehensive Employment and Training Act. Many of the national mission institutions serving low-income communities affected by the proposed cutbacks were hard pressed to provide supplemental services. The Board took exception to the military priorities of the new administration and warned against balancing the budget at the expense of the poor. "We urge balancing the Federal budget by converting our economy from one based on military research, development and production to one that is based upon peacetime needs of people, e.g., food, transportation and social services."[62]

The moves to build up the U.S. military during peacetime sent a foreboding message to constituents at home and mission partners abroad. In a proposed resolution on the subject of reinstituting the draft, the Board decried a growing dependence upon military solutions for foreign policy conflicts. "We must not permit a military response to be considered an answer to any problem. . . . We cannot risk the insanity of sending our youth to kill and be killed for oil, or a nuclear confrontation. We must now multiply our efforts to seek non-violent, non-military methods to secure justice, peace and reconciliation among the nations of the world."[63]

The Board pointed to conflicts in Central America where the churches were actively supporting the liberation struggles of their people from the forces of oppressive governments and demanded the cessation of any further U.S. military assistance for the regimes in El Salvador, Nicaragua, and Guatemala. To draw further public attention to conflicts in the region, the Board assisted a delegation of United Methodist bishops to travel to these countries (previously discussed in chapter 2). The delegation was hosted by the bishops of Methodist churches in Latin America and invited to enter into dialogue with church members and local community leaders. The bishops' statements and findings criticized U.S. Government policies. They were, in turn, subject to the criticism of organized political groups in the church who frequently complained about a United Methodist leadership bias for liberation theologies and causes. Their criticism took the same tone as a rather notorious U.S. State Department internal report known as the "Santa Fe Document," which blamed the churches for supporting and encouraging Latin American liberation movements.

Defending Policy Statements against Criticism

Prominent among the groups reacting to denominational engagement in U.S. social and foreign policy matters was the Washington-based Institute for Religion and Democracy (IRD). Funded largely by private foundations that supported conservative Republican policies and candidates, the leadership was a self-appointed group of political pundits with a church agenda. It recognized the significance of the voice of the churches in shaping public policy debate but disagreed with what it perceived to be a liberal slant. The IRD hired its own stable of analysts to counter the positions of mainline churches. But their public relations strategy was a constant stream of heavy-handed critiques of church policy statements and allegations that church agencies had abused church donors' intent by funding political causes and groups. The IRD became especially active whenever denominations met in legislative sessions and was sometimes successful in getting resolutions of its own authorship before these bodies for consideration. A conservative and partisan bias in the IRD political perspectives was easily discerned and readily dismissed in most discussions of the importance of encouraging a global Christian citizenship. Moreover, its proclivity for a pejorative branding of thoughtful church policy statements with claims of Christian infidelity wore thin. During the decades of the 1980s and 1990s, tension, more than enlightenment, was rising in the church constituency and the stakes increasing for those who sought to give leadership on controversial issues of human rights and public policy.

Conclusion

The resolutions and position papers prepared for adoption by The UMC or its agencies represented the social policy platform of the denomination. The process was more than an exercise in theoretical or academic polemics. The issues were grounded in the life experience of its globally diverse program constituency and leadership. Their articulation by the church gave voice to the voiceless communities of poor and oppressed people the church was seeking to serve.

The effectiveness of such teaching and advocacy required "walking the walk" as well as "talking the talk." Efforts at discrediting the church's advocacy fell silent when confronted by the extensive program experience of the denomination in social service ministries. Ministries of advocacy took root in the teachings of John Wesley that there is no holiness but social holiness.

When they need to help the church membership understand the urgency of the issues it addressed, however, advocates were vulnerable to relying too heavily upon "talk." Only as church members experienced the nature of the witness and the strength of the service of their denomination's ministries among the last and least of the world's population would they begin to appreciate its calls for seeking justice and harmony in the world. Bringing about this reality required new models of education that promoted awareness to the neighbors' sufferings. As previous generations perfected their skills at defining issues, the next generation in mission leadership must, it seemed, focus its efforts at communicating the vision of a new world in Christ by sharing the journey with those whom its church has joined in the struggle to make the vision real.

Communication begins with listening. Constituencies among the global membership of The UMC were still waiting to be heard. Among them were the many who had been on the receiving end of the church's mission and had yet to be recognized as full partners in witnessing to Christ's mission. United Methodist mission partners had stories to tell about how Christ's transforming work was evident within their communities. It was only when the quality of the church's witness in each place was declared and understood that The UMC would begin to experience the true nature of a global church. In time, the church will no doubt employ modern global communications technologies to invite the whole church into the process of witnessing to God's coming reign. The question remains, will it have the patience and wisdom to discern the good news expressed in diverse cultures and languages?

CHAPTER 12

A Survey of North America

*I*N RESPONSE TO the 1988 General Conference of The United Methodist Church (UMC), the general agencies and conferences of the church prepared for the observance of the quincentennial of the Columbian expedition to the hemisphere by declaring the year 1992 a "Year of a New Beginning." In a resolution prepared for the General Board of Global Ministries (GBGM), the thrust of a Christian observance of the historical moment was a call to confession:

> Because of our biblical faith and our social principles, United Methodists cannot ignore the fact that the events which started five hundred years ago were not a "discovery" but a conquest, not so much an exchange of cultures as an invasion by an occupying force, not so much a bringer of civilization as an imposition by force of a foreign culture and values on peoples who already had their own civilizations, history, culture, languages, and values. . . . We cannot ignore that the five centuries since Columbus's arrival have left a legacy of violence and unjust socio-political and economic/ecological systems in the western hemisphere which has oppressed especially women, children, indigenous peoples, and people of African descent.[1]

Officially, United Methodism was awakening to its moral responsibility for a history in which the churches were complicit with the aims of the conquerors: "Unfortunately, the role of the churches in these events was ambiguous at best. Evangelization provided the excuse for the domination of indigenous peoples and Africans and for the destruction of their culture and religion. Nevertheless, evangelization did take place, in spite of the manipulation of religion for their own purposes by the colonizers. The power of the Gospel of Christ to transcend human sinfulness was able to raise prophetic voices that denounced injustice and worked to alleviate the conditions of the oppressed. Still centuries later, Protestant denominations divided the tribes among themselves just as the colonial powers had earlier divided the land."

The context for mission in North America remained a society based upon the myth of cultural, racial, and religious superiority. If a new beginning were to occur, it would mean "turning away from past practices and habits based on exploitation, racism, and injustice. . . . [and] affirming, respecting, celebrating and seeking reconciliation with cultures other than those which are dominant in our societies, with particular attention to indigenous groups."[2]

Inclusiveness

The preferred internal strategy for The UMC to achieve this goal has been twofold — policy modifications and program priorities. The institutions of Methodism were creatures of the dominant culture and controlled by it. As minorities found their voice and demanded representation, policies aimed at ensuring inclusiveness were adopted. The general membership formula for general agencies of the church was one-third clergy, one-third laymen, and one-third laywomen. Among the pool of nominees from the jurisdictional conferences were to be a sufficient number of racial/ethnic members (Asian Americans, African Americans, Hispanics, and Native Americans) for them to compose 25 percent of the final membership selection. This reform was only "recommended," not mandated, but the *Discipline* provided latitude for achieving an inclusive membership. It permitted the selection of between five and twelve additional members for each agency to "perfect the representation of racial and ethnic minority persons" (also other categories — youth, young adults, older adults, and persons with handicapping conditions).[3]

While the guidelines for inclusiveness made the nominating and selection process for the general agencies more complex, The UMC was beginning to catch a glimpse of the multicultural institution it was becoming. Elections of a greater number of racial/ethnic and women members to the Council of Bishops added to the credibility of the commitment to an inclusive church. The continuing struggle with fulfilling and maintaining this commitment through proactive, antiracist strategies and policies is documented elsewhere in this volume. Only the persistent monitoring

The movement to provide access to persons with handicapping conditions led to improvements like the opportunity for them to worship, as these persons were doing at a San Antonio church in 1979. *(Photo courtesy of UM Archives and History)*

and challenging of the inherited behaviors of institutional racism served the mission of an inclusive church in the North American context.

Policies adopted by the general church would provide needed corrective measures in representative decision making, but program priorities were required for the rest of the connectional church to position itself to address the promised "new beginning" in respecting and receiving the blessings of persons of all cultures into the life and mission of The UMC. The missional priority on Strengthening and Developing Racial and Ethnic Local Churches is also recorded elsewhere in this volume. This program commitment has been widely respected by other Protestant churches in North America which have yet to gain a membership stake among population groups other than the descendants of traditional white, Euro-centered groups. It successfully focused on each of the individual racial/ethnic groups in the society that were experiencing either natural growth or an increase by immigration. The appropriateness of the homogeneity principle[4] of church growth, so often criticized when employed by mission organizations of the dominant white church culture, seemed to be readily accepted when working with oppressed groups or first-generation immigrant populations where language was a major issue in developing local communities of faith.

Multi-ethnic Ministries

As urban communities of North America became increasingly diverse, The UMC learned how to conduct a multicultural ministry. Families from many cultures were converging and investing in the neighborhoods of the great metropolitan areas. They were not showing any signs of submitting to the notion of assimilating into one dominant North American culture but favored instead keeping their ethnic identities intact.

United Methodist congregations in most multi-ethnic neighborhoods have struggled to maintain their existence. They have been part and parcel of these communities as they have weathered changes in original ethnic stock followed by declining economic vitality, housing conditions, public education, and other services. Pastoral appointment-making lacked a strategy for effective ministry in these contexts. They were viewed as "transitional communities" in which pastoral appointments either reflected the past no longer relevant or the future that had not yet taken hold. Too many ill-equipped pastors appointed to churches in such neighborhoods have concluded that their placement must be some form of punishment.

Strategies for ministry in the new multicultural communities were emerging by the end of the millennium. A growing number of pastors were choosing ministry where there was a strong potential for developing racially and ethnically diverse congregations. They were becoming part of a growing network of clergy and lay leaders who had experienced the blessing of the rich variety of spiritual gifts laid on their church altars by persons from a host of different cultural backgrounds. Some found as many as thirty or forty different nationalities in a single church community. A large percentage of the membership of these congregations comprised the sons and daughters of immigrant parents and the first generation in their families to be raised from childhood to maturity in the North American context. Because they were fluent in English and acculturated to the institutions of society, they did not require ethnic-language services of worship. Because they had not sacrificed the values of their ethnic upbringing, they chose to worship in settings where their distinctive cultural identity was valued and could be freely shared with persons from other cultural backgrounds.[5]

GBGM cultivated a linkage group of leaders of multi-ethnic congregations through the sponsorship of seminars, workshops, and an interactive computer network. In itself, the leaders in this group represented a new expression of the diverse nature of Christ's universal church. According to staff member Douglas Ruffle, "They are clearly committed to building churches of many cultures seeking their unity in Christ." The gathering of these congregations benefitted from a theological foundation, not simply an accident of anthropology or the practice of a given methodology. The multicultural church became "a foretaste and instrument of the coming reign of God . . . not to be equated with the kingdom, but . . . as a sign that points to it . . . a community that is an active agent in bringing about the justice and mercy that God intends for all creation."[6]

Multi-ethnic worship gatherings reflected the diversity of the whole people of God and became the occasions for celebrating the gift of unity:

> On a Sunday morning, Rebeca Trujillo was preaching at All Nations United Methodist Church. Rebeca chose the 23rd Psalm for the scripture lesson from which to preach. When she began, she looked across the congregation and saw a mix of people from over thirty nations and as many colors as Noah's rainbow. In this English speaking worship service, she invited her hearers to remember the opening lines of this most familiar Psalm. "When I was a child," said Rebeca, "I learned the words, 'El Señor es mi pastor, nada me faltará.' What other languages can we use to say these same words?" "The Lord is my Shepherd, I shall not want," said Bernice. "I learned that in Nebraska, where I grew up." Others began chiming in, reciting the famous line in Chinese, Tagalog, Urdu, Greek, French, Xona, and Twi. There were many languages, but one verse from the Bible held in common. After several more people shared, several in the congregation stood and began to applaud in what became an explosion of supportive, happy, celebrative affirmation that though they were many, they were one.[7]

Some treated the concept of "multiculturalism" as just another trend aimed at preserving any number of social institutions. Members of the United Methodist multi-ethnic network viewed their congregations as reflections of the New Testament disciple community described in Scriptures as a prophetic minority. They fulfilled a prophetic function within the institutional church by offering a contrast to the well-worn traditional patterns of life and worship among culturally homogenous groups of Christians. Theirs has been a spiritual journey of discovery through sharing differences and celebrating their newfound common life in Christ.

They have suffered the discrimination and disregard of the institutions of the society's dominant culture and have chosen a new form of community with interethnic sensitivities and the biblical concept of social justice. It may be the sign of fulfilling of The United Methodist mission commitment to make new beginnings at the turn of a new quincentenary or a new millennium in the Northern Hemisphere.

CHAPTER 13

The Mission Journey toward
a Global Church

Every local United Methodist Church has global connections and must recognize these connections. The grace discovered in Christ makes necessary a truly global vision and mission. . . . United Methodism enters its third century pursuing a vision. We sing with remembrance and anticipation, "'Tis grace has brought [us] safe thus far, and grace shall lead [us] home."[1]

$\mathscr{A}$T THE CLOSE of the twentieth century, globalization had become both a major fascination and frustration. The world community had been brought closer together by technologies of travel and communication, yet still had not found community. A global marketplace had emerged through the successful, however exploitive, ventures of large multinational corporations. An international economic order was ruled by global institutions without democratic representation. News and entertainment were broadcast around the globe at the sponsors' discretion. International crime syndicates and terror networks heightened international concern and anxiety.

Since every aspect of human life seemed to be discovering a global dimension, it was not unexpected to find The United Methodist Church (UMC) engaged in deliberations over a "global church." The UMC needed to discuss how to appropriate fully its missionary outreach into its organizational life. For many, the answer is structural. The most recent effort at reorganizing the denomination around global parameters was rejected by the 2000 General Conference. Similar discussions about a worldwide form of Methodism emerged from the Commission on the Status of Methodism Overseas of The Methodist Church and were placed on the agenda of the World Methodist Council by the General Conferences of The UMC in 1968 and 1970. The issue was dropped because this voluntary association of Methodist bodies did not see itself taking on the burden of reorganizing as a worldwide denomination.

For many church leaders, the aim of global restructuring of The UMC will successfully address what they see as a "disconnect" within the connectional family. There are various interpretations given to this general diagnosis, but when it comes to the global family it reveals the latent desire to orchestrate a reunion with those former mission churches that chose autonomy in the last several decades. For many of these churches, autonomy was a culmination of the maturation of the mission movement, which gave them birth and nurture until they were able to take on a life of their own. Forces of history, not only issues of denominational polity, fostered this freedom movement by the young churches.

A brief synopsis of the journey of these churches may help inform contemporary conversations about connectionalism and the global nature of The UMC as it is now experienced and what it may become.

The Journey toward Autonomy

The first three of the U.S.–related Methodist churches to seek their independence received their wish in 1930. The Brazil church wanted to elect its own bishop. The church in México responded to politically inspired national constitutional amendments on separation of church and state restricting foreign intervention in church affairs. Korean Methodists wished to unify mission from the two missionary branches of U.S. Methodism (North and South) in their country under a single Korean-led church, created in 1930 also. In addition, in Japan, during the Second World War, the government sought to control foreign religious groups and created a union of Protestant churches (the Kyodan) that was voluntarily ratified in the postwar period.

In 1948, General Conference created a quadrennial committee, the Commission on the Structure of Methodism Overseas (COSMOS), to perfect the structural arrangements of The Methodist Church to the conferences established through the historic mission outreach of the church.

The process of autonomy was provoked by the rising aspirations of churches that accompanied the dramatic rise of nationalism during the post–World War II period. A host of new nations, especially in Asia and Africa, emerged from the suffering of wartime destruction and domination. The virulence with which they threw off the vestiges of military authority and colonial control should have been anticipated. New nations were defined by new beginnings with new leaders in charge. Churches would soon make similar claims. Methodists in the Philippines, Burma (now Myanmar), Pakistan, and Liberia were among the first to consider an autonomous status to reflect their newfound spirit of nationalism. When General Conference responded by liberalizing the disciplinary provisions for the direct election of bishops from among national church leaders, Liberia and Philippines remained within central conference structures. Others chose autonomy.

Prompted by numerous requests for autonomy from churches under the central conference structure, the General Conference of 1964 instructed COSMOS to engage in a well-planned consultative process aimed at bringing specific recommendations to the 1968 General Conference.

"Autonomy" was the most definitive and compelling issue challenging the order of the church. COSMOS struggled with how to define and then how to court churches with ambitions for autonomy. Commissioners recognized the inadequacy of existing church structures in the face of changes taking place in the world: "Our structures are vulnerable to the danger of paternalism and over-dependence, thus impeding growth toward inter-dependence."[2]

From Latin America, the committee members heard voices translating autonomy into power to make decisions at local, national, or regional levels of the churches. From Africa, the appeal was for recognition of the legitimate right to elect leadership.

For the several conferences moving toward the structural option of autonomy, this direction reflected a freedom akin to the basic nature of the church. A consultation sponsored by COSMOS in the fall of 1966 at Green Lake, Wisconsin, brought together 250 participants, including 150 representatives of churches in the Methodist connection from Asia, Africa, Latin America, and Europe. This consultative body concluded: "In a real sense, autonomy is not granted or legislated for a church. It is not merely a question of organizational independence. Rather the church is free and at the same time bound to God. In expressing its mission effectively in each place, an autonomous church assumes mutual responsibility and lives in interdependence with other churches."[3]

The force and lasting influence of this trend toward self-determination could not be underestimated. When asked in a survey by the Council of Bishops at the outset of their contemplation of a global church structure in the 1989–1992 quadrennium, few autonomous church leaders expressed any interest in returning to the fold of the central conferences in their regions.

The Influence of the Ecumenical Movement

At the height of the ecumenical movement, most church bodies looked to the World Council of Churches (WCC), not their own denominational structures, to express the vision of a universal church. The 1962 New Delhi Assembly of the WCC placed a premium upon visible unity of the church as expressed by *each gathering* of baptized believers in *every place*. It did not start with recognition of any confessional, doctrinal, or denominational identity. It chose to identify and define the autonomy of all Christian communions, yet joined together in one universal fellowship with full responsibility for the ministry of the whole gospel.

So convincing was this ecumenical spirit at the time that the 1966 General Conference of The Methodist Church met, it heartily endorsed a report from COSMOS that read: "In this present time we feel God calling us *out* of our Methodist separateness into new patterns of Christian unity in the USA and in the churches outside the United States."[4]

This ecumenical perspective on the manifestation of the unity of the whole church in each place energized the discussion of autonomy as the preferred option for churches of the Methodist mission tradition. The 1966 consultation recommended to COSMOS that it "affirm that the move toward an autonomous structure on the part of Methodist Churches in different parts of the world is a *welcome(ed)* [sic] development.[5]

Why was autonomy a welcome development? The commission went beyond the dictionary for its answer:

> The dictionary defines "autonomy" as the power of self-government. Within the church, this does not mean "complete independence." No church is fully autonomous in that sense, rather every church stands under the Lordship of Christ and is bound by the guidance of the Holy Spirit. It does not mean that autonomy is not present in the existing

Mortimer Arias, a native of Uruguay, became the first bishop of the Methodist Church of Bolivia. He was imprisoned for forty days after a military coup in Bolivia in 1980. Later he became dean of the Latin American Biblical Seminary in San José, Costa Rica. *(Photo courtesy of UM Archives and History)*

Methodist structures. There is a sense in which every community of Christians has "autonomy" in its own inner spiritual life and relationship with God. However, it is also clear that structures may inhibit the expression of this inner "autonomy" in the external manifestation of autonomy. It does mean that every church lives in direct relationship with God and is free to interpret for itself what the Spirit is saying to it, without the assistance of a priest (or another group of people in another place). It is each church responding to the Holy Spirit in its own locale. Perhaps autonomy is to structure what the priesthood of all believers is to the community of believers. Autonomy is not just self-government, it also involves integrity. That is, autonomy involves responsibility for one's own life. This means that the church must take seriously the question of self-support and meaningful stewardship.[6]

In the discussions of autonomy, a high value was placed upon indigeneity as a mark of the developing church. "With its roots in the soil, and a structure suited to the people, the autonomous church would be able to work and witness more effectively in its national and cultural environment."[7] Autonomy promised to "release a new spiritual vitality within the churches and make for a more effective Christian witness to their nations and to the world."[8]

Prevailing Political Realities

A vigorous debate ensued at the 1966 Green Lake consultation over the legitimacy of national influences in determining autonomy. The report of COSMOS to the 1968 General Conference concluded that autonomy for the churches "is not a retreat into narrow nationalism; it is a move into a fuller responsibility for their own life."[9] The Cold War ideology was already presenting problems for churches in various political contexts where a church could not risk being seen as "a foreign body." The Methodist Conference in Cuba argued for its autonomy along these lines. In the countries of Eastern Europe there was little or no choice in the matter. While the conferences remained members of the central conference structure, socialist governments generally took over their administration and appointed leaders of the Methodist and other "free" churches. These developments fueled the speculation that the rising political forces of the day might overwhelm autonomous churches. Bishop James K. Mathews opined: "At a time of extreme nationalism, is it wise to put aside an international fellowship? The enemies of the Gospel would not dream of such a thing. This is a principal reason I have opposed the advocacy of autonomy unless it leads immediately to effective church union in a given area. Even then is there not a danger in exchanging one form of disunity for another, that is, national for denominational? Isolated churches run the risk of becoming mere tools of nationalism."[10]

In advocating autonomy, D.T. Niles of the Methodist Church in Ceylon (now Sri Lanka) told members of COSMOS that the "safeguard" against nationalism was to be found in maintaining an international fellowship with strong regional structures: "Both autonomy and internationalism must go together. . . . Churches effective in their regions . . . are at the same time safe-guarded against the dangers of nationalism and isolation by the creation of a structure that is theologically plural."[11]

The drafting committee at the Green Lake consultation recognized that "the single most important impulse to change results from the desire for greater *freedom* for the churches. . . . They should have more power in the churches overseas to write their own statement of faith, deal with issues related to their local situations, decide the number and type of general superintendency; and develop their own *Discipline*."[12]

The autonomous church was defined in the 1964 *Discipline* as a "self governing church in whose establishment The Methodist Church assisted and with which it is cooperating through its Board of Missions." The relationship between The Methodist Church and an autonomous church were "such as may be mutually agreed on by the two churches."[13]

Economic Complexities and Self-sufficiency

Autonomy is frequently associated with the notion of self-sufficiency. Newly independent churches in the early 1970s were forced to struggle with inherited systems of mission dependence established and enforced by mission boards in the developed countries. Before many of them could create and install their own plans, many emerging independent nations became victims of the global financial crisis. Wealthy oil-producing states had money to lend at low-interest rates, and developing nations needed capital. Limits on oil production and rising prices for this valuable commodity reduced the capital that developed nations had available for international investments. Faced with rising external indebtedness and only small amounts of hard currency to repay the loans, the borrowing nations' economies spiraled down. National budgets reflected austerity conditions. Government support for social services like education and health care was eliminated and churches were expected to pick up the slack. Survival amidst scarcity became the aim of most churches. The aim of self-sufficiency soon vanished.

The need for some form of continuing support from the missions board was anticipated in negotiations for autonomy. Financial trends in The UMC changed, however, making block grants for the basic support of the churches difficult to maintain. Mission donors began to express a preference for designated giving for specific mission projects. Underwriting church budgets was difficult to promote. Donors wished to know who benefitted from their mission contributions, and local projects provided more specific information about their needs and activities than church offices. These dynamics have affected all funding relationships, whether the partner was an autonomous church or one in a central conference relationship.

The issue of the financial crisis of partner churches is addressed in chapter 11 of this volume. The burden of financial support for the growing churches in the world mission relationship of The UMC cannot be supported locally and cannot be simply passed along for the connectional relationships of Methodism to handle. The complexities of international finance and the current trends in church fund-raising for mission development require a serious review in the face of growing needs for funding and the need to achieve a genuine mission partnership rather than control.

Reflections, Learnings, and Implications

What do these developments mean as The United Methodist Church confronts the reality of a global church?

Autonomy

The movement toward autonomy was not uniform nor did it receive unanimous endorsement. The most decisive and qualitative change that autonomy introduced to the churches and their conferences was ending their subordination to the General Conference of the church in the U.S. Ironically, some have chosen autonomy but still are dependent or continue to work in a close program relationship that diminishes their self-understanding and self-determining powers. Meanwhile, others remaining in the central conference structures have been able to exercise significant autonomy in decision making and operations.

So what is meant by "autonomy"? In mission relationships, pleading independence from the authority of the progenitor shapes the quest for autonomy. More attention is given to prosecuting the offenses of the "parent church" than developing the integrity of the mission of the newly autonomous church. And little respect is given to the need for the "parent church" to realize its own autonomy. A question that needs to be addressed is whether conversations about a global denominational structure are helping or hindering the shaping of a responsible Christian witness for the UMC in the North American context.

Autonomy assumes that each church will be free to allow its context to shape its life and ministry. But if each church is shaped by social context alone, what can be said of the distinctive witness of the universal church? The catholicity of the church, not merely its local autonomy or its denominational heritage, should be the starting point for discussions of a global church. The Lordship of Jesus Christ and the gift of a universal

Emiliana Aguilar, a Mayan in Guatemala, survived violence against her family during political oppression in her country and learned to become a videographer. She used her skills to chronicle the life stories of indigenous women and worked with the late Alva Cox, a staff member of GBGM. *(Photo courtesy of UM Archives and History)*

community of faith define the true nature of the church. The Christian faith expressed within this community is marked by accountability to a call to mission service to be celebrated by its members in each and every gathering. The church thrives when it realizes its interdependence, risks being in interactive dialogue, and strives to achieve some sense of mutuality in mission among all its members.

Mission and Evangelization

There is much to celebrate in the emergence of the churches from their missionary beginnings. The fact of the matter is that for the extensive reach of the mission of the church into so many countries, the new churches were for the most part tiny minority communities. In a few places, like the Pacific, evangelization methods led to the baptism of whole communities into the Christian faith. But a concentration of missionary activity in the Belgian Congo resulted in barely 25 percent of the population being reached for Christ by the time of independence. The work of evangelization in the region of sub-Saharan Africa had hardly begun. Churches in Asia were set against majority communities of other living faiths, namely, Hinduism, Buddhism, and Islam. Free churches in Europe existed in the shadows of state churches. In Latin America the dominance of the Roman Catholic tradition proscribed evangelization activities of all Protestants. Large indigenous communities with distinctive faith traditions of their own were unappreciated and difficult to penetrate.

Methodist Church statistics gathered for the COSMOS study process reported a membership in 1965 of 475,000 in Methodist churches in thirty countries (other than the U.S.) with a total population of 856 million. That is a penetration of less than one-half of 1 percent. For some of the smaller churches, discussion of independent organizational structures were almost beyond comprehension; still, the spirit of nationalism required independence. The recognition of church autonomy along with national sovereignty was more significant than actual membership strength or organizational merit. The value of a continuing relationship to a larger community at a regional or international level would most certainly reinforce a sense of identity and offer a connection to a shared stewardship of needed resources.

Ecumenism

While ecumenism is not the force it was in the era when missionary churches were moving into independence, the spirit of unity needs to be rekindled. This is especially true where church memberships constitute only small fractions of the total population. There the urgency of a united Christian witness surfaces with greater urgency. Visible manifestation of the unity of the church is still needed to arrest the scandal of division among the members of Christ's body but also to offer a living witness to the power in its ministry for the healing of the conflicts which are tearing apart communities, nations, and churches. How will a global United Methodist structure contribute to the strengthening of an ecumenical witness?

The Role of Culture

Some see the current stirring of passions of esteem and chauvinism in the world today as a unique history-shaping characteristic of the post–Cold War period. The political ideologies of Communism and capitalism no longer bind nations to one another. They are replaced by adherence to cultural loyalties with nationalistic overtones, which have a destructive potential as witnessed in Bosnia, Serbia, Albania, Kosovo, Armenia, Azerbaijan, and Chechnya. Rwanda, Burundi, Liberia, Angola, and Sierra Leone have suffered similar consequences when manipulations of nationalist, ethnic, or tribal differences erupted into violent conflicts.

The churches of the world are not without discrete ethnic backgrounds or other particularities that require affirmation. It is too easy to be drawn into the conflicting values in our pluralistic world and not offer vision and hope. A global expression of the church will seek to understand, appreciate, celebrate, and tolerate a host of differences while faithfully assuming the requirements of a life in a larger and common covenant aimed at making a qualitative difference in the world.

The challenge to the churches is to recognize that in each culture the revelation of Christ occurs with genuinely distinctive characteristics. The church of Jesus Christ is indeed the single expression of the whole body of Christ, but in *each* and *every* place. That unity which embraces divisions of culture, tribe, nationality, and caste within the churches as well as the nations of the world must prevail. A globally connected church promises a denominational togetherness, but settling for a global organizational chart without a sensitivity to issues of cultural diversity will entertain something less than a full and vital expression of Christ's church.

Economics and a Global Structure

The mission and evangelization efforts of the church have brought it into witness and service among communities of the world's poor. And most of the world's unevangelized people are economically poor. While traditional mission strategies incorporated new converts into faith communities through programs of nurture, education, agriculture, and economic development, most national economies have failed to prosper, leaving the many mission-related churches facing financial hardship.

If the future of United Methodism is within a common global church structure, issues of economic justice within the household will most certainly dominate every discussion, from foundations of faith to policies, programs, budgets, and structures. And with conditions in a global economy producing more poor communities, the mission of a global church must embrace the struggle for justice in solidarity with the poor. A global church structure needs to offer a model of economic justice through an effective plan for the sharing of resources and authority in its policymaking domains.

It is well that there be full candor on this point, for it seems to have been the stopping point for discussions in COSMOS which were moving toward a model of the world church. Proposals were drafted for semi-autonomous churches in the regions of the world. These churches would develop their own policies in regional and annual conferences and be drawn together periodically into a world Methodist conference to work on matters of church constitution, doctrine, and order and to address issues of prophetic justice. Conversations with British Methodism and the World Methodist Council were initiated. When the subject of responsibility for funding this global vision of Methodism arose, the project seems to have been dropped. For the churches related to "American Methodism," i.e., the U.S. church, the outcome was satellite autonomy without a supportive and accountable world connection. This deficiency is totally inconsistent with the history of connectional ministry in the Wesleyan tradition. Those conferences that chose this path have a right to feel disinherited.

The Search for Distinctiveness

Conversations about the global nature of The UMC need to be more frank and begin with less grandeur. Yes, The UMC is a "global church," but as one denominational expression within the universal church, it is relatively small (though not weak) and poor (though not limited). The position of the churches of the U.S. Methodist mission heritage is often precarious. Most of these churches still live in a dependent relationship to more affluent churches in the West. But the churches are alive and in most cases growing. They have a passion for the unfinished missionary task, which, in the Methodist tradition, requires a distinctive witness in the social and political life of their countries.

The special significance given to the church is the gospel it has received. It is a gospel that is the power of God unto salvation to all who will believe. The churches called Methodist are significant not because of what they have achieved, but because of the Christ—our human destiny—to whom they point. The task of the churches is great: to make the name of Christ known to the vast multitudes that do not know or have not heeded. In articulating this message, it must be made relevant in word and deed to the vast majority of this world whose lives are hanging in the balance of the continuous turmoil of social and political life. Sufficiency for this task is not in us but in Christ alone. With this knowledge, there should be no holding back of support within the larger community of faith, however it is structured. Whenever there is lack of material resources, the churches born of poverty will always lead the whole church back to a more simple and confident faith in God. Will the church follow?

Conclusion

Discussion of a "global church" is an adventure into what the church is becoming. The forces which shaped the debate within Methodism more than thirty years ago are still identifiable but with contemporary nuances. The UMC is being given an opportunity to affirm the kind of worldwide community of faith its mission has helped shape. Its mission should also define its future shape. Its mission calling should take the discourse far beyond organizational boundaries and privileges of membership. The mission of the church cannot afford to exclude any portion of the human family. The COSMOS process was fairly domesticated, with discussions focused on a purely institutional agenda. And its membership and participation reflected the last bastion of male dominance. These parameters for a contemporary discussion of the nature of a global church are hardly sufficient.

Becoming "global" assumes an inescapable commitment to the cause of world community. The quality of that kind of community is still under construction. It is generally acknowledged that existing structures can no longer handle the growing global network of economic and technological relationships. The International Monetary Fund and World Bank are not adequately defining the global future for humankind. Global structures should help individuals and communities understand their identity as global citizens and seek to enhance their well being through a growing international interdependence. What will be the capacity of a new global church structure for contributing to the needs of the global community? To global security through gaining respect for sovereignty of nations? To systems of international law to avoid wars and develop rules for international behaviors? To an economic world order promising a balance among nations and large transnational corporations that now dominate governments and protect the markets for the benefit of the wealthy? To the protection of the fragile ecosphere as required for assuring the quality of a fully human life? If the discussions of a global church do not include consideration of these matters, they will not lead to the creation of any global significance.

Tensions will mark the experience of building a global church. The future integrity of a global church will be tested in the process of discussing and defining it. If the process is open to critique and judgment of current mission performance and organizational support, there will be a virtual

José Míguez Bonino, a
Methodist theologian at
the Instituto Superior
Evangélico de Estudios
Teológicos (ISEDET) in
Buenos Aires, argued elo-
quently for autonomy of
the South American
churches. *(Photo courtesy of
UM Archives and History)*

explosion of new insights and ideas. If this tension is not a part of the experience, the product will be a failure.

Organizational prototypes for a global UMC will be hard to develop.
Because its present organizational culture and its financial security are
based within the context of the U.S., United Methodist leaders and other
Methodist church partners throughout the world will be wary of a pervad-
ing North American center of influence throughout a proposed structure.
José Míguez Bonino, renowned Latin American theologian, Methodist
minister, and professor emeritus of systematic theology at the Instituto
Superior Evangélico de Estudios Teológicos (ISEDET) in Buenos Aires,
Argentina, warns: "This is . . . the reason why Latin American churches
opted in the 1960s for the autonomous national church model instead of
the Central Conference model. They were frustrated in their attempt to
make a church of 10,000 members function on the basis of a 400-page
Discipline written for a 10,000,000-member church with a complex structure and vast monetary resources in a nation where it enjoyed general
recognition."[14]

The mission purpose of the church in the emerging global context should be affirmed in the future structure of The UMC. For the near term it appears that the church will continue to organize for its work without a great new revelation or vision to guide it. Through prayer and dialogue a new formation of the global experience of The UMC will ultimately emerge with new form and substance. The terms of the discussion are familiar:

- autonomy/freedom;
- culture/politics/ideology;
- selfhood/self-determination/self-sufficiency;
- dependence/independence/interdependence;
- power/authority — centralized/decentralized; and
- national/international/global.

This lexicon seems to have only paradoxical importance, for the church embraces all of the above and is not limited by having to choose any of the above. The church must remain open to the work of the Spirit around and beyond the administrative and policymaking structures and authority of the church. There is a distinct possibility of not one but a pluriform approach to expressing and appreciating life together in the Methodist family of the Christian world community. By its very nature the church is a community of those who have faith in the one God who is not constrained by ideas of the moment but realizes a mission for all humanity through those who humbly and obediently follow on the journey.

[Appendix]

Church Relationships through United Methodist Mission

Abbreviations

AC=annual conference
CC=central conference
CIEMAL=Consejo de Iglesias Evangelicas Metodistas de America Latina
DRC=Democratic Republic of the Congo
GBGM=General Board of Global Ministries of The United Methodist Church
MCCA=Methodist Church in the Caribbean and Americas
PRC=People's Republic of China
UMC=The United Methodist Church

Church Name	Region	Country	Relationship
All Africa Council of Churches	Africa	Kenya	Ecumenical Council
Protestant Church of Algeria	Africa	Algeria	Ecumenical Council
North Africa District of UMC	Africa	Algeria	Central and Southern Europe CC
UMC of Angola	Africa	Angola	Africa CC
UMC of Zimbabwe	Africa	Botswana	Mission of the Zimbabwe AC
UMC of Burundi	Africa	Burundi	East Africa AC CC
UMC of Cameroon	Africa	Cameroon	Mission of GBGM
UMC of Côte d'Ivoire	Africa	Côte d'Ivoire	West Africa CC
Church of Christ in the Congo	Africa	DRC	Ecumenical Council
UMC of the DRC	Africa	DRC	Congo CC
Methodist Church in the Gambia	Africa	The Gambia	Autonomous (British Methodist)

Church Name	Region	Country	Relationship
Methodist Church in Ghana	Africa	Ghana	Autonomous (British Methodist)
The Methodist Church in Kenya	Africa	Kenya	Autonomous/Covenant (British Methodist)
UMC of Liberia	Africa	Liberia	West Africa CC
Igreja Metodista Unida de Moçambique	Africa	Mozambique	Africa Central CC
The Methodist Church in Namibia	Africa	Namibia	Autonomous (British Methodist)
UMC of Nigeria	Africa	Nigeria	West Africa CC
Nigeria Methodist Church	Africa	Nigeria	Autonomous/Covenant (British Methodist)
UMC in Rwanda	Africa	Rwanda	Mission of East Africa CC
UMC of Senegal	Africa	Senegal	Mission of GBGM
UMC of Sierra Leone	Africa	Sierra Leone	West Africa CC
Methodist Church of Sierra Leone	Africa	Sierra Leone	Autonomous/Covenant (British Methodist)
Methodist Church of Southern Africa	Africa	South Africa	Autonomous (British Methodist)
Provisional UMC AC South Africa	Africa	South Africa	Zimbabwe AC CC
UMC of Tanzania	Africa	Tanzania	North Katanga AC CC
North Africa District of UMC	Africa	Tunisia	Central and Southern Europe CC
UMC of Uganda	Africa	Uganda	East Africa AC CC
UMC of the DRC	Africa	Zambia	Congo CC
UMC of Zimbabwe	Africa	Zimbabwe	Africa Central CC
International Afghan Mission	Asia (Central)	Afghanistan	Cooperative Mission
The Church of Bangladesh	Asia	Bangladesh	Independent
Cambodian Christian Methodist Association	Asia	Cambodia	Cooperative Mission
China Christian Council	Asia	PRC	Ecumenical
The Methodist Church Hong Kong	Asia	PRC	Affiliated Autonomous

Church Name	Region	Country	Relationship
The Church of Christ in China (Hong Kong)	Asia	PRC	Affiliated Autonomous
The Methodist Church in India	Asia	India	Affiliated Autonomous
Church of South India	Asia	India	United (British Methodist)
The Methodist Church of Indonesia	Asia	Indonesia	Affiliated Autonomous
Karo Batak Protestant Church	Asia	Indonesia	Autonomous
The United Church of Christ in Japan Kyodan	Asia	Japan	Affiliated United
UMC Mission in Laos	Asia	Laos	Mission of GBGM
The Methodist Church in Malaysia	Asia	Malaysia	Affiliated Autonomous
The Basel Christian Church in Malaysia	Asia	Malaysia	Independent/Covenant
The Methodist Church of the Union of Myanmar	Asia	Myanmar	Affiliated Autonomous
United Mission in Nepal	Asia	Nepal	Cooperative Mission
Methodist Mission in Nepal	Asia	Nepal	Mission of GBGM
Korean Christian Federation	Asia	North Korea	Independent/ Ecumenical
Church of Pakistan	Asia	Pakistan	Affiliated United
UMC of Philippines	Asia	Philippines	CC
The United Church of Christ in the Philippines	Asia	Philippines	Affiliated United
Evangelical Methodist Church in the Philippines	Asia	Philippines	Affiliated Autonomous
The Methodist Church in Singapore	Asia	Singapore	Affiliated Autonomous
National Council of Churches in Singapore	Asia	Singapore	Ecumenical Council
The Korean Methodist Church	Asia	South Korea	Affiliated Autonomous
National Council of Churches in Korea	Asia	South Korea	Ecumenical Council
The Methodist Church in Sri Lanka	Asia	Sri Lanka	Autonomous (British Methodist)

Church Name	Region	Country	Relationship
The Methodist Church in the Republic of China	Asia	Taiwan	Affiliated Autonomous
UMC Mission in Vietnam	Asia	Vietnam	Mission of GBGM
Uniting Church in Australia, National Assembly	Asia/ Pacific	Australia	United (British Methodist)
The Methodist Church in Fiji	Asia/ Pacific	Fiji	Independent
Église Évangelique en Nouvelle Caledonia	Asia/ Pacific	New Caledonia	Independent
The United Church in Papua New Guinea	Asia/ Pacific	Papua New Guinea	Independent
Methodist Church in Samoa	Asia/ Pacific	Samoa	Independent
The United Church in the Solomon Islands	Asia/ Pacific	Solomon Islands	Independent
Église Évangelique de Polynésie Française	Asia/ Pacific	Tahiti	Independent
Free Wesleyan Church of Tonga	Asia/ Pacific	Tonga	Independent
Presbyterian Church of Vanuatu	Asia/ Pacific	Vanuatu	Independent
Austria Provisional Annual Conference UMC	Europe	Austria	Central and Southern Europe CC
UMC in Belarus	Europe	Belarus	Mission of UMC Eurasia (Northern Europe CC)
Église Protestant Unie de Belgique	Europe	Belgium	Affiliated United
Bulgaria Provisional AC	Europe	Bulgaria	Central and Southern Europe CC
The UMC in the Czech and Slovak Republics	Europe	Czech & Slovak Republics	Central and Southern Europe CC
UMC in Denmark	Europe	Denmark	Northern Europe CC
UMC in Estonia	Europe	Estonia	Northern Europe CC
UMC in Finland (Finnish and Swedish)	Europe	Finland	Northern Europe CC

Church Name	Region	Country	Relationship
Die Evangelisch-methodistische Kirche	Europe	Germany	Germany CC
Hungary Provisional AC UMC	Europe	Hungary	Central and Southern Europe CC
Ecumenical Council of Churches Hungary	Europe	Hungary	Ecumenical Council
The Methodist Church of Ireland	Europe	Ireland	Autonomous (British Methodist)
Methodist Evangelical Church of Italy	Europe	Italy	Autonomous
UMC in Kazakhstan	Europe/ Central Asia	Kazakhstan	Mission of UMC Eurasia (Northern Europe CC)
UMC in Latvia	Europe	Latvia	Northern Europe CC
UMC in Lithuania	Europe	Lithuania	Northern Europe CC
Joint Church of Scotland/ Methodist Congregation of St. Andrews	Europe	Malta	Independent
UMC in Moldova	Europe	Moldova	Mission of UMC Eurasia (Northern Europe CC)
UMC in Norway	Europe	Norway	Northern Europe CC
UMC of Poland	Europe	Poland	Central and Southern Europe CC
Igreja Evangelical Metodista Portuguêsa	Europe	Portugal	Autonomous (British Methodist)
The United Methodist Church–Eurasia	Europe/ Central Asia	Russia	Northern Europe CC
Evangelical Church of Spain	Europe	Spain	Independent
Spanish Protestant Church	Europe	Spain	Independent
UMC in Sweden	Europe	Sweden	Northern Europe CC
Switzerland France AC UMC	Europe	Switzerland/ France	Central and Southern Europe CC
UMC in the Ukraine	Europe	Ukraine	Related to UMC Eurasia (Northern Europe CC)
The Methodist Church in Great Britain	Europe	United Kingdom	Concordat

Church Name	Region	Country	Relationship
Yugoslavia Provisional AC	Europe	Yugoslavia	Central and Southern Europe CC
Argentine Evangelical Methodist Church	South America	Argentina	Affiliated Autonomous
Evangelical Methodist Church in Bolivia	South America	Bolivia	Affiliated Autonomous
Igreja Metodista de Brazil	South America	Brazil	Affiliated Autonomous
Methodist Church of Chile	South America	Chile	Affiliated Autonomous
Comunidad Cristiana Metodista	South America	Colombia	Mission (UMC/CIEMAL)
United Evangelical Church of Ecuador	South America	Ecuador	Affiliated United
Guyana District Conference	South America	Guyana	Concordat MCCA
Methodist Church in Paraguay	South America	Paraguay	Mission (Igreja Metodista de Brazil)*
Methodist Church of Perú	South America	Perú	Affiliated Autonomous
Methodist Church in Uruguay	South America	Uruguay	Affiliated Autonomous
Communidad Cristiana Metodista	South America	Venezuela	Mission (UMC/CIEMAL)
Evangelical Methodist Church of Costa Rica	Central America	Costa Rica	Affiliated Autonomous
Evangelical Methodist Church of El Salvador	Central America	El Salvador	Mission (UMC/CIEMAL)
Iglesia Evangelical National Primitiva Metodista	Central America	Guatemala	Independent/Covenant
UMC Mission in Honduras	Central America	Honduras	Mission (UMC/CIEMAL)
Honduras Belize District MCCA	Central America	Honduras/Belize	Concordat MCCA

*The Methodist Church in Paraguay is a district of the autonomous Methodist Church of Brazil.

Church Name	Region	Country	Relationship
Methodist Church of México	North America	México	Concordat
Evangelical Methodist Church of Nicaragua	Central America	Nicaragua	Mission (UMC/CIEMAL)
Evangelical Methodist Church of Panamá	Central America	Panamá	Affiliated Autonomous
Panamá Costa Rica District MCCA	Central America	Panamá/Costa Rica	Concordat MCCA
Methodist Church in the Caribbean and the Americas (MCCA)	Caribbean	Caribbean	Concordat
Bahamas/Turks & Caicos Islands Conference	Caribbean	Caribbean	Concordat MCCA
South Caribbean District Conference	Caribbean	Caribbean	Concordat MCCA
Methodist Church in Cuba	Caribbean	Cuba	Affiliated Autonomous
Dominican Evangelical Church	Caribbean	Dominican Republic	Affiliated United
The Methodist Church in Haiti	Caribbean	Haiti	Concordat MCCA
Jamaica District Conference	Caribbean	Jamaica	Concordat MCCA
Leeward Islands District Conference	Caribbean	Leeward Islands	Concordat MCCA
Methodist Church of Puerto Rico	Caribbean	Puerto Rico	Concordat
Middle East Council of Churches	Middle East	Cyprus	Ecumenical
Middle East Council of Churches	Middle East	Egypt	Ecumenical
Episcopal Church in Jerusalem & Middle East	Middle East	Israel	Cooperative Mission
Middle East Council of Churches	Middle East	Israel	Ecumenical

[Notes]

Abbreviations: UMC for The United Methodist Church; GBGM for the General
Board of Global Ministries.

Board of Missions and Board of Global Ministries were titles for The UMC
mission board 1968–1972 and 1972–1976, respectively, before the adoption of "general" as an appellation for churchwide agencies in 1976.

1. Rising Expectations

1. "Partnership in God's Mission: Theology of Mission Statement," General
   Board of Global Ministries of The United Methodist Church, New York, 1986,
   pp. 10–11.
2. "A Union . . . And Much More," "New Church Born in Dallas, Largest Religious Merger in U.S. History, United Methodists Plan for Future," *Together*
   (July 1968): 6.
3. "A Union," p. 6.
4. "A Union," p. 6.
5. "A Union," p. 6.
6. "Report of the President," *Daily Journal*, Board of Missions, September 5–9,
   1968, Appendix A, p. 149. Note: *Daily Journal* was the official record of the respective boards meeting in the fall (annual) and in the spring.
7. James Forman, "The Black Manifesto," *World Outlook* (September 1969): 10–11.
   The terms "black" and "African American" are used interchangeably throughout this book.
8. The encounter between James Forman and the church agencies is described in
   more detail in chapter 7.
9. *Daily Journal*, Board of Missions, October 23–31, 1969, Appendix B, p. 60.
10. *Daily Journal*, Board of Missions, October 23–31, 1969, p. 37.
11. Comments of Galván in a presentation to the Board, *Daily Journal*, Board of
    Missions, October 21–30, 1970, p. 39.
12. Comments of Thomas Roughface in a presentation to the Board, *Daily Journal*,
    October 21–30, 1970, p. 44; Appendix J, p. 91.
13. Comments of Noley in a presentation to the Board, *Daily Journal*, October
    21–30, 1970, Appendix K, p. 94.
14. Comments of Banks in a report to the Board, *Daily Journal*, Board of Global
    Ministries, October 19–27, 1973, p. 35.

15. Comments of Robert W. Huie in a report to the Board, *Daily Journal*, Board of Missions, October 21–30, 1970, p. 32.

16. "Report of the Special Committee on Involvement of Young People," *Daily Journal*, Board of Missions, October 23–31, 1969, Appendix D, p. 61.

17. "Report of the Youth Task Force," *Daily Journal*, Board of Missions, October 23–31, 1969, Appendix E, p. 63.

18. "Report of Women's Division Highlights," *Daily Journal*, Board of Missions, September 1968, Appendix D, p. 166.

19. "Recommendations of the Ad Hoc Committee on Churchwomen's Liberation," *Daily Journal*, Board of Missions, October 20–30, 1971, Women's Division Minutes, Appendix G, p. 222.

20. Derby, unpublished report, "Where Have All the Women Gone?" p. 4.

21. "Summary Statement—Consultation on Single Women in Church and Society," *Daily Journal*, Board of Global Ministries, October 18–27, 1974, Women's Division Minutes, Appendix A, p. 308.

22. The development and impact of the missionary moratorium are discussed further in chapter 3.

23. "The Need for Structural Flexibility," a report to the Green Lake Consultation of the Commission on the Status of Methodism Overseas, October 28–November 4, 1966, Green Lake, Wisconsin, pp. 1, 2.

24. "Report of the President," *Daily Journal*, Board of Missions, October 5–9, 1968, p. 151.

25. *Daily Journal*, October 5–9, 1968, p. 51.

26. "Report of the Africa Bishops Consultation, Salisbury, Rhodesia," *Daily Journal*, Board of Global Ministries, October 10–18, 1974, World Division Minutes, Appendix G, p. 484.

27. The final section of this volume offers further reflection on the historical development of autonomous churches affiliated with The UMC for learnings that may inform the movement toward a global organizational structure.

28. *Daily Journal*, Board of Global Ministries, October 25–November 2, 1972, p. 180.

29. "Global Dialogue" (report of President Washburn and General Secretary Jones), *Daily Journal*, Board of Global Ministries, October 10–18, 1974, Appendix B, pp. 53–60.

30. "Report of the Committee on Policy and Program," *Daily Journal*, Board of Missions, October 23–31, 1969, National Division Minutes, p. 125.

31. "Report of the Associate General Secretary," *Daily Journal*, Board of Missions, October 23–31, 1969, National Division Minutes, pp. 121–122.

32. "Report of the General Treasurer," *Daily Journal*, GBGM, October 16–23, 1981, Appendix 18.

33. "Report of the President," *Daily Journal*, Board of Missions, September 5–9, 1968, p. 153.

34. "Report of World Development Task Force," *Daily Journal*, Board of Missions, October 23–31, 1969, p. 34.

35. "World Division Response to the Crisis in Black/White Relations," *Daily*

Journal, Board of Missions, October 23–31, 1969, World Division Minutes, Appendix B, pp. 263–264.

36. "World Division Response to Crisis," p. 263.

37. "Quadrennial Emphasis Report," *Daily Journal*, Board of Missions, October 23–31, 1969, World Division Minutes, Appendix C, pp. 266 ff.

38. "Report of the Education and Cultivation Division," *Daily Journal*, Board of Global Ministries, October 18–27, 1974, p. 146.

39. "1970 Annual Report — Quadrennial Emphasis," *Daily Journal*, Board of Missions, October 21–30, 1970, World Division Minutes, Appendix E, pp. 337 ff.

40. "Report of the Task Force to Experiment in Third World Awareness," *Daily Journal*, Board of Missions, October 21–30, 1970, Women's Division Minutes, pp. 265–267.

41. Stephen Rose, "O Lovable Edifices," *New World Outlook* (February 1968): 18.

42. Bonneau P. Murphy, "The House Is for God's Service," *New World Outlook* (February 1968): 17.

43. *The Book of Discipline of The United Methodist Church 2000* (Nashville: The United Methodist Publishing House, 2000), ¶ 212.1, pp. 128–129.

44. Statement on Vietnam, *Daily Journal*, Board of Missions, October 23–31, 1969, Women's Division Minutes, Appendix E, p. 246.

45. Statement on Vietnam, pp. 186–187.

46. Statement on Vietnam, pp. 186–187.

47. "Update on United States–Vietnam Relations," *Daily Journal*, Board of Global Ministries, October 17–25, 1975, pp. 108–113.

48. "Report of the General Secretary," *Daily Journal*, Board of Missions, September 5–9, 1968, pp. 155–158.

49. "Report of the Ombudsman," *Daily Journal*, Board of Missions, October 20–30, 1971, p. 45.

50. "Report of the Inter-Ethnic Task Force," *Daily Journal*, Board of Global Ministries, April 29–May 3, 1975, pp. 31–35.

51. "Institutional Racism," *Daily Journal*, Board of Global Ministries, March 16–22, 1976, p. 262.

52. "Report of the Board Task Force on Institutional Racism," *Daily Journal*, GBGM, April 26–31, 1977, p. 33.

53. "Report of the Board Ombudsman," *Daily Journal*, Board of Global Ministries, October 22–30, 1976, p. 53.

54. "Report of Committee to Eliminate Institutional Racism," *Daily Journal*, GBGM, April 10–18, 1992, p. 22.

55. Ronald G. Mitchell, missionary director of youth work in Sierra Leone and a United Methodist missionary, "Black Persons in Mission," *New World Outlook* (March 1978): 37.

56. "Report of the Inter-Ethnic Task Force," *Daily Journal*, GBGM, March 11–16, 1978, pp. 6–8.

57. "Report of the Inter-Ethnic Task Force," pp. 6–8.

58. "Report of the Committee to Eliminate Institutional Racism," *Daily Journal*, GBGM, March 7–13, 1981, pp. 26–28.

2. Latin America and the Caribbean

1. "Panel Presentation from Latin America," *Daily Journal*, Board of Missions, October 20–30, 1971, Appendix D, participants: Bishop Frederico Pagura, bishop of Methodist churches of Panamá and Costa Rica; Roberto E. Rios, superintendent of the Argentine Evangelical Methodist Church; Néstor Míguez, Argentine theology student; María Elena Reyes, executive secretary of Department of Social Action of the Methodist Church of México; the Reverend Joel Gajardo, Chilean theologian and former minister in the Presbyterian Church; the Reverend Jaime Bravo, a Bolivian Aymara Indian pastor and superintendent of the Evangelical Methodist Church in Bolivia; Father Gustavo Pérez-Ramirez, director of Colombian Institute for Social Development in Bogota, Colombia; and the Reverend Paulo Ayres Mattos, pastor of the Methodist Church in Cabo Frio State of Rio de Janeiro, Brazil.

2. "Illusion and Reality in Inter-American Relations," *Daily Journal*, Board of Missions, October 23–31, 1969, Appendix E, pp. 276 ff.

3. Conscientization is understood to be a process of bringing social or political issues to a higher level of awareness and/or to ethical judgment.

4. GBGM adopted several resolutions, including: "Human Rights in Central America" (March 1985), "Sanctuary Movement" (March 1985), "Peace Initiative for Central America" (October 1987), "U.S. Military in El Salvador" (March 1984), and "Military and Economic War against Nicaragua" (March 1985).

5. Dow Kirkpatrick, "What U.S. Protestants Need from Latin American Catholics," *New World Outlook* (September 1978): 21–24.

6. "What U.S. Protestants Need," pp. 21–24.

7. "Report from Visiting Latin American Methodist Bishops/Presidents," *Daily Journal*, GBGM, March 26–April 1, 1982, Appendix 15.

8. Christie R. House, "CIEMAL: A Church United," *New World Outlook* (July-August 1994): 30.

9. Tracy Early, "From Latin America, A Critical Look," *New World Outlook* (January 1984): 19.

10. "From Latin America," p. 18.

11. "From Latin America," p. 18.

12. Bishop Elías G. Galván, "Witnesses of Peace," *New World Outlook* (September-October 1989): 15.

13. Joyce Hill, "100 Years of Methodism in Cuba," *New World Outlook* (September 1982): 13.

14. Phil Wingeier-Rayo, "Christians in Cuba," *New World Outlook* (November-December 1993): 14.

15. James and JoAnn Goodwin, "The Methodist Church in Brazil – Living Out Liberation Theology in a New Plan for Life and Mission," *New World Outlook* (May 1986): 15.

16. Robert J. Harman, "Report to the Board of Directors," October 1994. Unpublished typescript in possession of author.

17. Gregory Beals, "The Church of the Poor," *New World Outlook* (February 1988): 28.

18. "Manifesto to the Nation," *New World Outlook* (October 1970): 499.

19. Peter J. McFarren, "Methodism in Bolivia: Interview with Bishop Rolando Villena," *New World Outlook* (July-August 1983): 18.

20. Paul Jeffrey, "Methodism in Latin America," *New World Outlook* (July-August 1988): 13.

21. McFarren, "Methodism in Bolivia," p. 18.

22. Beatriz Ferrari, "Evangelical Church of Uruguay," World Methodist Council Handbook, Lake Junaluska, North Carolina, pp. 141–142.

23. "Mission Memo," *New World Outlook* (September 1973): 369.

24. Charles Brewster, "He was Pastor to the Prisoners," *New World Outlook* (September 1974): 383–385.

25. "Critical Issues in Latin America — Chile," *New World Outlook* (October 1975): 455.

26. Raymond K. DeHainhut, "Bishop Frederico J. Pagura — Argentina, a Voice of Hope," *New World Outlook* (February 1987): 71.

27. Paul Jeffrey, "Methodist Partnership in Panama," *New World Outlook* (November–December 1992): 31.

28. B. Webber, "Methodism in Costa Rica," *New World Outlook* (March-April 1989): 77.

29. B. Webber, "Interviews with Roberto Diaz and Mortimer Arias," *New World Outlook* (July-August 1989): 38.

30. Webber, "Interviews," pp. 36–39.

31. See resolutions on Haiti by GBGM in the *Daily Journals* of October 1981, 1987, 1991, and 1993.

32. The 2004 General Conference also approved a concordat status with the Methodist Church of Puerto Rico.

33. Resolution on the Colonial Status of Puerto Rico, *Daily Journal*, GBGM, World Division Annual Meeting, October 15–23, 1991, p. 54.

3. Mission Personnel

1. "Partnership in God's Mission," p. 13.

2. Unpublished Report on the Bangkok Assembly of the World Council of Churches, January 31, 1973, available in the archives of GBGM.

3. "President's Report," *Daily Journal*, Board of Missions, September 5–9, 1968, p. 152.

4. Frederick Dale Bruner, *The Christian Century* (June 5, 1968): 751, cited in Bishop Wicke's report to the Board.

5. "President's Report," *Daily Journal*, September 5–9, 1968, p. 153.

6. Black Methodists for Church Renewal Position Paper, *Daily Journal*, Board of Missions, October 23–31, 1969, Appendix C, p. 61.

7. Ezekiel C. Makunike, "A Personal View from the Mission Field," *New World Outlook* (September-October 1990): 40.

8. Makunike, "Personal View," p. 41. Makunike recognized efforts of missionary Bishop Ralph E. Dodge, the first U.S. bishop elected by African United Meth-

odists, at developing national leadership by instituting scholarship programs for selected students to attend colleges and universities abroad. He also acknowledged the value of the contribution of mission schools: "Almost all national leaders in the post-colonial nations were trained in mission institutions. They fought to overthrow colonialism but not to overthrow the Gospel! No wonder Christianity is growing faster in Africa than in most other continents."

9. Arthur J. Moore, Jr., "Standing on the Promises 1965–1990," *New World Outlook* (September-October 1990): 17.

10. *Daily Journal*, Board of Missions, January 3–13, 1969, pp. 336–339.

11. "Recommendations of SCIMO Report," *Daily Journal*, Board of Missions, October 20–30, 1971, pp. 325–328.

12. Nacpil, "Mission but Not Missionaries," IDOC — International Documentation, #63, July 1974, p. 79.

13. Tracy Early, "A Talk with Maxime Rafransoa," *New World Outlook* (December 1981): 22.

14. "A Statement from the African Bishops of The United Methodist Church — Consultation in Salisbury, Rhodesia," *Daily Journal*, Board of Global Ministries, October 18–27, 1974, pp. 484–485.

15. "Recommendations of the Latin America Task Force," *Daily Journal*, Board of Missions, October 20–30, 1971, pp. 320–323.

16. "Rethinking the Missionary Role," *New World Outlook* (December 1987): 15.

17. "Report of World Division," *Daily Journal*, Board of Global Ministries, April 30, 1974, p. 107.

18. "Mission Resource Center Proposal," *Daily Journal*, GBGM, April 14–24, 1989, p. 6.

19. "Report of the Missionary Support Options Committee to the World Division," *Daily Journal*, Board of Global Ministries, October 17–25, 1975, pp. 612–615.

20. "Persons in Mission Report to the World Division," *Daily Journal*, Board of Global Ministries, October 18–27, 1974, Appendix D, pp. 471–478.

21. "Missionary to Us," *New World Outlook* (January 1974): 41–42.

22. George Daniels, "The Board and Me — Reflections on Ethnic Minorities in Mission," *New World Outlook* (September-October 1990): 36.

23. Tony Chapelle, "Black Community Developers," *New World Outlook* (November-December 1988): 36.

24. "10th Anniversary Resolution — Community Developers' Program," *Daily Journal*, GBGM, April 4–11, 1978, p. 9. In July 2004, the Northeastern Jurisdiction elected Marcus Matthews to the episcopacy. Matthews is a product of the community developers program, the first to be elected to this highest office of the church.

25. Betty Letzig, "Deaconesses Past and Future," *New World Outlook* (May-June 1992): 31.

26. "Reaffirming Mission at the Center of the Ecumenical Movement," Ioan Sauca, *International Review of Mission* 88 (January/April 1999): 52.

27. "Crusade Scholars 50th Anniversary Observance," *Daily Journal*, GBGM, March 28–April 5, 1995, p. 42.

28. "Crusade Scholars 25th Anniversary Observance," *Daily Journal*, Board of Missions, September 5–9, 1968, p. 166.

29. "Crusade Scholarship Committee Report," *Daily Journal*, Board of Global Ministries, October 19–27, 1973, p. 503.

30. Bill Matthews, "Fiji Crusade Scholar," *New World Outlook* (February 1980): 87.

31. "Report of Crusade Scholarship Committee," *Daily Journal*, Board of Global Ministries, October 18–27, 1974, p. 511.

32. For a description of the Kendall Program Fund, see *Daily Journal*, Board of Global Ministries, October 17–25, 1975, Health and Welfare Division minutes, p. 277.

33. "Phase I—Report and Recommendations to the Women's Division, March 1993," *Higher Education and Women in Africa*, p. 1.

34. Manuel Quintero, *Mission from the Reverse of History—A Brief History of Frontier Internship in Mission* (Geneva: Ecumenical Center in cooperation with the Latin American Council of Churches [*Consejo Latinoamericano de Iglesias*, or CLAI], 1998), pp. 8 ff.

35. Wingeier, "Recovering and Receiving the Bible," *New World Outlook* (July-August 1990): 13.

36. " . . . But, said God, hope, what a strange thing," *World Student Christian Federation Journal* (December 1995): 3.

37. Devotional message by Dr. Michael Watson, *Daily Journal*, Board of Global Ministries, October 21–30, 1970, pp. 40–41.

38. Watson, p. 41.

39. Watson, p. 41.

40. "Report on Persons in Mission," *Daily Journal*, Board of Global Ministries, October 18–24, 1974, World Division, Appendix D, pp. 476–477.

41. For an annotated biography and history, see Thomas L. Curtis, Sr., *From the Grass Roots: A History of United Methodist Volunteers in Mission* (Nashville: Abingdon Press, 2000).

42. As a mission executive, the author occasionally heard national and local church officials say, "We'll wait to see how much the volunteers accomplish before we decide about our contribution."

43. In a consultation with the Methodist Church in the Caribbean and the Americas, Board representatives were asked "Why do your teams not reflect the ethnic diversity in The United Methodist Church?" The dialogue prompted the Board to approve a policy statement on racial inclusiveness for all teams "which go out under the sponsorship of the General Board of Global Ministries." The Board also pledged its assistance to conference and jurisdictional groups in achieving this goal. See *Daily Journal*, GBGM, March 12–16, 1984, p. III 18.

44. "Health and Relief/Mission Volunteers Report of the Deputy General Secretary to the Program Area Meeting," October 20, 1998.

4. Africa

1. Investments and Southern Africa, *Daily Journal*, Board of Global Ministries, Women's Division, October 25–November 2, 1972, p. 504.

2. I. H. Bivens, "A Statement on Church Investment in South Africa," *Daily Journal*, Board of Global Ministries, March 24, 1973, Appendix L, p. 75. Bivens went on to note that "profits in South Africa range from 15 percent to 35 percent of capital investments because hundreds of thousands of Southern African blacks are forced to work or survive on the most menial wages."

3. "Resolution on Divestment and South Africa," *Daily Journal*, GBGM, October 18–25, 1985, pp. 48–49.

4. *Daily Journal*, GBGM, October 14–22, 1993, p. 39.

5. "The Transformational Role of the Church in Post-Liberation Angola," *Mission & Transformation in a Changing World: A Dialogue with Global Mission Colleagues* (New York: General Board of Global Ministries, 1998), p. 48.

6. "Why I Got into Politics — A Bishop's Testimony," *New World Outlook* (November 1976): 19–20.

7. "The Zimbabwe United Methodist Church," *World Methodist Council Handbook of Information* (Lake Junaluska, N.C.: World Methodist Council, 1997), p. 151.

8. The official listing of annual conferences at the time included "Rhodesia Annual Conference — Southern Rhodesia." Southern Rhodesia was declared "Rhodesia" in 1965.

9. Mary Collison and Don Collison, "Botswana," *New World Outlook* (March 1971): 123–128.

10. Frances Thompson, "Freedom for Mozambique," *New World Outlook* (March 1968): 17.

11. "Mission Memo," *New World Outlook* (April 1975): 160.

12. Marcella Kerr, "Free to Learn in Mozambique," *New World Outlook* (November 1975): 30.

13. Charles Brewster, "The Church in Angola Bounces Back," *New World Outlook* (January 1974): 10.

14. "Mission Memo," *New World Outlook* (October 1974): 422.

15. Edward B. Fiske, "The Church in the Congo," *New World Outlook* (June 1971): 348–349; and news article, no author, from same issue, "Bishop Withdraws Methodism from New Congolese Church," p. 414.

16. Dorothy Gilbert, "Profile of an African Bishop," *New World Outlook* (March 1974): 122–124.

17. Ralph E. Dodge, "An American Looks at Methodism in Liberia," *New World Outlook* (March 1981): 39.

18. James M. McGraw, "An Interview with Bishop Arthur F. Kulah," *New World Outlook* (March-April 1991): 19.

19. "Sierra Leone Re-union Plan Called Sacrifice of Autonomy," *New World Outlook* (February 1981): 92.

20. The establishment of these schools, as well as the EUB mission in both Sierra Leone and Nigeria, is described in J. Steven O'Malley, *"On the Journey Home"*:

The History of Mission of the Evangelical United Brethren Church, 1946–1968 (New York: General Board of Global Ministries, 2003).

21. Peter Marubitoba and Done Peer Dabale, "The UMC in Nigeria," *New World Outlook* (May–June 1994): 11–14.

22. Dean S. Gilliland, "In Nigeria, Religious Maturity Grows," *New World Outlook* (January 1977): 18–22.

23. The 2004 General Conference gave qualified approval to a petition from the Côte d'Ivoire Methodist Church to become a United Methodist Church. The approval is pending favorable action by the West Africa Central Conference. It also limits the representation of the Ivorian UMC to the 2008 General Conference and makes it assume financial support for its bishop until then.

24. Remarks made in a consultation between African church leaders and representatives of North American and European mission agency officials in Geneva, February 1995, recorded in personal documents of the author.

5. Corporate Dimensions of Grace

1. *Grace upon Grace: The Mission Statement of The United Methodist Church* (Nashville: Graded Press, 1990), p. 11.

2. Report of the General Secretary, *Daily Journal*, Board of Missions, September 5–9, 1968, pp. 155 ff.

3. Lewistin M. McCoy, "Progress Report on Quadrennial Emphasis," *Daily Journal*, Board of Missions, Biannual Meeting, January 3–13, 1969, pp. 354–355.

4. Among the cities selected were Salisbury and Freetown in Africa; Seoul-Inchon, Singapore, Calcutta, and Manila in Asia; and São Paulo, Buenos Aires, and Lima in South America. "1970 Report—Quadrennial Emphases," *Daily Journal*, Board of Missions, October 21–30, 1970, pp. 337–342.

5. McCoy, "Progress Report," p. 354.

6. "Issues in the 70s, Report of the Associate General Secretary," *Daily Journal*, Board of Missions, Biannual Meeting, January 3–13, 1969, pp. 326 ff. See the glossary for the definition of directors.

7. "Report on Quadrennial Emphasis," *Daily Journal*, Board of Missions, Biannual Meeting, January 3–13, 1969, p. 337.

8. "Report of the Interim Committee on Policy and Program," *Daily Journal*, Board of Global Ministries, March 24, 1973, p. 42.

9. Evangelization is distinguished from evangelism. The former entails a commitment to addressing the gospel to the needs of the whole person. It is more than proclamation or preaching. When churches in Latin America speak of evangelization they refer to a process of spiritual development in which believers are nurtured by the community of believers into Christian maturity and assume responsibility for the church's ongoing witness and service in the world.

10. "Tentative Indicators," *Daily Journal*, Board of Global Ministries, March 24, 1973, Appendix O.

11. "Report of Committee on Research and Development," *Daily Journal*, Board of Global Ministries, April 30, 1974, pp. 99–102.

12. "Report of Section III: Churches Renewed in Mission," World Conference on Salvation Today, World Council of Churches, Bangkok, Thailand, December 29, 1972–January 9, 1973, page 10 of unpublished section report.

13. Panel Presentation, Education and Cultivation Division, "Theological Basis of Mission," *Daily Journal*, Board of Global Ministries, October 19–27, 1973, pp. 151–152.

14. Address, *Daily Journal*, Board of Global Ministries, March 28, 1973, p. 27.

15. The formation of the independent Mission Society for United Methodists (MSUM) took place immediately before the 1984 General Conference. It was promoted as an alternative to GBGM, which the MSUM accused of failing to fulfill its primary responsibility of evangelistic mission through the sending of missionaries. This development was seen as a divisive action by the majority of the delegates to the conference, who voted in favor of a petition that reaffirmed GBGM as the "official" mission agency of the denomination. There was also strong support for the drafting of a denominational mission statement as a unifying activity that would help the church identify its foundations in the faith and its contemporary responsibility in mission. More on the role of the MSUM is presented in the rest of this chapter.

16. For the background and detailed development of the theology of mission statement, see Betty S. Gordon, "The Origin and Creation of a Theology of Mission Statement," Charles E. Cole, ed., *Initiatives for Mission, 1980–2002* (New York: General Board of Global Ministries, 2004).

17. See *Grace upon Grace*.

18. In 1972, the General Conference allocated $11,700,000 for the first year of the next quadrennium to the Board of Missions. The Board of Health and Welfare Ministries, which later became part of the Board of Missions, was allocated $491,000. The cumulative total was $12,191,000, or 55.68 percent of the $23.5 million for the World Service Fund. *Journal of the 1972 General Conference*, pp. 2029–2033. The actual amount received in 1973 was $10.9 million, about 24 percent of the Board's budget. *1976 Daily Christian Advocate, Advance Edition I*, p. 29. By contrast, the General Conference of 2000 allocated $27,393,000 to GBGM for the first year of the quadrennium, or 42.5 percent of the World Service Fund. *Daily Christan Advocate, Advance Edition*, vol. 1, p. 329, 2000 General Conference. The amount of World Service in the Board's budget for 2000 was approximately $25 million, or roughly 14 percent of the Board's operating expenditures. *Mission: A Commitment to Action, a Supplement to New World Outlook*, the 2000–2001 biennial report of GBGM, pp. 36–37.

19. The Women's Division "provided more than $40 million in total mission support in 2000," and "supported Board program and operations near or above the $20 million level." *Mission: A Commitment to Action*, p. 37. Total operating expenditures for 2001 were $174.7 million.

20. "Pastors' Consultation," pp. 172–173, *Daily Journal*, Board of Global Ministries, Education and Cultivation Division Minutes, October 19–27, 1973.

21. "Mission Statement," *2001 Program Offerings*, Scarritt-Bennett Center.

22. "Mission and Unity of the Church," *Daily Journal*, GBGM, April 14–21, 1989, pp. 36–37.

23. "R & D Committee Report, Mission Society Dialogue and Resolution," *Daily Journal*, GBGM, April 10–18, 1991, p. 36.

24. Dialogue Status Report, *Daily Journal*, GBGM, March 6–15, 1987, pp. 6–8.

25. Plenary Minutes, *Daily Journal*, GBGM, October 16–23, 1987, p. 42.

26. See Hunt, "The Challenge of Christian Mission in Islamic Southeast Asia," Charles E. Cole, ed., *Christian Mission in the Third Millennium* (New York: General Board of Global Ministries, 2004).

27. Progress Report on 10-Year Review, *Daily Journal*, Board of Global Ministries, October 22–30, 1976, Women's Division Minutes, pp. 372–374.

28. The divisions of the Board after 1972 General Conference included: World, National, Women's, Education and Cultivation, Ecumenical and Interreligious Concerns, Health and Welfare, and United Methodist Committee on Relief. Other program entities were Crusade Scholars and Mission Personnel.

29. Report of the Section of Studies and Interpretation, *Daily Journal*, Board of Global Ministries, Ecumenical and Interreligious Concerns Division, October 25–November 2, 1973, pp. 240–241.

30. *Baptism, Eucharist and Ministry* was a document issued for study and then approved as policy by the WCC unit on Faith and Order. The document provided guiding principles for member churches to recognize the rights of membership and participation in each others' ministries.

31. Robert L. Turnipseed, "Looking Ahead in Dialogue," *Daily Journal*, Board of Global Ministries, Ecumenical and Interreligious Concerns Division, October 18–27, 1974, pp. 133–136.

32. Location of EICD, *Daily Journal*, Board of Global Ministries, April 11–16, 1978, pp. 17–18.

33. Administrative Flexibility, *Daily Journal*, Board of Global Ministries, October 15–22, 1979, p. 62.

34. Committee on Research and Development, *Daily Journal*, GBGM, October 13–21, 1992, pp. 56–57.

35. See the glossary for definitions of elected and nonelected staff.

6. Asia

1. "Annual Statistical Table on Global Mission: 1989," *International Bulletin of Missionary Research* 13 (1989): 20–21.

2. This and the preceding quote are from Jones, "Celebrating the Faithfulness of the Christian Church in China and the Faithfulness of the Missionaries," a report on the 150th anniversary of Christian mission in China, *Daily Journal*, GBGM, October 20, 1997, Addendum C.

3. See "United States Church—China Relations," *The Book of Resolutions* (Nashville: United Methodist Publishing House, 1984), pp. 440–445. The resolution acknowledges the end of the missionary era and the responsibility of Chinese Christians to lead in the development of the Christian witness. It calls for repentance from past mistakes that linked the mission in China to detrimental political and economic forces. It invites United Methodists to reexamine their

mission relationships to China and to support initiatives by the China church that emphasize unity, not denominationalism; self-determination, not dependency; and economic equality, rather than disparities between rich and poor.

4. Gao Ying, "Challenges to Mission Work from Chinese Perspectives," *Mission & Transformation*, p. 70.

5. Jones, "Celebrating the Faithfulness."

6. David Barrett, *World Christian Encyclopedia* (Nairobi: Oxford University Press, 1982).

7. These shamanistic values and other aspects of Korean Christian religious phenomena are described extensively in Stephen S. Kim, "'Looking Forward Inwardly': The Future of the Korean Mission in the United States," *Christian Mission in the Third Millennium*.

8. "Human Rights Struggles in Korea," *Daily Journal*, Board of Global Ministries, October 22–30, 1976, Appendix D. Kim Dae Jung was a signer of this statement that was shared with the world church community by the National Council of Churches in Korea. Kim, a respected national political figure, was forced to live in exile in the early 1980s under threat of a death penalty judgment by the military government in Korea. He was elected president of the Republic of Korea in 1997.

9. Resolution on Korea, *Daily Journal*, GBGM, October 14–21, 1983, pp. 80–81.

10. Jubilee Celebration 1995 on Korea Reunification, *Daily Journal*, GBGM, October 14–21, 1994, p. 58.

11. Partnership in Mission Consultation Report, *Daily Journal*, Board of Missions, January 3–13, 1969, Appendix G.

12. See chapter 1 for a discussion of Korean-American church development strategies in The UMC.

13. Japan–North American Commission on Cooperative Mission, *Daily Journal*, Board of Global Ministries, October 25–November 2, 1972, Appendix B, p. 551.

14. *The World Guide 1999/2000* (Oxford, England: New International Publications, 1999), p. 457.

15. Gain on exchange is the difference in official rate of exchange and that received in private markets for strong international currencies such as the U.S. dollar, Euro, or U.K. pound. Contributions received by the MCI treasury in these currencies were booked at the market (higher rate) but remitted to projects at the official (lower) rate. The difference remained in the MCI treasury as a transaction or handling charge. While the amount received by the MCI on an individual transaction seemed minute, the annual income from all such transactions was quite substantial.

16. See chapter 9 for a discussion of the cooperative Methodist mission in Cambodia and Vietnam. See also Scott Sunquist, "Asian Mission to Asians," *Christian Mission in the Third Millennium*.

17. Robert Solomon, "A Southeast Asian Perspective on Mission and Transformation in the Post Cold War Era," *Mission & Transformation*, p. 58.

7. Aims of Mission

1. "The Aims of Mission," 1968 *Discipline* (Nashville: Methodist Publishing House, 1968), ¶ 1277, revised for inclusive language.

2. "World Division," 1972 *Discipline* (Nashville: The United Methodist Publishing House, 1972), ¶ 1158.1.

3. "The Episcopacy," 1968 *Discipline*, ¶ 387.

4. "Nature of the Superintendency," 1976 *Discipline* (Nashville: The United Methodist Publishing House, 1976), ¶ 501.

5. "What the Bishops' Call Is About," an undated communication from the Co-ordinating Committee of the Call, Church Center for the United Nations, New York.

6. "What the Bishops' Call Is About." See also Dodge, McIntyre et al., "Report of the Bishops' Call for Peace and the Self-development of Peoples," 1976 General Conference *Daily Christian Advocate*, pp. 44–48.

7. A pastoral letter, "The Challenge of Peace: God's Promise and Our Response," was issued in 1983.

8. United Methodist Council of Bishops, *In Defense of Creation—The Nuclear Crisis and a Just Peace* (Nashville: The United Methodist Publishing House, 1986), p. 12.

9. *In Defense of Creation.*

10. 1984 *Discipline* (Nashville: United Methodist Publishing House, 1984), ¶ 107.

11. Report of the Connectional Process Team, "Transformation Directions for the UMC for the 21st Century," December 3, 1999.

12. Council of Bishops of The United Methodist Church, "Children and Poverty: Episcopal Initiative—Biblical and Theological Foundations" (Nashville: The United Methodist Publishing House, 1996), pp. 1–3.

13. Task Force for the Bishops' Initiative on Children and Poverty, *Community with Children and the Poor: A Guide for Congregational Study* (Nashville: Cokesbury, 2003), p. 55.

14. *Community with Children and the Poor,* p. 7.

15. 1996 *Discipline* (Nashville: The United Methodist Publishing House, 1996), ¶ 703.9.

16. Executive Committee of the World Council of Churches, Resolution on World Food Crisis, *Daily Journal,* Board of Global Ministries, April 30, 1974, pp. 159–160.

17. "The World's Agenda and the Church's Priorities," *Daily Journal,* Board of Global Ministries, April 30, 1974, p. 158.

18. Report of the Interdivisional Task Force on World Hunger, *Daily Journal,* Board of Global Ministries, October 18–27, 1974, p. 37.

19. "Toward Solidarity with the World's Hungry: First Steps in a Coordinated Board of Global Ministries Response," *Daily Journal,* Board of Global Ministries, April 29–March 5, 1975, p. 233.

20. C. Dean Freudenberger, "Hunger and Rural Poverty—A Church Response," *New World Outlook* (March 1978): 32.

21. "Report on the Crisis in the Ethnic Minority Churches," *Daily Journal*, Board of Global Ministries, March 16–22, 1976, pp. 256–257.

22. Predecessors to the Oklahoma Indian Missionary Conference had existed since 1844 in the Methodist Episcopal Church. By the time of The UMC, Native Americans had become unhappy with the restrictions of the comity agreements. They appealed to General Conference to renounce these agreements as a form of denominational and governmental collusion. In 1980 General Conference approved a resolution objecting to the comity agreements and stating: "To be responsible for implementing a policy stating that The United Methodist Church is not a party to any international agreement that limits the ability of any Annual Conference in any jurisdiction to develop and resource programs of ministry of any kind among Native Americans, including the organization of local churches where necessary." "Comity Agreements Affecting Development of Native American Ministries by The United Methodist Church," 1980 *Book of Resolutions*, p. 137. In 1984 this statement was made a part of the responsibilities of GBGM. 1984 *Discipline*, ¶ 1403.m.

23. Denise Johnson Stovall, "Missional priority report marks ethnic-minority church progress," *United Methodist Reporter*, May 6, 1988.

24. Talbert, "Interview," *New World Outlook* (September 1986): 15.

25. Yolanda E. Rivas, "A Call to Repentance: An Ethnic Answer to the Missional Priority Program," *New World Outlook* (September 1983): 33.

26. Graham, "Black Persons in The United Methodist Church," *New World Outlook* (March 1978): 33.

27. The distribution of the missional priority funds to general agencies remained as follows: 45 percent to GBGM; 20 percent to GBOD; 20 percent to GBHEM; and 15 percent to GBCS.

28. The 1996 General Conference also approved *Come, Let Us Worship: Book of United Methodist Worship*, which bears the subscription on the front cover, *The Korean-English United Methodist Hymnal*, in Korean. This volume, which was completed in 2000, combined the hymnal with worship resources in Korean.

29. General and Judicial Administration Report No. 19, "Report of the GCOM Ethnic Local Church Concerns Support Group," *Advance Edition, Daily Christian Advocate*, 2000 General Conference, 1: 651.

30. The Asian American Language Ministries Study/Program included Asian subethnic groups: Cambodian, Chinese, Filipino, Formosan, Hmong, Japanese, Korean, Lao, Vietnamese, and South Asian (Indians, Pakistani, Sri Lankans, Bangladeshi, Indonesians, and Malaysians). Korean United Methodists, the largest of the Asian-American United Methodist constituency, responding to specific needs and issues within their own constituency, proposed the formation of an independent Council on Korean American Ministries that was approved by the 2000 General Conference. See chapter 1 for a description of this development.

31. "General Provisions," 1996 *Discipline*, ¶ 703.10.

32. Kurewa, "Church Growth and Development in Africa," *New World Outlook* (December 1979): 32–33.

33. Kurewa, "Church Growth," pp. 32–33.

34. Report of the Africa Church Growth and Development Committee Meeting, Monrovia, Liberia, March 1983, *Daily Journal*, GBGM, April 1983, Appendix 13.

35. Margaret Schiffert, "Church Growth and Development — A Conversation with Zimbabwe's Nathan Goto," *New World Outlook* (October 1983): 27.

36. "The Superintendency," 1996 *Discipline*, ¶ 407.3.

37. "Holy Boldness, A National Plan for Urban Ministry," 1996 Petition to the General Conference.

38. *Daily Christian Advocate*, April 27, 1996, p. 741.

39. Takenaka, "Urban Rural Mission in Asia," *Daily Journal*, Board of Global Ministries, October 19–27, 1973, p. 34.

40. See chapter 7 for a further reference to criticisms and concerted attacks on the WCC and NCC.

41. Report of Committee on Policy and Program, *Daily Journal*, Board of Missions, October 10–20, 1971, p. 40.

42. Report of the President, *Daily Journal*, Board of Missions, September 5–9, 1968, Appendix A.

43. "Letter from Nairobi," *Daily Journal*, GBGM, October 18–25, 1985, p. 9.

44. Report of the Health and Welfare Program Department, "Ecumenical Decade: Churches in Solidarity with Women," *Daily Journal*, GBGM, October 13–20, 1989, p. 28.

45. Report of the Committee on Ecumenical Relations, *Daily Journal*, Women's Division, Board of Missions, October 23–31, 1969, p. 183.

46. Decisions on funding of ecumenical projects by UMCOR had a higher level of representation and participation by ecumenical partners. Regional "round-tables" were conducted with the aid of the WCC. Project proposals were presented by the member churches and development partners in each region. The projects were screened, prioritized, and then selected by the individual "funding" partners for promotion.

47. Raiser, "A Fresh Ecumenical Vision," *Daily Journal*, GBGM, October 14–22, 1993, Addendum H.

48. The NCC ended the fiscal year 2000 with a major hole in its operating budget and minimal reserves upon which to draw. The UMC General Commission on Christian Unity and Interreligious Concerns monitored the financial administration of the council and suspended payments to the council from the General Church Interdenominational Cooperation Fund until spending was reduced and accountability for handling funds was increased. Church World Service, the council's relief and development arm, declared its financial independence from the council to assure continuance of its own program. Member churches were called to the rescue, and major grants, including $700,000 from The UMC, made it possible for a restructured and lighter-weight organization to begin a new fiscal year.

8. Europe

1. In 2000, European United Methodism was divided into three central conferences (Germany, Central and Southern Europe, and Northern Europe). Northern Europe comprised two episcopal areas—Oslo and Moscow—while the others had one each—Frankfurt and Zurich.

2. "Requests for Enabling Acts," *Journal*, 1970 General Conference of The United Methodist Church (Nashville: United Methodist Publishing House, 1970), p. 883.

3. Vilem Schneeberger, "The Church in Czechoslovakia," *New World Outlook* (October 1968): 490.

4. Hani Handschin, "Women and Mission in Central and Southern Europe," *Mission & Transformation*, p. 83.

5. When U.S. anti-Communist foreign policy discouraged contacts within Angola, GBGM support declined. Meanwhile, the Norway mission board continued to provide a formal United Methodist mission connection to the Angola UMC. Substantial material and financial assistance was provided, which the Angola church gratefully acknowledged with a subtle critique of the way in which United Methodists in the U.S. often allow political interests to preempt a faithful discipleship.

6. An overview of the future possibilities for Methodist/United Methodist mission in Europe, including Russia, may be found in James A. Dwyer, "The Future of Methodist Mission in Europe," *Christian Mission in the Third Millennium*.

9. Initiatives for a New Mission Age

1. "Partnership in God's Mission," p. 12.

2. J. Woodrow Hearn/Randolph Nugent, "USSR Mission—A Report and Recommendations (to the General Board of Global Ministries)," April 14, 1992, p. 10. *Daily Journal*, GBGM, April 10–18, 1991, Appendix. See also Hearn, "A Servant People to God's Creation, *Initiatives for Mission*.

3. Report of UMCOR, *Daily Journal*, GBGM, March 18–25, 1992, p. 45.

4. Spurgeon Dunnam III, "Report Regarding Shreveport, La., Delegation Visit to the USSR," September 17–29, 1991, *Daily Journal*, GBGM, October 15–23, 1991, Appendix.

5. Comments of Bishop Heinrich Bolleter (Zurich Episcopal Area) to GBGM at the annual meeting of the Board in October 1991. The World Division of the Board created a European United Methodist Task Force to establish dialogue with the European central conferences on strategies for the extended mission of the denomination to the former Soviet Union.

6. The UMC in the Ukraine is now a part of the Provisional Annual Conference of South Russia, Ukraine, and Moldovo, and the Central Conference for Northern Europe and Eurasia. Rev. Vuksta died in 2004. This information was provided by Urz Schweizer, assistant to the bishop of the Central and Southern Europe Central Conference and Peter Siegfried, Europe executive with GBGM, in a communication to the author, August 9, 2004.

7. Resolution, *Daily Journal*, GBGM, March 18–25, 1992, p. 51.

8. Talbert and Robbins, "United Methodist Delegation Visit to The Russian Orthodox Church, Moscow, January 21–22, 1993," p. 3, Appended to the *Daily Journal*, GBGM, March 18–28, 1993. United Methodist delegates to the meeting included Talbert, Robbins, Bishop Joseph H. Yeakel, president of the Council of Bishops, Minor, Nugent, and Harman. The Reverend Leonid Kishkovsky, ecumenical officer of the Orthodox Church in America, participated as an observer and adviser to the United Methodist delegation.

9. In 2001, a complete support package for beginning pastors provided a monthly salary of $150 with special allowances for housing, health care, pension, travel, children, and ministry site. The monthly package for experienced full-time pastors was $280 salary, with the same allowances. "Russia Initiative Update," August 2001. This source is a newsletter published by the Russia Initiative network in the U.S.

10. The participating seminaries included Iliff School of Theology, St. Paul School of Theology, Wesley Theological Seminary, Perkins School of Theology, and the Methodist Theological School in Ohio. Garrett-Evangelical Theological Seminary expressed an interest in participating. Asbury School of Theology, though not a member of the Advisory Committee, offered to recruit professors. The theological schools of the Korean Methodist Church continued to provide teachers and lecturers. For a full report on this partnership, see Sally Geis, "A Transformed People in a Transformed World," *Occasional Papers*, No. 93, September 1998, General Board of Higher Education and Ministry.

11. Robin W. Lovin memo to R. Bruce Weaver, "Russia Initiative," September 27, 2001.

12. The 2001 conference session was the first meeting of the United Methodist Eurasia Annual Conference, which attained the level of thirty-one ordained elders, forty probationary members, and eighteen local pastors. "Russia Initiative Update," August 2001.

13. Proposal to Establish a United States/Kazakhstan International Foundation on Radiation, Ecology and Health, *Daily Journal*, GBGM, March 28–April 5, 1995, Appendix.

14. Cathie Lyons, "Semipalatinsk: A Place of Weeping and a Place of Sorrow," *New World Outlook* (March-April 1994): 4.

15. Ministries in Kazakhstan, *Daily Journal*, GBGM, April 16–23, 1998, p. 5.

16. Program Proposal—A Primary Medical Care Center in Semipalatinsk, Kazakhstan, *Daily Journal*, GBGM, October 18–21, 1999, Addendum L.

17. "Master Plan for United Methodist Work in Honduras," an unpublished working paper of the GBGM staff steering committee for the Honduras Initiative.

18. From an interview with Dr. David Wu, assistant general secretary for congregational development in the Evangelization and Church Growth Program Area of GBGM, May 21, 2002.

19. From minutes of a meeting related to the establishment of the Bible Training School, cited in an interview with Wu, May 21, 2002.

20. Comments of Joon-Sik Park, professor at Methodist Theological School in Ohio, "Reflection on the Consultation on Mission and Evangelism in

Cambodia, January 7–15, 2001," an event sponsored by the GBGM program on Mission Evangelism.

21. "Senegal Mission Initiative," *Daily Journal*, GBGM, March 10–18, 1991, p. 52.

22. Presentation by Ndjungu at the Cumberland Wisconsin United Methodist Church, October 10, 2001.

23. "The Bishops' Appeal and Campaign for Africa," *Daily Journal*, GBGM, October 14–21, 1994, p. 33.

24. "The Bishops' Appeal and Campaign for Africa," *Daily Journal*, p. 33.

25. "The Context in Which Evangelization and Church Growth Are Being Carried out in East Africa," a presentation of Ndoricimpa, resident bishop of The United Methodist Church—East Africa Annual Conference, to the 2000 Consultation on Evangelization and Church Growth, GBGM, Nairobi, Kenya, June 2000.

26. "Offering Christ in the New Millennium—Opportunities and Challenges," Global Consultation on Evangelization and Church Growth, Emory University, Atlanta, Georgia, June 1999.

27. Two retired national mission executives, Norman Klump (former EUB) and Ed Carothers (former Methodist) were presented the Frank Mason North Award for their leadership in innovative urban ministry. Christiana Hena, the first United Methodist missionary to the post–Soviet Union, was given the Anna Eklund Award, named after the last Methodist missionary deaconess to leave Russia during the Bolshevik period. Maribeth Collins of Portland, Oregon, was awarded the Everett Stanton Collins award for her mission stewardship, including the family philanthropy that established the Collins Pension Fund benefitting United Methodist missionaries. The African Central Council Bishops were each recognized with the Peace Award for their leadership of African United Methodists into ministries of justice, reconciliation, and peace.

28. "Globalizing" refers to increasing its missionary cadre with recruits from countries other than the U.S.

29. *Report on National Consultation on AIDS Ministries* (Cincinnati: Mission Education and Cultivation Program Department, GBGM, June 1988).

30. Resolution, *Daily Journal*, GBGM, October 16–23, 1987, p. 61.

31. "Report and Recommendation of the Interagency Task Force on AIDS to the 1992 General Conference," *Daily Journal*, GBGM, October 15–23, 1991, Appendix G.

32. "Non Governmental Organization Program—Mission and Policy Statements," *Daily Journal*, GBGM, October 19–22, 1998, Addendum G. The pertinent disciplinary mandate is the 1996 *Discipline*, Part V, Chapter One, Section I, pp. 114–115.

33. "And Have They Come to Know Christ?" Report of the General Secretary, GBGM, April 3, 2000, p. 4.

34. "Presentation on Land Mines," *Daily Journal*, GBGM, October 18–21, 1999, p. 9.

35. "Comfort My People: Ministries with Women in Crisis," a program brochure published by GBGM about 1979.

36. Betty Letzig, "Expressions of Faith: A Background Paper on the Origins of Social Welfare Institutions Related to the National Program Division of GBGM of The United Methodist Church" (National Program Division, 1987), p. 39. The perspective of staff persons is attributed to the author's colleagues in the National Division.

37. Letzig, "Expressions of Faith," p. 41.

38. This report was cited in an "Update on Rural/Farm Crisis," September 15, 1987, by Gladys L. Campbell, executive secretary for Town and Country Ministries of GBGM.

39. *Daily Journal*, GBGM, April 12–19, 1985, pp. 37–38.

40. Peggy Billings, *Speaking Out in the Public Space: An Account of the Section of Christian Social Relations, 1968–1984* (New York: Women's Division, 1995), p. 82.

41. Rural Chaplains Association, Columbus, Ohio, *Rural Chaplain Report* 2 (Summer 1998): 7.

42. "National Comprehensive Plan for Town and Country Ministry of The United Methodist Church: Report to General Conference 2000," *Daily Christian Advocate Advance Edition*, 2000 General Conference (Nashville: United Methodist Publishing House, 2000), pp. 858–864.

10. Middle East/North Africa

1. See actions of the Board of Global Ministries and GBGM on Middle East matters taken at annual meetings 1973, 1982, 1983, 1986, 1989, 1990, 1991, 1993, and 1996 and spring meetings 1988, 1989, 1993, and 1996.

2. Johnson, "Starting Over in Algeria," *New World Outlook* (June 1979): 33.

11. New World Vision

1. "Partnership in God's Mission," p. 7.

2. "A Proposed Policy for the National Division in relating its work to the Social Welfare and Health Needs of the Nation," *Daily Journal*, Board of Missions, January 3–13, 1969, pp. 218–221.

3. "Health Care," *Daily Journal*, Women's Division, October 20–30, 1971, pp. 255–257.

4. "Health for All by the Year 2000," *Daily Journal*, GBGM, October 14–21, 1983, pp. 21–24.

5. For a report on the Women's Health program, see *Daily Journal*, GBGM, March 12–16, 1984, Appendix III.

6. "Health Care Delivery Polity Statement," *Daily Journal*, GBGM, October 15–22, 1979, pp. 32–36. The statement was developed and adopted by the Women's Division, National Division, and Health and Welfare Division before Board approval for recommendation to General Conference.

7. "A Pastoral Letter to the People Called Methodist," *Daily Journal*, GBGM, October 11–18, 1990, pp. 14–18.

8. Mabel Arole, "Comprehensive Community-Based Primary Health Care – Our Healing Mission," *New World Outlook* (January-February 1992): 21.

9. The story of the Emmanuel Community Center pilot project in Cochabamba, Bolivia, is included in a report on Comprehensive Community-Based Primary Health Care 1994–2000, by the staff of the Health and Relief Program Area of GBGM. The center developed from a local church base with members reflecting on needed services and then organizing around food programs, childcare, youth programs, employment, personal and family finance, and spiritual growth.

10. *Daily Journal*, Board of Global Ministries, October 17–25, 1975, p. 44.

11. *Daily Journal*, GBGM, April 11, 1978, p. 20.

12. *Daily Journal*, GBGM, October 15–22, 1979, pp. 19–31.

13. *Daily Journal*, GBGM, March 18–23, 1998, p. 48.

14. *Daily Journal*, GBGM, October 16, 1978, p. 47.

15. Sources for the history of the Nestlé boycott are: *Daily Journal*, GBGM annual meetings, October 1978, October 1982, and October 1984, spring meeting 1984, and a précis of Women's Division participation in the Nestlé boycott prepared by Women's Division staff Jennifer Washington, April 18, 2001.

16. The source for the Women's Division's advocacy for the rights of the child is a précis on the subject prepared by Jennifer Washington, April 18, 2001.

17. Billings, *Speaking Out in the Public Space*, pp. 30–32.

18. *Daily Journal*, Board of Missions, September 5–9, 1968, p. 132.

19. *Daily Journal*, Board of Missions, September 5–9, 1968, p. 164.

20. *Daily Journal*, GBGM, April 7–13, 1981, p. 19.

21. *Daily Journal*, GBGM, April 7–13, 1981, p. 20.

22. *Daily Journal*, GBGM, April 11, 1978, p. 22.

23. Correspondence on file in General Board of Global Ministries archives from the Reverend Tom McCallister, Winston County parish minister, Noxpater United Methodist Church, Noxpater, Mississippi, received May 19, 1983.

24. "Resolution on Justice Ministries and the Crisis in Civil Rights," *Daily Journal*, GBGM, October 15–22, 1982, p. 52.

25. "National Division Statement – Progress in the Case of Eddie James Carthan," October 20, 1983.

26. *Daily Journal*, GBGM, October 15–22, 1979, p. 38; March 18–25, 1980, p. 11.

27. *Daily Journal*, GBGM, April 7–13, 1981, pp. 7–8.

28. Consuelo Urquiza, *The Charter for Racial Justice: A History* (New York: Council on Interracial Books for Children, 1980). Urquiza was the secretary for racial justice of the Women's Division.

29. Press release, National Seminar, Woman's Division, Methodist Board of Missions, St. Paul School of Theology, Kansas City, Missouri, August 9, 1967.

30. *Daily Journal*, GBGM, April 7–13, 1981, pp. 21–24.

31. 1984 *Discipline*, ¶ 1434, p. 518.

32. *Daily Journal*, GBGM, April 7–13, 1981, pp. 21–24.

33. A resolution adopted by the 1984 General Conference of The UMC encouraged United Methodist congregations to "be a sanctuary for refugees from El Salvador and Guatemala." At least eight congregations publicly declared themselves to be sanctuaries, and many others provided support for refugees from Central America.

34. See Joyce Sohl, "Church Investments and South Africa," *Response* (April 1985): 34.

35. The Asia Pacific Center in Washington, D.C., is the result of progenitor groups of church-supported agencies working on U.S.–Korea foreign policy issues.

36. Billings, *Speaking Out in the Public Space*, p. 63.

37. The Rural Chaplains program of the United Methodist Rural Fellowship was created to provide crisis intervention services to churches and communities suffering from loss of economic assets and employment opportunities.

38. *Daily Journal*, GBGM, April 8–15, 1983, p. 19.

39. Peggy Billings, "The Global Economic Crisis Challenges Missions," *New World Outlook* (March 1986): 18.

40. *Daily Journal*, Board of Global Ministries, November 1, 1972, p. 196.

41. *Daily Journal*, Board of Global Ministries, October 19–27, 1973, p. 49.

42. *Daily Journal*, Board of Global Ministries, March 16–22, 1976, p. 276.

43. *Daily Journal*, Board of Global Ministries, March 12–19, 1985, pp. 39–41.

44. *Daily Journal*, Board of Missions, October 20–30, 1971, Appendix F, p. 335.

45. *Daily Journal*, Board of Global Ministries, March 24, 1973, pp. 39–41, 73.

46. *Daily Journal*, GBGM, April 11–13, 1978, pp. 34–35.

47. The interpretation of the global refugee crisis by Lilia Fernandez is found in a collection of her articles and other publications assembled by UMCOR entitled *UMCOR Refugee Ministries*.

48. "Women's Division Resolution on Haiti," *Response* (July/August 1992): 24.

49. "A Chronology of U.S. Response to Haitian Refugees," *Interpreter* (October 1992): 11.

50. "On Undocumented Migration: To Love the Sojourner, A Statement of Concern to United Methodists in the U.S.A." United Methodist Council of Bishops, meeting April 20, 1988, Kansas City, Missouri.

51. *Daily Journal*, Board of Missions, October 10–20, 1971, p. 156.

52. Text of resolution is cited in *Daily Journal*, Board of Global Ministries, October 19–27, 1973, p. 49.

53. *Daily Journal*, Board of Global Ministries, October 19–27, 1973, p. 49.

54. *Daily Journal*, GBGM, October 28–November 3, 1980, pp. 42–43.

55. "Justice, Peace, and Integrity of Creation—Final Document," World Council of Churches Central Committee, Geneva, Switzerland, March 25–30, 1990, p. 12.

56. John Hart, "Report from the Earth Summit," *New World Outlook* (September-October 1992): 7.

57. "Earth Summit Press Release," UN Conference on Environment and Development, UN Information Department, New York.

58. "Environmental Justice Issues," a memo prepared by Jennifer Washington, Women's Division staff, April 18, 2001.

59. *Daily Journal*, Board of Missions, Women's Division, October 23–31, 1969, p. 171.

60. *Daily Journal*, Board of Global Ministries, April 29–May 3, 1975, pp. 204–205.

61. *Daily Journal*, GBGM, October 15–22, 1979, pp. 13–14.

62. *Daily Journal*, GBGM, April 7–13, 1981, p. 20.

63. *Daily Journal*, GBGM, March 18–April 25, 1980, p. 19.

12. North America

1. "Resolution toward a New Beginning beyond 1992," *Daily Journal*, GBGM, October 15–23, 1991, pp. 36–41.

2. "Resolution," pp. 36–41.

3. "General Provisions," 1984 *Discipline*, ¶ 806.

4. The "homogeneity principle" of church growth theorizes that the most effective evangelism takes place within the same socio-demographic-ethnic groups. It has been criticized for being narrowly exclusive and aimed at preserving all-white congregations/denominations.

5. A survey among the 1.5 generation of Korean-American United Methodists revealed a church attendance preference for congregations with English-language services and a multi-ethnic membership. This generation of Korean Americans was not inclined toward attending churches with a Korean-language service or a single dominant ethnic membership base. The 1.5 generation refers to first-generation Koreans who were born in Korea but raised in the U.S. They acknowledged the inherited Korean cultural values of their parents while adopting those of the new context. See Task Force on Korean American Ministries: Report to General Conference 2000, *Daily Christian Advocate*, Advance Edition, vol 1, sec. 2, pp. 825–830.

6. Douglas Ruffle, "The Multi-cultural Church as Sign, Foretaste and Instrument," *Multi-ethnic Net Circular*, October 2000.

7. "Multi-cultural Church."

13. Mission Journey

1. "Grace upon Grace."

2. Unpublished report of the Green Lake Consultation submitted to the Commission on the Structure of Methodism Overseas (COSMOS), November 4, 1966. Located in Central Record Archives, General Board of Global Ministries, New York.

3. Report of the Green Lake Consultation.

4. "Findings of the Consultation on Methodist Church Overseas Structure," Green Lake Wisconsin, October 29–November 5, 1966.

5. "Findings of the Consultation." The odd term "welcome(ed)" was apparently an effort on the part of the authors to express both a present and past attitude toward ecumenism.

6. "Interpretation and Implications of the Green Lake Consultation on Methodist Church Overseas Structure," revised and approved by COSMOS Executive, December 14, 1966, p. 5.

7. "Interpretation and Implications," p. 5.

8. "Findings of the Consultation," p. 3.

9. "Findings of the Consultation," p. 3.

10. Mathews, "Whither World Methodism?" a presentation at a meeting of the American Section, World Methodist Council, Lake Junaluska, North Carolina, June 21, 1965.

11. Niles, "A World Methodist Conference of Churches," a memorandum prepared for COSMOS, August 1965. Niles also wrote: "It is simply one of the quirks of history that the modern discussion of autonomy for churches is following the same lines as independence for countries which once belonged to a colonial setup. . . . It is my firm belief that throughout the Church's history, the organizational units of church life were determined by the secular entities in which people were involved. If today in continents like Asia and Africa and South America, we urge that the churches become autonomous, we do so out of the realization that the word 'National' corresponds as nearly as we can make it to the context of obligation and mission in which the churches of these continents find themselves. To say the least, when our fellow Christians in America express their concern at what they call dangers of nationalism, that concern must sound misplaced to us who know the present center of gravity of church organization in America."

12. Preliminary Report of the Drafting Committee, Green Lake Consultation, November 1, 1966.

13. 1964 *Discipline* (Nashville, Methodist Publishing House, 1964), ¶ ¶ 600–605.

14. Bonino, "A Latin American Perspective on Challenges of Mission in the Post Cold War Era," *Mission & Transformation*, p. 41.

[Glossary]

Advance – "The program for promoting special gifts to missionary causes over and above apportioned World Service and other general funds and conference benevolences. Moneys given through this program are known as Advance special gifts" (Glossary, 1980 *Discipline*).

Cabinet – the body of senior staff members of GBGM with administrative responsibilities for major program areas/divisions of the Board. Not to be confused with the same term used for the resident bishop and district superintendents of an annual conference acting as a body.

Directors – individuals elected through annual conferences and jurisdictions for four-year terms of service to the voting membership of a United Methodist general board.

Elected Staff – all Cabinet and secondary level staff elected by the GBGM Board of Directors for administrative and supervisory duties within program and management areas/divisions of the Board.

General Board of Global Ministries (GBGM) – the program agency/board of The UMC authorized to implement responsibilities of mission outreach. (See explanation at the beginning of the notes to this volume for the different titles of the Board 1968–2000.)

General Council on Finance and Administration (GCFA) – the general church agency in The UMC to which all general church program and administrative agencies are accountable for financial operations between quadrennial sessions of the General Conference.

General Council on Ministries (GCOM) – the general church agency in The UMC to which all program agencies were accountable for fulfilling program mandates between the quadrennial sessions of the General Conference. The council was charged with evaluating and coordinating the programs of all general agencies and recommending levels of general church funding.

General Secretary – The chief executive officer of a general agency.

Itineracy – "The system of The United Methodist Church by which [ordained] ministers are appointed to their charges by the bishop and are under discipline to accept such appointment" (Glossary, 1980 *Discipline*).

Missional Priority – a program response to a critical need calling for a massive and sustained effort through primary attention and ordering or reordering of the program and budget at every level of the church. It must be approved by General Conference, which also establishes quadrennial general church funding requirements (2000 *Book of Discipline*, ¶ 703.9).

Mission Society for United Methodists (MSUM) — an unofficial organization created by individuals as an alternative to GBGM for recruiting and sending missionaries. It does not seek the blessing of the general church nor is it in any way accountable to the governance structures of the denomination.

Nonitinerating — Ordained ministers or other professionals in the church who are not subject to itinerancy.

NRSV — New Revised Standard Version translation of the Holy Bible.

Ombudsman — a staff person without program portfolio who investigates and seeks to adjudicate complaints or grievances of parties within an organization. In GBGM, the portfolio was designed to advance working relationships and programs addressing racial/ethnic minorities.

Program Agency/Board — an agency created by the General Conference of The United Methodist Church (UMC) to administer general church program mandates.

Research and Development Committee (Mission Development Committee) — a standing committee of the General Board of Global Ministries assigned responsibility for boardwide program planning, evaluation, and budgeting.

Special Program — a quadrennial emphasis, initiated by a general program agency, designed to respond to a distinct opportunity or need. It must be approved by General Conference and administered by the sponsoring agency with resources available within or generated by that agency (2000 *Discipline*, ¶ 703.10).

[Select Bibliography]

Following are suggestions for readings on mission philosophy and practice in the late twentieth century — with apologies to authors of many overlooked resources and especially those in countries and languages to which I do not have access.

The author.

Books, Monographs, and Papers

Bonk, Jonathan J., *Missions and Money–Affluence as a Western Missionary Problem* (Maryknoll, N.Y.: Orbis Press, 1992).

Bosch, David J., *Transforming Mission: Paradigm Shifts in Theology of Mission* (Maryknoll, N.Y.: Orbis Press, 1993).

Dudley, Carl S., *Where Have All the People Gone? New Choices for Old Churches* (New York: Pilgrim Press, 1979).

Duraisingh, Christopher, ed., *Called to One Hope–The Gospel in Diverse Cultures* (Geneva: World Council of Churches, 1998). See also "Gospel and Cultures Pamphlet Series" (Geneva: WCC Publications) for context-specific resources for this program of the WCC.

Escobar, Samuel, *Changing Tides: Latin America and World Mission Today* (Maryknoll, N.Y.: Orbis Press, 2002).

General Board of Global Ministries, *Mission & Transformation in a Changing World: A Dialogue with Global Mission Colleagues* (New York: General Board of Global Ministries, 1998).

_____, "Partnership in God's Mission: Theology of Mission Statement," General Board of Global Ministries of The United Methodist Church, New York, 1986.

Knitter, Paul F., *No Other Name? A Critical Survey of Christian Attitudes toward the World Religions* (Maryknoll, N.Y.: Orbis Press, 1985).

Phillips, James M. and Robert T. Coote, eds., *Toward the 21st Century in Christian Mission* (Grand Rapids: William B. Eerdmans, 1993).

Robert, Dana L. ed., *Gospel Bearers, Gender Barriers: Missionary Women in the Twentieth Century* (Maryknoll, N.Y.: Orbis Press, 2002).

Sanneh, Lamin, *Translating the Message* (Maryknoll, N.Y.: Orbis Press, 1990).

Senior, Donald and Carroll Stuhlmueller, *The Biblical Foundations for Mission* (Maryknoll, N.Y.: Orbis Press, 1983).

Sider, Ronald J., *One Sided Christianity? Uniting the Church to Heal a Lost and Broken World* (San Francisco: HarperCollins, 1993).

Spong, John Shelby, *Into the Whirlwind: The Future of the Church* (Minneapolis: Seabury Press, 1993).

Walls, Andrew F., *The Cross-Cultural Process in Christian History* (Maryknoll, N.Y.: Orbis Press, 2002).

White, Dale M., *Making A Just Peace–Human Rights and Domination Systems* (Nashville: Abingdon Press, 1998).

Wieser, Thomas, *Planning for Mission—Working Papers on the New Quest for Missionary Communities* (New York: The U.S. Conference for the World Council of Churches, 1966).

_____, *Whither Ecumenism? A Dialogue in the Transit Lounge of the Ecumenical Movement* (Geneva: World Council of Churches, 1986).

World Council of Churches, *Mission and Evangelism—An Ecumenical Affirmation* (Geneva: WCC Publications, 1983).

Yrigoyen, Charles, Jr. ed., *The Global Impact of the Wesleyan Traditions and Their Related Movements* (Lanham, Md.: Scarecrow Press, 2002).

Periodicals

The Ecumenical Review (published by the World Council of Churches, Geneva):
"Turn to God—Rejoice in Hope, Unfolding the Eighth Assembly Theme," 50 (April 1998).

The International Bulletin of Missionary Research (published by the Overseas Ministries Study Center, New Haven, Conn.):
Sanneh, Lamin, "A Resurgent Church in a Troubled Continent: Review Essay of Bengt Sundkler's *History of Mission in Africa*," (July 2001).
Shenk, Wilbert R. "Recasting Theology of Mission: Impulses from the Non-Western World," (July 2001).

International Review of Mission (published by the Conference on World Mission and Evangelism, World Council of Churches, Geneva):
"Mission at the Crossroads," 87 (April 1998).
"Mission in the Twenty First Century: Impulses from Salvador," 86 (January/April 1997).
Issues on Conference on World Mission and Evangelism, Salvador, Brazil, 1996:
"Mission 2000 —An Agenda," 86 (October 1997).
"Looking Towards Salvador," 84 (July 1995).
"Authentic Witness within Each Culture," 84 (October 1995).
"Gospel and Identity in Community," 85 (January 1996).
"Local Congregations in Pluralistic Societies" and "One Gospel—Diverse Expressions," 85 (April 1996).
"The San Antonio Conference," 78 (July/October 1989) [Conference on World Mission and Evangelism, San Antonio, Texas, 1989].
"Exploring God's Will," 78 (January 1989) [San Antonio Conference Subthemes].
Skreslet, Stan, "Emerging Trends in a Shifting Global Context—Mission in the New World Order," *Theology Today* 54 (July 1997).

[Permissions]

Used with permission of AP/WIDE WORLD PHOTOS: Anti-Vietnam demonstrations, p. 35; Biko funeral, p. 125.

Used with permission of the General Commission on Archives and History, The United Methodist Church: Aleut fishermen, Hispanic man, two African-American girls, cover; Photos of 1968 uniting conference, p. 3; Cain Felder and Tracey Jones, p. 10; César Chávez and Coretta King, p. 13; Lake Titicaca, cover, p. 67; Toge Fujihira photo of Esther Mabry, cover, p. 90; John Goodwin photo of US-2s protesting, cover, p. 98; deaconess, p. 104; Emilio de Carvalho, p. 127; Abel Muzorewa, p. 129; Onema Fama, p. 143; Randolph Nugent in Liberia, p. 146; Harry Haines, p. 248; Ezekiel Makunike, p. 161; Schools of Mission, p. 176; Joel N. Martínez, p. 199; K. H. Ting, p. 204; Lee Tai Young, p. 209; WSCF in Côte d'Ivoire, cover, p. 239; community worker Richard Abrams, p. 265; East Berlin cornerstone, p. 291; Lydia Istomina, p. 319; Cathie Lyons photo of radiated patient, Kazakhstan, p. 324; Roy I. Sano, p. 342; Theressa Hoover, p. 394; DeWitt, Morales, Pagura, p. 410; handicapping worshipping, p. 439; Mortimer Arias, p. 447; Aguilar videotaping, p. 451; José Miguez Bonino, p. 456.

Used with permission of the General Board of Global Ministries, The United Methodist Church: Charles Cole photos of Pinochet guard, p. 71; and *Aparición con vida*, p. 72; Christie R. House photo of mission volunteers, p. 117; Arole/Jamkhed, p. 389; all maps.

Used with permission of The Image Works: Intifada, p. 379; oil spill, p. 427.

Used with permission of Nebraska United Methodist Historical Center, Nebraska Wesleyan University, Lincoln, Nebraska: photo of Means and Noley, p. 14.

Used with permission of Robert J. Harman: African art, p. 262; Rüdiger Minor et al., p. 305; killing fields, p. 338.

Used with permission of United Methodist Communications (and United Methodist News Service): Mike Dubose photo of Bosnia mosque and church, p. 296; Jay Mallin photo of AIDS quilt, p. 360; Joan LeBarr photo of Dallas homeless, p. 153.

[Index]

Abrams, Richard: photo, 265.

Abuse: 369. *See also* substance abuse, women in crisis.

Advance for Christ and His Church: for Africa Church Growth and Development, 262; creation of, 173; and Russia Initiative, 312; and small church support, 365; for special program on substance abuse, 267–268; and world hunger, 252.

Adventist church: 330.

Advocacy: 18, 63. *See also* injustice, poor and poverty.

Affiliation: 21. *See also* appendix.

Africa: 123–150; and AIDS, 359, 361; black demand for Board staff to administer program in, 11; and children's ministries of UMC, 244; and consultation on mission theology, 170; and European churches' mission in, 289; and evangelization academies in, 352; and evangelization in sub-Saharan area of, 451; and global urban development, 30; and higher education for women, 111; and immigrants to Europe, 292–293; independence of countries of, 236, 445; and initiatives in, 344–350; and In Mission Together, 120; Korean mission to, 330; and land mines in, 365–366; and Millennium Fund projects in, 353–354; and new mission opportunities, 4; and Operation Classroom, 119–120; and racism in Europe, 288; and Senegal chosen for new mission initiative, 185; mentioned, 41, 101, 114, 116, 233, 251. *See also* photos, 125, 127, 129, 143, 146, 161, 239, 262; maps, 131, 139, 141.

Africa Central Conference: and bishops given Peace Award, 354 *n*27; and Burundi church made part of, 346; and episcopal elections, 140; and outreach to neighboring countries, 132; and Uganda visit, 348.

African Americans: and black church burnings, 406; and "Black Manifesto," 399; in Brazil, 62; and crisis in ethnic minority churches, 252–254; and demands on churches in 1968, 10–12; and discrimination against, 401–402; and economic development, 27; as farmers in South, 372, 373; French-speaking, 345; and hymnal supplement of, 257; and Ku Klux Klan resurgence, 405; and limits of ethnic minority missional priority for, 258; and limits of short-term programs for, 256; among nominees from jurisdictions, 438; omitted from early mission histories, xviii; and Philander Smith College, 109; and schools for, 110; and Strengthening the Black Church for the Twenty-First Century, 260. *See also* photos, cover, 10, 13, 90, 117, 146, 153, 265, 394.

African churches: appeal of to COSMOS for right to elect leaders, 445; bishops' statement of missionary deployment, 93; and central conference status, 22–23; and church growth and development program, 261; and evangelistic zeal of, 344; and German church relations, 292; and global conference on substance abuse, 268; and invitation to Communities of Shalom, 266; as partners on Health for All, 388.

Agricultural development: 357–358;

Please mail order with check payable to:
SERVICE CENTER
7820 READING ROAD CALLER NO 1800
CINCINNATI OH 45222-1800

Costs for shipping and handling for sale items:
$25 or less, add $5.35
$25.01–$60, add $6.65
$60.01–$100, add $8.05
Over $100, add 8.5%

For billed and credit card orders:
CALL TOLL FREE: 1-800-305-9857
FAX ORDERS: 1-513-761-3722
E-MAIL: orders@gbgm-umc.org
If billing is requested, a $2.00 billing fee will be added.

$ 14.95 PAPERBACK   STOCK # 3642

$ 21.95 HARDBACK   STOCK # 2878